■ The Iowa State Constitution

The Oxford Commentaries on the State Constitutions of the United States
G. Alan Tarr, Series Editor

Professor G. Alan Tarr, Director of the Center on State Constitutional Studies at Rutgers University, serves as General Editor for this important new series which in its entirety will cover each of the fifty states. Each volume of *The Oxford Commentaries on the State Constitutions of the United States* contains a historical overview of the state's constitutional development, plus a section-by-section analysis of the state's current constitution. Other features included in the volumes are the text of the state's constitution, together with a bibliographic essay, table of cases, and index. This series provides essential reference tools for those investigating state constitutional development and constitutional law.

The Iowa State Constitution

Second Edition

Todd E. Pettys

THE OXFORD COMMENTARIES ON THE STATE CONSTITUTIONS OF THE UNITED STATES
G. Alan Tarr, Series Editor

OXFORD
UNIVERSITY PRESS

OXFORD
UNIVERSITY PRESS

Oxford University Press is a department of the University of Oxford. It furthers the University's objective of excellence in research, scholarship, and education by publishing worldwide. Oxford is a registered trademark of Oxford University Press in the UK and certain other countries.

Published in the United States of America by Oxford University Press
198 Madison Avenue, New York, NY 10016, United States of America.

First Edition published in 1998 by Greenwood Press
Republished in 2011 by Oxford University Press

Library of Congress Cataloging-in-Publication Data

Names: Pettys, Todd E., author. | Iowa. Constitution (1857)
Title: The Iowa state constitution / Todd E. Pettys.
Description: Second edition. | New York, NY : Oxford University Press, 2018. |
Series: The Oxford Commentaries on the State Constitutions of the United States |
Includes bibliographical references and index.
Identifiers: LCCN 2017025947 | ISBN 9780190490836 ((hardback) : alk. paper)
Subjects: LCSH: Iowa. Constitution (1857) | Constitutions—Iowa. |
Constitutional law—Iowa. | Constitutional history—Iowa.
Classification: LCC KFI4601 1857.A6 S727 2017 | DDC 342.77702/3—dc23
LC record available at https://lccn.loc.gov/2017025947

Printed by Bridgeport National Bindery, Inc., United States of America

Note to Readers

This publication is designed to provide accurate and authoritative information in regard to the subject matter covered. It is based upon sources believed to be accurate and reliable and is intended to be current as of the time it was written. It is sold with the understanding that the publisher is not engaged in rendering legal, accounting, or other professional services. If legal advice or other expert assistance is required, the services of a competent professional person should be sought. Also, to confirm that the information has not been affected or changed by recent developments, traditional legal research techniques should be used, including checking primary sources where appropriate.

(Based on the Declaration of Principles jointly adopted by a Committee of the American Bar Association and a Committee of Publishers and Associations.)

For Lily, my Iowan

CONTENTS

■ SERIES FOREWORD

In 1776, following the declaration of independence from England, the former colonies began to draft their own constitutions. Their handiwork attracted widespread interest, and draft constitutions circulated up and down the Atlantic seaboard, as constitution-makers sought to benefit from the insights of their counterparts in sister states. In Europe, the new constitutions found a ready audience seeking enlightenment from the American experiments in self-government. Even the delegates to the Constitutional Convention of 1787, despite their reservations about the course of political developments in the states during the decade after independence, found much that was useful in the newly adopted constitutions. And when James Madison, fulfilling a pledge given during the ratification debates, drafted the federal Bill of Rights, he found his model in the famous Declaration of Rights of the Virginia Constitution.

By the 1900s, however, few people would have looked to state constitutions for enlightenment. Instead, a familiar litany of complaints was heard whenever state constitutions were mentioned. State constitutions were too long and too detailed, combining basic principles with policy prescriptions and prohibitions that had no place in the fundamental law of a state. By including such provisions, it was argued, state constitutions deprived state governments of the flexibility they needed to respond effectively in changing circumstances. This—among other factors—encouraged political reformers to look to the federal government, which was not plagued by such constitutional constraints, thereby shifting the locus of political initiative away from the states. Meanwhile, civil libertarians concluded that state bills of rights, at least as interpreted by state courts, did not adequately protect rights and therefore looked to the federal courts and the federal Bill of Rights for redress. As power and responsibility shifted from the states to Washington, so too did the attention of scholars, the legal community, and the general public.

During the early 1970s, however, state constitutions were "rediscovered." The immediate impetus for this rediscovery was President Richard Nixon's appointment of Warren Burger to succeed Earl Warren as Chief Justice of the United States Supreme Court. To civil libertarians, this appointment seemed to signal a decisive shift in the Supreme Court's jurisprudence, because Burger was expected to lead the Court away from the liberal activism that had characterized the Warren Court. They therefore sought ways to safeguard the gains they had achieved for defendants, racial minorities, and the poor during Warren's tenure from erosion by the Burger Court. In particular, they began to look to state bills of rights to secure the rights of defendants and to support other civil-liberties claims that they advanced in state courts.

The "new judicial federalism," as it came to be called, quite quickly advanced beyond its initial concern to evade the mandates of the Burger Court. Indeed, less than two decades after it originated, it became a nationwide phenomenon. For when judges and scholars turned their attention to state constitutions, they discovered an unsuspected richness. They found not only provisions that paralleled the federal Bill of Rights but also constitutional guarantees of the right to privacy and of gender equality, for example, that had no analogue in the U.S. Constitution. Careful examination of the text and history of state guarantees revealed important differences between even those provisions that most resembled federal guarantees and their federal counterparts. Looking beyond state declarations of rights, jurists and scholars discovered affirmative constitutional mandates to state governments to address such important policy concerns as education and housing. Taken altogether, these discoveries underlined the importance for the legal community of developing a better understanding of state constitutions.

Yet the renewed interest in state constitutions has not been limited to judges and lawyers. State constitutional reformers have renewed their efforts with notable success: since 1960, ten states have adopted new constitutions and several others have undertaken major constitutional revisions. These changes have usually resulted in more streamlined constitutions and more effective state governments. Also, in recent years political activists on both the left and the right have pursued their goals through state constitutional amendments, often enacted through the initiative process, under which policy proposals can be placed directly on the ballot for voters to endorse or reject. Scholars too have begun to rediscover how state constitutional history can illuminate changes in political thought and practice, providing a basis for theories about the dynamics of political change in America.

In this second edition, Todd E. Pettys has written a completely new treatise on the history and development of the Iowa Constitution, as well as a section-by-section analysis of the state's governing document as part of *The Oxford Commentaries on the State Constitutions of the United States*, a series which reflects the renewed interest in state constitutions and will contribute to our knowledge about them. Because the constitutional tradition of each state is distinctive, the volume begins with the history and development of constitutionalism in Iowa. It then provides the complete text of the state's current constitution, with each section accompanied by commentary that explains the provision and traces its origins and its interpretation by the courts and by other governmental bodies. Finally, the book concludes with a bibliographic essay, a table of cases cited in the volume, and a topical index.

G. Alan Tarr

ACKNOWLEDGMENTS

I am grateful to many people for the roles they played in helping me bring this book across the finish line. Thanks to Gail Agrawal, Eric Andersen, Barry Butler, and the Iowa Board of Regents for supporting my work on the manuscript; to Blair and Joan White and their sons, Blair and Brian, who created the chair that I am privileged to hold at the University of Iowa College of Law; to everyone at the University of Iowa Law Library and the State Historical Society of Iowa for fielding my questions and helping me chase down sources; to Pat Bauer, Marvin Bergman, Arthur Bonfield, Bill Hines, Shelly Kurtz, Caroline Sheerin, and Joe Yockey for critiquing drafts or talking with me about particular features of Iowa law; to Ross Andrews, who served as my energetic research assistant; to Alan Tarr, who brought me together with Oxford University Press for this project and served as my principal editor; and to Tony Lim and his colleagues at Oxford for their assistance and their faith. Most of all, I thank Caroline Sheerin and Lily Pettys Sheerin for the innumerable ways in which they sustain me.

Introduction

The story of the Iowa Constitution takes one on a journey through some of the most important transitions in American legal and political history—the transitions from the twilight years of Jacksonian democracy to the rise of the Republican party, from an era of explicit discrimination on the basis of race and sex to an era of textually proclaimed legal equality, and from skepticism about banks and paper money to reliance upon a national currency, to name just a few. Of course, Iowa's constitutional story is also rooted in the particularities of Iowa itself, beginning with Iowans' early geographic ambitions and the political commitments of the state's first generation of leaders.

Part I of this book broadly sketches the Iowa Constitution's origins and evolution. Part II turns to the history and meaning of each of the constitution's individual provisions. A brief bibliographic essay then introduces readers to the many resources available to those studying the Iowa Constitution. In the Table of Cases, the reader will find full citations to all of the cases referenced in the book. The book's account of judicial rulings is current through June 30, 2017; periodic updates will be provided on the author's website, www.todd-pettys.com.

PART ONE

The History of the Iowa Constitution

THE IOWA TERRITORY

Representing a small but resource-rich portion of the more than 800,000 square miles of land that the United States acquired from France in the Louisiana Purchase of 1803, the area that eventually would become Iowa was not the focus of sustained national attention until the 1830s. Under federal legislation enacted in 1804 and 1805, Iowa's future home was initially part of the enormous District (and then Territory) of Louisiana.[1] In 1812, Congress renamed that vast region the Territory of Missouri[2]—an arrangement that endured until 1821, when some of that real estate was carved out to create a new state bearing the Missouri name. A large expanse of land—including today's Iowa—then sat beyond the reach of any organized territorial government for more than a decade.[3] With Native

[1] Act of Mar. 26, 1804, ch. 38, § 12, 2 Stat. 283, 287 (establishing the District of Louisiana and placing it under the control of the Territory of Indiana); Act of Mar. 3, 1805, ch. 31, 2 Stat. 331 (converting the District of Louisiana to the Territory of Louisiana). In the 1804 statute's first section, Congress established the Territory of Orleans, the jurisdiction that would be admitted to the Union eight years later as the State of Louisiana.

[2] Act of June 4, 1812, ch. 95, 2 Stat. 743. The name change was prompted by the fact that a state bearing the Louisiana name had been admitted to the Union earlier that year.

[3] Cyrenus Cole, *A History of the People of Iowa* (Cedar Rapids: Torch Press, 1921), pp. 133–35. Of course, Congress did not ignore the region entirely. Under the Missouri Compromise of 1820, for

American tribes occupying much of the area and with white settlers scarce, there was no pressing reason for Congress to provide a regional government.

In the 1830s, wars and treaties forced Native Americans to abandon large swaths of hospitable terrain along the west side of the Mississippi River north of Missouri.[4] White settlers poured into the region to take advantage of the resulting opportunities. With those settlements came the need for legal order and governmental services. Congress's initial response came in 1834, when it appended the land that would become Iowa (as well as other portions of the region) to the Territory of Michigan.[5] No one, however, expected that arrangement to last; with the available modes of travel and communication being what they were, the territory's leaders could not responsively govern a growing population scattered over such a vast area. Recognizing those difficulties, as well as the fact that a state carrying the Michigan name was poised to join the Union as soon as a border dispute with the State of Ohio could be resolved, Congress created the Territory of Wisconsin in 1836, with borders extending over a region that today includes Iowa, Minnesota, Wisconsin, and much of the Dakotas.[6]

The Territory of Wisconsin's leaders initially set up shop in Belmont, and then began making plans for moving the capital to Madison, fifty miles farther northeast. For those settling closer to the Missouri border, the arrangement was only marginally more satisfactory than when they were part of the Territory of Michigan.[7] Eager to bring lawmakers farther south, at least temporarily, Jeremiah Smith—a financially successful, Burlington-based member of the territory's Legislative Assembly[8]—volunteered to build a capitol in Burlington to accommodate the legislators' meetings while awaiting construction of their Madison quarters. Due in part to the lack of amenities in Belmont, Smith's offer found a receptive audience. On December 3, 1836, the Legislative Assembly declared that the territory's permanent seat of government would be located in Madison, with future legislative sessions held in Burlington until the public buildings in Madison were ready for occupancy.[9]

---

example, Congress banned slavery in all of the territory north of the parallel of 36° 30′, except for the proposed State of Missouri. Act of Mar. 6, 1820, ch. 22, § 8, 3 Stat. 545.

[4] For a map showing Native Americans' incremental loss of land through treaties dating from 1824 through 1851, see Leland L. Sage, *A History of Iowa* (Ames: Iowa State University Press, 1974), p. 45.

[5] Act of June 28, 1834, ch. 98, 4 Stat. 701.

[6] Act of Apr. 20, 1836, ch. 54, 5 Stat. 10.

[7] Louis Pelzer, "The History and Principles of the Democratic Party of the Territory of Iowa," 6 *Iowa Journal of History & Politics* 3, 7–8 (1908) [hereinafter Pelzer, *Democratic Party*].

[8] *See generally* Philip D. Jordan, "Iowa's Puzzling Jeremiah Smiths," 45 *Annals of Iowa* 352 (1980) (telling the stories of two Iowa men named Jeremiah Smith).

[9] Act of Dec. 3, 1836, *Acts Passed at the First Session of the Legislative Assembly of the Territory of Wisconsin* (Belmont: James Clarke, 1836), p. 49.

Alas, the lawmakers' time in Burlington proved to be less convenient than they had hoped. In December 1837, just one month after the Legislative Assembly arrived, Smith's capitol and some of its neighboring structures burned down, leaving legislators to assemble in separate buildings while hastening their plans for departure. Those in and near Burlington had known from the beginning, however, that the legislature's presence in that southerly location was only a temporary arrangement. By November 1837—one month before the fire—representatives of the territory's southern counties had already adopted a resolution asking Congress to place them within a new territorial government.[10]

Responding favorably with legislation finalized on June 12, 1838, Congress created the Territory of Iowa, with boundaries encompassing all of the land possessed by Iowa today, as well as much of what would become Minnesota and the Dakotas.[11] The population in the district that later would become the State of Iowa then stood at approximately 22,000, roughly double the number who had lived there just two years earlier.[12] President Martin Van Buren appointed Robert Lucas—a fellow Democrat, the former governor of Ohio, and an intense, often uncompromising man—to serve as the new territory's first governor.[13] Lucas arrived in Burlington in August 1838 and soon agreed to make that city the territory's temporary capital. With no designated building in which to work, lawmakers rented space in the Old Zion Methodist Episcopal Church, situated a short walk from the shore of the Mississippi River.[14]

Lucas made it clear that he had large aspirations for the territory and its burgeoning population. In his opening message to the territory's Legislative Assembly, for example, Lucas urged lawmakers to find a site for a more permanent capital. The assembly complied, initiating a site-selection process in the spring of 1839 that resulted in the founding of Iowa City more than sixty miles northwest of Burlington on the bank of the Iowa River.[15] On July 4, 1840, Lucas

---

[10] Stanley H. Cravens, "Capitals and Capitols in Early Wisconsin," in *State of Wisconsin 1983–1984 Blue Book* (Madison: Wisconsin Legislative Reference Bureau, 1983), pp. 99, 116–17; Marie Haefner, "The Capital at Burlington," 18 *The Palimpsest* 98 (1937).

[11] Act of June 12, 1838, ch. 96, 5 Stat. 235. For an overview of the Territory of Iowa's governmental structures and powers, see Benjamin F. Shambaugh, *The Constitutions of Iowa* (Iowa City: State Historical Society of Iowa, 1934), pp. 74–98. For an account of the origins of the name "Iowa"—an account that runs through Lieutenant Albert Miller Lea, of the United States Dragoons—see Benjamin F. Shambaugh, "The Naming of Iowa," 16 *The Palimpsest* 81 (1935). For a history of Lea himself, see Ruth A. Gallaher, "Albert Miller Lea," 33 *Iowa Journal of History & Politics* 195 (1935).

[12] Sage, *supra* note 4, pp. 59, 310.

[13] For a profile of Lucas, see John C. Parish, "Robert Lucas," 3 *The Palimpsest* 233 (1922).

[14] An historical marker sits on the church's former site today, resting atop the church's lintel stone. For histories of the church, see J.A. Swisher, "Old Zion Church," 13 *The Palimpsest* 274 (1932); Edmund H. Waring, "Old Zion Church, Burlington, Iowa," 9 *Annals of Iowa* 524 (1910).

[15] Sage, *supra* note 4, pp. 62–63. To help travelers find their way from the established settlement in Dubuque to the territory's new capital, Lyman Dillon—the owner of a sawmill in Cascade—was

and others ceremonially laid the cornerstone for the grand structure that would become the Capitol.[16] (Known today as Old Capitol, it stands at the heart of the University of Iowa's campus and remains Iowa City's visual centerpiece.) Lawmakers would relocate from Burlington to Iowa City a year and a half later, while the Capitol's construction was still underway.[17]

In November 1839, Lucas made a second, even more consequential recommendation: that lawmakers lay the groundwork for statehood by seeking approval to call a constitutional convention.[18] Although popular in some quarters, a large number of the territory's residents did not quickly warm to the idea. Many feared statehood's tax burden, since local funds would be needed to pay the salaries and other operational costs of an autonomous new government.[19] Democrats were the territory's dominant political party, and so Whigs had additional reasons to prefer the status quo: why give Democrats the opportunity to control the convention in which the constitution would be written, as well as the new government that the constitution would create?[20] With taxation-wary Democrats finding common cause with Whigs, voters rejected the convention proposal by more than a 2-to-1 margin in August 1840.[21]

A few months later, William Henry Harrison, a Whig, defeated Martin Van Buren in the race for the nation's presidency.[22] Harrison appointed John Chambers, a fellow Whig, to serve as the Territory of Iowa's second governor. Breaking with his party, Chambers shared Lucas's belief that the territory should

---

retained to plow the nearly 100-mile path to Iowa City. John C. Parish, "The Old Military Road," 2 *The Palimpsest* 33 (1921). For short essays on Iowa City's founding and early years, see the twentieth volume of *The Palimpsest*, published in 1939. Looking at territorial governments' development more generally, historian Silvana Siddali points out that, "[b]ecause of the potential for conflict, territorial assemblies . . . often created new capitals in an unsettled area rather than destabilizing a fragile frontier society by awarding the prize to an existing town." Silvana R. Siddali, "'Principle, Interest and Patriotism All Combine': The Fight Over Iowa's Capital City," 64 *Annals of Iowa* 111, 117 (2005).

[16] Benjamin F. Shambaugh, *The Old Stone Capitol Remembers* (Iowa City: State Historical Society of Iowa, 1939), pp. 116–18. For more on the building, see Margaret N. Keyes, *Old Capitol: Portrait of an Iowa Landmark* (Iowa City: University of Iowa Press, 1988).

[17] Upon their arrival in Iowa City in December 1841, lawmakers met in a building owned by Walter Butler on the corner of Clinton and Washington streets. The Capitol entered service on December 5, 1842. Shambaugh, *supra* note 16, p. 32.

[18] Shambaugh, *Constitutions of Iowa, supra* note 11, pp. 99–100.

[19] In the public debates, this was the Whigs' leading argument against calling a convention. Louis Pelzer, "The History and Principles of the Whigs of the Territory of Iowa," 5 *Iowa Journal of History & Politics* 46, 63 (1907) [hereinafter Pelzer, *Whigs*].

[20] Robert Cook, *Baptism of Fire: The Republican Party in Iowa, 1838–1878* (Ames: Iowa State University Press, 1994), pp. 18–21 (discussing the fault lines between Democrats and Whigs).

[21] Shambaugh, *Constitutions of Iowa, supra* note 11, pp. 103–04.

[22] Although Whigs remained a political minority in Iowa, the Harrison campaign did a great deal to strengthen Iowa Whigs' political organization. Pelzer, *Whigs, supra* note 19, pp. 48–53.

pursue statehood. Like many Democrats in the Legislative Assembly, he perceived that the region's continued population growth, together with financial inducements that Congress was offering, might now prompt Iowans to appraise the advantages of statehood more favorably. The legislature submitted the convention question to voters a second time in August 1842, but voters again rejected it.[23] Chambers and others desiring statehood were undeterred. In 1844, the Legislative Assembly placed the issue on voters' ballots for a third time. In an election held that April, a majority of those voting finally relented.[24]

■ THE 1844 CONVENTION

The Territory of Iowa's first constitutional convention commenced in the Capitol in Iowa City on October 7, 1844. As Whigs had feared, Democrats were firmly in control, holding fifty-one of the convention's seventy-two seats.[25] The first issue that sparked a lengthy debate, however, was one that did not break along party lines: should they begin each of their daily sessions with a prayer? Muscatine County's Elijah Sells proposed that the delegates do precisely that. Evidently anticipating heavenly supplications of a lengthy variety, Dubuque County's Francis Gehon pointed out that the convention was costing taxpayers between $200 and $300 per day. There were better things than prayer, he said, on which to spend the public's money. Gehon was joined by Jonathan Hall, a Democrat who figures prominently in the story of Iowa's constitutional history. Hall suggested that those seeking divine assistance either say their prayers at home or arrive at the Capitol early to pray, so that the rest of the delegates could begin their work on time. The opposition to Sells's proposal did not sit well with Wapello County's William Chapman, who said that Gehon, Hall, and others were insulting all who believed that God's guidance would be needed throughout the convention. Rather than bring Sells's proposal to a vote, the delegates opted to table it indefinitely.[26] Their rhetorical knives nevertheless sharpened, the delegates moved on to more textually consequential disagreements.

Although the delegates' debates ranged across a large number of topics (as will be noted from time to time in Part II's discussion of individual constitutional

---

[23] For an account of the election, see Jack T. Johnson, "The Election of 1842," 23 *The Palimpsest* 241 (1942). Remarkably, one of the Whigs' arguments against calling a convention that year was that Iowa lacked a sufficient number of eminent leaders to staff a state government. Pelzer, *Democratic Party, supra* note 7, p. 21.

[24] Shambaugh, *Constitutions of Iowa, supra* note 11, pp. 105–17.

[25] *Fragments of the Debates of the Iowa Constitutional Conventions of 1844 and 1846*, ed. Benjamin F. Shambaugh (Iowa City: State Historical Society of Iowa, 1900) [hereinafter *1844 and 1846 Fragments*], pp. 408–10 (listing the delegates' names, party affiliations, states of origin, occupations, county residences, and number of years in the Territory of Iowa).

[26] *1844 and 1846 Fragments, supra* note 25, pp. 11–21.

provisions), four subjects—banks, race, judges, and state boundaries—drew especially noteworthy attention.[27]

Banks

At the heart of the banking controversy lay a single question: should Iowa's constitution permit the creation of "banks of issue"—that is, banks authorized to issue paper designed to circulate as currency? The Second Bank of the United States, founded in 1816, had been a reliable source of paper money, but that institution closed its doors in 1836—over the strenuous objection of Whigs—after President Andrew Jackson, a Democrat, vetoed legislation that would have renewed its charter.[28] Just when the Territory of Iowa was trying to find its footing, many Americans thus found themselves without a ready means of conducting economic transactions.[29]

Like other buyers and sellers in the United States and its territories, the Territory of Iowa's residents had little choice but to barter or to use either gold and silver (specie) or notes issued by chartered banks.[30] In theory, note-issuing banks were typically obliged to redeem their paper for specie on demand. But gold and silver were in short supply, and so one's ability to exchange a note for those coveted metals was far from certain. Indeed, in an effort to discourage redemption calls, some "wildcat" banks established themselves in unfamiliar and inaccessible locations (where wildcats were said to roam). Because there often was no way for buyers and sellers to be sure how much banks' paper was actually worth, they were left to speculate about the degree to which its face value should be discounted. Hoping to profit from that uncertainty, many banks added discounting services to their portfolios, offering specie or notes for other banks' notes at less than the latter's face value.[31] Although paper issued by other states' and territories' chartered banks was in circulation throughout the Territory of Iowa, the territory itself had only one chartered bank—the Miners' Bank of Dubuque, which the Territory of Wisconsin chartered in 1836[32] and the

---

[27] For a discussion of some of the leading issues and forces at play in constitutional conventions held in Iowa, Illinois, Indiana, Michigan, Minnesota, Ohio, and Wisconsin from the 1820s through the 1850s, see Silvana R. Siddali, *Frontier Democracy: Constitutional Conventions in the Old Northwest* (New York: Cambridge University Press, 2016).

[28] *See generally* Ralph C.H. Catterall, *The Second Bank of the United States* (Chicago: University of Chicago Press, 1903).

[29] Erling A. Erickson, *Banking in Frontier Iowa, 1836–1865* (Ames: Iowa State University Press, 1971), pp. 12–13.

[30] *See generally* Ruth A. Gallaher, "Money in Pioneer Iowa, 1835–1865," 32 *Iowa Journal of History & Politics* 3 (1934).

[31] Erickson, *supra* note 29, pp. 9–15.

[32] Act of Nov. 30, 1836, *Acts Passed at the First Session of the Legislative Assembly of the Territory of Wisconsin* (Belmont: James Clarke, 1836), p. 27.

Territory of Iowa inherited upon its creation in 1838. Yet that bank suffered persistent problems, ranging from specie shortages to bad loans to shady dealings of various kinds.[33] By the time the delegates convened in Iowa City in 1844, the failures of the Miners' Bank—together with the unreliability of notes issued by chartered banks located elsewhere—had done much to stoke anti-bank sentiment within the territory.[34]

In their debates about how best to fix the banking problem, the delegates divided into roughly three groups: Whigs, who strongly favored allowing banks of issue to operate in Iowa (and whose party had defined itself in significant part by its opposition to President Jackson's decision to kill the Second Bank of the United States); a faction of Democrats who believed that the legislature should be permitted to establish banks of issue under strictly defined circumstances; and "hard money" Democrats who believed that banks of issue should be constitutionally banned. Stephen Hempstead—a Democrat and farmer from Dubuque County who would become the State of Iowa's second governor in 1850—was among those wishing to ban banks of issue altogether. In his judgment, the banking business "was the most cunning scheme ever devised by mortal man for the purpose of swindling the people, plundering them of their substance and filling the land with misery, dishonesty, and crime."[35] Robert Lucas (the Territory of Iowa's first governor) and Gideon Bailey—Democrats representing Johnson County and Van Buren County, respectively—argued that the constitution should allow the people and their elected representatives to decide for themselves how to resolve the banking question.[36] Joseph Hawkins, a Whig from Henry County, agreed that it would be a mistake to "tie up the people's hands, while other States were issuing paper and sending it among us."[37] After a debate that spanned multiple days, the delegates voted 45 to 22 to produce a draft constitution that would permit the legislature to create banks, but only if the banks' charters were directly approved by Iowa voters at a general election.[38]

---

[33] Howard H. Preston, *History of Banking in Iowa* (Iowa City: State Historical Society of Iowa, 1922), pp. 10–30.

[34] Erickson, *supra* note 29, pp. 16–35. The Legislative Assembly repealed the bank's charter in 1845. Act of May 21, 1845, reprinted in *Acts and Resolutions Passed at the Several Sessions of the Territorial Legislature of Iowa 1840–1846* (Des Moines: Emory H. English, 1912) [hereinafter *1840–1846 Acts and Resolutions*], p. 564. The Iowa Supreme Court upheld the repeal in *Miners' Bank of Dubuque v. United States* (1848).

[35] *1844 and 1846 Fragments, supra* note 25, pp. 197–98.

[36] *1844 and 1846 Fragments, supra* note 25, pp. 74–77.

[37] *1844 and 1846 Fragments, supra* note 25, pp. 79–80.

[38] *1844 and 1846 Fragments, supra* note 25, p. 167.

Race

Issues of race also featured prominently in the delegates' discussions.[39] Although the Missouri Compromise of 1820 barred slavery in Iowa,[40] there were a variety of ways in which the territory's existing laws treated blacks far less favorably than whites. In one of its first enactments, for example, the territory's Legislative Assembly had declared that "no black or mulatto person shall be permitted to settle or reside in this Territory" unless he or she (1) had a judicially issued certificate attesting to his or her freedom and (2) posted a $500 bond, which would be forfeited if he or she was convicted "of any crime or misdemeanor against the penal laws of this Territory."[41] Only "free white male[s]" were permitted to vote in the territory's elections.[42] No "negro, mulatto, or Indian" was allowed to "be a witness in any court, or in any case against a white person."[43] Interracial marriages involving "white persons" were "illegal and void."[44]

On the sixth day of the convention, Henry County's George Hobson presented a petition from sixty-two citizens who wanted the delegates to adopt a provision granting people of color a wide range of rights, including the right to vote.[45] After an initial period of debate, the delegates appointed a thirteen-member committee to ponder the question of black suffrage, as well as to consider the wisdom and feasibility of banning blacks from settling in the new state altogether.[46] Three days later, Henry County's Jonathan Hall returned with the committee's report, announcing that they were firmly opposed to giving blacks the right to vote. He conceded that blacks and whites were equal "in a state of

---

[39] For accounts of the rights and experiences of blacks in early Iowa, see Leola Nelson Bergmann, "The Negro in Iowa," 46 *Iowa Journal of History & Politics* 3 (1948); Louis Pelzer, "The Negro and Slavery in Early Iowa," 2 *Iowa Journal of History & Politics* 471 (1904).

[40] Act of Mar. 6, 1820, ch. 22, § 8, 3 Stat. 545.

[41] Act of Jan. 21, 1839, ch. 24, *Revised Statutes of the Territory of Iowa* (Iowa City: Hughes & Williams, 1843) [hereinafter *1843 Revised Statutes*], p. 98. (The State of Iowa reprinted the *1843 Revised Statutes*, with different pagination, in 1911.) The legislation also made it a crime to "knowingly engage, or hire, or harbor" any "colored person" who had not met these requirements. For a discussion of the law's predecessors, see Robert R. Dykstra, *Bright Radical Star: Black Freedom and White Supremacy on the Hawkeye Frontier* (Ames: Iowa State University Press, 1993), pp. 24–27.

[42] Act Providing for and Regulating General Elections, § 12, *1843 Revised Statutes, supra* note 41, p. 248.

[43] Act of Feb. 10, 1843, ch. 112, § 37, *1843 Revised Statutes, supra* note 41, p. 475.

[44] Act of Jan. 6, 1840, ch. 100, § 13, *1843 Revised Statutes, supra* note 41, p. 436.

[45] *Journal of the Convention for the Formation of a Constitution for the State of Iowa* (Iowa City: Jesse Williams, 1845) [hereinafter *1844 Journal*], pp. 32–33. (Despite its 1845 publication date, this is the official journal of the Territory of Iowa's 1844 constitutional convention.) The delegates subsequently received another petition urging them to give people of color all of the "rights and privileges" enjoyed by whites. *See id.* p. 110.

[46] *1844 Journal, supra* note 45, p. 44; *1844 and 1846 Fragments, supra* note 25, pp. 26–29, 33.

nature," but said that this was "a mere abstract proposition." Women and children similarly possess "what we abstractly term unalienable rights," he said, and "yet they submit without complaint or murmur" and "[n]o one thinks of sympathizing with them in their deprivations." White men, Hall argued, are "not bound to unbar [the government's] doors and receive every vagrant who may take refuge in it." He predicted that, if Iowa allowed blacks to vote, "[t]he policy of other States would drive the whole black population of the Union upon us," and Iowa's whites would be overrun at the ballot box.[47] The cause of black suffrage never progressed any further at the 1844 convention. Blacks' only small victory on this front came when the delegates declined to take any decisive action on the suggestion by Francis Gehon that the convention adopt a resolution stating that the General Assembly "never shall entertain petitions in regard to negro suffrage."[48]

With respect to the committee's other agenda item, Hall reported (without elaboration) that the committee did not favor trying to exclude non-whites from the state. Many in the convention, however, were of a different mind. By a vote of 32 to 21, the delegates initially endorsed the motion of Edward Langworthy—a miner and Democrat from Dubuque County—to include a provision directing the General Assembly to adopt legislation aimed at preventing "blacks and mulattoes" from settling in Iowa.[49] When the matter came up for discussion in a subsequent session, Langworthy argued that, without such a provision, Iowa would "have all the broken-down negroes of Missouri overrunning us." Van Buren County's Gideon Bailey agreed that "the people of Iowa did not want negroes swarming among them." By the narrow vote of 32 to 35, however, the delegates ultimately rejected Langworthy's proposal.[50] Because the voting delegates' identities were not recorded for the first of the two votes, one cannot say

---

[47] *1844 Journal, supra* note 45, pp. 52–54.

[48] *1844 Journal, supra* note 45, p. 121; *1844 and 1846 Fragments, supra* note 25, p. 123.

[49] *1844 and 1846 Fragments, supra* note 25, p. 66.

[50] The vote did not end all talk of racial exclusion in Iowa. Seven years later, for example, Billy G. Haun—a Democrat—introduced a bill in the Iowa house that would explicitly bar blacks from settling in Iowa. The measure passed the house and proceeded to the senate. In that chamber, one of Haun's opponents successfully inserted a provision stating that the legislation would not become effective until published "in the *Iowa True Democrat*, a weekly newspaper published in Mount Pleasant." Unbeknownst to Haun and his allies, that newspaper was an anti-slavery publication. The measure passed the senate, was approved in its amended form by the house, and signed by Governor Stephen Hempstead. Act of Feb. 5, 1851, ch. 72, 1851 Iowa Acts 172. The newspaper, of course, refused to publish the statute, leaving its legal status in some doubt. Thirteen years to the day after its purported enactment, the General Assembly repealed the measure while simultaneously expressing uncertainty about whether it had fully held the status of law in the first place. Act of Feb. 5, 1864, ch. 7, 1864 Iowa Acts 6. For good discussions of those events, see Richard, Lord Acton & Patricia Nassif Acton, "A Legal History of African-Americans: From the Iowa Territory to the State Sesquicentennial, 1838–1996," in *Outside In: African-American History in Iowa, 1838–2000*, ed. Bill Silag (Des Moines: State Historical Society of Iowa, 2001), pp. 61–89; Dykstra, *supra* note 41, pp. 110–13, 198–200.

whether the thirty-two exclusionists largely held together as a block and were simply outnumbered by newly participating delegates in the second vote, or whether a number of Langworthy's initial supporters subsequently abandoned his proposal. We do know, however, that at least one delegate fell into the latter camp. James Grant—a Scott County lawyer and Democrat—told the delegates that, although he had initially voted in favor of Langworthy's proposal because he "was as anxious as anyone to keep negroes out of the State," he had reluctantly concluded that the provision probably violated the U.S. Constitution and could doom Iowa's bid for statehood.[51]

In the end, the document that the 1844 delegates produced declared that only white men would be eligible to vote,[52] serve in the General Assembly,[53] and serve in the militia,[54] and only whites would be eligible to be counted for purposes of legislative apportionment.[55]

Judges

With respect to judges, the central point on which the delegates divided was whether members of the bench should be chosen by the legislature or by Iowa voters. (Nomination by the executive—the arrangement under the federal system—was never seriously considered.) The Committee on the Judiciary, chaired by Jonathan Hall, proposed that all judges seeking seats on the state's supreme and district courts "be elected by the joint vote of the Senate and House of Representatives."[56] Urging his colleagues to reject that proposal, John Fletcher—a farmer and Democrat from Muscatine County—filed a report on behalf of a minority of the judiciary committee,[57] arguing that the people were entirely capable of making these decisions, that no advantage would be gained from delegating the selection responsibility to legislators, and that judges' dependence upon the people's favor would provide "a most salutary restraint against any deviation from the path of duty."[58] Elijah Sells and Gideon Bailey were among those who believed that, far from having a beneficial influence, making judges directly dependent upon the will of the larger electorate would foster judicial bias and corruption. At the suggestion of Stephen Hempstead, the delegates compromised by deciding to allow the legislature to select the

---

[51] *1844 and 1846 Fragments, supra* note 25, pp. 155–56. For additional description and analysis of the debate, see Dykstra, *supra* note 41, pp. 52–67.

[52] *1844 Journal, supra* note 45, p. 190.

[53] *1844 Journal, supra* note 45, p. 191.

[54] *1844 Journal, supra* note 45, p. 198.

[55] *1844 Journal, supra* note 45, p. 194.

[56] *1844 Journal, supra* note 45, p. 35.

[57] *1844 Journal, supra* note 45, pp. 65–67.

[58] *1844 and 1846 Fragments, supra* note 25, pp. 113, 192–95.

members of the supreme court and Iowa voters to select the members of the district courts. As Washington County's William Harrison put it just prior to the delegates' vote, this divided approach would give the new state an opportunity to experiment with two different selection methods and thereby learn through experience whether one was preferable to the other.[59]

State Boundaries

The fourth issue that sparked a particularly noteworthy discussion—and proved to be more consequential than the delegates anticipated at the time—was where to place the proposed new state's boundaries. Back in November 1839, when first urging the Territory of Iowa's lawmakers to begin moving down the path toward statehood, Governor Robert Lucas had proposed boundaries that seemed sensible to him, based largely upon the location of various rivers.[60] Now a Johnson County delegate to the constitutional convention, Lucas was a member of the Committee on State Boundaries. On the convention's fourth day, the committee proposed boundaries—commonly referred to as "the Lucas boundaries"—that largely matched those that Lucas had advocated five years earlier.[61] Comparing those boundaries to the ones that ultimately defined the State of Iowa, the observer finds two key differences: Lucas's plan would have sliced off the northwest corner of today's Iowa, and the northern boundary would have been formed by two meandering legs of a triangle, with their apex extending all the way up to today's St. Paul, Minnesota.[62] A handful of delegates proposed different boundaries, focusing particularly on the north (due in part to uncertainty about where particular rivers were situated) and on the south (due in part to uncertainty about the location of the adjacent State of Missouri's northern border—uncertainty that had nearly led to armed conflict between residents of Missouri and the Territory of Iowa in earlier years, and that would not be fully resolved until the U.S. Supreme Court's 1849 ruling in *Missouri v. Iowa*).[63] Nevertheless, with minor alterations in verbiage, the delegates ultimately embraced the Lucas boundaries.

---

[59] *1844 and 1846 Fragments*, *supra* note 25, pp. 104–05, 110, 115–16, 118–19.

[60] Erik M. Eriksson, "The Boundaries of Iowa," 25 *Iowa Journal of History & Politics* 163, 207–08 (1927).

[61] *1844 Journal*, *supra* note 45, pp. 17–18; Eriksson, *supra* note 60, pp. 208–10; Sage, *supra* note 4, p. 85.

[62] For a set of colored maps nicely illustrating the various boundaries that will be referenced throughout this discussion, see Benjamin F. Shambaugh, "Maps Illustrative of the Boundary History of Iowa," 2 *Iowa Journal of History & Politics* 369, 377–80 (1904).

[63] *1844 and 1846 Fragments*, *supra* note 25, pp. 22–24, 30–33, 135–36, 182–88. For discussions of the boundary conflict between Iowa and Missouri, see Derek R. Everett, "To Shed Our Blood for Our Beloved Territory: The Iowa-Missouri Borderland," 67 *Annals of Iowa* 269 (2008); Carol J. Kraus, "A Study in Border Confrontation: The Iowa-Missouri Boundary Dispute," 40 *Annals of Iowa* 81 (1969).

On November 1, 1844, the convention adjourned. Whether because they genuinely believed the draft contained fatal weaknesses or because they did not want Democrats to control the new government that the proposed constitution would establish, Whigs worked hard in the ensuing months to defeat ratification. Iowa City's William Penn Clarke—a journalist and attorney who plays a prominent role in Iowa's constitutional story—was among the Whig leaders who believed that the political tide would soon turn in their party's favor, and that Whigs' political interests would thus best be served by thwarting ratification of a constitution until after the Democrats' power had waned.[64] Whigs' criticisms ranged across a broad spectrum of areas, from the draft's requirement that banks' charters be approved by a vote of the people, to the draft's provision for popularly electing district judges, to other matters. Some of the territory's residents continued to resist the very idea of statehood, arguing that it would entail unjustifiably heavy tax burdens.[65]

At the same time that the Territory of Iowa's residents were immersed in the ratification debate, members of Congress were also scrutinizing the document. In December 1844, copies of the draft constitution had been presented in both chambers of Congress in conjunction with the territory's application for statehood. Congress's practice at that time was to admit slave states and free states in opposite pairs (hoping thereby to forestall a definitive resolution of the slavery question), and since 1838 the proposed slave state of Florida had been awaiting a free-state application partner. In the early months of 1845, Congress produced legislation that would bring both Iowa and Florida into the Union. Congress's approval of Iowa's application for statehood had just one catch: Iowans would need to accept less generous state boundaries than those proposed in the draft constitution. Southern states had been satisfied with the Lucas boundaries; they were not eager to see the west divided into numerous small states that would carry heavy voting power in Congress on issues concerning slavery and other matters of interest to the South. Southern states' political adversaries, of course, found the idea of small western states appealing precisely because of the national political power those states could wield. Counting themselves among the latter group, Representative Alexander Duncan and Senator Samuel Vinton, both of Ohio, helped lead the charge for drawing Iowa's boundaries more sparingly than the delegates to the 1844 convention had proposed. Congress concluded that Iowa could enter the Union only if it accepted the more constrained borders that the French-American explorer Joseph ("Jean-Nicolas") Nicollet had proposed in an 1843 report he produced following his travels in the upper Mississippi basin on behalf of the War Department's Bureau of Topographical

[64] Sage, *supra* note 4, p. 88.

[65] Shambaugh, *Constitutions of Iowa, supra* note 11, pp. 168–73.

Engineers.[66] On March 3, 1845, President John Tyler signed Congress's conclusion into law.[67]

When news of Congress's actions reached the Territory of Iowa, the proposed constitution's opponents found themselves armed with new ammunition. The pending ratification vote had been structured in such a way that a "Yes" vote would signal a voter's willingness to accept any conditions that Congress had attached when approving the application for statehood.[68] Finding the Nicollet boundaries unacceptably confining, a number of leading Democrats thus joined Whigs in publicly opposing ratification. The Territory of Iowa's delegate to Congress—a Democrat named Augustus Dodge, to whom our attention will be returning—took the contrary view, urging Iowans to ratify the proposed constitution and accept the Nicollet boundaries; he had initially favored the Lucas boundaries proposed in the convention's draft, but believed Congress would never budge on the issue.[69] On April 7, 1845, more than 13,000 voters passed judgment on the proposed constitution and the Nicollet boundaries—and a majority rejected them by a 996-vote margin.[70] Over Governor Chambers's veto, the Legislative Assembly gave voters one more chance to assent in August of that same year, but—by a 421-vote margin amidst heavier turnout—voters again sent the document and the Nicollet boundaries down to defeat.[71]

■ THE 1846 CONVENTION

When the Territory of Iowa's Legislative Assembly gathered in Iowa City for a new session in December 1845, they brought with them the conviction that, although voters had rejected the proposed constitution, they still desired statehood. Joined by James Clarke—a Democrat who had represented Des Moines

---

[66] Eriksson, *supra* note 60, pp. 212–15; Sage, *supra* note 4, pp. 86–87. For a map comparing the Nicollet boundaries to those that define the State of Iowa's contours today, see Shambaugh, *supra* note 62, p. 380. For Nicollet's account of why he drew the boundaries as he did, see Jean Nicolas Nicollet, "The Nicollet Boundaries," 9 *The Palimpsest* 170 (1928). For a profile of Nicollet himself, see Ruth A. Gallaher, "J.N. Nicollet, Map Maker," 26 *The Palimpsest* 289 (1945).

[67] Act of Mar. 3, 1845, ch. 48, 5 Stat. 742.

[68] Shambaugh, *Constitutions of Iowa*, *supra* note 11, pp. 157–58.

[69] Sage, *supra* note 4, p. 88. Dodge subsequently came under withering criticism for failing to persuade Congress to accept the Lucas boundaries. For a discussion of Dodge's actions in Congress and their political aftermath, see Louis Pelzer, *Augustus Caesar Dodge* (Iowa City: State Historical Society of Iowa, 1908), pp. 112–21.

[70] The vote was 6,023 in favor and 7,019 against. Richard, Lord Acton & Patricia Nassif Acton, *To Go Free: A Treasury of Iowa's Legal Heritage* (Ames: Iowa State University Press, 1995), p. 53.

[71] The vote was 7,235 in favor and 7,656 against. Governor's Message of Dec. 3, 1846, reprinted in 1 *Documentary Material Relating to the History of Iowa*, ed. Benjamin F. Shambaugh (Iowa City: State Historical Society of Iowa, 1897) [hereinafter *Documentary Material*], pp. 183–84.

County at the 1844 convention and whom President James Polk had installed as the territory's third governor in November 1845—the Legislative Assembly called for an election of delegates to a second constitutional convention.[72] Perhaps signaling a belief that Iowans would accept the 1844 draft if it were changed in only a few significant ways, the legislature determined that thirty-two delegates would suffice for the second convention, less than half the number who had attended in 1844. In the ensuing April 1846 elections, Democrats once again trounced the Whigs, securing twenty-two of the convention's seats.[73]

Assembling in the Capitol in Iowa City, the delegates began their work on May 4, 1846. They adjourned only fifteen days later, completing their labors in roughly half the time of their predecessors. Many portions of the draft they produced were textually or functionally identical to the draft written two years earlier. For example, the delegates to the 1846 convention copied the 1844 document's provisions making only white men eligible to vote,[74] serve in the General Assembly,[75] and serve in the militia,[76] and making only whites eligible to be counted for purposes of legislative apportionment.[77] To pick just three additional examples, the delegates in 1846 copied almost verbatim the lengthy bill of rights that the 1844 convention had produced,[78] the 1844 provisions stating that the General Assembly would choose the Iowa Supreme Court's justices and ordinary voters would choose the district courts' judges,[79] and the 1844 provision making it difficult for the state to incur more than $100,000 in aggregate debt.[80]

Of course, the delegates did make some changes. A few of those alterations addressed matters that, while small in the grand scheme of things, had nevertheless been controversial during the prior ratification debates. The 1844 draft, for example, would not have allowed the senate to choose its own president; rather, a separately elected lieutenant governor was to serve that function. The delegates

---

[72] Act of Jan. 17, 1846, reprinted in *1840–1846 Acts and Resolutions, supra* note 34, p. 669. Learning from the 1844 experience, the legislature this time made it clear that the delegates' draft constitution was not to be presented to Congress until after it had been ratified by the people. *Id.* § 8.

[73] *1844 and 1846 Fragments, supra* note 25, pp. 414–15.

[74] *Compare* Iowa Const. of 1846, art. III, § 1, *with 1844 Journal, supra* note 45, p. 190.

[75] *Compare* Iowa Const. of 1846, art. IV, §§ 4, 5, *with 1844 Journal, supra* note 45, p. 191.

[76] *Compare* Iowa Const. of 1846, art. VII, § 1, *with 1844 Journal, supra* note 45, p. 198.

[77] *Compare* Iowa Const. of 1846, art. IV, § 31, *with 1844 Journal, supra* note 45, p. 194.

[78] The delegates made only two notable changes to the bill of rights: they added a provision barring those who engaged in dueling from ever holding public office, Iowa Const. of 1846, art. II, § 5, and they omitted an 1844 provision giving juries the right "to determine the law" in libel prosecutions, *compare id.* § 7 *with 1844 Journal, supra* note 45, p. 188.

[79] *Compare* Iowa Const. of 1846, art. VI, §§ 4, 5 *with 1844 Journal, supra* note 45, p. 198.

[80] *Compare* Iowa Const. of 1846, art. VIII, *with 1844 Journal, supra* note 45, p. 199.

to the 1846 convention opted to omit the position of lieutenant governor altogether and to allow senators to choose their own leader.[81]

Three changes they made proved to be especially consequential. First, rather than allow banks of issue to operate in Iowa so long as their charters had been approved by the electorate, the delegates to the 1846 convention opted to take an even stricter approach to the currency problem. The 1846 text flatly barred all persons and entities from "exercising the privileges of banking, or creating paper to circulate as money."[82] The delegates' approval of that provision proceeded almost entirely along party lines, with only one Whig—Van Buren County's Erastus Hoskins—voting in the affirmative and no Democrat voting in opposition.[83]

The second change concerned constitutional amendments. The 1844 draft proposed two separate paths for altering the constitution: (1) making additions or deletions specifically proposed by the General Assembly and approved by the electorate and (2) calling a constitutional convention. The delegates to the 1846 convention opted to take the first option off the table.[84] That decision had enormous implications. To pick what will prove to be an appropriate example, let us imagine that Iowans were soon to conclude that they had made a mistake when they entirely banned banks of issue from operating in the state. The 1846 text would not allow them simply to amend the unwise provision; instead, a full constitutional convention would be required.

The third major change concerned the proposed new state's geographic borders, the issue on which Congress and the Territory of Iowa's voters had previously butted heads. By the time the delegates arrived in Iowa City for the second convention, a solution to that problem had already begun to take shape. Shortly after the 1844 draft's defeat at the polls, Augustus Dodge—the Territory of Iowa's delegate to Congress—urged the nation's lawmakers to amend the March 1845 legislation requiring statehood-seeking Iowans to accept the Nicollet boundaries. Illinois Representative Stephen Douglas—chair of the House Committee on Territories—was sympathetic to Dodge's plea. On March 27, 1846, Douglas proposed a compromise between the Lucas and Nicollet boundaries. Under his plan, (1) the state's western boundary would reach all the way to the Missouri and Big Sioux rivers, a line much farther to the west than the Nicollet plan would have set (and, in the northwest corner, farther west than even the Lucas plan had contemplated), and (2) the state's northern boundary would be set at the

---

[81] Shambaugh, *Constitutions of Iowa, supra* note 11, pp. 194–98 (noting this and other differences between the 1844 and 1846 texts).

[82] Iowa Const. of 1846, art. IX, § 1.

[83] *Journal of the Convention for the Formation of a Constitution for the State of Iowa* (Iowa City: Abraham H. Palmer, 1846) [hereinafter *1846 Journal*], pp. 86, 102.

[84] Iowa Const. of 1846, art. XI.

parallel of 43° 30′, a line farther south than either the Nicollet plan or the Lucas plan would have established.[85]

While that proposal was circulating in Congress, the Territory of Iowa's second constitutional convention commenced in Iowa City. Due to the rudimentary nature of communication technology at the time, the delegates did not have up-to-date information about how Douglas's March 27 proposal was faring in the House and Senate. Nevertheless, on the delegates' second day of work, the Committee on Boundaries (chaired by Scott County's James Grant, who had represented that same county at the 1844 convention) proposed that the convention set the western boundary at the Missouri and Big Sioux rivers and the northern boundary at 43° 30′—the same western and northern boundaries that Douglas had proposed.[86] By an 8-to-22 vote, the delegates initially rejected that proposal, insisting instead on the more expansive Lucas boundaries that the 1844 convention had endorsed.[87] Six days later, Van Buren County's William Steele asked his colleagues to revisit that decision and to accept the more modest boundaries that Douglas had sketched. After a period of deliberation, the delegates agreed that Douglas's proposal was acceptable.[88]

Three weeks after the 1846 convention adjourned, Congress took up action on the Douglas plan. By that time, Douglas and his colleagues knew that the delegates to the Iowa convention had agreed to accept the compromise boundary lines. Some in Congress continued to argue that the territories ought to be divided into even smaller states in order to counterbalance southern states' voting power, but this time those arguments were unavailing. Concluding that Douglas and the delegates to the 1846 convention had found an acceptable balance between the nation's sectional concerns and Iowans' geographically expansive ambitions, Congress approved those boundaries on August 1. At the suggestion of Representative James Bowlin, of Missouri, Congress employed precisely the same boundary-defining language that appeared in the draft produced by the 1846 convention.[89] On August 4, 1846, President Polk signed the bill into law.[90]

As it happens, the Territory of Iowa's voters cast their ballots on the question of ratification on August 3, just one day before President Polk signed Congress's boundary-setting legislation. Whether voters would accept the proposed constitution was far from certain. A powerful recitation of the case

---

[85] Eriksson, *supra* note 60, p. 222.

[86] *1846 Journal, supra* note 83, p. 28.

[87] *1846 Journal, supra* note 83, pp. 39, 48–49.

[88] *1846 Journal, supra* note 83, pp. 87–88, 102.

[89] *Congressional Globe*, 29th Cong., 1st Sess. (1846), pp. 938–41; Eriksson, *supra* note 60, pp. 223–27; Pelzer, *supra* note 69, pp. 126–27.

[90] Act of Aug. 4, 1846, ch. 82, 9 Stat. 52.

against ratification appeared in a lengthy (and, as will be seen, largely prescient) essay published by *The Iowa Standard* on June 20, 1846.[91] The essay's author was William Penn Clarke, the Whig whose opposition to the 1844 convention's draft we have already noted, and who was now seeking election to the Territory of Iowa's Legislative Assembly.[92] In Clarke's judgment, the proposed constitution contained numerous fatal mistakes, first among which was the absolute ban on banks of issue—a ban that rendered Iowa's currency-users dependent upon the solvency and integrity of other states' institutions. Clarke believed the delegates also had erred by sharply limiting the state's ability to finance internal improvements with debt, by using popular elections as the mode of choosing district courts' judges, by making conventions the lone permissible method of amending the constitution's text, and by establishing boundaries that rendered Iowa City an inconveniently located state capital. On the last of those issues, Clarke predicted that there soon would be a movement to shift the state capital to the west, in the direction of "the Raccoon Forks" and the "Desmoines River," and that, to make that change palatable in Iowa City, "we shall probably be promised a State University, or something of that character."

In the August 3 election, Iowa voters ratified the proposed constitution by an exceptionally thin margin (9,492 to 9,036).[93] Given the closeness of that vote and the nature of some of the issues that Clarke had flagged, it does not come as a surprise to learn that the state would call a third constitutional convention less than a dozen years later. Iowans nevertheless finally had a constitution. In the Territory of Iowa's final months, voters went about the business of staffing the government that their new constitution prescribed. In an election held on October 26, 1846, Democrats easily won control of the General Assembly, and a Democrat—Ansel Briggs—was elected to serve as the new state's first governor.[94] Two months later—on December 28, 1846—President Polk signed legislation making Iowa the Union's twenty-ninth state,[95] home to approximately 100,000 people.[96]

---

[91] *1844 and 1846 Fragments, supra* note 25, pp. 347–65 (reprinting the essay).

[92] At the time he wrote the essay, he was aligned with the Whigs. By 1857, when he was elected to Iowa's third constitutional convention, he was a Republican. For an introduction to Clarke, see Erik McKinley Eriksson, "William Penn Clarke," 25 *Iowa Journal of History & Politics* 3 (1927). For a brief glimpse of his later political career, see Tyler Anbinder, "William Penn Clarke and the Know-Nothing Movement: a Document," 52 *Annals of Iowa* 43 (1994).

[93] *1844 and 1846 Fragments, supra* note 25, pp. 371–73 (reprinting Governor James Clarke's announcement of the election results).

[94] Shambaugh, *Constitutions of Iowa, supra* note 11, p. 210.

[95] Act of Dec. 28, 1846, ch. 1, 9 Stat. 117.

[96] Sage, *supra* note 4, p. 310.

THE 1857 CONVENTION

Over the ensuing decade, Iowa's population quintupled, rising to nearly 520,000 by 1856.[97] Agricultural production soared, as well.[98] At the same time, the state was awash with currency issued by other states' and territories' chartered banks, with much of that paper carrying little or uncertain value. Some of Iowa's businesses and municipal governments issued scrip to finance their operations, obtaining specie, services, or other things of value in exchange for paper entitling future bearers to payment. This practice helped to provide Iowans with a source of paper currency, but it sometimes proved unreliable and, in any event, was insufficient to meet the demand.[99] Whigs argued that the new constitution's anti-banking provision was forcing the state and its residents into an unsustainable financial position, but—given the impressive gains in Iowa's population and productivity—this economic argument struggled to find traction.[100] In the gubernatorial election of 1850, for example, Iowans chose Stephen Hempstead, one of the Democrats who had strongly opposed banks of issue during his service as a delegate to the 1846 convention.[101]

By 1854, however, a historic political shift was underway in many portions of the country. Within Iowa, the shift was fueled, in part, by an alliance that emerged on the issue of slavery between two Democrats in the United States Senate: Iowa's own Augustus Dodge—formerly the Territory of Iowa's delegate to Congress—and Stephen Douglas, of Illinois. During his prior service in the House, Douglas proposed the Iowa boundaries on which Congress and the delegates to the 1846 convention ultimately settled. Now a member of the Senate and exerting his influence on other matters, Douglas insisted that the Missouri Compromise of 1820 be repealed. Under that legislation, Congress had banned slavery in all of the former Louisiana territory north of the parallel of 36° 30′, except for the State of Missouri.[102] Douglas argued that the residents of new states and territories—Kansas and Nebraska among them—were entitled to decidc for themselves whether to permit slavery within their borders. Delivering an unequivocal speech on the floor of the Senate, Dodge came powerfully to Douglas's aid, arguing that the Missouri Compromise was an unconstitutional and "dangerous assumption[] of power," that "[s]ocial and political equality between two races which are created so different is an abhorrent thought," that power-seeking abolitionists were chiefly to blame for the miserable conditions

---

[97] Sage, *supra* note 4, p. 310.

[98] Preston, *supra* note 33, pp. 45–46.

[99] Preston, *supra* note 33, pp. 65–68.

[100] Cook, *supra* note 20, pp. 39–41.

[101] Preston, *supra* note 33, pp. 70–71.

[102] Act of Mar. 6, 1820, ch. 22, § 8, 3 Stat. 545.

in which many southern slaves lived, and that Douglas's legislation would likely improve the lives of many blacks.[103] Douglas prevailed, securing passage of the Kansas-Nebraska Act.[104]

Outraged by Democrats' retreat from the Missouri Compromise, Iowa Whigs nominated James Grimes—an unapologetic defender of that thirty-four-year-old legislation—to oppose Hempstead in the governor's race, and Whigs ran with new energy for seats in the Iowa legislature, as well. In the August 1854 elections, Iowa voters gave Grimes the governorship and gave Whigs firm control of the house of representatives, and left Democrats with only a slim majority in the senate. In January 1855, the legislature placed the Whigs' favored candidates on the Iowa Supreme Court and—amidst much procedural drama—removed Dodge from the U.S. Senate and replaced him with James Harlan, a strong opponent of slavery who had been serving as president of Iowa Wesleyan University.[105]

The Whig party itself nationally unraveled during this period, and many Iowa Whigs—including Governor Grimes—realigned themselves with the newly emerging Republican party.[106] Republicans would quickly establish themselves

---

[103] *Congressional Globe*, Appendix, 33rd Cong., 1st Sess. (1854), pp. 375–83. Dodge's willingness to tolerate slavery was certainly not news to Iowans; previously, for example, Dodge had strongly defended the federal Fugitive Slave Act. Joel H. Silbey, "Proslavery Sentiment in Iowa, 1838–1861," 55 *Iowa Journal of History* 289, 302–05 (1957). But Dodge's 1854 alliance with Douglas came at a time when some Iowans' views about southern slavery were beginning to shift. Moreover, the repeal of the Missouri Compromise threatened to bring dramatic upheaval to some of Iowa's neighboring regions.

[104] Act of May 30, 1854, ch. 59, 10 Stat. 277. Iowa's other senator—George Jones, also a Democrat—joined Dodge and Douglas in voting for the legislation. Cole, *supra* note 3, p. 266. *See generally* Nicole Etcheson, *Bleeding Kansas: Contested Liberty in the Civil War Era* (Lawrence: University Press of Kansas, 2004); P. Orman Ray, *The Repeal of the Missouri Compromise: Its Origin and Authorship* (Boston: J.S. Canner and Co., 1965).

[105] Pelzer, *Democratic Party, supra* note 7, pp. 204–13. Because the Seventeenth Amendment to the U.S. Constitution was not added until more than half a century later, these events transpired at a time when state legislatures chose United States Senators. *See* U. S. Const. art. I, § 3, cl. 1. For information concerning political parties' representation in the Iowa General Assembly from session to session beginning in 1846, see Frank J. Stork & Cynthia A. Clingan, *The Iowa General Assembly: Our Legislative Heritage, 1846–1980* (Des Moines: Iowa Senate, 1980), pp. 5–8, available at https://www.legis.iowa.gov/docs/publications/BB/696310.pdf.

[106] *See generally* Cook, *supra* note 20, pp. 31–71; William J. Petersen, *The Story of Iowa: The Progress of an American State* (New York: Lewis Historical Publishing Co., 1952), pp. 390–97; David S. Sparks, "The Birth of the Republican Party in Iowa, 1854–1856," 54 *Iowa Journal of History* 1 (1956). Governor Grimes was among the Republican party's leading Iowa founders. Sage, *supra* note 4, pp. 130–32. As for the Whigs, their national demise was prominently signaled by the presidential election of 1852, in which their candidate—General Winfield Scott—was resoundingly defeated by Franklin Pierce. Thomas J. Rowland, *Franklin B. Pierce: The Twilight of Jacksonian Democracy* (New York: Nova Science Publishers, Inc., 2012), pp. 74–78.

as a powerful political force in the state, losing the governorship only once between 1854 and 1932. For purposes of Iowa's constitutional story, however, the most significant consequence of the 1854 election was immediately apparent: the Democratic party, so firmly in control at the 1844 and 1846 constitutional conventions, had lost its grip on power.[107]

For nearly a decade, frequently citing the need for in-state banks of issue, Whigs and even some Democrats had been pressing for a convention, influenced in part by the essay that William Penn Clarke had written in opposition to the 1846 constitution's adoption. The Democrats' electoral losses in 1854 finally gave those desiring change the opening they needed. On January 24, 1855, Governor Grimes signed legislation calling for a vote on whether to call a convention.[108] The following August, Iowans authorized a third convention by more than a 2-to-1 margin, with 32,790 voting in favor and 14,162 opposed. Of the thirty-six delegates whom voters elected three months later, twenty-one were Republicans and fifteen were Democrats.[109] These were the individuals who would write the constitutional text that, as amended, remains in force today.

* * *

On January 19, 1857, the delegates were gaveled to order in the Capitol in Iowa City. Because the legislature was still in session, the delegates assembled in the supreme court room on the building's first floor. By the end of the convention's third day, the delegates had selected their officers, agreed upon the convention's procedural rules, and staffed twelve standing committees. They also had entertained invitations from the cities of Davenport and Dubuque to move the convention to either of those locations.[110] Those invitations were not easily dismissed; because the General Assembly was still in session, the Capitol was crowded and public accommodations in Iowa City were tight. Scott County's George Ells complained, for example, that "[h]alf of the members of the Convention have to sleep three in a bed, and two on a bunk, in consequence of the want of good

---

[107] For a more complete discussion of the reasons for the Democrats' losses during this period, see David S. Sparks, "The Decline of the Democratic Party in Iowa, 1850–1860," 53 *Iowa Journal of History* 1 (1955).

[108] Act of Jan. 24, 1855, ch. 78, 1855 Iowa Acts 114.

[109] Petersen, *supra* note 106, p. 397.

[110] *Journal of the Constitutional Convention of the State of Iowa* (Muscatine: John Mahin, 1857) [hereinafter *1857 Journal*], pp. 3–29. They also had chosen as First Messenger a young man championed by the Republicans (James Hawkins, described as "an orphan boy who is endeavoring to educate himself"), rather than the young man proposed by the Democrats (Willis Conrad, "poor and unfortunate, having broken his hips not long since"). *The Debates of the Constitutional Convention of the State of Iowa* (Davenport: Luse, Lane & Co., 1857) [hereinafter *1857 Debates*], vol. 1, pp. 7–8. Hawkins later ran into trouble with members of both parties for being obstinate and discourteous. *Id.* at pp. 275–76.

accommodations here."[111] Jonathan Hall—a Democrat who had served prominently in the Territory of Iowa's 1844 convention, had served for one year as a member of the Iowa Supreme Court, and was now representing Des Moines County at the convention—complained that the hotel service was not up to par. "This city was created for the purpose of holding meetings here, Legislatures and Conventions," he said, "and the people have got into the habit of treating all who come here like sheep who are to be shorn."[112] After a lengthy debate, however, the delegates opted to indefinitely postpone taking any action on the question of relocation.[113] They continued to carry out their work in the supreme court room until January 30, by which time the General Assembly had adjourned and the much larger senate chamber directly above them had become available. The delegates briefly argued about how to assign seats in that capacious space, ultimately agreeing to draw lots, with each delegate going upstairs and choosing from among the available locations when his number was drawn.[114]

The convention ran from January 19 through March 5, a period three times the length of the 1846 convention. Over the course of those six and a half weeks, the delegates took action on scores of issues, as will be noted often in Part II's discussion of individual constitutional provisions. For example, they shifted responsibility for choosing supreme court justices from the General Assembly to the electorate at large,[115] they reduced the governor's term of office from four years to two,[116] and they increased the state's debt cap from $100,000 to $250,000.[117]

Special attention is owed to the delegates' handling of several particular topics: banks, race, the locations of the seat of government and the State University of Iowa, and constitutional amendments.

Banks

As the Iowa Supreme Court would observe nearly thirty years later, "[t]he great evil of the constitution of 1846, in the public estimation of the time, was the

---

111 *1857 Debates, supra* note 110, vol. 1, p. 12.

112 *1857 Debates, supra* note 110, vol. 1, p. 13.

113 *1857 Debates, supra* note 110, vol. 1, p. 22.

114 *1857 Debates, supra* note 110, vol. 1, pp. 81–82. The following day, the delegates approved a resolution banning smoking in the chamber. *Id.* at p. 115.

115 *Compare* Iowa Const. of 1857, art. V, § 3, *with* Iowa Const. of 1846, art. VI, § 3. The 1846 constitution had given the legislature responsibility for choosing supreme court justices and the electorate responsibility for choosing district court judges. At the 1857 convention, no one pushed hard for allowing the legislature to retain the justice-selecting power. Instead, the debate focused on whether supreme court justices should be elected in statewide or district elections. *See 1857 Debates, supra* note 110, vol. 1, pp. 115–17, 449–55.

116 *Compare* Iowa Const. of 1857, art. IV, § 2, *with* Iowa Const. of 1846, art. V, § 2.

117 *Compare* Iowa Const. art. VII, § 2, *with* Iowa Const. of 1846, art. VIII, § 1.

prohibition therein contained of banks with power to issue bills to circulate as money" (*Allen v. Clayton*, 1884). Speaking on the floor of the convention, Daniel Solomon—a Democrat, lawyer, and delegate from Mills County—summarized the problem this way:

> [T]oo much of that which passes for a circulating medium is not money, [but rather] consists of mere empty, void promises-to-pay, coming from some quarter, we know not where, but tending to inflate the money market, and create an unhealthy excitement in the public mind. We are surrounded by all kinds of banks, and if we do not have any of our own, we are flooded with the bank paper of other people, the character of which we do not know.[118]

With the bipartisan support of twenty-nine of the convention's thirty-six members, the delegates concluded that the state should cautiously shift course.[119] The constitution they produced authorizes the General Assembly to adopt legislation permitting banks of issue to do business within Iowa's borders, but such legislation becomes effective only if it is approved by Iowa voters at a general or special election.[120] The constitution imposes strict requirements to ensure that a bank's notes are of reliable value; it makes a bank's shareholders doubly responsible for liabilities that the bank incurs during the period when those shareholders own the bank's shares; it gives a bank's billholders priority over other creditors if a bank becomes insolvent; and it bars banks from suspending specie payments.[121] Reflecting the delegates' desire to maximize the General Assembly's options for dealing with Iowans' banking needs, the 1857 constitution also authorizes the state to establish its own multi-branch bank, "founded on an actual specie basis."[122]

Although each of these provisions remains within the text of the Iowa Constitution, none of them plays a role in Iowa banking law today. In the 1860s, as part of an effort to establish a national currency and to build a network of federally organized banks, Congress imposed a ten-percent tax on the amount of all state-bank bills "paid out by" any state or national bank.[123] As economists Milton

---

[118] *1857 Debates, supra* note 110, vol. 1, p. 350.

[119] *1857 Debates, supra* note 110, vol. 2, pp. 1022–25 (reporting the final vote).

[120] Iowa Const. art. VIII, § 5.

[121] Iowa Const. art. VIII, §§ 8, 9, 10, 11.

[122] Iowa Const. art. VIII, §§ 6, 7.

[123] Act of Mar. 3, 1865, ch. 78, § 6, 13 Stat. 469, 484. That legislation followed the National Banking Acts of 1863 and 1864. *See* Act of Feb. 25, 1863, ch. 58, 12 Stat. 665; Act of June 3, 1864, ch. 106, 13 Stat. 99. Among many other things, the 1863 and 1864 legislation allowed individuals meeting specified requirements to establish banking associations; it authorized those associations to issue federally authorized notes as currency; it required all associations organized under this legislation to honor at par value the notes they had issued; and it invited banks organized under state law to reorganize under this legislation as federal entities.

Friedman and Anna Jacobson Schwartz put it, that legislation had the effect of "denying state banks *de facto* the privilege of note issue."[124] Moreover, in *Allen v. Clayton* (1884), the Iowa Supreme Court concluded that each of the constitution's banking provisions is concerned only with entities that "issue bills to circulate as money." As a result, the banking clauses of the Iowa Constitution—the focus of so much attention and political drama in the mid-nineteenth century—are now functionally obsolete.

Race

No overarching question provoked more heated disagreements among the delegates than whether the constitution should confer new rights upon people of color. Even within the Republican camp, delegates were not always of the same mind. The fact that one opposed the geographic spread of slavery did not necessarily mean that one favored full legal equality for blacks, or even that one favored the abolition of slavery in the South.

The convention's most vocally persistent proponent of blacks' rights was Henry County's Rufus Clarke, a thirty-seven-year-old lawyer and Republican who had come to Iowa from Connecticut six years earlier.[125] It was Clarke who, at the end of the delegates' second week of work, prompted the convention's first extended debate about race. On the agenda that day was the provision that ultimately became Section 22 of Article I, providing newly arriving "[f]oreigners" with the same property rights "as native born citizens." Clarke proposed adding a clause that would secure the property rights of American-born racial minorities, without regard to whether those individuals were legally regarded as citizens of America or any of its states.[126]

A number of delegates condemned Clarke's idea. George Gillaspy—a Kentucky-born Democrat from Wapello County and a man "of almost giant proportions"[127]—said, for example, that far from wishing to encourage blacks to come to Iowa, he "would today vote for a proposition, if it was before this Convention, to exclude the negro forever from coming into this State." Heartily agreeing, Amos Harris—a lawyer and Democrat from Appanoose County—said that he later would propose a constitutional provision that would indeed "prevent those negroes not already here from becoming residents of this State," just like the provision that the delegates to the 1844 convention nearly

[124] Milton Friedman & Anna Jacobson Schwartz, *A Monetary History of the United States: 1867–1960* (Princeton: Princeton University Press, 1963), pp. 18–19.

[125] For a brief introduction to Clarke, see Dykstra, *supra* note 41, p. 161.

[126] *1857 Debates*, *supra* note 110, vol. 1, p. 129.

[127] William M. Donnel, *Pioneers of Marion County* (Des Moines: Republican Steam Printing House, 1872), p. 149.

endorsed.[128] Harris said that he did not want to strip property rights from racial minorities who already resided in Iowa, but neither did he want to encourage more non-whites to come. "I am proud to think that the [Democratic] party to which I belong is the white man's party, and seeks to promote the interests of the white man," Harris said. "I do not wish to make this State a hospital for the worn out negroes of the South." Des Moines County's Jonathan Hall also opposed Clarke's proposal, arguing that Iowa law already protected blacks' property rights and that Clarke's amendment would cause a "boiling over" within the state.[129]

Rufus Clarke replied that, regardless of the current state of the law, he wished to guard against future instances of the kinds of racially discriminatory legislation that could be found in other states. Hoping to stay one step ahead of federal law, Clarke predicted (inaccurately) that, in the case of freedom-seeking Dred Scott—a case that was pending before the U.S. Supreme Court and would be decided just five weeks later, one day after the convention closed (*Scott v. Sandford*, 1857)—the Court would rule that blacks are American citizens and are consequently entitled to all of the privileges and immunities of state citizenship under Article IV of the U.S. Constitution.[130]

The last word in this particular debate fell to William Penn Clarke, the former Whig who had written against the 1846 constitution's ratification and who was now a Republican representing Johnson County and serving as the Iowa Supreme Court's reporter. Clarke would later aid the underground railroad and would help John Brown elude capture in Iowa City,[131] but at the 1857 convention he

[128] *1857 Debates, supra* note 110, vol. 1, p. 130. In one of the delegates' final sessions, Harris followed through on that promise, proposing that the constitution declare that (1) "[n]o negro or mulatto shall come into the state, after the adoption of this constitution," and (2) those who employed negroes or mulattos or encouraged them to remain in Iowa would pay a fine. Harris's proposal was set aside and never revisited. *1857 Debates, supra* note 110, vol. 2, p. 913. Harris modeled his proposal on Article XIII of the Indiana Constitution of 1851.

[129] *1857 Debates, supra* note 110, vol. 1, pp. 131–34. Hall's assessment of blacks' property rights surely carried great weight among his colleagues; he had argued numerous cases before the Iowa Supreme Court and had served as a justice on that court from early 1854 until early 1855. Edward H. Stiles, "Judge Jonathan C. Hall," 9 *Annals of Iowa* 18, 22, 30 (1907).

[130] *1857 Debates, supra* note 110, vol. 1, pp. 132–33, 137. Clarke's confidence about the outcome in *Dred Scott* might have flowed, in part, from the Supreme Court of the Territory of Iowa's 1839 ruling in *In re Ralph,* holding that—by virtue of the Missouri Compromise—a slave ceased to be property when his Missouri-based owner voluntarily permitted him to reside in the Territory of Iowa. For an engaging discussion of *In re Ralph,* supplemented by photocopies of some of the relevant documents, see Acton & Acton, *supra* note 70, pp. 40–48.

[131] Eriksson, *supra* note 92, pp. 42–44; Jacob Van Ek, "Underground Railroad in Iowa," 2 *The Palimpsest* 129, 132–33 (1921); Benjamin F. Gue, *History of Iowa* (New York: Century History Co., 1903), vol. 1, pp. 373–83. For excellent, thorough treatments of the underground railroad in Iowa and of the battle against slavery in the Midwest, see Lowell J. Soike, *Necessary Courage: Iowa's Underground Railroad in the Struggle Against Slavery* (Iowa City: University of Iowa Press, 2013), and Lowell J. Soike,

did not always support Rufus Clarke's efforts to ensure blacks' legal equality.[132] He argued that blacks already enjoyed full property rights under Iowa law, that Iowa's judges would uphold those rights, and that the delegates' debate was undesirably encouraging them to divide along party lines. Immediately upon the conclusion of those remarks, the delegates soundly rejected Rufus Clarke's proposal, with only eight delegates voting in its favor.[133]

The next racial issue to provoke a lengthy debate concerned whether non-whites should be permitted to testify as witnesses in judicial proceedings. The state legislature previously had declared that "an indian, a negro, a mulatto or black person shall not be allowed to give testimony in any cause wherein a white person is a party."[134] The Iowa Supreme Court enforced that statutory bar even when white defendants wished to call a black witness to testify against a black plaintiff (*Motts v. Usher*, 1855). On December 22, 1856, however—just one month before the 1857 convention began—the legislature repealed that racial restriction.[135] Recognizing that what the legislature gives the legislature may take away, some delegates were eager to elevate racial minorities' testimonial rights to a constitutional level. Rufus Clarke led the charge, proposing that the delegates add a provision to Section 4 of Article I, ensuring that no person could be deemed incompetent to testify in any court "in consequence of his belonging to any particular sect, class or party of men."[136]

Opponents once again denounced Clarke for evidently trying to attract "blacks and mulattoes" to the state. George Gillaspy, for example, said that he believed Iowans had sent delegates to the convention to "provide for the white race first" and that, upon hearing Clarke's suggestion, he detected "a nigger in the wood-pile." Clarke readily confirmed that his objective was racial equality, and said that "sneers" and "cries of 'nigger' will not influence me any more than the passing of the idle wind." He explained that, while his purpose was not necessarily to lure blacks to Iowa, he certainly did want to "spread upon our constitution principles that every man, wherever he may be on the whole face of the

Busy in the Cause: Iowa, the Free-State Struggle in the West, and the Prelude to the Civil War (Lincoln & London: University of Nebraska Press, 2014). For shorter discussions of John Brown, the underground railroad, and anti-slavery forces in Iowa, see the various pieces collected in the State Historical Society of Iowa's *Iowa Heritage Illustrated*, vol. 90:2 (Summer 2009), as well as G. Galin Berrier, "The Underground Railroad in Iowa," in *Outside In, supra* note 50, pp. 44–59.

132 Nor were these two men on friendly terms. In a debate about a different matter, for example, William Penn Clarke said that "if the intelligence and capacity of the gentleman from Henry [County] were at all equal to his arrogance and presumption, he would be a very useful man upon this floor." *1857 Debates, supra* note 110, vol. 1, pp. 366–67.

133 *1857 Debates, supra* note 110, vol. 1, pp. 129–38.

134 Code of Iowa (1851), § 2388.

135 Act of Dec. 22, 1856, ch. 19, 1857 Iowa Acts 15.

136 *1857 Debates, supra* note 110, vol. 1, p. 172.

earth, may say, there is a land where I can go and have my rights and my liberty secure."[137]

After many hours of discussion, Jefferson County's James Wilson—a young lawyer and Republican who later would serve in both houses of Congress and would co-author the Thirteenth Amendment banning slavery—worried aloud that Clarke's amendment might doom the new constitution at the polls. Clarke's proposal was then soundly defeated by an 11-to-22 vote, with no Democrat voting in its favor and with several Republicans voting against it.[138] Undeterred, Clarke returned with what was essentially the same proposal in slightly altered language. After another lengthy exchange, the delegates referred the matter to a committee consisting of Rufus Clarke, James Wilson, and Amos Harris.[139] Nearly three weeks later, the committee reported that it had been unable to reach agreement: Wilson believed other constitutional provisions would secure blacks' testimonial rights, Clarke believed his amendment was necessary to make those rights inviolable, and Harris feared that Clarke's approach would signal to voters that the constitution had been "especially framed" for the benefit of persons of color.[140]

With a politically savvy proposal that he offered the following day, William Penn Clarke brought the convention's discussion of Section 4 to a close. He suggested declaring that litigants are entitled to use the testimony of any disinterested, potentially knowledgeable witness.[141] Rather than frame the constitutional guarantee from the perspective of non-whites who wished to testify, he thus framed it from the perspective of litigants—many of whom would be white, as in 1855's *Motts v. Usher*—who sometimes would need the testimony of racial minorities in order to vindicate their own rights.[142] The delegates approved Clarke's proposal by the narrow margin of 18 to 17, with no Democrat voting in its favor.[143]

Race-focused concerns also lay behind the delegates' drafting of the provision guaranteeing individuals a trial by "an impartial jury" in certain kinds of cases.[144]

---

[137] *1857 Debates, supra* note 110, vol. 1, pp. 172–73.

[138] *1857 Debates, supra* note 110, vol. 1, p. 180.

[139] *1857 Debates, supra* note 110, vol. 1, pp. 180, 200, 226. One week later, word arrived that 199 individuals from Muscatine County had signed a petition urging the delegates not to strip blacks of their newly acquired statutory right to testify in judicial proceedings. *Id.* at p. 395. The petition was referred to the committee on which Clarke, Wilson, and Harris sat.

[140] *1857 Debates, supra* note 110, vol. 2, pp. 651–55.

[141] *1857 Debates, supra* note 110, vol. 2, p. 735.

[142] The seeds for that approach had been planted three weeks earlier, when George Ells—a bookseller and Republican from Scott County—observed that barring non-whites from testifying would "violate the constitutional right of white citizens, in all cases when the testimony of a colored person is necessary to the defense of their lives, liberty or property." *1857 Debates, supra* note 110, vol. 1, p. 175.

[143] *1857 Debates, supra* note 110, vol. 2, p. 735.

[144] Iowa Const. art. I, § 10.

The 1846 constitution had promised jury trials "[i]n all criminal prosecutions."[145] At the 1857 convention, one day after the delegates' first round of debate regarding non-whites' ability to testify in judicial proceedings, Rufus Clarke proposed expanding the jury-trial right to include "all cases involving the life or liberty of an individual." The delegates quickly gave their tentative approval.[146] Three weeks later, however, Amos Harris launched an effort to strike Clarke's language. He argued that the clause's chief purpose—problematically, in his view—was to ensure that fugitive slaves received a jury trial to determine whether they should be returned to the states from which they had fled. That evidently had indeed been among Rufus Clarke's objectives: he did not deny Harris's claim, and other delegates rose in defense of providing fugitive slaves with precisely that form of protection. Allamakee County's John Clark, for example, insisted that Iowans would not be a "sovereign people" if they did not have the power to offer jury trials to fugitive slaves found within their borders. If the federal Fugitive Slave Act of 1850 did not permit a state jury to determine whether a slave should be returned, he said, then that statute itself was likely unconstitutional. Jonathan Hall vehemently disagreed, arguing that the U.S. Constitution gave Congress full control over matters concerning fugitive slaves and that the delegates would be "sow[ing] the seeds of treason" if they put anything in the state constitution that authorized interference with the fugitive-slave regime that Congress had established.[147] Harris and Hall failed to persuade their colleagues. By a vote of 21 to 14—and without the support of any Democrat—the convention opted to retain the language that Rufus Clarke had helped place there.[148]

Disagreements about race reared their head again in the delegates' handling of the militia. Under the state's 1846 constitution, militia membership was limited to "white male citizens between the ages of eighteen and forty-five years."[149] At the 1857 convention, Clayton County's Alpheus Scott—a real-estate agent and Republican—proposed that the delegates remove that racial restriction, so that black Iowans could participate in "defending their own common country with us." His motion drew resistance, however, from Rufus Clarke. Clarke said that, because his opponents in the convention had blocked other attempts to level the racial playing field, it would be unjust to force black men to defend the

---

[145] Iowa Const. of 1846, art. II, § 10.

[146] *1857 Debates, supra* note 110, vol. 1, p. 201.

[147] In 1842, the U.S. Supreme Court had determined in *Prigg v. Pennsylvania* that the power to legislate on matters concerning fugitive slaves was "exclusive in the national government."

[148] *1857 Debates, supra* note 110, vol. 2, pp. 736–41. With the nation's ratification of the Thirteenth Amendment banning slavery coming less than a decade later, there was little opportunity to put Clarke's clause to work for fugitive slaves. As explained in Part II's discussion of Article I, Section 10, however, the clause remains significant because it appears to extend Section 10's reach to cases that might not be covered by the U.S. Constitution's Sixth Amendment.

[149] Iowa Const. of 1846, art. VII, § 1.

institutions that oppressed them. The delegates rejected Scott's motion by an unrecorded margin.[150]

Issues of race appeared yet again in the delegates' discussion of public education.[151] Under existing statutory law, only whites were entitled to attend the state's publicly funded schools, and property owned by non-whites was "exempt from taxation for school purposes."[152] Albert Marvin and George Ells—Republicans from Jones County and Scott County, respectively—recommended that the delegates include some variation of a provision requiring the legislature to make publicly funded schools available to "all" of the state's children. Marvin argued that it was in every Iowan's best interest to ensure that black and white children alike received the intellectual and moral benefits of education. George Gillaspy responded with a vitriolic speech, saying that he and his constituents were irrevocably opposed to allowing "blacks, mulattoes and Indians" to attend the same public schools as white children, and that only white children should have a constitutional right to an education at the public's expense. If white and black children were allowed to attend school together, he said, white children might perceive "that the negroes are as good as they are." William Penn Clarke replied that "the Great Father of all . . . has given the negro the same mind, and the same moral faculties that He has to the white" and that it was the state's "duty to provide for the education of all classes of people in the State." Unmoved, Gillaspy proposed that the constitution explicitly limit educational rights to "white children."[153]

Jefferson County's James Wilson pointed out that there was nothing in Marvin's and Ells's proposals that would require the state to place black and white children in the same schools; if legislators preferred to establish racially segregated schools, Wilson said, they could do so. Jonathan Hall replied that, so long as whites and blacks were indeed educated separately, he would be willing to guarantee all children access to a public education. "[I]f the negroes and Indians are permitted to live and settle in Iowa," Hall reasoned, "the first thing

---

150 *1857 Debates, supra* note 110, vol. 1, pp. 641–42; *1857 Journal, supra* note 110, p. 232.

151 Muscatine County's John Parvin (a Republican) had raised the question of blacks' education early in the convention, proposing that the Committee on Education and School Lands "inquire into the expediency of making provision for the education of the children of blacks and mulattoes." With virtually no debate, the delegates agreed to ask the committee to consider the matter. The vote fell almost entirely along party lines; the only delegate to break from his party was Jeremiah Hollingsworth—a Republican from Keokuk County—who voted against Parvin's suggestion. *1857 Debates, supra* note 110, vol. 1, p. 62. Parvin's desire to educate non-whites may have played a role in his subsequent defeat in a state senatorial race. Dykstra, *supra* note 41, p. 192.

152 Code of Iowa (1851), §§ 1127, 1160. Prior legislation had similarly declared that publicly funded schools "shall be open and free alike to all white persons in the district between the ages of five and twenty-one years." Act of Jan. 24, 1847, ch. 99, § 6, 1846 Iowa Acts 110.

153 *1857 Debates, supra* note 110, vol. 2, pp. 825–32.

I want to have done is to take them and educate them. . . . [T]hey are not fit to be here without some education." After further discussion, the delegates rejected Gillaspy's whites-only proposal by a vote of 10 to 22. By the mirror-image vote of 22 to 10, the delegates then agreed to require the state to provide an education to "all the youths of the state"—a phrase that includes black children within its scope but does not explicitly declare that black and white children must be permitted to attend the same schools.[154]

Most noteworthy of all were the delegates' exchanges about black suffrage. At the beginning of the 1857 convention's second week, the Committee on the Right of Suffrage proposed that the 1846 constitution's voting provisions be carried forward unchanged,[155] including that constitution's conferral of voting rights only upon "white male citizen[s] of the United States."[156] On this issue, Rufus Clarke found himself in a bind. He personally favored giving blacks the right to vote, but he feared that stripping the new constitution of its most prominent racial exclusion might prompt voters to reject the document at the polls. In his view, it was better to have a new constitution with racial restrictions than to leave the 1846 constitution in force.[157] To resolve that quandary, Clarke proposed that the delegates retain the whites-only language in the constitution's voting-rights provision, but that, at the time of the statewide ratification vote, voters separately be asked whether that provision's racial restriction should be jettisoned.[158]

The delegates created a special, five-member committee to consider Clarke's idea. Clarke himself was named one of that committee's members, as was Jonathan Hall—the Democrat who, at the Territory of Iowa's 1844 convention,

---

[154] *1857 Debates, supra* note 110, vol. 2, pp. 832–37. *See* Iowa Const. of 1857, art. IX, div. 1, § 12; Arnie Cooper, "A Stony Road: Black Education in Iowa, 1838–1860," 48 *Annals of Iowa* 113, 126–28 (1986). One year later, the General Assembly enacted a statute directing local school officials to "provide for the education of the colored youth, in separate schools, except in cases where by the unanimous consent of the persons sending to the school in the sub-district, they may be permitted to attend with the white youth." Act of Mar. 12, 1858, ch. 52, § 30, 1858 Iowa Acts 57, 65. Nine months later, the Iowa Supreme Court struck that entire statute down on the ground that the General Assembly had intruded upon the domain of the state board of education. *District Township of the City of Dubuque v. City of Dubuque* (1858). Subsequent legislation concerning Iowa's schools omitted any explicit reference to race. For a discussion of those developments, and for the ruling declaring it statutorily and constitutionally impermissible for school officials to segregate Iowa's schools by race, see *Clark v. Board of Directors* (1868). For a discussion of the board of education, see Part II's treatment of Article IX. For an overarching discussion of race and public education in Iowa, covering the period from the state's founding until the end of the twentieth century, see Hal S. Chase, "'You Live What You Learn': The African-American Presence in Iowa Education, 1839–2000," in *Outside In, supra* note 50, pp. 134–63.

[155] *1857 Debates, supra* note 110, vol. 1, p. 36.

[156] Iowa Const. of 1846, art. III, § 1.

[157] *1857 Debates, supra* note 110, vol. 2, pp. 669, 677–80.

[158] *1857 Debates, supra* note 110, vol. 1, pp. 45–46.

had spoken insistently against giving blacks the right to vote.[159] Nearly three weeks later, a Clarke-led majority of the committee issued a recommendation even broader than the one Clarke had initially floated: the committee proposed that voters casting ballots on ratification be separately asked whether the word "white" should be removed from each place it appeared in the constitution. Jasper County's Harvey Skiff—a banker, Republican, and fellow member of the special committee—proposed that Iowa voters instead be presented with the narrower question that Clarke had initially proposed: should voting rights continue to be restricted to whites? Jonathan Hall expressed confidence that most Iowans would reject any such invitation, he provided the delegates with the text of the remarks he had made against racial equality at the 1844 convention, and he urged his colleagues not to present voters with *any* freestanding questions about race.[160]

In their lengthy discussion of those options,[161] the delegates all agreed that a majority of Iowans would insist upon retaining the existing constitution's racial restrictions, particularly the one denying blacks the right to vote. The question on which the delegates divided was whether the issue should be placed on voters' ballots anyway. Many Republicans believed that it should. Rufus Clarke, for example, conceded that Iowans would likely vote against racial equality in this particular election, but argued that asking voters to speak to the issue now would help hasten "the day . . . when the people of this State shall not be afraid to carry out to the letter the true intent and spirit of every iota of the true democratic creed."[162] David Bunker—a farmer and Republican from Washington County—was initially unenthusiastic about presenting voters with questions about race, but he ultimately changed his mind. The ratification vote could be close, Bunker reasoned, and—even if the proponents of racial equality were small in number—their badly needed "Yes" votes on ratification might be more easily secured if they were given a separate opportunity to condemn one or more of the text's explicitly racist provisions.[163]

At least initially, some of the convention's Republicans were less eager to press forward with the ballot initiative. In his first remarks on the question, William Penn Clarke said that the Republican party had never taken a position on black suffrage, that the party was doing itself great political damage by appearing to champion that cause, that only about three hundred blacks resided in the state and none of them had demanded the right to vote, and that "[n]o man believes that [the cause of black suffrage] can command a respectable vote in the State."[164]

---

159 *1857 Debates, supra* note 110, vol. 1, pp. 217–19.

160 *1857 Debates, supra* note 110, vol. 2, pp. 649–50, 664–65.

161 *1857 Debates, supra* note 110, vol. 2, pp. 666–718, 888–912.

162 *1857 Debates, supra* note 110, vol. 2, pp. 666–72.

163 *1857 Debates, supra* note 110, vol. 2, p. 911.

164 *1857 Debates, supra* note 110, vol. 2, pp. 675–76.

After hearing further discussion of the matter, however, Clarke concluded that the Democrats in the convention were more loyal to southern proponents of slavery than to the Iowa voters who might wish to be heard on an important issue, and that he should join his fellow Republicans by voting in favor of giving Iowans a chance to cast ballots on black suffrage. Clarke hastened to add that, when the day of the election arrived, he would cast his own ballot against giving non-whites the right to vote.[165]

The convention's Democrats uniformly opposed asking voters any question focused on racial equality. Delaware County's John Peters said, for example, that the ballot initiative would be a waste of time and money, since even "the most earnest advocate of the proposition here says that there is no possibility of its being adopted."[166] Marion County's Hiram Gibson believed he owed it to his constituents not to "insult" them by asking "if they believed the negro was as good as they."[167] Jonathan Hall accused Republicans—both in Iowa and nationally—of attempting to build their new political party by fanning the flames of disagreement among Americans about slavery and the rights of blacks. Because no one doubted that Iowans would reject any invitation to strike the word "white" from the constitution, Hall said, the sole purpose of the vote would be to give Iowa Republicans a party-building opportunity.[168]

After several days of debate, the delegates accepted Harvey Skiff's recommendation that Iowa voters be asked to express their views about blacks' right to vote, but not about other matters of racial equality.[169] The measure passed by a vote of 20 to 13, without the support of a single Democrat and without the opposition of a single Republican. Iowa voters thus would be presented with two questions: whether to ratify the proposed constitution and whether to extend voting rights to black men.

The State Capital and the State University

The same westward migration that doomed Burlington's status as the Territory of Iowa's capital ultimately doomed Iowa City's status as the capital of the State of Iowa. The 1846 constitution had declared that Iowa City would "be the Seat of Government of the State of Iowa, until removed by law," thereby leaving the General Assembly free to move the capital to a different location.[170] In his essay opposing the 1846 constitution's ratification, William Penn Clarke had predicted

---

165 *1857 Debates, supra* note 110, vol. 2, pp. 888–905.

166 *1857 Debates, supra* note 110, vol. 2, p. 680.

167 *1857 Debates, supra* note 110, vol. 2, p. 697.

168 *1857 Debates, supra* note 110, vol. 2, pp. 687–94.

169 *1857 Debates, supra* note 110, vol. 2, pp. 912–17. The delegates placed the measure in Section 14 of Article XII.

170 Iowa Const. of 1846, art. XIII, § 8.

that the capital would be moved westward and that Iowa City would be offered a university in exchange. That is precisely how things played out. On February 22, 1847, the General Assembly appointed a group of commissioners to find a suitable new site for the capital at or near the state's geographic center.[171] Three days later, the General Assembly enacted legislation declaring that "there shall be established at Iowa City . . . an institution to be called the 'State University of Iowa'" and giving the university "[t]he public buildings at Iowa City, together with the ten acres of land on which the same are situated."[172]

In the ensuing months and years, several communities—Fort Des Moines, Pella, and Oskaloosa prominent among them—lobbied hard to win the capital.[173] By 1855, the legislature had settled upon the Des Moines location.[174] Some Iowans nevertheless continued to agitate for different possible sites, and so it fell to the delegates to the 1857 constitutional convention to try to bring closure to the matter.

David Palmer—a lawyer and Democrat from Davis County—suggested the provision that appears today in Article XI, Section 8, permanently establishing Des Moines as the state capital and Iowa City as the home of the State University of Iowa, popularly known since the 1960s as the University of Iowa.[175] The Committee on Miscellaneous Subjects had already proposed declaring that the university would be permanently established in Iowa City and could use the Capitol (in which the delegates themselves were working) when the building was not needed for other state purposes.[176] But the delegates initially rejected that recommendation, with Hardin County's Sheldon Winchester arguing that the constitution should not speak to such "local matters" and Lee County's Edward Johnston suggesting that the provision would be better placed in Article IX, which deals with education.[177] Palmer pressed the matter, adding Des

---

171 Act of Feb. 22, 1847, ch. 71, 1847 Iowa Acts 85.

172 Act of Feb. 25, 1847, ch. 125, 1847 Iowa Acts 188. For an account of the ensuing efforts to raise money for the university and to open the institution's doors to students, see J.L. Pickard, "Historical Sketch of the State University of Iowa," 4 *Annals of Iowa* 1 (1899).

173 John E. Briggs, "The Removal of the Capital from Iowa City to Des Moines," 14 *Iowa Journal of History & Politics* 56, 73–90 (1916).

174 Act of Jan. 25, 1855, ch. 72, 1855 Iowa Acts 105 (directing five commissioners to locate a suitable site for "relocat[ing] the Seat of Government of this State" to a place "within two miles of the junction of the Des Moines and Raccoon rivers in Polk county"). *See generally* Siddali, *supra* note 27, p. 134 (observing that Des Moines' "proximity to the geographic center of the state and its claims of health and the fertility of its hinterlands brought it to the forefront of the capital city debates."

175 *1857 Debates, supra* note 110, vol. 2, p. 877. For an explanation of the university's naming conventions, see David McCartney, "What's in a Name? For the University of Iowa, Lots of History and a Little Confusion," *Univ. of Iowa Spectator* (Dec. 2010), available at http://spectator.uiowa.edu/2010/december/oldgold.html.

176 *1857 Debates, supra* note 110, vol. 2, p. 648.

177 *1857 Debates, supra* note 110, vol. 2, pp. 801, 811.

Moines' permanent receipt of the state capital to the mix. Following a discussion about whether Iowa voters should be asked to weigh in directly on these issues and about the disadvantages of having what Rufus Clarke called "a capitol on wheels," the delegates accepted Palmer's recommendation by a 20-to-15 vote—a vote that, unlike many others, did not break cleanly along party lines.[178]

Constitutional Amendments

As has been noted, the 1846 constitution's outright ban on banks of issue was widely regarded as that document's greatest defect needing speedy revision. Under the terms of that same document, however, the only way to change the constitution's text was by calling a constitutional convention.[179] At the 1857 convention, the Committee on Amendments recommended that the General Assembly continue to hold the power to propose constitutional conventions, but that this power be supplemented with two additional paths to constitutional change: that voters be given an opportunity every ten years to call for a convention and that the General Assembly have the power (when acting in successive sessions, with an intervening general election) to propose individual amendments on which Iowa voters may then pass judgment. After making small-scale revisions of various kinds, the delegates approved the committee's proposal by a vote of 21 to 12. Sheldon Winchester—a young merchant from Hardin County—was the only Republican to vote against it, while Daniel Solomon—a young lawyer from Mills County—was the only Democrat to vote in its favor.[180]

* * *

The convention adjourned on March 5, giving Iowans until the election scheduled for August 3 to debate whether the proposed new constitution should be ratified and whether non-white men should be added to the state's electorate. Democrats strongly opposed both proposals. Regarding ratification, they argued that (among other things) the constitution would open the state's doors to scheming bankers, the proposed increase in the state's debt limit—from $100,000 to $250,000—would facilitate financially irresponsible legislation, and Republicans' decision to place black suffrage on the ballot was a signal that the new constitution was drafted with an eye toward conferring new legal rights upon people of color.[181] By the close vote of 40,311 to 38,681, Iowans

---

[178] *1857 Debates, supra* note 110, vol. 2, pp. 922–34. By the end of that calendar year, the capital had moved to Des Moines. Briggs, *supra* note 173, pp. 93–94.

[179] Iowa Const. of 1846, art. XI.

[180] *1857 Debates, supra* note 110, vol. 2, pp. 1030–33.

[181] For a collection of editorials written for and against ratification, see "Contemporary Editorial Opinion of the 1857 Constitution," 55 *Iowa Journal of History* 115 (1957).

nevertheless ratified the document.[182] With respect to the separate ballot question concerning black suffrage, the election results were far more lopsided, just as the delegates to the convention had anticipated: 8,479 voted in favor of striking the word "white" from the new constitution's voting-rights provision, but 49,267 said it should be retained.[183] Those tallies prompt one to wonder whether Washington County's David Bunker got it right at the convention when he predicted that a successful ratification vote might be secured only if those favoring electoral equality were given an opportunity to condemn at least part of the document's explicit racism.[184] The ultimate margin of victory for ratification was only 1,630 votes. Of the 8,479 voters who supported black suffrage, might there have been at least twenty percent who voted to ratify the constitution but would have voted differently if they had not been able to declare that black men should be given the right to vote?[185] Regardless, Iowa finally had the constitution that, as amended, remains in force today.

■ SUBSEQUENT AMENDMENTS

In the decades that have elapsed since the 1857 constitution's adoption, Iowans have repeatedly declined their constitutionally mandated decennial opportunities to call for another constitutional convention.[186] Iowa voters have, however, ratified numerous amendments that the General Assembly has proposed.[187]

---

[182] Proclamation by Governor James W. Grimes (Sept. 3, 1857). A copy of the handwritten proclamation is available at http://www.statelibraryofiowa.org/services/collections/law-library/iacon/iacons. For county-by-county voting results, see *Constitution of the State of Iowa with Subsequent Amendments* (Iowa Secretary of State, 1893), p. 2, available at http://publications.iowa.gov/9996/1/iowa_constitution_1857002.pdf.

[183] Acton & Acton, *supra* note 70, p. 92. Note that more than 21,000 voters who cast ballots on ratification failed to cast ballots on black suffrage. One partial explanation for that difference might lie in the fact that the two measures were presented to voters on separate pieces of paper, to be deposited in separate boxes. Dykstra, *supra* note 41, pp. 178–79. Perhaps some voters felt that they couldn't be bothered to complete two separate ballots. Perhaps others had not yet made up their minds about whether black men should be permitted to vote.

[184] *1857 Debates, supra* note 110, vol. 2, p. 911.

[185] For an example of empirical analysis of such matters, see Dykstra, *supra* note 41, pp. 177–91.

[186] *See* Iowa Const. art. X, § 3 (stating that, at a general election held every ten years, voters must be presented with the following question: "Shall there be a convention to revise the constitution, and propose amendment or amendments to same?"). Iowa voters responded affirmatively to the invitation in 1920. *Iowa Official Register, 1921–1922*, pp. 482–83, available at https://www.legis.iowa.gov/archives/register. Subsequent legislation evidently satisfied many who had desired a convention, however, and so legislators opted not to call one and no outcry ensued. Charles W. Wiggins, "Constitutional Convention Issue in Iowa (1960)," 40 *Annals of Iowa* 171, 171 (1970).

[187] *See* Iowa Const. art. X, § 1 (stating that the General Assembly may propose specific constitutional amendments to Iowa voters, so long as those amendments are approved by successive legislatures with

Among the most important are amendments concerning race, women's rights, the composition of the General Assembly, the leadership of the executive branch, and the means by which judicial vacancies are filled.

Race

Recall that, at the 1857 convention, Henry County's Rufus Clarke tried to lay the groundwork for removing the word "white" from each place it appeared in the proposed new constitution. Through amendments adopted in 1868 and 1880, Clarke's goal was finally achieved.

Upon returning from the Civil War's battlefields in the mid-1860s, scores of black Iowans who had fought against the Confederacy lobbied for the right to vote.[188] Many Iowa Republicans began to rally around that cause during a convention held in Des Moines in June 1865.[189] Black suffrage received a further boost on January 11, 1866, when newly re-elected Governor William Stone, a Republican, used a portion of his inaugural address to urge lawmakers to launch the amendment process necessary to extend the franchise to black men:

> In the darkest hour of the late struggle for the Union, seven hundred of these black citizens stepped forward to fill the quota of Iowa under the President's call for troops.... Have we that degree of moral courage which will enable us to recognize the services of these black veterans, and do them justice?...
>
> ...I earnestly press upon your attention the expediency of proposing an amendment to the Constitution for striking out the word "white" from the article on suffrage, in order that, in due time, this much agitated question shall be submitted directly to the people, for their ultimate and final decision.[190]

Governor Stone's entreaty was consistent with a growing national recognition that the victorious North could not successfully push a program of suffrage reform on the South while still—in free states like Iowa—continuing to withhold voting rights from blacks.[191]

---

an intervening general election). The State Library of Iowa maintains an online list of those amendments. State Library of Iowa, "Amendments to the Constitution," http://www.statelibraryofiowa.org/services/collections/law-library/iaconst/amends.

[188] Dykstra, *supra* note 41, pp. 218–19. For discussions of Iowa politics during the Civil War years, see Cook, *supra* note 20, pp. 136–56; Robert R. Dykstra, "Iowans and the Politics of Race in America, 1857–1880," in *Iowa History Reader*, ed. Marvin Bergman (Iowa City: University of Iowa Press, 1996), ch. 7.

[189] Cook, *supra* note 20, pp. 160–65.

[190] Governor William H. Stone, Second Inaugural Address (Jan. 11, 1866), reprinted in *Messages and Proclamations of the Governors of Iowa*, ed. Benjamin F. Shambaugh (Iowa City: State Historical Society of Iowa, 1903), vol. 3, pp. 65, 84–86.

[191] William S. McFeely, *Grant: A Biography* (New York: W.W. Norton & Co., 1981), pp. 278–79.

Two weeks after Governor Stone's address, Iowa ratified the Thirteenth Amendment to the U.S. Constitution, banning slavery.[192] Two months after that—over the objection of nearly all of its Democratic members—the Republican-dominated General Assembly adopted a resolution proposing to amend the constitution by removing the word "white" not only from the provision concerning voter eligibility but also from the provisions concerning membership in the militia and counting inhabitants for purposes of legislative apportionment.[193] Racist candidates tried to leverage those proposed amendments against Republicans in the general election later that fall, but Iowa voters responded by giving Republicans an overwhelming victory.[194]

Under the terms of the 1857 constitution, Iowa voters could not be asked to approve the proposed amendments unless the legislature reaffirmed its commitment to those changes during its next session.[195] In February 1868, Alexander Clark and other black leaders in Iowa held what one historian described as the state's first "colored convention," aimed at encouraging the General Assembly to approve the pending amendments.[196] On March 31 of that same year, the General Assembly did precisely that, thereby ensuring that voters would be asked to consent to the amendments later that fall.[197] Several days later, the General Assembly voted to ratify the Fourteenth Amendment to the U.S. Constitution,[198] a watershed amendment that (among other things) confers citizenship upon all native-born and naturalized persons regardless of their race and bars each state from "deny[ing] to any person within its jurisdiction the equal protection of the laws." Two weeks after those momentous votes, the Iowa Supreme Court issued one of its most famous rulings to date, holding—in a case brought by Alexander Clark[199]—that the state's constitution and statutes required public-school officials to grant equal admission to black and white children (*Clark v. Board of Directors*, 1868).

On November 3, 1868—eleven years after refusing by nearly a 6-to-1 margin to give blacks the right to vote—Iowans ratified the amendments that the

---

[192] Joint Resolution No. 1 (Jan. 24, 1866), 1866 Iowa Acts 163.

[193] Resolution of Apr. 2, 1866, ch. 98, 1866 Iowa Acts 106. For discussions of the legislature's vote, see Cook, *supra* note 20, pp. 190–91; Dykstra, *supra* note 41, pp. 218–19.

[194] Dykstra, *supra* note 41, pp. 221–22.

[195] Iowa Const. art. X, § 1.

[196] Ruth A. Gallaher, "A Colored Convention," 2 *The Palimpsest* 178 (1921).

[197] Joint Resolution No. 11 (Mar. 31, 1868), 1868 Iowa Acts 290.

[198] Joint Resolution No. 15 (Apr. 3, 1868), 1868 Iowa Acts 293.

[199] For an introduction to Alexander Clark—Iowa's most prominent black leader during that era, and an energetic contributor to the work of the Republican party—see Leslie A. Schwalm, *Emancipation's Diaspora: Race and Reconstruction in the Upper Midwest* (Chapel Hill: University of North Carolina Press, 2009), pp. 36, 120–21, 171–73, 188–91.

General Assembly had proposed.[200] The only remaining constitutional provision in which the restrictive term "white" continued to appear was in the section describing eligibility for service in the General Assembly. In 1880, after a legislative campaign that for the first time saw a significant number of the General Assembly's Democrats cast votes in support of blacks' rights,[201] Iowa voters finally removed that remaining vestige of the 1857 constitution's explicit racism.[202]

Women's Rights

Like its 1846 predecessor, the 1857 constitution explicitly discriminated against women: under Section 1 of Article II, only men were permitted to vote; under Section 4 of Article III, only men were permitted to serve in the General Assembly; and under Section 1 of Article VI, only men were members of the militia. (The last of those restrictions remains in the constitution's text today.) The political and moral wisdom of those exclusions was not the subject of historically preserved debate at any of Iowa's three constitutional conventions. The most prominent reference to sex discrimination came from Jonathan Hall at the 1844 convention, when he used the law's treatment of women (and children) to rationalize denying blacks the right to vote:

> [T]he infant is not entitled to liberty or the pursuits of happiness until he arrives at the age of twenty-one years. Females by the arbitrary rules of society are excluded and debarred from many things which males consider rights and high privileges—such as the elective franchise, holding office, &c. Now in these cases the female and infant are denied what we abstractly term unalienable rights, and they submit without complaint or murmur. No one thinks of sympathizing with them in their deprivations. The philanthropist has never had occasion to commiserate their fate, still it is in those respects the same as the citizen of color. The

---

[200] Proclamation of Governor Samuel Merrill (Dec. 8, 1868), reprinted in *Documentary Material, supra* note 71, vol. 1, pp. 265–67; Dykstra, *supra* note 41, pp. 224–29. The amended texts appear today in Article II, Section 1; Article III, Section 35; and Article VI, Section 1. Two years later, Iowa voted to ratify the Fifteenth Amendment to the U.S. Constitution, barring states from withholding voting rights from American citizens on grounds of race. Joint Resolution No. 3 (Feb. 3, 1870), 1870 Iowa Acts 242.

[201] Dykstra, *supra* note 41, pp. 229–37. In 1870, the General Assembly had approved a resolution proposing to amend the constitution by lifting the racial restriction on those eligible to serve in that legislative body. Joint Resolution No. 19 (Apr. 12, 1870), 1870 Iowa Acts 256. In its next session, however, the legislature failed to approve the resolution again, and so the measure died until being resurrected later that decade.

[202] The vote was 90,237 in favor and 51,943 opposed. Certificate of the Board of State Canvassers (Dec. 3, 1880), reprinted in *Documentary Material, supra* note 71, vol. 1, p. 272. The amended provision appears today in Article III, Section 4.

> negro is surely no better than our wives and children, and should not excite sympathy when they desire the political rights which they are deprived of.[203]

Constitutional change for Iowa's women proved to be a long time in coming. Elizabeth Cady Stanton, Lucy Stone, and other nationally prominent suffragists had hoped that, once the North prevailed in the Civil War and blacks' status as citizens had been secured, many abolitionists would direct their energies toward securing women's equal access to the ballot.[204] Legislative conversations about allowing women in Iowa to vote did indeed begin with the ratification of the Thirteenth Amendment (banning slavery) in 1866, the ratification of the Fourteenth Amendment and its Equal Protection Clause in 1868, the extension of voting rights to Iowa's black men in that same year, and the national movement for black suffrage that would produce the Fifteenth Amendment in 1870. In 1866 and 1868—the years in which Iowa's General Assembly proposed amendments removing the word "white" from most of the locations in which it appeared in the Iowa Constitution—some of Iowa's legislators considered extending the franchise to women. The issue, however, was never brought to a vote.[205]

By 1870, it seemed that the tide was poised to turn. Just a few weeks after enacting legislation that opened the legal profession to women and to men of color,[206] the General Assembly proposed constitutional amendments that would allow women to vote and to serve in the General Assembly.[207] At a convention organized by Joseph Dugdale in Mount Pleasant two months later, suffragists created the Iowa Woman Suffrage Association (later renamed the Iowa Equal Suffrage Association) to help ensure the pending amendments' successful ratification.[208] Over the course of the following year, Susan B. Anthony, Lucy Stone, and Mary Livermore delivered lectures across the state, urging Iowans to support women's rights.[209] In the ensuing 1872 legislative session, however, the senate refused to endorse the amendments, and so, under the terms of Article X, the measure died before reaching the electorate.[210] In 1874, the General Assembly

---

[203] *1844 Journal*, *supra* note 45, pp. 52–53.

[204] Louise R. Noun, *Strong-Minded Women: The Emergence of the Woman-Suffrage Movement in Iowa* (Ames: Iowa State University Press, 1969), pp. 32, 36–37.

[205] Ruth A. Gallaher, *Legal and Political Status of Women in Iowa: An Historical Account of the Rights of Women in Iowa from 1838 to 1918* (Iowa City: State Historical Society of Iowa, 1918), pp. 177–79; Noun, *supra* note 204, pp. 42–44, 84–87.

[206] Act of Mar. 8, 1870, ch. 21, 1870 Iowa Acts 21. A prior statute had limited the legal profession to white men. Act of Mar. 12, 1858, ch. 44, 1858 Iowa Acts 51.

[207] Joint Resolution No. 14 (Apr. 4, 1870), 1870 Iowa Acts 252. For an account of the legislative debate, see Noun, *supra* note 204, pp. 128–32.

[208] Gallaher, *supra* note 205, pp. 184–85, 193; Noun, *supra* note 204, pp. 133–40.

[209] Noun, *supra* note 204, pp. 158–64.

[210] Noun, *supra* note 204, pp. 211–22.

approved another resolution proposing the same two amendments,[211] but the senate killed them once again in the following session. The opposition flowed from numerous sources. There were many in Iowa and elsewhere who believed, for example, that granting women the right to vote would ultimately lead to the abolition of marriage and the dissolution of the social order.[212] In an effort to distinguish the cases of women and black men, some argued that women should not have the right to vote because they did not bear arms in military conflicts.[213] Opponents of prohibition further argued that, if women were permitted to vote, they would cast their ballots in ways adverse to the sale and possession of alcohol.[214]

In nearly every legislative session over the course of the next four decades, equal-rights advocates asked the Iowa legislature to initiate the amendment process necessary to expand the franchise.[215] It nevertheless was not until 1913 that the General Assembly once again proposed an amendment that would grant women the right to vote.[216] Unlike the proposed amendments of 1870 and 1874, the 1913 package did not include eligibility for service in the General Assembly. The legislature approved the suffrage amendment again during its ensuing session, thereby finally sending the issue to Iowa's voters.[217] The Iowa Equal Suffrage Association and the president of the National American Woman Suffrage Association—Iowa-raised Carrie Chapman Catt—campaigned hard to persuade Iowans to approve the amendment.[218] On June 5, 1916, the measure was nevertheless defeated by a vote of 162,849 to 172,990, with the heaviest opposition coming from the state's anti-temperance counties.[219] Following

---

[211] Joint Resolution No. 18 (Mar. 13, 1874), 1874 Iowa Acts 85.

[212] Gallaher, *supra* note 205, pp. 180–88; Noun, *supra* note 204, pp. 177–97.

[213] Noun, *supra* note 204, pp. 200–02.

[214] Christine Mastalio, *Women's Suffrage in Iowa: A Sneak Peek of a New Digital Collection*, http://sdrc.lib.uiowa.edu/exhibits/suffrage/IAWomenSuffrage.pdf, p. 5. This creative University of Iowa website is worth a visit.

[215] Those efforts occasionally yielded small gains. In 1894, for example, the General Assembly enacted legislation giving women the right to vote in local elections concerning bonds, debts, and taxes. Act of Apr. 13, 1894, ch. 39, 1894 Iowa Acts 47.

[216] Joint Resolution No. 6 (Mar. 15, 1913), 1913 Iowa Acts 426.

[217] Joint Resolution No. 7 (Mar. 6, 1915), 1915 Iowa Acts 41.

[218] For Catt's own account of that campaign—an account that weaves together the politics of alcohol, paved roads, voter fraud, and women's right to vote—see Carrie Chapman Catt & Nellie Rogers Shuler, *Woman Suffrage and Politics: The Inner Story of the Suffrage Movement* (New York: Charles Scribner's Sons, 1926), pp. 211–26.

[219] *Iowa Official Register, 1917–1918*, pp. 462–481, available at https://www.legis.iowa.gov/archives/register. In its next session, the legislature once again proposed an amendment giving women the right to vote. Resolution of Apr. 5, 1917, ch. 153, 1917 Iowa Acts 171. The issue was not publicized as required by law prior to the ensuing general election, however, and so the amendment process was sent back, yet again, to square one. Gallaher, *supra* note 205, p. 221.

an investigation, the pro-suffrage Woman's Christian Temperance Union concluded that thousands of illegitimate anti-suffrage ballots had been counted on the anti-suffrage side of the ledger.[220]

It ultimately was by virtue of an amendment to the *federal* constitution that Iowa women finally won a share of the franchise. On July 2, 1919, with the encouragement of Governor William Harding, the Iowa legislature voted overwhelmingly to ratify the Nineteenth Amendment to the U.S. Constitution, barring each state from denying the right to vote "on account of sex."[221] By August of the following year, a sufficient number of other states had similarly granted their approval, thereby completing the ratification process. By virtue of the federal constitution's supremacy, Iowa's constitutional provision denying women the right to vote was rendered inoperative. Half a century later, when ratifying an amendment targeted at giving the General Assembly the power to define the state and county residency requirements for voter eligibility, Iowa voters finally removed the word "male" from the text of Iowa's suffrage provision.[222]

There have been two additional sex-related amendments to the Iowa Constitution. First, in 1926, Iowa voters approved an amendment striking the word "male" from the constitution's description of those eligible to serve in the General Assembly.[223] Women were thereby finally permitted to serve in the state legislature.

The story of Iowa's most recent sex-related amendment is intertwined with the national debate that emerged in the 1970s about whether to add the Equal Rights Amendment to the U.S. Constitution. That proposed federal amendment would have declared that "[e]quality of rights under the law shall not be denied or abridged by the United States or by any state on account of sex." Iowa was one of the first states in the nation to vote to ratify that amendment, doing so in March 1972, just days after the proposal left Congress's hands.[224] As the years

---

[220] Gallaher, *supra* note 205, pp. 219–20; Noun, *supra* note 204, p. 257.

[221] The vote in the house was 96 to 5 (with seven not voting). Iowa State House Journal: Special Session (July 2, 1919), pp. 12–13. The vote in the senate was 48 to 0 (with two not voting). Iowa State Senate Journal: Special Session (July 2, 1919), pp. 15–16. Even prior to the General Assembly's July 2 vote, 1919 had been an eventful year in Iowa on the issue of women's voting rights. On March 28, the legislature once again proposed to amend the Iowa Constitution by giving women the right to vote. Resolution of Mar. 28, 1919, ch. 110, 1919 Iowa Acts 116. On April 25, the General Assembly enacted legislation giving women a right to vote in presidential elections. Act of Apr. 25, 1919, ch. 353, 1919 Iowa Acts 459.

[222] The vote on the 1970 amendment was 300,119 to 141,091. *Iowa Official Register, 1971–1972*, pp. 173–75, available at https://www.legis.iowa.gov/archives/register. The amended text appears in Article II, Section 1.

[223] The vote on the 1926 amendment was 239,999 to 133,929. *Iowa Official Register, 1927–1928*, p. 39, available at https://www.legis.iowa.gov/archives/register. The amended text appears in Article III, Section 4.

[224] Joint Resolution, ch. 1140, 1972 Iowa Acts 525.

passed, however, it became clear that the amendment might not secure approval from a sufficient number of additional states. The amendment's opponents had found political traction by arguing, for example, that the amendment would result in unisex bathrooms, abortion on demand, and same-sex marriage.[225] Iowa's General Assembly nevertheless remained persuaded that constitutional change was necessary to secure the rights of women. In 1978 and 1979, legislators proposed an amendment to the Iowa Constitution that would make two changes to the document's text: (1) it would add the words "and women" to the opening clause of Article I, Section 1, thereby declaring that "[a]ll men *and women* are, by nature, free and equal, and have certain inalienable rights," and (2) it would declare that "[n]either the State nor any of its political subdivisions shall, on the basis of gender, deny or restrict the equality of rights under the law." In that same joint resolution, the legislators declared that it was their intention that gender classifications be permitted when "necessary to accomplish a compelling state interest."[226] In 1980, Iowa voters rejected that amendment by a vote of 468,708 to 591,925.[227] In 1989 and 1991 (after the federal Equal Rights Amendment had been rejected), the General Assembly returned with the same proposed amendment that Iowans had rejected in 1980, though this time the legislators did not declare any intention regarding the test by which gender classifications would be judged.[228] In 1992, Iowa voters rejected that amendment by a vote of 557,918 to 604,839.[229] In 1995 and 1997, the General Assembly returned a third time, this time proposing merely the first enumerated change listed above—namely, adding "and women" to the constitutional phrase describing those human beings who "are, by nature, free and equal, and have certain inalienable rights." Iowans ratified that watered-down proposal by a vote of 654,419 to 128,589.[230]

---

[225] For a nicely contextualized account of the ratification battle, see Reva B. Siegel, "Constitutional Culture, Social Movement Conflict and Constitutional Change: The Case of the De Facto ERA," 94 *California Law Review* 1323, 1378–414 (2006).

[226] Joint Resolution, ch. 1205, 1978 Iowa Acts 1024; Joint Resolution, ch. 170, 1979 Iowa Acts 478.

[227] *Iowa Official Register, 1981–1982*, pp. 154–55, available at https://www.legis.iowa.gov/archives/register.

[228] Joint Resolution, ch. 327, 1989 Iowa Acts 1024; Joint Resolution, ch. 272, 1991 Iowa Acts 856.

[229] *Iowa Official Register, 1993–1994*, p. 449, available at https://www.legis.iowa.gov/archives/register. For an account of the failed 1980 and 1992 pro-amendment campaigns, see the loose-leaf publication issued by the Feminist Majority Foundation titled *New Strategies, Old Obstacles in the Fight for Equality: An Analysis of the 1992 Iowa Equal Rights Amendment Campaign* (Los Angeles: Feminist Majority Foundation, 1993). As indicated by its title, most of the report focuses on the 1992 campaign. On pages 7–9, however, the authors also provide a brief recap of the 1980 campaign.

[230] *Iowa Official Register, 1999–2000*, p. 440, available at https://www.legis.iowa.gov/archives/register.

Composition of the General Assembly

Under the original text of the 1857 constitution, population and county lines both played important roles in determining the apportionment of seats in the General Assembly. Based upon periodic censuses,[231] seats in the senate were to be "apportioned among the several counties, according to the number of white inhabitants in each," and seats in the house similarly were to be "apportioned among the several counties and representative districts of the State, according to the number of white inhabitants in each."[232] (As explained above, amendments approved in 1868 removed the word "white" from both of those clauses.) No representative district could contain more than four counties, each district was to be assigned at least one representative, and no county could be divided when drawing the districts' lines.[233] Counties with especially high population counts (calculated using a ratio that the General Assembly was to devise) could each receive one additional representative.[234] Seats in the senate and house of representatives were capped at fifty and one hundred, respectively.[235]

The 1857 constitution's apportionment scheme permitted notable variations in the number of constituents that those in either legislative chamber represented, but amendments approved in 1904 and 1928 made matters even worse. The 1904 amendment fixed the total number of seats in the senate at fifty and capped the permissible number of seats in the house at 108. Senate seats were to be allocated based upon the population in each of the state's "counties or [senatorial] districts." In the house, however, concerns about population took a distant back seat to county lines. Each of the state's ninety-nine counties was to constitute one representative district, each county-district was to be assigned one representative in the house, and up to nine county-districts could each receive a second representative if they had especially high population counts.[236] Voters in sparsely populated counties thus would enjoy significantly stronger per-capita legislative representation than voters in heavily populated counties. The 1928 amendment secured a comparable arrangement in the senate, declaring that no

---

[231] The 1857 text required the state to conduct its own periodic census. Iowa Const. of 1857, art. III, § 33. Recognizing that the federal census rendered the state effort unnecessary, Iowa voters removed this provision in 1936. *Iowa Official Register, 1937–1938*, p. 510, available at https://www.legis.iowa.gov/archives/register.

[232] Iowa Const. of 1857, art. III, §§ 34, 35.

[233] Iowa Const. of 1857, art. III, §§ 35, 37.

[234] Iowa Const. of 1857, art. III, §§ 35, 36.

[235] Iowa Const. of 1857, art. III, § 35.

[236] For the text of the amendment, see *Iowa Official Register, 1905*, p. 16, available at https://www.legis.iowa.gov/archives/register.

county could be represented by more than one senator.[237] Even if a county were stuffed to the gills with inhabitants, it could have no greater voting strength in the senate than Iowa's most lightly populated county.

Although county lines thus played decisive roles in the amended constitution's apportionment scheme, the constitution—both in 1857 and as subsequently altered—did require reapportionment following each periodic census to ensure that at least some account would be taken of geographic shifts in population density. Even here, however, heavily populated regions were disadvantaged. Because many of the General Assembly's rural legislators were satisfied with an arrangement that permitted them to wield power disproportionate to the small constituencies they represented, the constitution's reapportionment mandate was perpetually ignored.[238] That failure to respond to population shifts, together with the constitution's heavy reliance upon county lines, yielded a General Assembly that was grossly malapportioned. The 1960 census revealed, for example, that six of Iowa's fifty senatorial districts had populations of less than 25,000 each, while five districts were each home to more than 100,000.[239] Matters were no better in the house. Adams County and Ringgold County—each with fewer than 8,000 people—had one representative apiece, for example, while Polk County—home to more than 260,000 people—had only two.[240]

Due to the legislature's longstanding failure to solve the problem, apportionment emerged as a leading issue in the election of 1960, when Iowa voters were asked (as they are asked every ten years, pursuant to Article X) whether they favored calling a constitutional convention. Proponents of constitutional change formed the Citizens Committee for a Constitutional Convention to coordinate the effort to secure an affirmative answer to that question. By a vote of 470,257 to 534,628, however, the convention proposal was defeated, due in part to heavy opposition in the state's rural areas.[241]

In 1961 and 1963, the General Assembly proposed an apportionment amendment that would implement what was popularly known as "the Shaff Plan" (or, among its opponents, "the Shaft Plan"), named for Senator David Shaff, one of the plan's chief sponsors. The proposed amendment would (1) divide the state into fifty-eight senatorial districts of roughly equal populations, with one senator

---

[237] For the text of the amendment, see *Iowa Official Register, 1929–1930*, p. 39, available at https://www.legis.iowa.gov/archives/register.

[238] Dorothy Schwieder, *Iowa: The Middle Land* (Iowa City: University of Iowa Press, 1996), p. 298.

[239] Wiggins, *supra* note 186, p. 173.

[240] Sage, *supra* note 4, pp. 311, 323.

[241] Wiggins, *supra* note 186, pp. 180–89; Charles W. Wiggins, "The Post World War II Legislative Reapportionment Battle in Iowa Politics," in *Patterns and Perspectives in Iowa History*, ed. Dorothy Schwieder (Ames: Iowa State University Press, 1973), pp. 403, 409–17; *Iowa Official Register, 1961–1962*, pp. 368–69, available at https://www.legis.iowa.gov/archives/register.

to be elected from each, and (2) reduce the number of representatives to ninety-nine, with each of the state's ninety-nine counties electing one—and only one—representative, regardless of the size of its population.[242] One of the General Assembly's chambers would be apportioned based upon population, in other words, and the other would be apportioned based entirely upon county lines. Many Democrats (whose base tended to live in urban areas) and many urban Republicans opposed the Shaff Plan, while many rural Republicans favored it because of the increased strength it would give them in the house. In an election held on December 3, 1963, Iowa voters rejected the proposed amendment by a vote of 190,424 to 272,382, with urban voters forming a large share of the negative vote.[243]

By the time the Shaff Plan had been defeated, it was clear that the legislature could not simply revert to its prior pattern of ignoring the state's apportionment problem. In 1962, the U.S. Supreme Court had ruled in *Baker v. Carr* that federal courts could take jurisdiction of claims that states' apportionment schemes violated the Equal Protection Clause of the U.S. Constitution's Fourteenth Amendment. Two citizens of Polk County had accordingly launched federal litigation in Iowa, alleging that Iowa's apportionment arrangement violated their equal-protection rights by giving far less weight to their votes than to those of individuals residing in less populous counties. Six months before the Shaff Plan was presented to the state's voters, the federal district court determined that Iowa's existing apportionment scheme violated the Equal Protection Clause (*Davis v. Synhorst I*, 1963). Because a statewide ratification vote on the Shaff Plan was then pending, however, and because the court did not want to pass judgment on that plan unnecessarily, the court opted to refrain from making any decisions about appropriate remedies until after the election had been held. In January 1964—two months after the Shaff Plan's electoral defeat—the court reiterated that the state's existing apportionment scheme violated the federal constitution and urged the state's lawmakers to convene a special session aimed at solving the problem (*Davis v. Synhorst II*, 1964).

The General Assembly promptly convened in a special session and responded in two ways. First, the legislature proposed to amend the constitution by apportioning both the house and the senate using a mixture of county lines and population, with one hundred seats in the house and fifty seats in the senate.[244] Second, pending approval of that amendment, lawmakers adopted a temporary apportionment plan under which urban areas would receive somewhat

---

[242] Joint Resolution, ch. 344, 1961 Iowa Acts 345; Joint Resolution, ch. 371, 1963 Iowa Acts 560.

[243] *Iowa Official Register, 1965–1966*, p. 416, available at https://www.legis.iowa.gov/archives/register; Wiggins, *supra* note 241, pp. 417–18. In heavily populated Polk County, for example, the vote was 7,214 in favor and 38,600 opposed.

[244] Joint Resolution, ch. 31, 1964 Iowa Acts 38 (special session); Wiggins, *supra* note 241, p. 419.

increased representation in both chambers.[245] Shortly thereafter, in a four-paragraph ruling issued in March 1964, the federal district court indicated that the state's temporary apportionment plan was an improvement over the status quo and that—absent further guidance from the U.S. Supreme Court—there was no reason for the federal court to declare that plan unconstitutional (*Davis v. Synhorst III*, 1964).

Three months later—on June 16, 1964—the U.S. Supreme Court issued a game-changing ruling in *Reynolds v. Sims*. Pointing out that "[l]egislators represent people, not trees or acres," the *Reynolds* Court held that, under the Equal Protection Clause, representation in *both* chambers of a state's bicameral legislative body must be apportioned based primarily upon population, so that, in both house and senate elections, the weight of a person's vote does not substantially vary from one part of the state to another. *Reynolds* provided the guidance that the federal district court in Iowa previously believed it had lacked. In a ruling handed down in February 1965, the district court found that the temporary apportionment plan currently in place violated the Equal Protection Clause (*Davis v. Cameron*, 1965). The court's rationale made it clear that, if later given an opportunity, the court likely would also strike down the constitutional amendment that the legislature had proposed one year earlier. Rather than impose its own judicially crafted remedy, however, the court once again urged the General Assembly to solve the problem for itself.

In 1965, with the federal judiciary having left lawmakers with no clear alternative, the General Assembly finally proposed a constitutional amendment that placed population at the heart of the apportionment formula for both legislative chambers.[246] The proposed amendment capped membership in the senate at fifty and membership in the house at one hundred, and it did not require that any regard be paid to county lines when drawing legislative districts.[247] Importantly, the amendment also gave the Iowa Supreme Court jurisdiction to review any apportionment plan that the General Assembly adopts, as well as the power to craft its own apportionment plan for the state either if the court concludes that a plan adopted by the legislature is defective or if the legislature altogether fails to put together an apportionment plan in a timely fashion following a federal decennial census. The amendment was approved by the legislature once again in 1967[248] and, on November 5, 1968, was approved by Iowa voters by a vote of 469,449 to 263,886.[249] An amendment approved in 1970 put the final

[245] Act of Mar. 23, 1964, ch. 1, 1964 Iowa Acts 1 (special session); Wiggins, *supra* note 241, p. 419.

[246] Joint Resolution, ch. 473, 1965 Iowa Acts 877 (codified today at Iowa Const. art. III, § 34).

[247] When drawing federal congressional districts, however, counties cannot be divided. Iowa Const. art. III, § 37.

[248] Joint Resolution, ch. 463, 1967 Iowa Acts 856.

[249] *Iowa Official Register, 1969–1970*, pp. 361–63, available at https://www.legis.iowa.gov/archives/register. The amendment's text appears today in Article III, Sections 6, 34, 35, 36, and 37.

constitutional piece of the puzzle into place, stating that each senatorial district may be represented by only one senator and each representative district may be represented by only one representative.[250]

Iowa voters' ratification of those amendments did not bring a permanent end to the state's reapportionment battles, but the judiciary's power to be intensively involved in the process helps to ensure that gross malapportionment is a thing of the past. The 1969 apportionment plan that the legislature adopted immediately following the 1968 amendment's approval, for example, was struck down by the Iowa Supreme Court for having districts with constitutionally impermissible population variances (*In re Legislative Districting of General Assembly*, 1970), as was the plan that the General Assembly adopted in 1971 in a purported effort to cure the 1969 plan's defects (*In re Legislative Districting of General Assembly*, 1972).[251] At the conclusion of the latter ruling, the court declared that, pursuant to the map-drawing power that the 1968 amendment had given it, the court itself would "proceed immediately to the development and adoption of a decennial apportionment plan which in our judgment will comply with constitutional requirements." As a result of the plan that the Iowa Supreme Court devised, Iowa became what one writer described as "the most equitably apportioned legislature in the Union."[252]

Leadership of the Executive Branch

Under Iowa's first constitution, ratified in 1846, the governor served a four-year term,[253] there was no lieutenant governor, and—in the event of the governor's death or departure—the gubernatorial line of succession consisted of the secretary of state, the president of the senate, and the speaker of the house of representatives, in that order.[254] Over the more than a century and a half that have elapsed since that constitution's adoption, the structure of Iowa's executive-branch leadership has undergone noteworthy changes.

---

[250] *Iowa Official Register, 1971–1972*, pp. 173–75, available at https://www.legis.iowa.gov/archives/register; Wiggins, *supra* note 241, pp. 420–22. The amendment's text appears in Article III, Section 39. The 1970 amendment was a response to the Iowa Supreme Court's declaration in *Kruidenier v. McCulloch* (1966) that, absent unusual circumstances, "[a]ny scheme of legislative apportionment in which there are multimember districts and single-member districts in the same house impairs the right of a resident of a single-member district to have the laws operate uniformly as guaranteed by section 6, Article I, of the Constitution of Iowa."

[251] For a discussion of these cases, see Wiggins, *supra* note 241, pp. 425–29.

[252] Wiggins, *supra* note 241, p. 450 (citing an analysis published in "42 States Reapportion: Plans Are 'Final' in 21," *The American Legislator* (May 1972), p. 2).

[253] Iowa Const. of 1846, art. V, § 2.

[254] Iowa Const. of 1846, art. V, §§ 18, 19.

The first set of alterations came at the 1857 convention. When that convention's Committee on the Executive presented a draft of executive-branch provisions in the middle of the convention's second week, it made clear that it knew the existing four-year term was controversial: the committee simply left the governor's term of service blank, acknowledging that the delegates would want to discuss the matter.[255] In a subsequent session, attorney Harvey Skiff proposed that the blank be filled with the word "two," while former Muscatine mayor John Parvin proposed that it be filled with "four." Without recorded debate, Parvin's motion prevailed by a vote of 18 to 13.[256] The following morning, however, the four-year plan ran into trouble, with Wapello County's George Gillaspy among those leading the attack. Gillaspy argued that there was no reason to allow the governor to serve longer than the secretary of state, the state auditor (whom Gillaspy believed might prove to be "of more importance to the people" than the governor), and members of the house of representatives, all of whom were slated to serve two-year terms. He further contended that a four-year term did not provide sufficient democratic accountability in a rapidly changing and growing state, and that two years was plenty of time for a person to demonstrate that he ought to be re-elected. Davis County's David Palmer added that the position was not one for which significant government experience was necessary, and that Iowa ought to maximize the number of service-minded people who could take their turn in the office.[257] Evidently persuaded by such arguments, the delegates voted 23 to 9 to reduce the governor's term to two years.[258]

The delegates to the 1857 convention also concluded that Iowa would be better off having a lieutenant governor elected to serve as the senate's president and to stand first in the line of gubernatorial succession.[259] Under the scheme that the delegates established, the governor and lieutenant governor were to be elected separately—voters were to be instructed to "designate for whom they vote as Governor, and for whom as Lieutenant Governor."[260] Political antagonists thus could find themselves holding the state's two highest executive positions, with the lieutenant governor waiting in the wings to succeed the governor in the event of a vacancy in that office. Although politically divided gubernatorial outcomes were rare, they did sometimes occur, as they did, for example, in successive elections in the 1980s, when Democratic lieutenant governors were elected to serve with a Republican governor.[261]

---

[255] *1857 Debates, supra* note 110, vol. 1, p. 76.

[256] *1857 Debates, supra* note 110, vol. 1, p. 579.

[257] *1857 Debates, supra* note 110, vol. 1, p. 590.

[258] *1857 Journal, supra* note 110, p. 216.

[259] Iowa Const. of 1857, art. IV, §§ 17, 18.

[260] Iowa Const. of 1857, art. IV, § 3.

[261] Wikipedia (an erratic source that is useful here) provides a color-coded chart showing the political results of all Iowa elections for governor and lieutenant governor from 1858 to the present. *See* https://en.wikipedia.org/wiki/List_of_lieutenant_governors_of_Iowa.

Iowa voters have changed the 1857 structure in two prominent ways.[262] First, in 1972, Iowans ratified an amendment extending the governor's and lieutenant governor's terms to four years, just as the governor's term had been under the 1846 constitution.[263] Second, under an amendment ratified in 1988, a candidate for either governor or lieutenant governor must run as a team with an individual seeking the other office, and voters are not allowed to split their ballots between members of two competing teams.[264] This ensures that the governor and lieutenant governor serving at any given moment in time will at least begin their terms in office as allies, rather than as antagonists. An additional amendment approved in 1988 states that the lieutenant governor shall perform the duties that are assigned to him or her by law, as well as any duties assigned by the governor.[265] Today, pursuant to Senate Rules 52 and 53, the senate elects its own president and president pro tempore.[266]

Filling Judicial Vacancies

Recall that, at the Territory of Iowa's 1844 convention, the delegates proposed that the legislature select the members of the supreme court and that Iowa voters select the members of the district courts. The 1846 constitution adopted precisely that arrangement.[267] In keeping with a trend that swept the nation in the mid-nineteenth century, the delegates to the 1857 convention shifted responsibility

---

[262] In 1952, Iowa voters ratified an amendment that added a further nuance to the gubernatorial line of succession: if the governor, the lieutenant governor, the president of the senate, and the speaker of the house all become unable to serve, the justices of the Iowa Supreme Court are to convene the General Assembly, and the state's legislators are then to choose a new governor and lieutenant governor. *Iowa Official Register, 1953–1954*, p. 461, available at https://www.legis.iowa.gov/archives/register. Although the 1952 amendment was subsequently repealed and replaced in a package of amendments approved in 1988, the 1988 replacement retained this succession arrangement, and it remains in place today in Article IV, Section 19.

[263] *Iowa Official Register, 1973–1974*, p. 381, available at https://www.legis.iowa.gov/archives/register. The amendment appears today in Article IV, Section 2. For contemporaneous coverage of Iowans' decision, see Richard Doak, "Iowa Voters Face Issues of Lottery, Judges, Office Term," *Des Moines Register*, Oct. 8, 1972, at 1B; Editorial, "For Improved Iowa Government," *Des Moines Register*, Oct. 15, 1972, at 10C. Although the 1972 amendment was subsequently repealed and replaced in a package of amendments approved in 1988, the 1988 replacement retained this feature of the 1972 amendment and it remains in place today. Iowa Const. art. IV, § 2.

[264] *Iowa Official Register, 1989–1990*, pp. 291–92, available at https://www.legis.iowa.gov/archives/register. The amendment appears today in Article IV, Section 3.

[265] *Iowa Official Register, 1989–1990*, p. 292, available at https://www.legis.iowa.gov/archives/register. The amendment appears today in Article IV, Section 18.

[266] The senate's rules are available at https://www.legis.iowa.gov/docs/publications/SR/644148.pdf.

[267] Iowa Const. of 1846, art. VI, §§ 3, 4.

for choosing supreme court justices from the General Assembly to ordinary voters.[268] For more than a century thereafter, popular elections remained the vehicle by which the state filled all of its judicial vacancies.

In 1914, Albert Kales—a law professor at Northwestern University and co-founder of the American Judicature Society—urged states to abandon the widespread practice of filling judicial vacancies through elections.[269] He recommended that states establish nonpartisan bodies for the task of nominating slates of qualified individuals to fill those vacancies, with one politically accountable decision-maker then appointing new judges from the short lists that the nonpartisan bodies prepared. Recognizing that including an opportunity for voter input would be essential to make the merit-selection plan politically saleable among Progressives, Kales and his allies added judicial-retention elections to the mix, whereby appointed judges would appear on voters' ballots, unopposed, after a short initial term of service and again periodically thereafter. In 1940, Missouri became the first state to adopt the model Kales had described; the merit-selection and retention-election system is thus often referred to as "the Missouri Plan."[270]

In the 1950s, the virtues of the Missouri Plan began to impress themselves upon a variety of Iowans. In the closing pages of a 1957 book, for example, a University of Iowa political scientist suggested that, even though the state's judicial elections often were not contested, lawmakers could improve the quality of Iowa's judges—especially in the lower courts—if they shifted to a system of "[a]ppointment of judges by the governor with Bar Association aid."[271] A fully developed endorsement of the Missouri Plan came the following year, with an article that Harvey Uhlenhopp—a district court judge who formerly had served in the General Assembly—published in the *Iowa Law Review*.[272] Judge Uhlenhopp argued that (among other things) "[p]opular election, rather than careful selection, is a poor way to fill posts involving professional qualifications," "the most popular candidates not infrequently turn out to be the most incompetent judges," lawyers should play a role in judicial selection but should not

---

[268] Iowa Const. of 1857, art. V, § 3.

[269] Albert M. Kales, *Unpopular Government in the United States* (Chicago: University of Chicago Press, 1914), pp. 225–51.

[270] Susan B. Carbon, "Judicial Retention Elections: Are They Serving Their Intended Purpose?," 64 *Judicature* 210, 215, 220–21, 233 (1980); G. Alan Tarr, "Do Retention Elections Work?," 74 *Missouri Law Review* 605, 607–09 (2009); Glenn R. Winters, "The Merit Plan for Judicial Selection and Tenure—Its Historical Development," 7 *Duquesne Law Review* 61, 65–71 (1968).

[271] Russell M. Ross, *The Government and Administration of Iowa* (New York: Thomas Y. Crowell Co., 1957), p. 356.

[272] Harvey Uhlenhopp, "Judicial Reorganization in Iowa," 44 *Iowa Law Review* 6 (1958). At different points in his life, Uhlenhopp was a county attorney, he served in the General Assembly, he was a district court judge, and he was a justice on the Iowa Supreme Court.

control the entire process, and, although no "system is perfect, . . . students of the subject generally agree that the best selection system yet devised is the one conceived by Albert Kales in 1914."[273]

Judge Uhlenhopp's argument quickly found fertile ground. In 1959—just one year after the *Iowa Law Review* article appeared—the General Assembly proposed an amendment that would bring the Missouri Plan to Iowa.[274] Under the legislature's proposal, the governor would appoint individuals to fill judicial vacancies, drawing from short lists of nominees submitted by newly created judicial nominating commissions. There would be two such commissions—one for vacancies on the supreme court and one for vacancies on district courts. Until July 4, 1973 (and thereafter unless changed by law), the two commissions' memberships would be composed of equal numbers of individuals appointed by the governor and individuals elected by the state's licensed attorneys, and each commission would be chaired by a senior member of the bench. Following their appointment, judges would stand unopposed in retention elections after a short period of service and then again at established intervals thereafter. The General Assembly reaffirmed its commitment to these changes during its ensuing session, thereby sending the amendment to the state's electorate for a final assessment.[275]

In a special election held on June 4, 1962, Iowa voters granted their approval by a vote of 158,279 to 118,215.[276] In the years since Iowans adopted this new vacancy-filling system, judges have routinely prevailed in their retention elections, with three prominent exceptions that all occurred in the same unusual year: in 2010, Iowa voters removed three members of the Iowa Supreme Court who had joined the court's unanimous conclusion in *Varnum v. Brien* (2009) that a state statute barring same-sex marriage violated the Iowa Constitution.[277]

* * *

As the *Varnum* ruling illustrates, the world has changed in many ways since 1857, when thirty-six delegates gathered in Iowa City to draft the constitution

---

[273] Uhlenhopp, *supra* note 272, pp. 55–72.

[274] Joint Resolution, ch. 420, 1959 Iowa Acts 549.

[275] Joint Resolution, ch. 343, 1961 Iowa Acts 343.

[276] *Iowa Official Register, 1963–1964*, pp. 366–67, available at https://www.legis.iowa.gov/archives/register. The text of the amendment appears today in Article V, Sections 15, 16, 17, and 18.

[277] For a history of the 2010 retention election, see Todd E. Pettys, "Letter from Iowa: Same-Sex Marriage and the Ouster of Three Justices," 59 *Kansas Law Review* 715 (2011). For a history of the retention election of 2012, in which a fourth *Varnum* justice was retained, see Todd E. Pettys, "Retention Redux: Iowa 2012," 14 *Journal of Appellate Practice & Process* 47 (2013). The remaining three *Varnum* justices were retained in the election of 2016. *See* Iowa Secretary of State, "General Election 2016: Judicial," located under an unwieldy URL at https://sos.iowa.gov/.

that, as amended, remains in force today. For more than a century and a half now, litigants have called upon Iowa's courts to resolve disagreements about the Iowa Constitution's requirements and implications. By virtue of that perennial litigation, the remainder of Iowa's constitutional story has been told, in large part, by Iowa's judges. It is to those judicial rulings that we principally turn in Part II.

PART TWO

The Iowa Constitution and Commentary

Part II provides a provision-by-provision analysis of the Iowa Constitution. Full citations to the referenced cases appear in the Table of Cases near the end of the book. The book's account of judicial rulings is current through June 30, 2017; periodic updates will be provided on the author's website, www.todd-pettys.com.

At the time of this writing, the Iowa Code Editor (housed within Iowa's Legislative Services Agency) hopes to conform the state's future printings of the Iowa Constitution to the text of the handwritten document that was signed by the delegates to Iowa's 1857 constitutional convention. Prior code editors deviated from the handwritten text in various ways. Those variances are likely inconsequential; they typically concern such matters as whether to capitalize the terms "General Assembly" and "State." Even if all of those variances are indeed negligible, this book aims to provide a version of the Iowa Constitution that is faithful to the 1857 handwritten text. This book also aims to be faithful to the original text of all constitutional amendments. Such faithfulness unavoidably yields occasional inconsistencies; some amendments, for example, refer to the General Assembly using a lowercase "g" and "a," while those two words are typically capitalized in the 1857 document. Images of the 1857 handwritten text and the text of subsequent amendments are presented online by the State Library of Iowa.[1]

For many years, the Iowa Code Editor and other publishers have inserted titles for each enumerated section of the constitution. (The title assigned for Article I, Section 1, for example, is "Rights of persons.") Those titles were not written by the delegates to the 1857 convention and are not themselves part of the ratified constitution. One should not make the mistake, therefore, of attaching constitutional significance to those titles' phrasings. This book nevertheless retains those titles for such guidance as they may provide the reader.

---

[1] *See* State Library of Iowa, "Constitutions," http://www.statelibraryofiowa.org/services/collections/law-library/iacon/iacons (presenting the 1857 handwritten text and other iterations of the Iowa Constitution); State Library of Iowa, "Amendments to the Constitution," http://www.statelibraryofiowa.org/services/collections/law-library/iaconst/amends (presenting a chronological list of all constitutional amendments).

Preamble and Boundaries

Preamble.

WE THE PEOPLE OF THE STATE OF IOWA, grateful to the Supreme Being for the blessings hitherto enjoyed, and feeling our dependence on Him for a continuation of those blessings, do ordain and establish a free and independent government, by the name of the State of Iowa, the boundaries whereof shall be as follows:

Like nearly every other state constitution in the United States,[1] the Iowa Constitution begins by acknowledging a deity and by articulating the document's overarching ambitions. Consistent with the general understanding of preambles at the time of the constitution's adoption and with the U.S. Supreme Court's treatment of the U.S. Constitution's own preamble,[2] the Iowa Supreme Court has never given the state constitution's preamble independent legal effect.

[1] *See generally* Robert L. Maddex, *State Constitutions of the United States* (Washington, D.C.: Congressional Quarterly, 1998).

[2] Joseph Story, *Commentaries on the Constitution of the United States*, vol. 1 (Boston: Hilliard, Gray, & Co., 1833), § 221; *Jacobson v. Massachusetts* (1905).

In the preamble to the 1844 draft constitution that the Territory of Iowa's voters rejected, the document's framers expressed Iowans' gratitude to "the Supreme Ruler of the universe."[3] The 1844 text also borrowed heavily from the preamble to the U.S. Constitution and from the Declaration of Independence, stating that the constitution's overarching purposes were "to establish justice, insure tranquility, provide for the common defense, promote the general welfare, [and] secure to ourselves and our posterity the rights of life, liberty, and the pursuit of happiness." At the 1846 convention that yielded Iowa's first constitution, the delegates made two notable changes: they changed "the Supreme Ruler of the universe" to "the Supreme Being," and they removed the purposive language that their predecessors had borrowed from revered national texts. The fragmentary historical record does not reveal why the delegates made those changes. On the second day of the 1846 convention, James Grant—a young lawyer who had come to Iowa from North Carolina—presented a draft of the preamble on behalf of the Committee on Boundaries and Bill of Rights.[4] The committee's draft already reflected the changes noted here, and the delegates ultimately approved those changes without any historically recorded debate. The 1846 language was carried forward to the 1857 constitution that remains in force today.

Boundaries.

Beginning in the middle of the main channel of the Mississippi River, at a point due East of the middle of the mouth of the main channel of the Des Moines River, thence up the middle of the main channel of the said Des Moines River, to a point on said river where the Northern boundary line of the State of Missouri—as established by the constitution of that State—adopted June 12th, 1820—crosses the said middle of the main channel of the said Des Moines River; thence Westwardly along the said Northern boundary line of the State of Missouri, as established at the time aforesaid, until an extension of said line intersects the middle of the main channel of the Missouri River; thence up the middle of the main channel of the said Missouri River to a point opposite the middle of the main channel of the Big Sioux River, according to Nicollett's Map; thence up the main channel of the said Big Sioux River, according to the said map, until it is intersected by the parallel of forty three degrees and thirty minutes North latitude; thence East along said parallel of forty three degrees and thirty minutes until said parallel intersects the middle of the main channel of the Mississippi River; thence down the middle of the main channel of said Mississippi River to the place of beginning.

---

[3] That language was included at the urging of Caleb Campbell, a farmer from Washington County. *Fragments of the Debates of the Iowa Constitutional Conventions of 1844 and 1846*, ed. Benjamin F. Shambaugh (Iowa City: State Historical Society of Iowa, 1900), p. 34.

[4] *Journal of the Convention for the Formation of a Constitution for the State of Iowa* (Iowa City: Abraham H. Palmer, 1846), p. 28.

As Part I explains in greater detail, the state's boundaries were among the most contentious issues surrounding the efforts of those within the Territory of Iowa to adopt a constitution and secure statehood. The draft constitution produced by the 1844 convention proposed boundaries that were significantly more expansive than those described above. After Congress rejected those boundaries, the 1846 convention embraced the more constrained boundaries that continue to define the state's geographic reach under the 1857 constitution.

Legal questions concerning Iowa's borders have reached the U.S. Supreme Court on a number of occasions. In an 1849 ruling concerning the state's southern boundary, for example, the Court resolved a controversy between Iowa and Missouri about which of them could rightfully claim a stretch of land more than ten miles wide and about two hundred miles long (*Missouri v. Iowa*). The dispute initially arose between Missouri and the federal government before Iowa joined the Union; Iowa inherited a stake in the matter by virtue of its constitutional dependence upon the location of Missouri's northern border. The controversy flowed from uncertainties about the relevance of a boundary line previously established by federal treaties with the Great and Little Osage nations and about the meaning of the Missouri constitution's ambiguous reference to "the rapids of the River Des Moines" in the provision setting forth that state's own boundaries. The dispute nearly led to armed conflict, but the Court's ruling put the matter to rest.[5]

In 1892, the Court settled a controversy between Iowa and Nebraska about whether gradual changes in the location of the middle of the Missouri River's main channel resulted in a new boundary between the two states, such that one state gained property while the other lost it (*Nebraska v. Iowa*). In keeping with long-established principles concerning riparian disputes in other settings, the Court held that gradual changes in the midpoint's location ("accretions") do indeed result in a new boundary line, but sudden changes ("avulsions") do not.[6]

In 1893, facing a dispute between Iowa and Illinois about how much of each state-connecting bridge the two states could respectively tax, the Court ruled that the boundary lay at the midpoint of the Mississippi River's main navigable channel, and not (as Iowa had ambitiously contended) at the midpoint of the

---

[5] For discussions of the dispute, see Erik M. Eriksson, "The Boundaries of Iowa," 25 *Iowa Journal of History & Politics* 163 (1927); Derek R. Everett, "To Shed Our Blood for Our Beloved Territory: The Iowa-Missouri Borderland," 67 *Annals of Iowa* 269 (2008); Carol J. Kraus, "A Study in Border Confrontation: The Iowa-Missouri Boundary Dispute," 40 *Annals of Iowa* 81 (1969).

[6] The two states entered a compact in 1943, establishing a more stable boundary. That compact generated litigation of its own (*Nebraska v. Iowa*, 1972). As a matter of federal law, the Court incorporates state-law standards when determining whether a change in a river's contours is the result of accretion or avulsion (*Wilson v. Omaha Indian Tribe*, 1979, concerning Iowa and the Missouri River).

river's entire width (*Iowa v. Illinois*).[7] The Court reasoned that the two states should have equal access to navigation on the river.

Iowa courts have had many occasions to grapple with boundary issues, some of them involving controversies about whether changes in the path of the stubbornly peripatetic Missouri River resulted from boundary-shifting accretion or from boundary-preserving avulsion (*State v. Simmons*, 1980; *Jeffrey v. Grosvenor*, 1968; *Kitteridge v. Ritter*, 1915). Because such inquiries are fact-intensive, the Iowa Supreme Court has commonly deferred heavily to trial courts' factual findings.

Although the Iowa Constitution fixes some of the state's boundaries at the midpoints of various rivers' main channels, it does not rigidly bar the state from extending its regulatory reach to those rivers' far sides. When admitting Iowa into the Union, Congress granted Iowa concurrent jurisdiction "on the river[s]" that helped to form the state's boundaries.[8] Iowa's legislators and judges have interpreted that statute as giving the state's lawmakers the power to regulate activities of numerous kinds on those rivers, regardless of where on the rivers they occur. In *State v. LeGear* (1984), for example, the Iowa Supreme Court held that the state could prosecute a man for murder after he threw a woman from a bridge into the Missouri River, and that it did not matter whether he committed his crime on the Iowa or Nebraska side of the boundary line. That 1984 ruling flowed from a series of earlier cases. In *State v. Mullen* (1872), for example, the Iowa court held that state authorities could prosecute an individual who was running a prostitution operation on a boat in shallow water on Illinois's side of the river. The court said that restricting Iowa's criminal jurisdiction to the midpoint of the river's main navigable channel would set the stage for future factual uncertainties about precisely where on the river alleged criminal activities occurred. Similarly, in *State v. Moyers* (1912), the Iowa court found that the state could prosecute a person for engaging in unlicensed fishing on the Mississippi River, no matter where on the river he had cast his nets. The court acknowledged that the ruling would create complications for the would-be fisherman who might have to obtain fishing licenses from two different states in order to fish on a single river, but the court said this was the unavoidable implication of *Mullen*'s sound logic. The court applied the same rule against a duck hunter in *State v. Rorris* (1937).

When state officials have tried to extend their reach to comparatively permanent structures on an adjoining state's side of a boundary river, however, the Iowa Supreme Court has held that Iowa lacks jurisdiction. In *Buck v. Ellenbolt* (1892), for example, the court ruled that the state could not prosecute a person for

[7] For the Iowa Supreme Court's application of that standard to a bridge-taxation case, see *Chicago & Northwestern Railway Co. v. City of Clinton* (1893).

[8] Act of Mar. 3, 1845, ch. 48, § 3, 5 Stat. 742. The Iowa legislature has claimed such concurrent jurisdiction. Iowa Code § 1.3.

selling intoxicating alcohol from a building located on an island on Illinois's side of the Mississippi River, and in *Gilbert v. Moline Water Power & Manufacturing Co.* (1866), the court held that the state could not regulate a dam that spanned the Mississippi River from Illinois's mainland to an Illinois island. *Gilbert* laid the groundwork for the distinction on which subsequent rulings would turn, finding that there is an important difference between boats (whose precise locations on a river at a given moment in time may be difficult to determine, and over which Iowa and an adjoining state may thus sensibly exercise concurrent jurisdiction) and fixed structures that rest more or less permanently on one state's side of the boundary line.

Article I

Bill of Rights

Section 1.
Rights of persons.

All men and women are, by nature, free and equal, and have certain inalienable rights—among which are those of enjoying and defending life and liberty, acquiring, possessing and protecting property, and pursuing and obtaining safety and happiness.

Section 1 of the Bill of Rights declares some of the basic principles on which the United States and the State of Iowa were founded, and it tantalizingly refers to certain rights that cannot be taken away. In Iowa's first constitution, ratified in 1846, Section 1 was substantively framed just as it appears here, with two exceptions: it did not refer explicitly to women, and it said "free and independent," rather than "free and equal."[1] The 1846 convention's journal contains no indication that the provision's language was ever debated at that gathering, a fact that is not surprising given the degree to which it echoes familiar language found in the Declaration of Independence and in many early states' constitutions.[2]

On the tenth day of the 1857 convention, David Bunker—a farmer from Washington County who had served in Iowa's territorial and state

[1] Iowa Const. of 1846, art. II, § 1.

[2] *See*, e.g., Mass. Const. of 1780, pt. 1, art. I; Va. Const. of 1776, § 1; Vt. Const. of 1777, ch. I, § 1.

legislatures—proposed striking the word "independent" and replacing it with "equal." He argued that no person is truly independent in the sense of being fully beyond others' control, but that "all men are, by nature, perfectly equal in the use of whatever Nature's God has bestowed upon them."[3] After Allamakee County's John Clark replied that the existing text "comprehends everything that we can claim by the laws of nature and Nature's God," the delegates rejected Bunker's suggestion.[4] Bunker had nevertheless planted the seed of an idea. Three weeks later, when Henry County's Rufus Clarke presented the work of a committee tasked with reviewing Section 1 and a handful of other provisions, he announced that the committee was embracing Bunker's proposal.[5] Appanoose County's Amos Harris resisted the change on the grounds that the term "independent" better captured the natural order of things and that other states had used "independent" more frequently than "equal" in their constitutions' corresponding clauses.[6] Despite their disagreement, both Bunker and Harris said that the convention's ultimate choice between the two terms was unlikely to have practical consequences.[7] By a vote of 20 to 15, the delegates approved the change.[8] Iowa voters brought Section 1 into its current form nearly a century and a half later, when in 1998 they approved the General Assembly's proposal to add "and women" to the provision's opening clause.

History has largely vindicated Bunker's and Harris's prediction that the convention's acceptance or rejection of the term "equal" would be inconsequential. Although principles of equality loom large in modern American constitutionalism, it is Section 6—not Section 1—that principally functions today as the Iowa Constitution's equal protection provision. To be sure, one can find cases in which the Iowa Supreme Court cited Section 1, but not Section 6, for dispositive equality principles. For example, in *Coger v. North Western Union Packet Co.* (1875)—a celebrated case in which the court ruled against a steamboat operator

[3] *The Debates of the Constitutional Convention of the State of Iowa* (Davenport: Luse, Lane & Co., 1857) [hereinafter *1857 Debates*], vol. 1, p. 103. When describing the drafting histories underlying the Iowa Constitution's various provisions, this book often refers to a small number of essential sources. In addition to the two volumes of the *1857 Debates*, these sources include *Fragments of the Debates of the Iowa Constitutional Conventions of 1844 and 1846*, ed. Benjamin F. Shambaugh (Iowa City: State Historical Society of Iowa, 1900) [hereinafter *1844 and 1846 Fragments*]; *Journal of the Constitutional Convention of the State of Iowa* (Muscatine: John Mahin, 1857) [hereinafter *1857 Journal*]; *Journal of the Convention for the Formation of a Constitution for the State of Iowa* (Iowa City: Abraham H. Palmer, 1846) [hereinafter *1846 Journal*]; and *Journal of the Convention for the Formation of a Constitution for the State of Iowa* (Iowa City: Jesse Williams, 1845) [hereinafter *1844 Journal*], which—despite its publication date—is the journal of the Territory of Iowa's 1844 constitutional convention.

[4] *1857 Debates, supra* note 3, vol. 1, p. 104.

[5] *1857 Debates, supra* note 3, vol. 2, p. 651.

[6] *1857 Debates, supra* note 3, vol. 2, pp. 652–53.

[7] *1857 Debates, supra* note 3, vol. 2, pp. 733–34.

[8] *1857 Journal, supra* note 3, pp. 258–59.

that mistreated a female passenger who was "partly of African descent"—the court cited Section 1's opening clause for the proposition that rights cannot be "denied on the ground of race or color." Nevertheless, Section 1's more common role in the law of equality today is to articulate a premise on which Section 6's protections are built. A more detailed discussion of the Iowa Supreme Court's equal protection jurisprudence appears in this volume's treatment of Section 6. Similarly, although practitioners and judges often cite Sections 1 and 9 as a pair when discussing due process disputes concerning life, liberty, and property, it is Section 9 that serves as the dominant text, and so this volume will examine Iowa's due process jurisprudence in its treatment of that section. The focus here will be on the legal work that Section 1 accomplishes in its own right.

Section 1 does most of its independent work through the Inalienable Rights Clause. That provision provides at least a modicum of protection for common-law rights that predate the Iowa Constitution. Two cases—both with wonderfully Midwestern facts—illustrate plaintiffs' successful deployment of the clause.[9] The older of the two is 1915's *State v. Osborne*. The Marshalltown Buggy Company had sent representatives to the Westerly Feed Barn in Indianola, to sell roughly two dozen buggies for $65 each. The company's officials were cited for violating a state statute requiring temporary or transient merchants to provide a bond and obtain a license before commencing business in a city if they planned to run their operation from a building or other structure. Declaring that "[t]he constitutional right to life and liberty and to acquire, possess and enjoy property is not a mere glittering generality without substance or meaning," the Iowa Supreme Court concluded that the General Assembly's desire to shield permanent local merchants from transient competition did not justify the burden on the buggy company's effort to do business in Indianola.

Nearly a century later, a Section 1 plaintiff similarly prevailed in *Gacke v. Pork Xtra, L.L.C.* (2004). Twenty-two years after Joseph and Linda Gacke moved onto a tract of rural property, Pork Xtra built two hog-confinement facilities about 1,300 feet away. The Gackes claimed that the powerful odors emanating from those facilities were a nuisance and had driven down the value of their property. In its defense, Pork Xtra relied upon a state statute that granted animal-feeding operations immunity against nuisance actions like the one the Gackes had brought. The Iowa Supreme Court found that, as applied to the Gackes, the statute violated Section 1. Citing pre-constitution cases, the court first determined that the Gackes had a common-law right to use and enjoy their land free from noxious odors. The court then acknowledged that Section 1 does not place such rights far beyond the reach of the legislature; rather, the state's exercise of its police powers must simply be nonarbitrary and reasonable. The court nevertheless concluded that, while the immunity statute bore a reasonable relationship

---

[9] For a discussion of additional cases, as well as an overarching review of the Iowa Supreme Court's approach to the Inalienable Rights Clause, see *City of Sioux City v. Jacobsma* (2015).

to the state's permissible goal of promoting animal agriculture, the application of the statute to the Gackes was "unduly oppressive" because the Gackes derived no benefit from the hog operation, they had lived on their land (and had spent a substantial amount of money improving it) long before Pork Xtra arrived on the scene, and the hog facilities' odors "significantly impaired" the Gackes' enjoyment of their property.

Because the standard of review under Section 1 is highly deferential to government actors, it is far easier to find cases in which Iowa courts have rejected inalienable-rights claims. Finding the given laws permissible, the Iowa Supreme Court has rejected challenges to (among other things) a city ordinance that made vehicle owners liable for their vehicles' involvement in speeding violations detected by automated traffic-enforcement equipment (*City of Sioux City v. Jacobsma*, 2015), a statute providing borrowers with only limited protection against businesses making "payday loans" (*Midwest Check Cashing, Inc. v. Richey*, 2007), the state's denial of bail to alleged sexually violent predators facing civil-commitment proceedings (*Atwood v. Vilsack*, 2006), a trial court's decision to hold in contempt a drug-crime defendant who—based upon an unsubstantiated fear for his and his family's safety—refused to answer questions on cross-examination regarding the identity of his drug supplier (*Gibb v. Hansen*, 1979), a city council's refusal to permit the construction of a modular home due to concerns about the adequacy of the home's foundation (*Bennett v. Guthridge*, 1975), a statute barring used-car dealers from operating on Sundays (*Diamond Auto Sales, Inc. v. Erbe*, 1960), and a statute barring retailers and wholesalers from selling cigarettes at below-cost prices (*May's Drug Stores v. State Tax Commission*, 1950). The court has further held that, whatever the scope of one's property rights under Section 1, there is no inalienable right to control what happens to one's property after one's death (*In re Estate of Emerson*, 1921).

Section 2.
Political power.

All political power is inherent in the people. Government is instituted for the protection, security, and benefit of the people, and they have the right, at all times, to alter or reform the same, whenever the public good may require it.

By emphasizing the sovereign power of ordinary individuals, Section 2—like Section 1—declares some of Iowa's and the United States' most fundamental constitutional principles. On the fourth day of the 1844 convention, the Committee on the Bill of Rights proposed Section 2 in precisely the same form that it takes today.[10] It was carried forward, without any historically documented debate, in the 1846 convention's draft of what would become Iowa's

[10] *1844 Journal*, *supra* note 3, p. 19.

first constitution. Animated by some of the fundamental political convictions that had helped fuel the American Revolution more than half a century earlier, Section 2's drafters borrowed the provision's language from the Declaration of Independence (which proclaimed, for example, that "it is the right of the people to alter or to abolish" their form of government) and from other states' constitutions.[11]

At Iowa's 1857 convention, Section 2 was briefly swept up in the delegates' long-running debate about the degree to which Iowa should try to attract and retain corporations in the state. In the convention's second week, the Committee on the Preamble and Bill of Rights announced that it wished to add a clause to Section 2 declaring that "no privileges or immunities shall ever be granted that may not be altered, revoked or repealed by the General Assembly."[12] George Ells, a Scott County bookseller, suggested providing instead that "no special privileges or immunities shall ever be granted that may not be altered, revoked, or repealed, by the General Assembly, by a vote of two-thirds of each house."[13] Numerous delegates opposed both possible additions to Section 2, saying that either of them would discourage corporations from investing in railroads and other internal improvements, lest they begin costly operations only to have the legislature subsequently revoke the privileges that entitled them to undertake and complete the work.[14] Ells and others argued in response that, through their elected leaders, the sovereign people should retain the power to revoke corporate privileges in those rare instances in which the "privileged classes" abuse their legislatively granted powers. Henry County's Rufus Clarke said that he supported Ells's proposed addition but believed it would be better placed elsewhere in the constitution.[15] It did indeed ultimately appear elsewhere—in Article VIII, Section 12. By the time the 1857 convention ended, therefore, Section 2 remained in the same form that the 1844 convention had put it.

Notwithstanding the important principles it proclaims, the Iowa Supreme Court has relied upon Section 2 in only a small handful of cases. Perhaps the earliest was the Iowa Supreme Court's 1870 ruling in *Stewart v. Board of Supervisors*, in which the court relied in part upon Section 2 to underscore the principle that the judiciary is not authorized to overturn an act of the sovereign people's elected leaders unless the conflict between that act and the people's written constitution is "clear [and] palpable." The Iowa court also leaned upon Section 2 in 1915's *Barr v. Cardell*, holding (in an era of judicial elections) that voters are entitled to write in the names of their preferred judicial candidates if those candidates' names are not already listed on voters' ballots.

---

[11] *See*, e.g., Ky. Const. of 1799, art. X, § 2; Va. Const. of 1776, §§ 2, 3.

[12] *1857 Journal*, *supra* note 3, p. 65.

[13] *1857 Journal*, *supra* note 3, p. 106.

[14] *1857 Debates*, *supra* note 3, vol. 1, pp. 143–72.

[15] *1857 Debates*, *supra* note 3, vol. 1, p. 168.

Somewhat more common have been cases in which the court has rejected claims that Section 2 authorizes the sovereign people or their elected leaders to make law through means other than those that have been lawfully approved. In *Koehler v. Hill* (1883), for example, the court declared invalid a proposed amendment to the constitution banning the manufacture and use of alcoholic beverages—notwithstanding the fact that the proposed amendment had won a strong majority at the polls—because the General Assembly had not followed the constitutionally prescribed amendment procedures. In *Waugh v. Shirer* (1933), the court rejected the claim that Section 2 bars the legislature from providing that a county may issue bonds only if those bonds have been approved by a sixty percent supermajority vote. And in *Anderson v. Secretary of State* (2001), the court held that a citizen cannot bypass the General Assembly and demand that the Secretary of State place proposed measures on statewide ballots.

Conversely, Section 2 does not restrict the General Assembly's ability to use lawfully approved means to amend or repeal prior legislation. In *Bechtel v. City of Des Moines* (1975), a group of citizens advanced the curious claim that certain provisions of Iowa's Home Rule Act violated Section 2, apparently on the theory that the General Assembly could not alter statutes affecting cities. The Iowa Supreme Court predictably held that Section 2 does not shield previously enacted statutes from the reach of differently minded legislators.

Section 3.
Religion.

The General Assembly shall make no law respecting an establishment of religion, or prohibiting the free exercise thereof; nor shall any person be compelled to attend any place of worship, pay tithes, taxes, or other rates for building or repairing places of worship, or the maintenance of any minister, or ministry.

Sections 3 and 4 help to secure some of Iowans' important religious rights. With the inconsequential exception of referring to the state's legislative body as the "General Assembly" rather than the "legislature" (a change made at the 1846 convention), Section 3 stands in the same form that the Committee on the Bill of Rights proposed on the 1844 convention's fourth day.[16] The committee's framing of Section 3 did not provoke any documented debate, perhaps in part because there was nothing particularly novel about it. The establishment and free-exercise language was drawn directly from the U.S. Constitution's First Amendment, while the language after the semicolon was largely borrowed from state constitutions that dated back to the nation's founding.[17] The only noteworthy observation made about Section 3 at Iowa's 1844 convention may have been George Hepner's suggestion—during the delegates' debate about whether to

[16] *1844 Journal, supra* note 3, p. 19.

[17] *See*, e.g., N.J. Const. of 1776, § XVIII.

open each of their daily sessions with a prayer—that forcing delegates to attend such prayers would be inconsistent with Section 3's values.[18] If the historical records are accurate, Section 3 similarly received virtually no attention at the 1857 convention, save for a brief discussion on the convention's penultimate day about whether the text should say "*the* establishment of religion," rather than "*an* establishment of religion." The delegates declined to make that change, perhaps persuaded by Rufus Clarke's observation that the existing wording might provide broader protection because it could not be interpreted as narrowly referring only to one particular religion.[19]

Many of the Iowa Supreme Court's Section 3 cases come from the nineteenth and early twentieth centuries, before the U.S. Supreme Court held that the Fourteenth Amendment's Due Process Clause brings the First Amendment's establishment and free-exercise clauses to bear upon the states.[20] In several of those early Iowa cases, the court tended to read Section 3's Establishment Clause quite narrowly. In 1877, for example, the court in *Trustees of Griswold College v. State* upheld a tax exemption for a bishop's residence at a religious college, devoting just one conclusory sentence to the possibility that, because tax exemptions are subsidized by other taxpayers, the exemption at issue here entailed religion-supporting "taxes" in violation of one of Section 3's latter provisions. In 1878's *Davis v. Boget*, the court held that taxpayer-supported school facilities could be used for religious services during non-school hours, because the burden on taxpayers "would never amount to any appreciable sum." And in 1884, the court held in *Moore v. Monroe* that Section 3 did not bar public school teachers from beginning their school days with Bible readings, the Lord's Prayer, and religious songs, so long as children were not compelled to attend those activities. Yet Section 3 Establishment Clause plaintiffs in that era did not always leave the court empty-handed. In its 1918 ruling in *Knowlton v. Baumhover*, for example, the Iowa Supreme Court held that taxpayer funds could not be used to support a school operated by the Roman Catholic Church even though it was the only school located in that particular community.

When interpreting Section 3 in the modern period—that is, the period in which the First Amendment's religion clauses bind the states, and not merely the federal government—the Iowa Supreme Court has relied heavily upon the U.S. Supreme Court's First Amendment case law. In 1990's *Hope Evangelical Lutheran Church v. Iowa Department of Revenue & Finance*, for example, the court relied entirely upon federal precedent when rejecting the plaintiff church's objection to the state's use tax, even though the church had sought relief on both state and federal free-exercise grounds.

---

[18] *1844 and 1846 Fragments, supra* note 3, pp. 17–18.

[19] *1857 Debates, supra* note 3, vol. 2, p. 1007.

[20] *See Everson v. Board of Education* (1947) (Establishment Clause); *Cantwell v. Connecticut* (1940) (Free Exercise Clause).

The court has largely pushed aside any suggestion that the language appearing after Section 3's semicolon—that is, the language that goes beyond that of the First Amendment—adds anything of consequence. In *Rudd v. Ray* (1976), for example, taxpayers challenged the state's practice of paying chaplains to serve in the Iowa State Penitentiary. The trial court had found the practice permissible under the First Amendment but impermissible under Section 3, given the latter's explicit prohibition on using taxes for "the maintenance of any minister." But the Iowa Supreme Court reversed, finding that the framers intended the text after the semicolon merely to recite some of the specific evils of state-established churches—evils that Section 3's Establishment Clause presumably forbade by its own force—and that the practice of paying chaplains was a permissible accommodation for incarcerated believers who were not free to leave the prison grounds to attend religious services of their own choosing.

In recent years, however, there have been flickering indications that the Iowa Supreme Court might one day find daylight between Section 3 and the religion clauses of the First Amendment. In its 2009 ruling in *Varnum v. Brien* striking down the state's ban on same-sex marriage, the court cited Section 3 for the proposition that no branch of the government can take sides in religious disputes. That proposition is unremarkable as a matter of First Amendment doctrine, but the court said nothing about that federal text. That silence, while perhaps inconsequential, at least stands in contrast to the court's almost inevitable prior practice of subordinating Section 3 to the First Amendment. Three years later, in *Mitchell County v. Zimmerman* (2012), the court vaguely hinted that Section 3's scope might not be coextensive with that of the First Amendment. A member of a Mennonite congregation challenged a county ordinance banning steel wheels on public roads, saying that it violated his rights under both Section 3 and the First Amendment. Striking the law down, the court relied entirely upon the U.S. Supreme Court's First Amendment analytic framework. Rather than add Section 3 as an additional basis for its holding, the court dropped a footnote saying that it was declining to decide whether the law violated the Iowa Constitution. The court thereby acknowledged the possibility that legislation that is impermissible under either the state or the federal text might be permissible under the other.

Although not citing Section 3, there are a number of cases in which religious-freedom values have prompted the Iowa Supreme Court to decline to take control over parties' purely ecclesiastical disputes. These include, for example, challenges to the expulsion of church members (*Marks v. Estate of Hartgerink*, 1995; *Brown v. Mt. Olive Baptist Church*, 1963; *Sale v. First Regular Baptist Church*, 1883) and challenges to a congregation's choice of leaders (*Third Missionary Baptist Church v. Garrett*, 1968).[21] The court has also said, however,

---

[21] For a First Amendment ruling by the U.S. Supreme Court embracing a "ministerial exception" to anti-discrimination laws, see *Hosanna-Tabor Evangelical Lutheran Church & School v. EEOC* (2012).

that "courts do have authority to ascertain if action taken, even though ecclesiastical in nature, was by a duly authorized board or body" (*Third Missionary Baptist Church v. Garrett*, 1968), and that it is free to resolve disputes concerning "civil, contract, and property rights which are involved in or arise from a church controversy" (*Kliebenstein v. Iowa Conference of the United Methodist Church*, 2003). In *Kliebenstein*, for example, the court permitted a church member to sue a church official for defamation after the official sent a letter to local individuals outside the church community saying that the plaintiff had the destructive "spirit of Satan."[22] And, in its 1883 ruling in *Bird v. St. Mark's Church*, the court enforced a minister's contractual salary rights after other church leaders cut his annual pay to alleviate budget pressures.

Section 4.
Religious test—witnesses.

No religious test shall be required as a qualification for any office, or public trust, and no person shall be deprived of any of his rights, privileges, or capacities, or disqualified from the performance of any of his public or private duties, or rendered incompetent to give evidence in any court of law or equity, in consequence of his opinions on the subject of religion; and any party to any judicial proceeding shall have the right to use as a witness, or take the testimony of, any other person not disqualified on account of interest, who may be cognizant of any fact material to the case; and parties to suits may be witnesses, as provided by law.

Section 4 continues Section 3's focus on religious rights, then turns to litigants' right to rely upon the witnesses of their choosing. The delegates to Iowa's constitutional conventions never publicly considered permitting religious tests for public office or positions of public trust. The U.S. Constitution bars religious tests for those who wish to hold office or positions of public trust under federal law,[23] and Iowa's constitutional framers evinced no desire to take a different approach. Neither do the conventions' records suggest that the delegates ever considered authorizing broad-ranging deprivations of rights, privileges, and the like on religious grounds. Instead, the delegates focused almost all of their Section 4 energies on questions concerning witnesses in court proceedings. The primary issue in 1844 was religion; in 1857, it was race.

On the 1844 convention's fourth day, the Committee on the Bill of Rights presented its draft of Section 4. The committee's proposal consisted of what appears today prior to Section 4's first semicolon, absent the provision regarding witnesses' competency.[24] William Galbraith—a twenty-seven-year-old lawyer,

---

[22] The court found that the reference to Satan had a secular meaning, and that the case thus did not exclusively involve matters of church doctrine.

[23] U.S. Const. art. VI, cl. 3.

[24] *1844 Journal, supra* note 3, p. 19.

who, one year earlier, had become the first of his profession to settle in Wapello County—proposed adding a provision stating that a person could never be declared incompetent to testify in judicial proceedings due to his or her religious beliefs. Ralph Lowe—an attorney from Muscatine County, who would later become Iowa's fourth governor and would serve as a justice on the Iowa Supreme Court—led those opposing Galbraith's proposal, arguing that a person's oath is meaningless if he or she does not believe in a deity who will respond unfavorably if the person fails to testify truthfully.[25] Lowe's position was not unusual; one of the day's leading national treatises, for example, similarly insisted that "[a]theists . . . and all infidels, that is, those who profess no religion that can bind their consciences to speak truth, are rejected as incompetent to testify as witnesses."[26] Lowe's opposition nevertheless failed to find traction among his colleagues, and Galbraith's addition was approved.[27] The 1844 convention thus produced all of the text that one finds today before Section 4's first semicolon.

The text that appears *after* Section 4's first semicolon was added in 1857. The debate about Section 4 at that convention focused almost entirely on whether the provision's scope should be broadened to ensure that no one would be barred from the witness chair on racial grounds. The delegates' discussion and ultimate resolution of that issue are chronicled in Part I.

Section 4 has not been the focus of frequent litigation in the modern era. Much of the relevant case law dates to the nineteenth century and merely confirms that Section 4 means what it says. In the decade immediately following the constitution's adoption, for example, the Iowa Supreme Court handed down a pair of rulings confirming that, regardless of whether jointly indicted defendants are tried separately or together, the constitution abolished the common-law rule barring such defendants from testifying in one another's favor (*State v. Gigher*, 1867; *State v. Nash*, 1859). In 1914's *Meikle v. Hobson*, the Iowa court similarly observed that Section 4's final clause rejected the common-law rule barring litigants from testifying in their own behalf.

Notwithstanding Section 4's broad testimonial protections, the provision does not push the General Assembly entirely out of play. In *Kilburn v. Mullen* (1867), for example, the Iowa Supreme Court held that Section 4 permits the legislature to bar the testimony of any person—in this case, an eight-year-old child—who is not able to appreciate the gravity of the oath that witnesses are

[25] *1844 and 1846 Fragments, supra* note 3, pp. 25, 38–39.

[26] Simon Greenleaf, *A Treatise on the Law of Evidence* (2d ed. 1844), vol. 1, § 368.

[27] *1844 and 1846 Fragments, supra* note 3, p. 25. Lowe revisited the issue a few days later, proposing that Galbraith's language be replaced with a more generally framed guarantee that "no person shall be denied the enjoyment of any civil right, merely on account of his religious principles." *1844 Journal, supra* note 3, p. 48. In Lowe's view, that language would have left courts free to bar atheists from the witness stand on the ground that they could not take a meaningful oath. The delegates decisively rejected Lowe's proposal by a vote of 9 to 59. *1844 Journal, supra* note 3, p. 48.

asked to take. The court further held in *Karney v. Paisley* (1862) that Section 4 gives the legislature significant latitude to define those "interests" that, by Section 4's own terms, render a person incompetent to testify.[28] The *Karney* court sustained a statute that barred spouses from calling one another as supporting witnesses in judicial proceedings, a rule that the General Assembly subsequently abandoned.[29]

With respect to religion, most of the cases are, again, many decades old. The Iowa Supreme Court held in 1881, for example, that although Section 4 does not permit a person to be deemed incompetent to testify by virtue of his religious beliefs, such beliefs may be used for impeachment so long as the evidence of the witness's religious beliefs comes from a source other than the witness's own testimony (*Searcy v. Miller*, 1881).[30] That impeachment rule has long since been abandoned. Under Rule 5.610 of the Iowa Rules of Evidence—just as under the corresponding provision of the Federal Rules of Evidence—impeachment on religious grounds is now impermissible.

Section 5.
Dueling.

[Repealed.]

Like the 1846 constitution before it, the 1857 constitution declared that "[a]ny citizen of this State who may hereafter be engaged, either directly, or indirectly, in a duel, either as principal, or accessory before the fact, shall forever be disqualified from holding any office under the Constitution and laws of this State." Iowans removed the provision in 1992, evidently on the belief that it no longer served a useful function.[31]

Section 6.
Laws uniform.

All laws of a general nature shall have a uniform operation; the General Assembly shall not grant to any Citizen, or class of Citizens, privileges or immunities, which, upon the same terms shall not equally belong to all Citizens.

Section 6, which contains the Iowa Constitution's central provisions concerning equality, traces its roots to Iowa's first constitution. That 1846 document

---

[28] *See also Donnell v. Braden* (1886) (upholding an interest-defining statute against a Section 4 attack).

[29] Iowa Code § 622.8.

[30] *See also Dedric v. Hopson* (1883) (barring cross-examination of a witness concerning his belief in "a future conscious state of existence"); *State v. Elliott* (1877) (stating that evidence of a witness's religious beliefs may be offered to impeach his or her credibility).

[31] Jon Yates, "Amendment on Duel Law Up for Vote," *Daily Iowan*, Oct. 27, 1992, p. A2.

simply declared that "[a]ll laws of a general nature shall have a uniform operation."[32] At the 1857 convention, the delegates added the language that now appears after the semicolon. As for why they made that change, the historical record is remarkably thin. On the thirteenth day of the convention, the additional text was proposed by Republican John Edwards, a lawyer who would later serve as Iowa's Speaker of the House before leaving to join the Union army in the Civil War. The record suggests that, when asked to explain the amendment, Edwards simply restated the proposed new language. Evidently satisfied by that opaque response, the delegates approved the change.[33]

Reinforced by Section 1's acknowledgment of people's natural equality, Section 6 functions today as the Iowa Constitution's equal protection clause; it simply is worded differently than the equal protection provision that was added to the U.S. Constitution when the Fourteenth Amendment was ratified eleven years later (*King v. State*, 2012). Many decades would pass, however, before Section 6 began to do meaningful work. In 1906's *McGuire v. Chicago, Burlington & Quincy Railroad Co.*, for example, the Iowa Supreme Court characterized the provision as legally superfluous, stating that it "[c]ertainly . . . place[s] no narrower restriction upon the legislative power" than the Fourteenth Amendment. Today, the Iowa Supreme Court acknowledges that it may interpret Section 6 differently than the U.S. Supreme Court interprets the Fourteenth Amendment, but the court almost always declines to chart its own path.[34] Like the federal provision, therefore, Section 6 leaves the legislature with tremendous latitude to treat groups of people differently in nearly all areas of social and economic life, so long as the differing treatment is a rational means of trying to achieve some legitimate, "realistically conceivable" government purpose (*Doe v. New London Community School District*, 2014; *Perkins v. Board of Supervisors*, 2001).[35] Under

---

[32] The 1846 constitution, in turn, carried the language over from the draft of the 1844 constitution that the Territory of Iowa's voters had rejected. The fragmentary records of the 1844 and 1846 conventions do not illuminate the framers' intentions underlying this provision.

[33] *1857 Debates*, *supra* note 3, vol. 1, pp. 200–01. Elsewhere in the historical record, one finds possible clues to Edwards's motivation. On more than one occasion, Edwards spoke powerfully against slavery and its concomitants; it is possible that he thought additional constitutional language was necessary to ensure racial equality under the law. *See, e.g.*, *id.* at vol. 2, pp. 834–35 (arguing that children of African descent should be assured a public education); *id.* at pp. 680–86 (condemning slavery and arguing that those of African descent should be permitted to testify as witnesses in trials). Even Edwards, however, sometimes stopped short of advocating full racial equality. *See id.* at p. 836 ("Whether it is expedient to give the unfortunate negro who is in our midst all the privileges we enjoy, I am not prepared to say. . . . For myself, I am willing to stand upon the ground that the noble Henry Clay occupied—never to use my influence for the extension of slavery.").

[34] *See, e.g.*, *In the Interest of A.W.* (2007); *Sherman v. Pella Corp.* (1998); *Krull v. Thermogas Co.* (1994).

[35] *See also Residential & Agricultural Advisory Committee, LLC v. Dyersville City Council* (2016) (breaking the rational-basis analysis down into three steps, with the first requiring a "realistically conceivable" governmental purpose that serves a legitimate state interest, the second requiring that the

that highly deferential form of review, Iowa's courts have permitted scores of legislative distinctions, such as those imposing differing limits on legal claims against municipalities and private entities (*Doe v. New London Community School District*, 2014) and differing punishments for crimes that, at first blush, might seem comparably harmful (*State v. Jorgensen*, 2009; *State v. Bell*, 1997).

On occasion, however, the Iowa Supreme Court has found that Section 6 demands a more aggressive application of rational-basis review than the Fourteenth Amendment requires.[36] In *Racing Association of Central Iowa v. Fitzgerald* (2004), for example, the Iowa court examined the legislature's decision to tax gambling receipts at racetracks at nearly twice the rate it taxed gambling receipts on riverboats. In an earlier phase of the litigation, the court had declared the taxation scheme irrational under both Section 6 and the Fourteenth Amendment. On certiorari, the federal Supreme Court unanimously ruled that the legislation easily survived rational-basis review under the Fourteenth Amendment; it was a rational means, the Court said, of achieving such conceivable legislative purposes as promoting the economic development of river communities and preserving the state's riverboat history.[37] On remand, the Iowa Supreme Court said that it was free to interpret Section 6 differently, either by adopting a different analytic framework or by applying the federal Supreme Court's framework in a different manner. Choosing the latter course, the Iowa court found the fit between means and conceivable ends far too loose to be rational and so struck the legislation down. The court has subsequently emphasized that, when evaluating whether the government's means are sufficiently related to its ends, the key question is whether the means are "extremely" overinclusive or underinclusive (*LSCP, LLLP v. Kay-Decker*, 2015).

Like its federal counterpart, the Iowa Supreme Court sometimes applies a heightened, far more skeptical form of scrutiny, demanding either an important government purpose and substantially related means (in the case of intermediate

---

conceivable governmental purpose have a "basis in fact," and the third requiring that there be a nonarbitrary relationship between the conceivable governmental purpose and the challenged classification). Of course, if the legislature is not treating similarly situated people differently, there is no equal protection claim at all. *Timberland Partners XXI v. Iowa Department of Revenue* (2008).

[36] *See, e.g., Bierkamp v. Rogers* (1980) (finding Iowa's guest statute unconstitutionally irrational under Section 6 while acknowledging that the statute did not violate the Fourteenth Amendment under U.S. Supreme Court precedent). In other cases, the Iowa Supreme Court has used rational-basis review to strike down legislation under *both* Section 6 and the Fourteenth Amendment. *See, e.g., Chicago & Northwestern Railway Co. v. Fachman* (1963) (striking down a law that singled out railway corporations for criminal penalties if they did not pay their employees at least every eighteen days). In still other cases, the Iowa court has relied upon Section 6 to strike down legislation under rational-basis review, saying nothing about what the Fourteenth Amendment might require. *See, e.g., Collins v. State Board of Social Welfare* (1957) (striking down a welfare law that treated needy children less favorably if they resided in homes with numerous other needy children).

[37] *Racing Association of Central Iowa v. Fitzgerald* (2003).

scrutiny) or a compelling government purpose and narrowly tailored means (in the case of strict scrutiny). The Iowa court applies heightened scrutiny only if a legislative classification hinders some people's ability to exercise a fundamental right or if the legislature has made a suspect classification (*Hawkins v. Preisser*, 1978). When determining whether either of those preconditions to heightened scrutiny has been met, the Iowa court typically proceeds in lockstep with the U.S. Supreme Court.[38] State (and federal) equal protection cases involving fundamental rights are rare; such rights are themselves usually constitutional in nature and thus wield significant government-restraining power of their own, making it unnecessary to invoke equal protection principles. Heightened review is thus most commonly deployed when the government makes suspect classifications, treating people differently based upon traits that often have more to do with unfair prejudice or stereotypes than legitimate policymaking. Just as under federal law, sex-based classifications are the paradigmatic example of a classification warranting intermediate scrutiny under Section 6 (*Sherman v. Pella Corp.*, 1998), while racial classifications are the leading example of a classification warranting strict scrutiny (*In the Interest of A.W.*, 2007).

In what will long stand as one of the Iowa Supreme Court's most famous Section 6 rulings, the court held in *Varnum v. Brien* (2009) that legislative classifications based upon sexual orientation warrant at least intermediate scrutiny, and that the state's ban on same-sex marriage could not survive that rigorous analysis.[39] The court found that sexual-orientation classifications are suspect because gays and lesbians have long been on the receiving end of invidious discrimination, one's sexual orientation bears no relationship to one's ability to make societal contributions and thus is unlikely to warrant the legislature's attention, one's sexual orientation is either impossible or very difficult to change, and gays and lesbians often lack the political power necessary to defeat discrimination against them in the political realm. The court then found that refusing to permit same-sex marriages was not substantially related to any important government purpose. The ruling provoked a strong political backlash; as noted in this volume's treatment of Article V, Section 17, Iowa voters removed three of the Iowa Supreme Court's seven members in the judicial retention elections held the following year.

When a government official has violated a person's equal protection rights and there is no adequate statutory remedy for the violation, the person may

[38] *See, e.g.*, *King v. State* (2012) (embracing the federal methodology for identifying fundamental rights); *Varnum v. Brien* (2009) (relying upon federal precedent to identify the hallmarks of suspect classifications).

[39] *See also Gartner v. Iowa Department of Public Health* (2013) (holding that, when a woman in a same-sex marriage bears a child, the state violates Section 6 if it refuses to list the birth mother's spouse as a parent on the child's birth certificate).

bring a constitutional cause of action for damages against the government official (*Godfrey v. State*, 2017).

Section 7.
Liberty of speech and press.

Every person may speak, write, and publish his sentiments on all subjects, being responsible for the abuse of that right. No law shall be passed to restrain or abridge the liberty of speech, or of the press. In all prosecutions or indictments for libel, the truth may be given in evidence to the jury, and if it appear to the jury that the matter charged as libellous was true, and was published with good motives and for justifiable ends, the party shall be acquitted.

Section 7 provides a degree of protection for the freedoms of speech and the press (although, as we shall see, that protection is less robust than one might initially think), and then lays out some of the rules for libel lawsuits—that is, lawsuits charging that someone's false statements have damaged one's reputation. The 1844 convention produced largely the text that appears here, with one addition: after the closing word "acquitted," the delegates inserted a semicolon and declared that "the jury shall have the right to determine the law and the fact." That additional language was not included when the 1844 convention's Committee on the Bill of Rights produced its initial draft of the provision,[40] but was instead added later at the suggestion of Lee County's O.S.X. Peck.[41] The vote on Peck's motion was close—34 to 32—but the convention's spotty records do not reveal why the delegates were so narrowly divided. It is clear, however, that the entirety of the provision—including Peck's added phrase—was borrowed from other states' constitutions, rather than fashioned from scratch in Iowa City.[42]

In the draft that the 1846 convention's Committee on the Bill of Rights presented on the delegates' second day of work, Peck's language did not appear.[43] Without any documented explanation of the reasons for that change, the 1846 convention accepted the committee's draft and placed Section 7 in the form one finds it today. The 1857 convention later carried Section 7 forward, unchanged.[44] By that point, Section 7's final sentence echoed, almost verbatim, a provision that the Iowa legislature had placed in the Iowa Code.[45]

The U.S. Constitution's First Amendment protects the freedoms of speech and the press, and through the Fourteenth Amendment's Due Process Clause those provisions have restricted state and local governments (and not merely

---

[40] *1844 Journal, supra* note 3, p. 19.

[41] *1844 Journal, supra* note 3, p. 177.

[42] *See,* e.g., Mich. Const. of 1835, art. I, § 7; Miss. Const. of 1832, art. I, §§ 6–8; N.Y. Const. of 1821, art. VII, § 8. New York was O.S.X. Peck's state of origin.

[43] *1846 Journal, supra* note 3, p. 29.

[44] *1857 Debates, supra* note 3, vol. 1, pp. 118, 201; *id.* at vol. 2, pp. 1006–08.

[45] Code of Iowa (1851), § 2769.

the federal government) since the early twentieth century.[46] That extension of the First Amendment's reach, coupled with the Iowa Supreme Court's interpretation of Section 7 over the past half century, has gone a long way toward rendering Section 7 superfluous. The Iowa Supreme Court has determined that Section 7 "generally imposes the same restrictions on the regulation of speech as does the federal constitution" (*State v. Milner*, 1997)[47] and that the same is true with respect to the freedom of the press (*Des Moines Register & Tribune Co. v. Osmundson*, 1976). Iowa's courts and lawyers thus routinely rely upon federal First Amendment precedents when interpreting Section 7, to the extent they take notice of Section 7 at all. Iowa's appellate courts have relied almost entirely upon federal First Amendment cases when adjudicating such things as the rights of abortion protestors (*Emma Goldman Clinic v. Holman*, 2006), the constitutionality of a law punishing price fixing (*State v. Blyth*, 1975), the rights of persons distributing leaflets at a private shopping mall (*City of West Des Moines v. Engler*, 2002), the public's right to attend pretrial proceedings in criminal cases (*Iowa Freedom of Information Council v. Wifvat*, 1983), a reporter's claim of privilege (*Winegard v. Oxberger*, 1977), and the permissible reach of a regulation governing campaign-finance disclosures (*Iowans for Tax Relief v. Campaign Finance Disclosure Commission*, 1983).

To the extent there are any differences between the protections afforded by Section 7 and the First Amendment, the Iowa provision's "responsible for the abuse" clause likely works to make Section 7 less meaningful in Iowans' lives. Relying in part upon that clause in *Bierman v. Weier* (2013), for example, the Iowa Supreme Court rejected the argument that Section 7 "provides defendants in defamation cases with *more* protection than the United States Constitution."[48] The *Bierman* court approvingly cited the Utah Supreme Court's thoughtful discussion of the history of states' abuse clauses, demonstrating that state constitutions' framers gravitated toward such provisions in the nineteenth century in order to strengthen legislatures' ability to impose consequences upon those who produced problematic expression.[49] If the First Amendment does not protect the speech at issue in a given case, therefore, it is unlikely that Section 7 would provide the speaker with a more favorable outcome.

Even in cases in which it has not invoked Iowa's abuse clause, the Iowa Supreme Court has sometimes taken a notably narrow view of Section 7's speech protections. In 1974's *State v. Farrell*, for example, the court upheld a

---

[46] *Gitlow v. New York* (1925) (speech); *Near v. Minnesota* (1931) (press).

[47] *Milner* has been cited often for that proposition. *See, e.g., In re Adoption of S.J.D.* (2002).

[48] In *Jones v. Palmer Communications* (1989), abrogated in part on other grounds by *Schlegel v. Ottumwa Courier* (1998), the Iowa Supreme Court again relied upon Section 7's abuse clause to narrowly construe a defamation defendant's constitutional rights.

[49] *See American Bush v. City of South Salt Lake* (Utah 2006) (discussing states' movement away from *Cato's Letters* liberalism toward Blackstonian conservatism).

college student's conviction for burning an American flag during a war protest, finding that there was a risk of a breach of the peace, that any such risk need not be imminent to justify suppression of the student's expression, and that the student "manifested a total disregard for the flag as a symbol of patriotism, and by the same token espoused disunity."[50] The U.S. Supreme Court took a far more permissive approach to a protestor's flag burning fifteen years later in *Texas v. Johnson* (1989), striking down Texas's flag-desecration statute as an unjustifiable content-based regulation of expression.

In at least one case, however, the Iowa Supreme Court's reading of Section 7 helped to chart a broadly speech-favoring path that the U.S. Supreme Court would later take. In its 1901 ruling in *Cherry v. Des Moines Leader*, the Iowa court anticipated by more than half a century the important principle that the U.S. Supreme Court would make famous in *New York Times v. Sullivan* (1964)—namely, that public figures receive notably less protection than private figures against defamation (or, to put it differently, that it is legally much safer to say unpleasant things about public figures than it is to say such things about private figures).

Like the U.S. Supreme Court (*Valentine v. Chrestensen*, 1942), the Iowa Supreme Court was initially dismissive of commercial-speech claims. In 1894's *State v. Bair*,[51] for example, the court cursorily rejected an itinerant pharmacist's free-expression claim, finding that his efforts to advertise his services had nothing to do with "the rights intended to be secured" by Section 7. The court similarly upheld a law restricting dentists' ability to advertise their services in *Craven v. Bierring* (1936). Today, as in other areas of free-speech law, the court adjudicates Section 7 commercial-speech cases under the First Amendment standards declared by the U.S. Supreme Court (*Iowa Supreme Court Board of Professional Conduct & Ethics v. Kirlin*, 1997).

In the modern era, therefore, the focus in Iowa's free-expression cases is squarely on the First Amendment. That fact is nicely summed up by the defense attorneys' actions in 2014's *Bertrand v. Mullin*. *Bertrand* was a high-profile defamation case concerning Democrats' campaign speech in a bitter 2010 battle between Democratic and Republican candidates for a seat in the state legislature. As the Iowa Supreme Court noted, the Democrats relied entirely (and successfully) upon the First Amendment for their defense, not even bothering to raise an argument under Section 7.

---

[50] One year earlier, finding no risk of a breach of the peace, the court had overturned a war protestor's conviction for displaying an American flag upside down in his window, with a peace symbol visually superimposed over (but unattached to) the flag. *State v. Kool* (1973).

[51] In some printings of the case, the pharmacist's last name is spelled "Blair."

Section 8.
Personal security—searches and seizures.

The right of the people to be secure in their persons, houses, papers and effects, against unreasonable seizures and searches shall not be violated; and no warrant shall issue but on probable cause, supported by oath or affirmation, particularly describing the place to be searched, and the persons and things to be seized.

Nearly identical to the U.S. Constitution's Fourth Amendment, Section 8 helps to protect people and their property from being unreasonably searched or seized by government officials. (Section 8 places a semicolon between its unreasonableness and warrant provisions, while the Fourth Amendment uses a comma; it is not clear whether that difference is significant.[52]) Given its close tracking of the Fourth Amendment's celebrated language, it is not surprising that Section 8 was not controversial at any of Iowa's constitutional conventions. The Territory of Iowa's 1844 convention largely put the provision into the form it takes today, with one notable exception: the closing clause referred to "papers," rather than "persons." The 1846 convention carried that formulation forward without any documented debate. At the 1857 convention, the delegates changed "papers" to "persons" and thereby brought that portion of Section 8 into line with the text of the Fourth Amendment.[53]

---

[52] The 1846 constitution placed a comma in that location. For reasons that the historical record does not clearly explain, the delegates to the 1857 convention changed the comma to a semicolon. The Iowa Supreme Court has speculated about the punctuation mark's significance (*State v. Short*, 2014; *State v. Ochoa*, 2010). It appears unlikely that the delegates themselves believed the change in punctuation was substantively consequential. When the Committee on the Preamble and Bill of Rights first presented the list of changes that it was proposing to make to the 1846 text, the change to Section 8 was not among them. *1857 Debates, supra* note 3, vol. 1, p. 64. When the committee took Section 8 to the floor of the convention for discussion several days later, the comma had been changed to a semicolon. *Id.* at p. 201. The change did not provoke any historically documented discussion. One possibility is that, merely as a stylistic matter, they added the semicolon to bring the provision more closely into line with the text of other state constitutions with which they were familiar. The New Jersey Constitution of 1844, for example, placed a semicolon between the unreasonableness and warrant clauses of its nearly identically worded provision. N.J. Const. of 1844, art. I, § 6. Perhaps more significantly, parallels may be drawn with the constitutions of states formerly called home by members of the committee that drafted Section 8. The Connecticut Constitution of 1818—the constitution of the state that produced George Ells, the committee's chair—similarly used a semicolon. Conn. Const. of 1818, art. I, § 8. The same may be said of the Ohio Constitution of 1851. Ohio Const. of 1851, art. I, § 14. Ohio was formerly home to committee members Aylett Cotton and Timothy Day. (The committee's other two members—John Clark and Sheldon Winchester—came to Iowa from New York, a state whose constitution lacked a search-and-seizure clause until the twentieth century.) In any event, the delegates' loose handling of punctuation in other settings—see, for example, the commentary on Article VII, Section 3—should caution against making strong assumptions about the intended significance of an otherwise unexplained punctuational choice.

[53] *1857 Debates, supra* note 3, vol. 1, p. 119.

In recent years, Section 8 has emerged as one of the primary focal points in the Iowa Supreme Court's internal debate about when, as a matter of state constitutional law, it should reject doctrines that the U.S. Supreme Court has developed under parallel provisions of the U.S. Constitution. Rather than summarize the many ways in which the Iowa Supreme Court has interpreted Section 8 in a manner that generally tracks the complex law of the Fourth Amendment, the following commentary thus focuses on the Iowa court's recent—and internally controversial—movement toward analytic independence.

In 1949, the U.S. Supreme Court held in *Wolf v. Colorado* that the Fourteenth Amendment's Due Process Clause brings the Fourth Amendment to bear upon the states. Twelve years later, it held in *Mapp v. Ohio* (1961) that states also must honor the exclusionary rule—the rule that, at trial, prosecutors cannot introduce evidence that was obtained in violation of a defendant's Fourth Amendment rights. Prior to those landmark rulings, the Iowa Supreme Court had embraced its freedom to interpret Section 8 independently, and from 1923 forward it had "definitively" rejected the federal exclusionary rule (*State ex rel. Kuble v. Bisignano*, 1947).[54]

After *Mapp* came down, the Iowa Supreme Court not only followed the dictates of that ruling but also entered a period in which it routinely equated the requirements of Section 8 with those of the Fourth Amendment. In 1992's *State v. Strong*, for example—a case in which, without a warrant, law-enforcement officers had ordered the defendant's stomach pumped, on suspicion that he swallowed crack cocaine during his arrest—the defendant raised claims under both Section 8 and the Fourth Amendment. Observing that it had "consistently interpreted the scope and purpose of article I, section 8, of the Iowa Constitution to track with federal interpretations of the Fourth Amendment," the court rejected Strong's claims, relying heavily upon the analytic framework devised by the federal Supreme Court. In numerous additional cases, the Iowa court reiterated that the requirements of Section 8 and the Fourth Amendment were coextensive.[55]

Around the start of the twenty-first century, the Iowa Supreme Court began to shift its stance. In these cases, the court explicitly acknowledged its power to interpret Section 8 differently than the Fourth Amendment, and inquired whether the parties before them had offered any reasons for the court to deviate from the U.S. Supreme Court's path. In most cases, the court found that the parties had not provided any such reasons—nor was the court able to identify such reasons by its own lights—and so the court interpreted the two provisions identically, driven powerfully by the federal Supreme Court's holdings.[56] With

---

[54] The court traced Iowa's rejection of the exclusionary rule to *State v. Tonn* (1923). Prior to *Tonn*, the court had embraced the exclusionary rule. *See*, e.g., *State v. Sheridan* (1903).

[55] *See*, e.g., *State v. Grant* (2000); *State v. Loyd* (1995).

[56] *See*, e.g., *State v. Nitcher* (2006); *State v. Hoskins* (2006); *State v. Carter* (2005); *State v. McCoy* (2005); *State v. Reinders* (2004); *State v. Lewis* (2004); *State v. Legg* (2001). Even during this

its 2000 ruling in *State v. Cline,* however, the court's interest in analytic independence began to bear fruit. The U.S. Supreme Court had found (and still holds) that there is a good-faith exception to the exclusionary rule, such that evidence obtained in violation of the Fourth Amendment is admissible at trial if law-enforcement officers relied in good faith upon a defective search warrant (*United States v. Leon,* 1984) or an unconstitutional state statute (*Illinois v. Krull,* 1987). In *Cline,* the Iowa Supreme Court rejected the good-faith exception as a matter of state law, finding that the exclusionary rule provides an important remedy for Section 8 violations and helps to protect the courts' integrity, and is not merely a means (as the federal Supreme Court has said) of deterring officers from violating the law in unreasonable ways.

Ten years later, in *State v. Ochoa* (2010), the Iowa court turned to whether Section 8 bars a police officer from conducting a warrantless, suspicionless search of a parolee's hotel room pursuant to a provision of the state's standard agreement with parolees. That standard agreement provided that "any parole officer or law enforcement officer" could search parolees and their property and residences at any time and for any reason. After citing numerous scholarly articles on states' constitutional independence, the court noted that, in a majority of the states, supreme courts had afforded greater protections under their states' search-and-seizure clauses than the federal Supreme Court had afforded under the Fourth Amendment. Building on *Cline* and other cases, the court then declared its independence from federal Fourth Amendment precedent, saying that it would give federal rulings "respectful consideration," but would decide whether to follow those rulings based "solely upon [their] ability to persuade us with the[ir] reasoning." Finding that the leading U.S. Supreme Court case on parolees' Fourth Amendment rights (*Samson v. California,* 2006) was "fundamentally flawed," the *Ochoa* court rejected that federal precedent and held that "a parolee may not be subjected to broad, warrantless searches by a general law enforcement officer without any particularized suspicion or limitations to the scope of the search." The court also found that, in this particular case, the state had waived any argument that Ochoa had surrendered his Section 8 rights by signing the standard parole agreement. (The court left open the possibility that a limited, warrantless search by a parole officer might be permissible under the "special needs doctrine"—a possibility that the court briefly revisited in *State v. Kern* (2013) and then embraced in *State v. King* (2015).[57])

Shortly after *Ochoa* came down, three new justices joined the Iowa Supreme Court: Justices Edward Mansfield, Thomas Waterman, and Bruce Zager. With those additions came disagreement about the circumstances in which Iowa

period, however, the court sometimes returned to summarily declaring that Section 8 and the Fourth Amendment were coextensive. *See, e.g., State v. Carter* (2007).

[57] The court extended the special-needs doctrine to limited, warrantless searches by *probation* officers in *State v. Brooks* (2016).

should reject the federal Supreme Court's Fourth Amendment doctrines. In 2011's *State v. Pals*, for example, the court engaged in a lengthy discussion of federal and state precedents on the proper analysis to be applied when determining whether a person validly consented to an automobile search after being pulled over for a minor infraction. After reciting reasons to be skeptical about one of the U.S. Supreme Court's leading cases in this area (*Schneckloth v. Bustamonte*, 1973), a majority of the Iowa court opted to postpone deciding whether to embrace *Schneckloth*'s totality-of-the-circumstances test, concluding instead that, on an aggressive application of that test, the consent given in this case was invalid. But the decision was not unanimous. Justice Waterman filed a dissent, arguing that the court had been too eager to depart from federal precedent and that, under a faithful application of the relevant state and federal cases, the consent given in this instance was sufficient to authorize the search.

In *State v. Baldon* (2013) two years later, prosecutors relied squarely on the argument that the state had waived in *Ochoa*—namely, that by signing the state's standard parole agreement, a parolee voluntarily waives his Section 8 rights. Finding no U.S. Supreme Court precedent squarely on point, and reiterating its power to interpret Section 8 differently than the Fourth Amendment in any event, the court found that parolees lack meaningful bargaining power when deciding whether to sign the state's agreement, and that the defendant in this case had not voluntarily relinquished his constitutional rights. Justice Brent Appel (the author of *Ochoa*) wrote a lengthy special concurrence, reciting reasons why "we jealously reserve our right to construe our state constitution independently of decisions of the United States Supreme Court interpreting parallel provisions of the Federal Constitution." Joined by Justice Waterman, Justice Mansfield dissented, arguing that the *Ochoa* court had erred by treating Supreme Court precedent "as just another dish on the menu" and that—regardless of *Ochoa*'s wisdom—the defendant's acceptance of the terms of the standard parole agreement was sufficient to authorize the search that had occurred here.

Disagreement about Section 8's relationship to the Fourth Amendment prompted the justices to split once again in 2014's *State v. Short*. The case involved the Section 8 rights of a probationer whose residence law-enforcement officers had searched under a defective warrant. Finding that the federal Supreme Court had undesirably watered down the Fourth Amendment's warrant requirement, the majority (led by Justice Appel) rejected a line of federal precedent and held that, in this case, the absence of a valid warrant rendered the search illegal under Section 8. Chief Justice Mark Cady filed a special concurrence "to emphasize the importance of independently interpreting our Iowa Constitution." Justices Waterman and Mansfield each filed dissents, expressing misgivings about the court's departures from federal Fourth Amendment precedent. Justice Zager also dissented, arguing that the search here was permissible.

The justices divided again in 2015's *State v. Gaskins*, with the majority rejecting a facet of a U.S. Supreme Court ruling concerning searches incident to arrest

(*Arizona v. Gant,* 2009), and with Justices Waterman, Mansfield, and Zager arguing in dissent that the court's rejection of federal precedent was unwise. Attorneys representing the State of Iowa weighed in on the overarching issue of fidelity to U.S. Supreme Court case law, arguing that, when state and federal constitutional provisions closely track one another, the Iowa court should depart from federal precedent only when certain criteria are met. The dissenters embraced the state's argument, but the majority rejected it, with Justice Appel filing a special concurrence elaborating at length on his reasons for finding the state's proposed criteria unacceptable. The tone of the competing opinions indicated that the justices' disagreements had only grown sharper.

The same 4–3 split re-emerged two years later in *State v. Coleman* (2017). In that case, an officer had pulled a car over on suspicion of a traffic offense, but then quickly determined that the suspected offense had not occurred. Rather than allow the driver to proceed on his way, however, the officer asked the driver to produce his driver's license, registration, and proof of insurance. Upon reviewing those documents, the officer determined that the driver was driving while barred, in violation of Iowa law. Led by Justice Appel, the court concluded that Section 8 obliged the officer to end the traffic stop once he no longer had a reasonable suspicion that any violation of the law had occurred. Joined by Justices Mansfield and Zager, Justice Waterman dissented, arguing that the majority had broken with both federal and Iowa precedent.

Some important Section 8 issues remain unresolved. The Iowa Supreme Court has not yet determined, for example, "whether [Section 8] requires a knowing and intelligent waiver of rights to authorize a warrantless search" (*State v. Jackson,* 2016). Nor has the court determined "whether a warrantless search is valid under our state constitution when the individual who consented to a search of a premises had apparent authority, but not actual authority, to consent to a search of a closed container on that premises" (*State v. Jackson,* 2016). (In *Jackson,* Justice Appel indicated that he believed such a search violates Section 8; Justices Mansfield, Waterman, and Zager took the contrary view.)

Section 9.
Right of trial by jury—due process of law.

The right of trial by jury shall remain inviolate; but the General Assembly may authorize trial by a jury of a less number than twelve men in inferior courts; but no person shall be deprived of life, liberty, or property, without due process of law.

Echoing some of the language of the U.S. Constitution's Fifth, Sixth, Seventh, and Fourteenth Amendments, Section 9 helps to protect Iowans' basic due process rights, including their right to jury trial. (Section 10 speaks specifically to criminal defendants' rights, including their right to trial by an impartial jury.) In the draft constitution that the 1844 convention produced, the bill of rights contained a jury-trial provision that was substantively identical to what appears here, but it conspicuously did not contain a due process clause. The same was true of Iowa's first constitution, ratified in 1846. At the beginning of the 1857 convention's second week, the Committee on the Preamble and Bill of Rights announced that it was proposing to add a due process clause to the end of Section 9.[58] When the issue came up for discussion a few days later, Scott County's George Ells explained that the committee had pulled the clause's language directly from the U.S. Constitution. He said that he hoped the clause would be more effective than its federal counterpart, given that, through its fugitive-slave laws, Congress had been running "rough-shod over the necks of freemen."[59] Alpheus Scott—a real-estate agent from Clayton County—questioned whether the addition was truly necessary, given that the Fifth Amendment to the U.S. Constitution did indeed already contain a due process clause. After a delegate with legal training explained that the Fifth Amendment purported to bind only the federal government and placed no restrictions on the states, the convention approved the addition.[60] Eleven years later, the nation ratified the Fourteenth Amendment, declaring as a matter of federal law that no state can "deprive any person of life, liberty, or property, without due process of law."

Right to trial by jury.

The Sixth Amendment to the U.S. Constitution gives criminal defendants the right to trial "by an impartial jury," a right that is echoed in Section 10 of Iowa's Bill of Rights. This volume accordingly focuses on jury-trial rights in *criminal* cases in its discussion of Section 10. The U.S. Constitution's Seventh Amendment provides a right to trial by jury in *civil* cases in which twenty dollars or more are at stake. The Seventh Amendment is one of the few provisions of the federal Bill of Rights that the U.S. Supreme Court has not applied to the states through the Fourteenth Amendment. States thus have significant latitude to structure civil jury trials as they see fit, making Section 9's jury-trial clause of particular interest for Iowans.

Section 9's declaration that the "right of trial by jury shall remain inviolate" might lead one to think that litigants are entitled to jury trials in civil proceedings of all kinds. The Iowa Supreme Court, however, has taken a narrower view of the provision. Based on its review of the common law, for example, the Iowa court has ruled that the legislature may refuse to provide jury trials in cases involving only small monetary amounts (*Iowa National Mutual Insurance Co.*

---

[58] *1857 Debates, supra* note 3, vol. 1, pp. 64, 100.

[59] *1857 Debates, supra* note 3, vol. 1, pp. 101–02.

[60] *1857 Debates, supra* note 3, vol. 1, p. 119.

v. Mitchell, 1981). The court has also held that there is no jury-trial right in "special proceedings" (*Green v. Smith,* 1900),[61] such as cases involving judicial review of administrative agencies' actions (*O'Hara v. State,* 2002), cases seeking to have someone civilly committed due to mental illness (*In re Brewer,* 1937), or cases seeking to have a juvenile declared delinquent (*In the Interest of Johnson,* 1977). There similarly is no right to a jury trial in cases that are essentially equitable in nature, such as shareholder derivative suits (*Weltzin v. Nail,* 2000). But when there *is* a right to trial by jury, Iowa's high court strongly protects it. A trial court goes too far, for example, if it denies a jury trial as a sanction for failing to obey a discovery order (*R.E. Morris Investments, Inc. v. Lind,* 1981).

Although the Iowa Supreme Court has relied heavily upon historical practices when determining whether a litigant has a right to a jury trial in a particular kind of civil proceeding, the court also has declared that, when it comes to the mechanics of jury trials, it need not rigidly adhere to the rules that existed when Iowans ratified Section 9 in the mid-nineteenth century. In *Pitcher v. Lakes Amusement Co.* (1975), for example, the court held that the General Assembly may authorize non-unanimous verdicts in civil cases. Similarly, in 1921's *State v. Walker,* the court rejected a defendant's complaint about having women serve on his jury. Even though Section 9 refers to jurors as "men," the court found a dispositive relationship between eligibility to vote and eligibility to serve as a juror.

Due process.

The Iowa Supreme Court has repeatedly acknowledged that it has the power to interpret Section 9's Due Process Clause differently than the U.S. Supreme Court interprets the counterpart text in the Fourteenth Amendment. The Iowa court has pointed to George Ells's comments at the 1857 convention as "powerful evidence" that the constitution's framers did not want Iowa law to "simply mirror federal court interpretations" (*State v. Short,* 2014). To date, however, the court has declined to blaze its own due process path. It has said that, unless a litigant proposes a different analytic framework, the court will regard Section 9's requirements "as identical" to those of the U.S. Constitution (*State v. Reyes,* 2008). The Iowa court has thus followed the federal Supreme Court when deciding whether a protected life, liberty, or property interest is at stake, and when deciding whether such an interest has been deprived without constitutionally adequate due process (*Nguyen v. State,* 2016; *State v. Willard,* 2008; *In the Interest*

---

[61] The General Assembly has defined a "special" proceeding as a civil action that is *not* "a proceeding in a court of justice in which one party, known as the plaintiff, demands against another party, known as the defendant, the enforcement or protection of a private right, or the prevention or redress of a private wrong," or seeks "the recovery of a penalty or forfeiture." Iowa Code § 611.2.

of A.M.H., 1994). Like its federal counterpart, the Iowa Supreme Court has also determined that, absent adequate statutory remedies, a person can bring a constitutional cause of action for damages against a government official who has violated the person's due process rights (*Godfrey v. State*, 2017).

Just as under the U.S. Constitution, Section 9 due process claims can be divided into two categories: procedural and substantive. With respect to *procedural* due process claims—claims that a person was not afforded the procedures that he or she was constitutionally owed when the state deprived the person of a life, liberty, or property interest—the Iowa Supreme Court (like the U.S. Supreme Court) has distinguished between criminal and civil settings. A defendant challenging a state's criminal procedural rules can ordinarily prevail only by showing that it was "fundamentally unfair"—a judgment made with an eye toward historical practice, contemporary consensus, and the totality of the circumstances—for the government to refuse to provide the desired procedural protections (*State v. Becker*, 2012).[62] In civil settings, Iowa courts typically determine what procedures are owed using the balancing test made famous by the federal Supreme Court in *Mathews v. Eldridge* (1976). Under that analysis, a court weighs the private interests at stake, the governmental interests at stake, and the risk that an incorrect decision will be made unless additional procedures are provided (*F.K. v. Iowa District Court*, 2001). As a general matter, due process requires that the government give a person "notice" and "a meaningful opportunity to be heard" when it wishes to deprive that person of a life, liberty, or property interest (*Residential & Agricultural Advisory Committee, LLC v. Dyersville City Council*, 2016).

Federal law thus pervades Iowa's procedural due process cases. In recent years, for example, Iowa's appellate courts have invoked the federal tests for such inquiries as whether legislation adequately notifies individuals of what the law does and does not permit (*State v. Showens*, 2014; *State v. Feregrino*, 2008; *State v. Bower*, 2006), whether the state can require a prisoner who has not been convicted of a sex offense to participate in a sex-offender treatment program (*Dykstra v. Iowa District Court*, 2010), and whether the state's definition of the insanity defense impermissibly bars jurors from considering crucial factors (*State v. Kehoe*, 2011). Moreover, even though Section 9 does not expressly limit its reach to those cases in which the deprivation of life, liberty, or property has resulted from *the state's* action or inaction, the Iowa court has followed federal precedent and held that state involvement is indeed necessary to bring Section 9 into play (*Putensen v. Hawkeye Bank*, 1997).

With respect to *substantive* due process claims—claims that a given deprivation is impermissible regardless of the procedural protections that the government

---

[62] The *Becker* court relied in part upon the analytic framework developed by the U.S. Supreme Court in *Medina v. California* (1992).

provides—Iowa courts have again largely followed the U.S. Supreme Court's lead. Citing federal precedent, the Iowa Supreme Court has said that it ordinarily will defer heavily to the government, upholding its actions so long as there is a "reasonable fit" between the government's goals and the means by which it is pursuing them (*Zaber v. City of Dubuque*, 2010). The courts will ratchet the standard of review up to strict scrutiny—demanding a compelling governmental objective and narrowly tailored means—only if a "fundamental" right is at stake or if the government is engaging in behavior that "shocks the conscience" (*King v. State*, 2012; *State v. Seering*, 2005). Rights are deemed fundamental only if they are "'deeply rooted in this Nation's history and tradition,' and 'implicit in the concept of ordered liberty,' such that 'neither liberty nor justice would exist if they were sacrificed'" (*Sanchez v. State*, 2005 (quoting the U.S. Supreme Court's *Washington v. Glucksberg*, 1997)). Just as under federal law, substantive due process claims brought under Section 9 almost inevitably fail. In *Atwood v. Vilsack* (2006), for example, the Iowa Supreme Court ruled that the government may deny pretrial bail to persons believed to be sexually violent predators, even if strict scrutiny applies. (Cases concerning those who commit—or who are believed likely to commit—sexually violent offenses have generated numerous holdings concerning substantive and procedural due process issues; for an overview, see *In re Detention of Anderson* (2017).) The Iowa court's 2001 ruling in *Santi v. Santi*—holding that Section 9 bars the state from forcing fit married persons to accommodate grandparents' desire to visit their grandchildren—provides a rare example of a substantive due process claimant prevailing.

Under the U.S. Constitution, a woman's right to obtain an abortion is among the most famous (and controversial) examples of a substantive due process right. The Iowa Supreme Court has not yet determined whether there is a similar right under the Iowa Constitution (*Planned Parenthood of the Heartland, Inc. v. Iowa Board of Medicine*, 2015). The court has acknowledged, however, that individuals have a fundamental right to procreate (*McQuistion v. City of Clinton*, 2015).

One final point about Section 9's Due Process Clause warrants mention. Unlike the U.S. Constitution, the Iowa Constitution does not contain a provision granting individuals the right not to testify against themselves. The Iowa Supreme Court has held, however, that the privilege against self-incrimination is implicit in Section 9's guarantee of due process (*State v. Height*, 1902). The delegates' failure to include any explicit provision on the matter in the state's constitution is a little mysterious. At the 1857 convention, the Committee on the Preamble and Bill of Rights proposed that a provision be added to the end of Section 11 stating, "Nor shall any person be compelled in any criminal prosecution to be a witness against himself."[63] The delegates initially approved that

[63] *1857 Debates, supra* note 3, vol. 1, pp. 100, 102; *1857 Journal, supra* note 3, p. 65.

addition, apparently without debate.[64] At the end of that day's work, however, Section 11 was referred to the Committee on the Judiciary to resolve disagreements regarding Section 11's provision concerning grand juries.[65] When that committee returned to the delegates with the product of their labors, the language concerning self-incrimination had been removed.[66] The omission did not provoke any historically documented discussion.

Section 10.
Rights of persons accused.

In all criminal prosecutions, and in cases involving the life, or liberty of an individual the accused shall have a right to a speedy and public trial by an impartial jury; to be informed of the accusation against him, to have a copy of the same when demanded; to be confronted with the witnesses against him; to have compulsory process for his witnesses; and, to have the assistance of counsel.

Section 10 provides criminal defendants with a cluster of important procedural rights, closely tracking much of the language of the Sixth Amendment to the U.S. Constitution. Many of Section 10's provisions appeared in the 1844 convention's draft and were carried forward in the constitution that Iowans ratified in 1846. As it stood at that time, Section 10 lacked the phrase "and in cases involving the life, or liberty of an individual," it did not require that the accused's trial be "public," and it did not require that the accused be given a copy of the accusations against him upon request. The delegates to the 1857 convention made all three of those changes. The third was initially proposed by Amos Harris, a lawyer from Appanoose County. He acknowledged that courts already routinely provided defendants with copies of the accusations against them, but he believed that the right should not "depend upon the courtesy of the court."[67] The delegates' attention then shifted to other matters, however, and Harris's suggestion temporarily fell by the wayside. In a subsequent session, Henry County's Rufus Clarke revived Harris's idea and proposed the other two additions, as well. As Part I explains, the historical record suggests that a primary reason Clarke proposed expanding the jury-trial right to include "cases involving the life, or liberty of an individual" was to ensure that fugitive slaves received a jury trial in Iowa to determine whether they should be returned to the states from which they had fled. Even though slavery has long since been abolished, Clarke's addition remains significant because it appears to extend Section 10's reach to cases that might not be covered by the federal Constitution's Sixth Amendment (*State*

[64] *1857 Debates, supra* note 3, vol. 1, p. 124.

[65] *1857 Debates, supra* note 3, vol. 1, p. 140.

[66] *1857 Debates, supra* note 3, vol. 1, p. 201; *1857 Journal, supra* note 3, p. 112.

[67] *1857 Debates, supra* note 3, vol. 1, pp. 119–20.

v. Young, 2015).[68] In *Young,* for example, the court relied in part upon the "cases involving the life or liberty" language to rule that Section 10 provides criminal defendants with a right to the assistance of counsel in all misdemeanor prosecutions that carry the possibility of imprisonment.

Speedy and public trial.

Like Section 10, the U.S. Constitution's Sixth Amendment grants criminal defendants a "right to a speedy and public trial." The U.S. Supreme Court has held that both of those requirements protect fundamental rights and that—by virtue of the Fourteenth Amendment's Due Process Clause—all states must honor them (*Klopfer v. North Carolina,* 1967 (speedy); *In re Oliver,* 1948 (public)). The purposes of the state and federal speediness requirements are to alleviate the anxiety created by a prolonged threat of criminal conviction, to ensure the prompt administration of justice, and to protect defendants against the loss of exculpatory evidence (*State v. Miller,* 2012). Section 10's and the Sixth Amendment's speediness requirements are implemented in Iowa today by Rule 2.33 of the Iowa Rules of Criminal Procedure. That rule declares that the state's policy is to ensure that criminal prosecutions are "concluded at the earliest possible time consistent with a fair trial to both parties," and then prescribes a variety of deadlines. The Iowa Supreme Court has held that Rule 2.33's demands are more stringent than those of the Sixth Amendment and Section 10 (*State v. Nelson,* 1999), and so litigation on timeliness now typically proceeds under that procedural rule, rather than under either of the constitutional provisions. *State v. McNeal* (2017) nicely illustrates the point.

The requirement of public access is based upon the longstanding belief that "publicity serves as a buttress against unjust prosecution and aids greatly in insuring the accused the fair trial to which he is entitled" (*State v. Lawrence,* 1969). A trial's publicity might, for example, discourage witnesses from lying, bring the proceedings to the attention of knowledgeable witnesses of whom the defendant had not been aware, or discourage the judge from using voice inflections or other techniques to sway the jury's judgment unfairly. When interpreting Section 10's requirement that criminal trials be public, the Iowa Supreme Court has applied the Sixth Amendment's analytic framework. In a 1985 ruling, for example, the justices relied upon federal Supreme Court precedent to find that the trial court had erred when it excluded the public during the testimony of a ten-year-old girl who allegedly had been the victim of sexual abuse (*State v. Hightower,* 1985).[69] The Iowa court has not looked solely to federal precedent,

---

[68] Soon after the 1857 constitution's ratification, the Iowa Supreme Court rejected the notion that the clause only benefited fugitive slaves (*Ex parte Grace,* 1861).

[69] The *Hightower* court relied upon the U.S. Supreme Court's ruling in *Waller v. Georgia* (1984). The Iowa court reached the same conclusion on comparable facts in *State v. Klem* (1989).

however. In a 1979 case, for example—a case in which the trial had been held in the basement of a post office pending repairs to the courtroom—the court relied upon a Virginia ruling when finding that the small size of the facility did not violate the defendant's Section 10 rights (*State v. Jones*, 1979). The test, the court said, "is not whether the courtroom is large enough to seat everyone who wants to attend, but whether the public has freedom of access to it."

Impartial jury.

At the 1857 convention, the Committee on the Preamble and Bill of Rights proposed requiring that a criminal defendant's trial be held in "the county or district in which the offense is alleged to have been committed," reasoning (as Scott County's George Ells explained) that this would place a defendant's trial in the location "where the witnesses live, where the facts are all known, and where he is likely to have a more fair and impartial trial, than if taken to a distant part of the State."[70] A number of delegates resisted, however, saying that existing law already granted defendants a right to be tried where the alleged wrongs occurred, and that the General Assembly should be left free to make appropriate adjustments in the future. The key, they said, was simply to guarantee defendants an impartial jury. Evidently persuaded, the delegates rejected the committee's proposal.[71]

The U.S. Supreme Court has held that, through the Fourteenth Amendment's Due Process Clause, the Sixth Amendment's guarantee of trial by an impartial jury applies in state criminal proceedings (*Duncan v. Louisiana*, 1968).[72] The Iowa Supreme Court has not analytically distinguished between Section 10's and the Sixth Amendment's parallel jury provisions. The court has said, for example, that both texts assure criminal defendants that their juries will be drawn from pools representing a "fair cross-section of the community" (*State v. Jones*, 1992). Similarly, when faced with a claim that prosecutors violated both the Sixth Amendment and Section 10 by using their preemptory challenges to remove racial minorities from a jury, the Iowa court applied the familiar analysis prescribed by the federal Supreme Court in *Batson v. Kentucky* (1986), making no distinction between the state and federal constitutions' demands (*State v. Veal*, 1997). The court has also applied the federal standards when deciding whether the likelihood of juror bias necessitated changing a criminal trial's venue (*State v. Veal*, 1997).

---

[70] *1857 Debates, supra* note 3, vol. 1, p. 102.

[71] *1857 Debates, supra* note 3, vol. 1, pp. 119–24.

[72] The U.S. Supreme Court has, however, given states a bit of freedom to deviate from some of the federal rules. Under *Apodaca v. Oregon* (1972), non-unanimous juries can convict in state criminal cases, even though unanimity is required in federal criminal cases. If a state's criminal jury consists of only six people, however, they may convict only if unanimous (*Burch v. Louisiana*, 1979).

Informed of the accusation.

The U.S. Constitution's Sixth Amendment protects criminal defendants' right "to be informed of the nature and cause of the accusation." The federal Supreme Court has indicated that, through the Fourteenth Amendment's Due Process Clause, this provision applies in state criminal proceedings (*In re Oliver*, 1948). Constitutional litigation in Iowa under the comparable portion of Section 10 now appears to be nonexistent. Rules 2.4 and 2.5 of the Iowa Rules of Criminal Procedure require prosecutors to provide specified kinds of information concerning criminal charges and the evidence on which those charges are based, regardless of whether the charges are brought pursuant to an indictment by a grand jury (Rule 2.4) or an "information" prepared by the prosecutor (Rule 2.5). By complying with those rules, state officials satisfy their Section 10 obligations—obligations that older cases minimized by indicating that prosecutors were required merely to inform defendants of "the gist" of the crimes with which they had been charged (*State v. Neuhart*, 1940; *State v. McDougal*, 1922).

Confronting adverse witnesses.

Like Section 10, the Sixth Amendment gives a criminal defendant the right "to be confronted with the witnesses against him." The U.S. Supreme Court has held that, through the Fourteenth Amendment's Due Process Clause, the Sixth Amendment confrontation entitlement applies in states' criminal proceedings (*Pointer v. Texas*, 1965). The chief purpose of the confrontation right is to maximize the likelihood that jurors will have an opportunity to observe witnesses' demeanor while those witnesses are being cross-examined, under oath, by the defendant (*State v. Shearon*, 2003). Although the Iowa Supreme Court has stressed that it has the power to interpret Iowa's Confrontation Clause differently than the federal Supreme Court interprets the corresponding clause of the Sixth Amendment, it has not yet exercised that power. In 2014's *State v. Kennedy*, for example, the court observed that the defendant himself had relied entirely upon federal precedent when making his argument, and so the court relied upon that same precedent when determining which of a variety of documents were testimonial—that is, prepared under circumstances that would lead a reasonable person to believe the documents would be used at a trial—and thus constitutionally inadmissible because the defendant had not had an opportunity to cross-examine the individuals who prepared them.[73]

---

[73] The court has taken the same approach on other occasions. *See*, e.g., *In the Interest of J.C.* (2016); *State v. Shipley* (2008).

Compulsory process for witnesses.

The U.S. Constitution's Sixth Amendment protects a criminal defendant's right "to have compulsory process for obtaining witnesses in his favor," a right that the U.S. Supreme Court has held is fundamental and thus applies in state and federal proceedings alike (*Washington v. Texas,* 1967). Iowa's appellate courts have not distinguished between the federal and state constitutions' compulsory-process clauses. Recognizing the guarantee's close relationship with basic due process principles, the Iowa Supreme Court has said that the compulsory-process right's central function is to protect an accused person's ability "to present a defense" (*State v. Fox,* 1992). Like most constitutional rights, the right to present the witnesses of one's choosing is not absolute. A trial court, for example, has the discretionary power to refuse to permit a defendant to call to the stand witnesses who are incarcerated (*State v. Kennedy,* 1866)[74] or who have already indicated that they will invoke their federal Fifth Amendment right not to give self-incriminating testimony (*State v. Bedwell,* 1987). A defendant's Section 10 rights are similarly not violated when his or her trial proceeds without a desired witness who is geographically located beyond the state's borders and thus beyond the trial court's jurisdictional reach (*State v. Sieren,* 1961).

Assistance of counsel.

The Sixth Amendment states that, "[i]n all criminal prosecutions, the accused shall enjoy the right . . . to have the Assistance of Counsel for his defence," and the U.S. Supreme Court has held that, through the Fourteenth Amendment's Due Process Clause, this provision applies in state criminal proceedings (*Gideon v. Wainwright,* 1963). The purpose of Section 10's guarantee is similar to that of the Sixth Amendment's: "to correct the imbalance between the position of an accused and the powerful forces of the State in a criminal prosecution" (*State v. Newsom,* 1987). With *State v. Young* (2015) standing as a notable exception—a case in which the court held that criminal defendants have a right to counsel in all misdemeanor prosecutions carrying the possibility of imprisonment—Iowa's courts have frequently interpreted the two provisions to mean the same thing. Just as under federal law (*United States v. Wade,* 1967), for example, the right to counsel under Section 10 applies at all "critical stages" of a defendant's proceeding (*State v. Boggs,* 2007). But some members of the Iowa Supreme Court have recently indicated a desire to move toward greater analytic independence. Under federal law, an individual's Sixth Amendment right to counsel does not attach until judicial proceedings have been launched against him or her (*Rothgery v. Gillespie County,* 2008). In 2016's *State v. Senn*—a case concerning a person's desire to consult privately with counsel about whether to submit to a chemical

---

[74] *See also Hahn v. State* (1981) (extending that rule to postconviction proceedings).

blood test following an arrest for driving under the influence of alcohol—Iowa's justices divided on whether the same is true under Section 10, with three justices arguing that it is not, three justices arguing that it is, and Chief Justice Cady declining to reach the issue. On one point in this regard, however, the justices have agreed: "[T]here is no right to counsel based solely on the presence and the assistance of a prosecuting attorney during an investigatory police interview" (*State v. Green*, 2017).

Both the Sixth Amendment and Section 10 guarantee a defendant the *effective* assistance of counsel. The Iowa Supreme Court acknowledges that it has the power to develop its own analytic framework for ineffective-assistance claims under Section 10 but, to date, no defendant has successfully argued that a different framework is indeed appropriate. Iowa's courts thus routinely apply the federal standards developed in *Strickland v. Washington* (1984) and its progeny. In 2015's *State v. Halverson*, for example, the Iowa court noted that the defendant had not proposed a framework other than *Strickland*'s, and so the court proceeded to ask whether the defendant's attorney had failed to perform an essential duty and, if so, whether the defendant had been prejudiced as a result. The federal Supreme Court typically formulates the first of those two questions a little differently, asking whether the attorney's performance "fell below an objective standard of reasonableness" (*Strickland v. Washington*, 1984), but, to date, the different phrasing does not appear to matter. Indeed, the Iowa Supreme Court often invokes the federal language when explaining what it means by failing an "essential duty" (*Nguyen v. State*, 2016; *State v. Schlitter*, 2016; *State v. Ondayog*, 2006). When articulating the second prong of the ineffective-assistance analysis, the Iowa court closely tracks the language of the federal standard, requiring that the defendant prove prejudice by demonstrating that there is a reasonable probability that the outcome of the defendant's proceeding would have been different if the attorney had competently performed (*State v. Ambrose*, 2015; *State v. Enderle*, 2007).

Section 11.
When indictment necessary—grand jury.

All offenses less than felony and in which the maximum permissible imprisonment does not exceed thirty days shall be tried summarily before an officer authorized by law, on information under oath, without indictment, or the intervention of a grand jury, saving to the defendant the right of appeal; and no person shall be held to answer for any higher criminal offense;[75] unless on

---

[75] The handwritten document signed by the delegates to the 1857 constitution contains an evidently inappropriate semicolon here, rather than a comma. *See* State Library of Iowa, "Constitutions," http://www.statelibraryofiowa.org/services/collections/law-library/iacon/iacons (presenting the handwritten copy and other iterations of the Iowa Constitution). The text of the constitution that appears in the appendix to the *1857 Journal*, *supra* note 3, contains a comma, as does the version of the constitution published in recent iterations of the Iowa Code.

presentment or indictment by a grand jury, except in cases arising in the army, or navy, or in the militia, when in actual service, in time of war or public danger.

The grand jury may consist of any number of members not less than five, nor more than fifteen, as the General Assembly may by law provide, or the General Assembly may provide for holding persons to answer for any criminal offense without the intervention of a grand jury.

Section 11 focuses primarily on the means by which criminal prosecutions may be launched. With exceptions for certain cases arising from the armed forces, the U.S. Constitution's Fifth Amendment states that "[n]o person shall be held to answer for a capital, or otherwise infamous crime, unless on presentment or indictment of a Grand Jury." Because this is among the few provisions of the federal Bill of Rights that the U.S. Supreme Court has *not* deemed applicable to the states through the Fourteenth Amendment (*Hurtado v. California*, 1884), states are free to decide for themselves what role, if any, grand juries must play in initiating state criminal prosecutions.

In Iowa's 1857 constitution, the text of Section 11 differed from what one sees above in four noteworthy ways: crimes for which the punishment did not exceed $100 were among those for which summary proceedings were permitted, without any grand jury participation; justices of the peace were authorized to adjudicate minor offenses; nothing was said about the size of grand juries; and the General Assembly was not authorized to eliminate grand juries' role in criminal prosecutions altogether. In 1884, Iowa voters intervened in the latter two areas by adding what appears today as Section 11's second paragraph. Under prior law, grand juries were larger and their participation was required to launch prosecutions for almost all serious offenses (*Jones v. McClaughry*, 1915). (At the 1857 convention, Davis County's David Palmer had declared that he would be willing to authorize the legislature to eliminate grand juries, but the idea failed to gain traction among his colleagues.[76]) In 1998, Iowa voters removed the clause concerning crimes punishable by fines of $100 or less and the reference to justices of the peace.[77]

Because its provisions are relatively straightforward, Section 11 has not been the focus of extensive litigation. A few points nevertheless warrant emphasis. First, the last clause of Section 11's second paragraph trumps the first paragraph's declaration that most "higher criminal offenses" may be prosecuted only with a grand jury's involvement. If the General Assembly wishes to eliminate grand juries even for serious crimes, it may do so (*State v. Hillsman*, 1979; *Jones v. McClaughry*, 1915). (Under the law as it stands today, a prosecutor contemplating launching a criminal prosecution is free to decide for himself or herself

---

[76] *1857 Debates*, *supra* note 3, vol. 1, pp. 124–25.

[77] In 1972, the General Assembly abolished the position of justice of the peace. For more on the rise and fall of that position, see the commentary on Article XI, Section 1.

whether to seek an indictment by a grand jury.[78]) The court has indicated that a prosecutor may initiate a prosecution even if a grand jury considered the case and declined to issue an indictment (*State v. Lint*, 1978). Second, with respect to minor crimes, the Iowa court has held that, even though Section 11 states that such crimes "*shall* be tried *summarily* before an officer authorized by law," the General Assembly may authorize jury trials (*Marzen v. Klousia*, 1982).[79] Finally, with respect to the clause declaring that minor crimes may be prosecuted "on information under oath," the Iowa Supreme Court has said that the person providing the essential factual information must indeed take an oath before an officer authorized to administer oaths; an unsworn declaration of facts is insufficient (*City of Cedar Rapids v. Atsinger*, 2000).

Section 12.
Twice tried—bail.

No person shall after acquittal, be tried for the same offence. All persons shall, before conviction, be bailable, by sufficient sureties, except for capital offenses where the proof is evident, or the presumption great.

Apart from some minor differences in punctuation, Section 12 still stands today in the same form that the delegates to the 1844 convention placed it. The records of that convention, as well as those of the 1846 and 1857 conventions, provide no indication that the provision was ever the subject of any significant debate.

Tried for the same offense.

The U.S. Constitution's Fifth Amendment states that no person may "be subject for the same offence to be twice put in jeopardy of life or limb." The U.S. Supreme Court has held that the Double Jeopardy Clause applies to the states through the Due Process Clause of the Fourteenth Amendment (*Benton v. Maryland*, 1969). The Court has also said that the Fifth Amendment's ban on double jeopardy provides three basic protections: "It protects against a second prosecution for the same offense after acquittal. It protects against a second prosecution for the same offense after conviction. And it protects against multiple punishments for the same offense" (*North Carolina v. Pearce*, 1969). The text of Section 12 is considerably narrower, overlapping only with the first of the federal text's three functions—namely, barring post-acquittal prosecutions for the same crime (*State v. Velez*, 2013; *State v. Franzen*, 1993). With respect to the limited domain in which Section 12 operates, the Iowa Supreme Court has indicated that it follows the federal standards for adjudicating double-jeopardy

---

[78] Iowa R. Crim. Proc. 2.4, 2.5.

[79] Interested readers should consult the *Marzen* court's discussion of its holding's relationship to the jury-trial rights protected by Sections 9 and 10.

claims (*State v. Miller*, 2000). In those cases, Iowa's high court has relied primarily upon federal precedent and upon its own past efforts to interpret that precedent (*In the Interest of Z.S.*, 2009; *State v. Taft*, 1993). Moreover, the General Assembly has statutorily provided double-jeopardy protections that extend beyond those explicitly afforded by Section 12.[80] For all of those reasons, this portion of Section 12 does not currently carry independent significance.[81]

Bail.

Section 12 provides one of the Iowa Bill of Rights' two provisions on bail, the other being Section 17's ban on "[e]xcessive bail." Bail provides a means by which criminal defendants can obtain physical freedom prior to the time when they must appear in court, while nevertheless assuring the government that they will indeed appear in court when required. Because defendants often do not themselves have the funds required to pay the full bail amount, they frequently rely upon sureties of one form or another—individuals or entities who agree to be financially liable if the defendant ultimately fails to appear.[82] In 1978's *State v. Zylstra*, the Iowa Supreme Court explained the system this way:

> A court admits a defendant to bail in order to assure his appearance in court. In assuming the position of bail the surety becomes obligated to produce the accused in open court when his presence is required. Stated otherwise, when the State releases a defendant from confinement it commits him to the exclusive custody of his surety, who becomes "the jailer of his own choosing." If the surety fails to produce its principal at the appointed time, a judgment shall be entered by the court.

Perhaps because the area is closely regulated by statute,[83] Section 12's bail clause has not been frequently litigated. The most useful starting point for many who are studying this area of the law will be 2003's *State v. Briggs*.[84] In that case, the Iowa Supreme Court provided a historical overview of the bail system, tracing it from its medieval roots (when a surety personally took custody of a defendant and appeared in court in the defendant's place if the defendant ultimately could

---

[80] Iowa Code § 701.9; ch. 816.

[81] For an early example of a criminal defendant prevailing under Section 12, see *State v. Tweedy* (1860).

[82] For an example of a surety being forced to pay on a bond when a defendant failed to appear for trial, see *State v. Benedict* (1944).

[83] Iowa Code ch. 811.

[84] *See also State v. Sandy* (1908) ("Technically considered, bail is the delivery of a person to the sureties on his bond, he being supposed to continue in their friendly custody instead of jail; so that the sureties on the bail bond become the bailees or custodians of the person of their principal, and may at any time, before the entry of forfeiture or possibly, judgment, be exonerated by his surrender as provided by statute.").

not be located) up to the present day (when commercial bail bondsmen are prevalent, giving defendants an opportunity to finance their freedom by paying a bondsman only a portion of the bail amount set by the court). The *Briggs* court found that, at the time of Section 12's adoption, commercial bonding was only beginning to emerge, and so the "sufficient sureties" clause was not intended to guarantee defendants access to a commercial bail bond; rather, it was intended merely to ensure that defendants would have access to a surety "of some form." So long as the bail amount does not "absolutely bar" a defendant from using "a surety of some form," cash-only bail—such as the $6,500 in cash required of the woman seeking pretrial freedom in *Briggs*—is permissible.

By its terms, Section 12 permits the state to deny bail in a capital case if "the proof is evident, or the presumption great." If the state does wish to deny bail on these grounds, it bears the burden of proving that there is strong evidence that the defendant committed a capital crime (*Ford v. Dilley*, 1916). Iowa has abolished the death penalty, and so, strictly speaking, there are no "capital offenses" in this state. The Iowa Supreme Court has thus suggested in dictum that the viability of this portion of Section 12 "is at best doubtful" (*State v. Fowler*, 1976).[85] The question is not a pressing one today, however, because the General Assembly has opted to make preconviction bail broadly available.[86]

Section 12's assurance of bail eligibility does not apply in civil proceedings. Its benefits do not extend, for example, to individuals awaiting a determination of whether they should be civilly committed as sexually violent predators (*Atwood v. Vilsack*, 2006).

Section 13.
Habeas corpus.

The writ of habeas corpus shall not be suspended, or refused when application is made as required by law, unless in case of rebellion, or invasion the public safety may require it.

With roots extending back to the era of Magna Carta, the writ of habeas corpus is one of the Anglo-American legal tradition's most revered remedies for illegal confinement or restraint by government officials. The writ's historic importance is reflected in the U.S. Constitution's Suspension Clause, which declares that "[t]he Privilege of the Writ of Habeas Corpus shall not be suspended, unless

---

[85] A defendant advanced this argument in *State v. Fuhrmann* (1978), but the court declined to address it. Interpreting comparable provisions of their own state constitutions, other states' courts have concluded that, if the death penalty has been abolished, these provisions are inoperative. *See*, e.g., *Ex parte Ball* (Kan. 1920); *State v. Pett* (Minn. 1958); *City of Sioux Falls v. Marshall* (S.D. 1925); *In re Petition of Perry* (Wis. 1865). *Ex parte Ball* contains a useful discussion of the provision's origins in Anglo-American law.

[86] Iowa Code § 811.1.

when in Cases of Rebellion or Invasion the public Safety may require it."[87] The constitutional texts produced by Iowa's 1844 and 1846 conventions contained substantively similar language.

The delegates to the 1857 convention placed Section 13 into its current form, adding the phrase "or refused when application is made as required by law." That addition was first proposed by Johnson County's William Penn Clarke, who said that he had heard accounts of cases in other states in which courts had ignored lawful habeas applications. But some delegates resisted. Muscatine County's John Parvin said that the language was superfluous, while Des Moines County's Jonathan Hall argued that judges should not have to issue writs and thereby launch the full habeas adjudication process when they know that, on the merits, they ultimately will refuse to provide the remedy. (When a court issues the writ, it is not thereby ordering the confined person released; rather, it is launching an adjudicative process to determine whether the confinement is lawful.) Clarke replied that his amendment would help to facilitate meaningful appellate review: if a judge issued the writ but then denied relief following a hearing, the case could readily be reviewed on appeal; but if a judge refused to issue the writ altogether, the petitioner might have to seek a writ of mandamus to force the judge to issue the writ—and mandamus can itself be a difficult remedy to obtain because it is appropriate only when the person to whom the mandamus writ is issued has abused his or her discretion. By the close vote of 14 to 16, the delegates rejected Clarke's proposal.[88] At the end of that same day, however, Clarke successfully suggested that Section 13 be referred to the Committee on the Judicial Department, on which he sat.[89] Three days later, Clarke presented the same amendment on behalf of that committee, and the delegates approved it without any historically documented debate.[90]

Prior to 1970, Iowa provided two ways in which persons convicted of state crimes could challenge the government's power to restrain their liberty: a direct appeal or a civil suit seeking the writ of habeas corpus. The procedures for habeas litigation were (and still are) statutorily prescribed by Chapter 663 of the Iowa Code. The legal landscape changed in 1970, when the General Assembly adopted the Uniform Post-Conviction Procedure Act and thereby provided a third avenue for challenging the government's power to incarcerate or otherwise restrain a person.[91] (That legislation was originally codified in Chapter 663A and appears today in Chapter 822—something to keep in mind when searching for relevant case law.) If the person seeking relief has been "convicted of, or sentenced for, a public offense," Chapter 822's collateral remedies are exclusive;

---

[87] U.S. Const. art. I, § 9, cl. 2.

[88] *1857 Debates, supra* note 3, vol. 1, pp. 125–26.

[89] *1857 Journal, supra* note 3, p. 104.

[90] *1857 Debates, supra* note 3, vol. 1, p. 202; *1857 Journal, supra* note 3, p. 112.

[91] Act of Apr. 13, 1970, ch. 1276, 1970 Iowa Acts 395.

habeas relief under Chapter 663 is unavailable.[92] The Iowa Supreme Court has held that, because Chapter 822 provides an "equivalent substitute" for the habeas writ, that legislation's postconviction procedures may indeed replace the habeas writ for persons convicted of (or sentenced for) criminal conduct. Chapter 822 is, in other words, "an implementation of the right of habeas corpus, not an abrogation or suspension of it" (*McElhaney v. Auger*, 1976).

By virtue of the state's adoption of the Uniform Post-Conviction Procedure Act, most of the state's habeas cases predate 1970. In those cases, Iowa's courts generally followed the longstanding Anglo-American rule that the purpose of the habeas writ was not to provide a vehicle for reviewing allegations of trial error that were reviewable on appeal, nor was its purpose to provide an occasion for reviewing claims of innocence based upon newly discovered evidence (*Gibson v. Lainson*, 1953). Rather, the writ's central function was to provide a means of challenging the jurisdiction of the court in which the petitioner was convicted or sentenced (*Bell v. Lainson*, 1956). That jurisdictional focus was not as narrow, however, as it might first appear. In the mid-twentieth century, the Iowa Supreme Court noted that the U.S. Supreme Court had been broadening the *federal* habeas writ's availability to include an expanding range of constitutional challenges to criminal defendants' convictions and sentences, under a broad understanding of the kinds of claims that were jurisdictional in nature (*Sewell v. Lainson*, 1953). The Iowa court signaled that it intended to take the same approach. Before postconviction legislation arrived on the scene, for example, the Iowa Supreme Court held that a prisoner could use the habeas writ to claim ineffective assistance of counsel at trial (*Buteaux v. Bennett*, 1964) or to claim that he was denied due process when the trial court allowed prosecutors to tell the jury that the prisoner had previously entered and withdrawn a guilty plea (*Ely v. Haugh*, 1969).

With Chapter 822 now filling the postconviction territory, the writ of habeas corpus is an appropriate remedy in an exceptionally small number of circumstances. The Iowa Supreme Court has said, for example, that habeas proceedings under Chapter 663 *might* be an appropriate vehicle for challenging a state criminal proceeding resulting in a deferred judgment, if state officials are restraining the petitioner's liberty as a result of that judgment (*State v. Hernandez-Galarza*, 2015). (The possible availability of habeas relief in the deferred-judgment setting flows in part from the fact that a deferred judgment is not a conviction for a public offense within the meaning of Chapter 822, and thus does not provide an occasion for postconviction relief pursuant to that legislation (*Daughenbaugh v. State*, 2011).) Wholly apart from the criminal law setting, the Iowa court has found that habeas is a constitutionally appropriate remedy when one wishes to

[92] Iowa Code § 822.1.

challenge a child's current custody arrangement (*Doan Thi Hoang Anh v. Nelson*, 1976; *Lamar v. Zimmerman*, 1969).

Even within the narrow realm within which the habeas writ may properly be deployed, the General Assembly has some latitude to place limits on the writ's availability without fear of suspending the writ in violation of Section 13. Pointing out that Section 13 ensures the writ will be available in cases in which "application is made *as required by law*," for example, the Iowa Supreme Court has held that the General Assembly may impose a reasonable statute of limitations in habeas and postconviction-procedure cases alike (*Davis v. State*, 1989). The legislature also may withhold evidentiary hearings in cases in which the pleadings make it clear that the petitioner is not entitled to relief (*McElhaney v. Auger*, 1976).

Section 14.
Military.

The military shall be subordinate to the civil power. No standing army shall be kept up by the State in time of peace; and in time of war, no appropriation for a standing army shall be for a longer time than two years.

Section 14 contains unmistakable echoes of the widespread belief among the nation's founders that standing armies pose a threat to freedom because, among other things, they might be tempted to take control of the territory by force. The text of Section 14 still stands in the same form that the delegates to the 1844 convention placed it. The provision's substance was drawn from some of the nation's oldest state constitutions,[93] while the two-year limit on wartime appropriations for a standing army mirrors the U.S. Constitution's declaration in Article I, Section 8, that "no Appropriation of Money to [support Armies] shall be for a longer term than two Years." At the 1857 convention, the only documented discussion of Section 14 came when Appanoose County's Amos Harris proposed an amendment that would have rearranged the existing words in inconsequential ways, but also would have added a provision declaring, "The people have the right to bear arms in defence of their persons, property, and the State."[94] Without any documented debate, the delegates rejected that proposal.

Section 14 has never been the subject of reported appellate litigation.

Section 15.
Quartering soldiers.

No soldier shall, in time of peace, be quartered in any house without the consent of the owner, nor in time of war except in the manner prescribed by law.

---

[93] *See, e.g.*, Penn. Const. of 1776, § XIII; Va. Const. of 1776, § 13.

[94] *1857 Debates*, *supra* note 3, vol. 1, p. 126.

Section 15 continues Section 14's theme of warding off problems that could be caused by aggressive military authorities. With only minor typographical differences, Section 15 is identical to the text of the Third Amendment to the U.S. Constitution. Section 15 was not the subject of historically documented debate at any of Iowa's three constitutional conventions and has never been the subject of reported appellate litigation.

Section 16.
Treason.

Treason against the State shall consist only in levying war against it, adhering to its enemies, or giving them aid and comfort. No person shall be convicted of treason, unless on the evidence of two witnesses to the same overt act, or confession in open Court.

Section 16 provides a narrow definition of treason—a serious offense for which execution has historically been regarded as an appropriate punishment—and lays out some procedural protections aimed at ensuring that no one is too easily convicted of the crime. The provision is substantively identical to Article III, Section 3, of the U.S. Constitution. The only record of debate about Section 16 at any of Iowa's three constitutional conventions comes from the Territory of Iowa's first attempt to draft a constitution in 1844. At that convention, Henry County's Jonathan Hall proposed adding a provision to the end of the above text stating, "and no person shall be convicted of treason, when the act committed and charged as treason has been done in accordance with the will of a majority of the people, expressed by a vote prior to the commission of the act." The delegates rejected Hall's proposal by a vote of 14 to 54.[95] Section 16 has never been the subject of reported appellate litigation.

Section 17.
Bail—punishments.

Excessive bail shall not be required; excessive fines shall not be imposed, and cruel and unusual punishments shall not be inflicted.

With its ban on unjustifiably high bail amounts, Section 17 contains one of the Iowa Bill of Rights' two bail provisions, the other being Section 12's declaration that each person has a preconviction right to bail unless there is strong evidence that he or she committed a capital offense. Section 17 also limits the government's power to punish wrongdoers, stating that fines cannot be "excessive" and that "cruel and unusual punishments" cannot be imposed. Setting aside minor differences in wording, Section 17 is phrased in terms that are substantively identical to the U.S. Constitution's Eighth Amendment, which, in

---

[95] *1844 Journal, supra* note 3, p. 56.

turn, was closely modeled on Section 10 of the 1689 English Bill of Rights. With one inconsequential difference in punctuation, Section 17 stands in the same form that the delegates to the Territory of Iowa's 1844 constitutional convention placed it. It was not the subject of documented debate at that convention or at the conventions that followed in 1846 and 1857.

Excessive bail.

The U.S. Supreme Court has never clearly held that the Eighth Amendment's ban on excessive bail applies to the states, though the Court has indicated in dictum that it does (*Schilb v. Kuebel,* 1971). Regardless of whether that provision binds Iowa officials, when interpreting Section 17 the Iowa Supreme Court has sought guidance from the federal Supreme Court's treatment of the Eighth Amendment. Guided by federal precedent and by standards prescribed by Iowa's General Assembly,[96] the Iowa court has said that, when adjudicating an excessive-bail claim, the central inquiry is whether the person's bail amount is excessive in relation to the government's objectives of ensuring the person's later appearance in court and protecting the public against harms that the person might inflict while not in the government's custody (*State v. Briggs,* 2003). In dictum, the court has acknowledged the possibility that, under unspecified circumstances, cash-only bail might violate Section 17 (*State v. Briggs,* 2003).

Excessive fines.

The federal Supreme Court has never squarely decided whether the Eighth Amendment's ban on excessive fines applies to the states, and in dicta it has sent mixed signals.[97] The Iowa Supreme Court nevertheless routinely looks to federal precedent for guidance when interpreting Section 17. Drawing from federal case law, the Iowa court has said that, when adjudicating an excessive-fine claim, "[t]he touchstone of the inquiry . . . is based on the principle of proportionality"; a fine is excessive only if it is "grossly disproportionate to the gravity of the offense committed" (*State v. Klawonn,* 2000). As that language implies, the court gives "substantial deference to our legislators' choice of penalties for criminal offenses" (*State v. Izzolena,* 2000).

In 1994's *Spaur v. Owens-Corning Fiberglas Corp.,* the Iowa court held that Section 17's Excessive Fines Clause does not apply if the state is not a party

---

[96] Iowa Code § 811.2.

[97] *McDonald v. City of Chicago* (2010) (listing the ban on excessive fines as one of the few provisions of the Bill of Rights that has not been deemed applicable to the states); *Cooperman Industries, Inc. v. Leatherman Tool Group, Inc.* (2001) (stating in dictum that the ban on excessive fines applies to the states).

to the litigation, and that Section 17 remains inapplicable even if the private plaintiff will have to give a portion of any proceeds it collects to a state-run fund that has been established to serve a particular governmental purpose. (The *Spaur* court left open the possibility that the outcome in that case might have been different if the state's share of the financial award were to be placed in the state's general treasury.) In a subsequent case—*State v. Izzolena* (2000)—the Iowa Supreme Court found that a court-ordered monetary payment constitutes a "fine" within the meaning of Section 17 only if at least part of its purpose is to serve one or more punitive objectives, such as deterrence or retribution. Because one of the reasons the General Assembly requires convicted criminals to pay victim restitution in certain instances is to punish criminals for their conduct, the *Izzolena* court said, victim-restitution awards payable to private parties bring Section 17 into play. The *Izzolena* court looked specifically at Section 910.3B of the Iowa Code, which mandates payment of at least $150,000 in restitution when a person commits a felony resulting in the death of another person. Given "the gravity of the offenses covered under the statute," the court concluded that Section 910.3B did not facially violate Section 17. Building on *Izzolena,* the court ruled in *State v. Richardson* (2017)—a case concerning a felon who committed her crime at the age of fifteen—that the same statute "does not on its face violate the excessive fines clause of the Iowa Constitution as it relates to juvenile homicide offenders." Just as it had in prior cases,[98] the court in *Richardson* also rejected an as-applied challenge to a $150,000 victim-restitution order.[99]

The same gross-disproportionality analysis applies when the government uses civil forfeiture proceedings to seize property in response to the property owner's criminal conduct: the value of the forfeited property cannot be grossly disproportionate to the severity of the underlying criminal offense (*In re Property Seized from Terrell,* 2002). In the *Terrell* case, for example, the Iowa Supreme Court affirmed the forfeiture of a $9,000 automobile used during a burglary. In another case, the Iowa Court of Appeals (in an unpublished ruling) rejected the state's effort to take a $30,000 truck used by a person serving as the lookout during a drug transaction (*In re Property Seized from Flores,* 2006).

[98] *See State v. Klawonn* (2000); *State v. Rohm* (2000).

[99] The court rejected another as-applied challenge concerning a juvenile offender's $150,000 victim-restitution order in *State v. Breeden* (2017), handed down the same day as *Richardson.* In both cases, the court emphasized that it was not determining whether Section 910.3B "could be unconstitutional as applied to a juvenile homicide offender because of her specific payment plan" or whether "a juvenile homicide offender could show a restitution payment plan so deprives her of the opportunity for rehabilitation as to undermine the guarantees of" *State v. Ragland* (2013), *State v. Lyle* (2014), and other cases discussed below concerning juvenile offenders' rights under Section 17's Cruel and Unusual Punishments Clause.

Cruel and unusual punishments.

In 1962, the U.S. Supreme Court held that the Eighth Amendment's identically worded ban on cruel and unusual punishments applies to the states through the Due Process Clause of the Fourteenth Amendment (*Robinson v. California*). Prior to that ruling, the Iowa Supreme Court often paid little regard to federal precedent in its Section 17 cases. In 1922, for example, it almost exclusively cited other state courts' rulings when holding that execution by hanging is a permissible form of punishment for first-degree murder (*State v. Burris*). In 1955, the Iowa court did not cite any federal cases at all when holding that it was not unreasonable—and thus not unconstitutional—for the General Assembly to punish bribery in athletics contests with a fine of up to $10,000 and imprisonment for a period of up to ten years (*State v. Di Paglia*). The U.S. Supreme Court's 1962 ruling in *Robinson* changed things dramatically. In its first wave of post-incorporation Section 17 cases, the Iowa Supreme Court was highly reluctant—"in part out of a desire for consistency"—to ignore the federal Supreme Court's interpretation of the Eighth Amendment (*State v. Ramirez*, 1999). When articulating the general framework for its Section 17 analysis, the Iowa court carefully echoed federal precedent, explaining that it should defer substantially to the General Assembly's determination of appropriate punishments, and that a punishment violates Section 17 only if it is "grossly disproportionate" to the crime for which it has been imposed or if it "inflicts torture [or] is otherwise barbaric" (*State v. Cronkhite*, 2000).

In 2009's *State v. Bruegger*, the Iowa Supreme Court announced a move toward somewhat greater analytic independence for Section 17 claims. The court said that it would continue to apply the same legal standards that the federal Supreme Court applies under the Eighth Amendment, unless a defendant successfully argues that Section 17 demands a different framework. Drawing inspiration from its equal protection rulings under Article I, Section 6, however, the court said that it would apply those federal standards "more stringent[ly]," so that "review of criminal sentences for 'gross disproportionality' under the Iowa Constitution [w]ould not be a 'toothless' review." The court then found—in tension with some of the federal Supreme Court cases in place at that time and with some of its own prior rulings—that, at least in "rare" cases, individuals should be allowed to argue that, given the individualized circumstances of their own crimes, the legislatively prescribed punishments they received were grossly disproportionate to their offenses. The court found that the present case—involving a man who had received a twenty-five-year sentence for statutory rape, after he engaged in sexual intercourse at the age of twenty-one with a fifteen-year-old girl who purported to consent—was one of those rare cases, and so remanded for a resentencing hearing.

Three years later, after the federal Supreme Court in *Graham v. Florida* (2010) had further clarified its own analytic principles, the Iowa Supreme

Court held that defendants are *always* permitted to argue that, in light of their individualized circumstances, the punishments they received were grossly disproportionate to their crimes (*State v. Oliver*, 2012). If an individualized assessment suggests that the punishment in a given case does indeed seem grossly disproportionate, a court is then to make intrajurisdictional and interjurisdictional comparisons, looking to see how the defendant's punishment compares to the sentences imposed for other crimes in Iowa and how the defendant's punishment compares to the sentences imposed for the same or similar crimes in other jurisdictions. The court reiterated that the test for gross disproportionality is "more stringent" under Section 17 than it is under the Eighth Amendment. The court also explained that it nevertheless will be rare that an individualized assessment suggests gross disproportionality, and thus it will be rare that a court must make intrajurisdictional and interjurisdictional comparisons. For recent applications of *Oliver*'s framework in cases concerning juvenile offenders—cases in which the state prevailed—see *State v. Propps* (2017) and *State v. Graham* (2017).

Tracking the U.S. Supreme Court's interpretation of the Eighth Amendment, the Iowa Supreme Court held in 2017's *State v. Richardson* that Section 17's Cruel and Unusual Punishments Clause concerns "punishment of a physical nature, such as confinement," and does not concern "punitive financial measures," such as fines and mandatory restitution. "If the cruel and unusual punishment clause also limited fines [and mandatory restitution]," the court explained, "the excessive fines clause would be duplicative and unneeded."

Much of the action under Section 17 in recent years has concerned sentences imposed upon individuals who were juveniles when they committed their crimes. In early cases, the Iowa Supreme Court did not draw a significant line between juveniles and adults. In 1894, for example, the Iowa Supreme Court set aside its reservations about the defendant's "youth" and "lack of mental development" and upheld the death sentence for a boy who had committed murder at the age of sixteen (*State v. Dooley*).[100] Spurred on in part by changes in the U.S. Supreme Court's own jurisprudence, the Iowa court today draws important distinctions between those who commit their crimes while minors and those who do not. A trio of rulings handed down in 2013 were the first in a series of important new milestones in this area of Iowa law. In *State v. Ragland*, the Iowa Supreme Court took a close look at the federal Supreme Court's 2012 declaration in *Miller v. Alabama* that the Eighth Amendment demands an individualized sentencing hearing when determining whether a juvenile offender should be sentenced to life in prison without possibility of parole. The *Ragland* court held that *Miller* applies retroactively and that Section 17 itself makes the same

[100] For a brief history of James Dooley's crime and execution, see Dick Haws, *Iowa and the Death Penalty: A Troubled Relationship (1834–1965)*, ch. 12 (self-published, 2010).

demand as *Miller*. The court further held that Jeffrey Ragland's sentence of a minimum of sixty years in prison for a murder he committed at the age of seventeen was the functional equivalent of a sentence of life in prison without possibility of parole, and that Ragland was thus entitled to an individualized resentencing hearing. In two other rulings handed down the same day, the court held that individualized resentencing hearings were required for an inmate who had been sentenced to a minimum of fifty-two years in prison for crimes he committed at the age of sixteen (*State v. Null*, 2013) and for an inmate who had been sentenced to a minimum of thirty-five years in prison for crimes she committed at the age of seventeen (*State v. Pearson*, 2013). In both cases, the court elaborated on the various factors that a sentencing court should consider, such as the defendant's maturity and capacity for rehabilitation.

Those 2013 rulings helped set the stage for three landmark decisions. In 2014's *State v. Lyle*, the court declared—over the dissent of three justices—that in *all* cases involving defendants who were minors when they committed their crimes, Section 17 forbids statutorily prescribed mandatory minimum sentences of incarceration; courts cannot be stripped of their discretionary power to sentence juvenile offenders in a manner that is appropriate for those offenders' particular circumstances.[101] The *Lyle* court also recited factors that judges must consider when imposing these sentences. In 2016's *State v. Sweet*—and over the dissent of the same three justices—the court held that Section 17 categorically bans life-without-possibility-of-parole sentences for those who commit their crimes prior to the age of eighteen.[102] As support, the court relied heavily upon the difficulty of determining whether juvenile offenders are irreparably corrupt and thus beyond the likely reach of rehabilitation. That determination is better made, the court said, by parole boards later in offenders' lives.[103] In 2017's *State v. Roby*, the court held that Section 17 does not bar judges themselves from sentencing juvenile offenders to mandatory minimum terms of incarceration. The *Roby* court emphasized, however, that such sentences must be imposed in accordance with the sentencing factors recited in *Lyle*, and the

[101] The *Lyle* ruling triggered resentencing proceedings for dozens of previously sentenced juvenile offenders. In *Breeden v. Iowa Department of Corrections* (2016), the Iowa Supreme Court resolved a statutory dispute about how to calculate the earned-time (or good-behavior) credits for those offenders.

[102] The court decided subsequent cases on comparable grounds. *State v. Louisell* (2015); *State v. Querrey* (2015).

[103] In 2015's *State v. Seats*, the court had declined to say whether Section 17 categorically bans *all* sentences of life in prison without possibility of parole for juvenile offenders. The court instead chose to underscore the various factors that a sentencing court must consider before imposing that particular sentence. Justice Hecht filed a concurring opinion, arguing that Section 17 does categorically prohibit sentencing juveniles to life without parole, while the three dissenters—Justices Mansfield, Waterman, and Zager—argued that Section 17 permits such sentences as a general matter and permitted such a sentence in this particular case.

court elaborated on those factors in ways emphasizing their juvenile-favoring stringency.[104]

The Iowa Supreme Court is continuing to work out the details of its Section 17 juvenile-sentencing jurisprudence. In *State v. Propps* (2017), a plurality of the court concluded that, "when an indeterminate sentence is given that contains no mandatory minimum sentence and allows a juvenile to be immediately eligible for parole," Section 17 is not violated. In these circumstances, Justice Bruce Zager wrote, "the juvenile defendant's behavior in prison dictates when parole will be available—with the potential for immediate parole if rehabilitation, maturity, and reform have been demonstrated." In *State v. Graham* (2017), the court unanimously held that Section 17 permitted a juvenile sex offender to be given a lifetime sentence of parole. The court in *Graham* emphasized that the parole board was statutorily authorized to release the offender from his sentence after a period of ten years. The offender in that case had not challenged the portion of his sentence requiring that his parole extend a minimum of ten years, so the court did not address its constitutional propriety. The court also noted that the facts of the case did not require the justices to "consider the constitutionality of a de facto refusal of the parole board to ever consider release of lifetime parole for juvenile sex offenders."

Section 18.
Eminent domain—drainage ditches and levees.

Private property shall not be taken for public use without just compensation first being made, or secured to be made to the owner thereof, as soon as the damages shall be assessed by a jury, who shall not take into consideration any advantages that may result to said owner on account of the improvement for which it is taken.

The general assembly, however, may pass laws permitting the owners of lands to construct drains, ditches, and levees for agricultural, sanitary or mining purposes across the lands of others, and provide for the organization of drainage districts, vest the proper authorities with power to construct and maintain levees, drains and ditches and to keep in repair all drains, ditches, and levees heretofore constructed under the laws of the state, by special assessments upon the property benefitted thereby. The general assembly may provide by law for the condemnation of such real estate as shall be necessary for the construction and maintenance of such drains, ditches and levees, and prescribe the method of making such condemnation.

---

[104] Over the dissent of the same three justices who dissented in *Lyle* and *Sweet*, the *Roby* court found that the district court had not properly applied the *Lyle* factors when sentencing a juvenile offender. That voting pattern recurred in another case decided the same day, with the 4-3 court requiring resentencing of a juvenile offender in compliance with *Roby*'s elaboration upon the *Lyle* factors (*State v. Majors*, 2017).

Section 18 requires the government to pay for any property that it takes from private owners for the larger community's use, and it also lays out several provisions aimed at facilitating the construction and maintenance of drains, ditches, and levees. In the draft constitution that emerged from the 1844 convention, the entirety of what is numbered today as Section 18 closely tracked the language of the Fifth Amendment to the U.S. Constitution, simply stating that "[p]rivate property shall not be taken for public use, without just compensation." Iowa's first constitution, produced by the convention of 1846, retained that same phrasing.[105] The delegates to the 1857 convention put the first paragraph of Section 18 into the form it takes today. Iowa voters added Section 18's second paragraph in 1908.[106]

In an early session of the 1857 convention, the Committee on the Preamble and Bill of Rights announced that it proposed to add a provision to Section 18 stating:

> Private roads may be opened in the manner prescribed by law, but in every case, the necessity of the road, and the amount of damages sustained by the opening thereof, shall first be determined by a jury of disinterested free-holders; and such amount, together with the expenses of the proceedings, shall be paid by the person or persons benefitted thereby, before said road shall be opened.[107]

When that proposal came to the floor for discussion, Allamakee County's John Clark—a lawyer who had come to Iowa from New York—endorsed the committee's amendment, citing a New York case in which a court had held that the state constitution's public-use requirement barred the government from taking private property to build a private road. Amos Harris—a lawyer from Appanoose County—indicated that he intended to offer an alternative amendment at a later time. Perhaps believing they might find Harris's amendment more appealing, the delegates rejected the committee's proposal.[108]

One week later, aided by a couple of drafting suggestions made during the course of the delegates' discussion, Harris proposed amending Section 18 to read as it now appears in its first paragraph.[109] He said that he had seen great

---

[105] Iowa Const. of 1846, art. II, § 18.

[106] The Iowa Supreme Court had previously upheld legislation establishing a process by which landowners could prompt the construction of drains on other people's land. *See, e.g., Oliver v. Monona County* (1902). Fears persisted, however, that railroads or other landowners might ultimately prevail in a case challenging such processes, and so the amendment was adopted to put the matter to rest. *See* "Law for Drainage Is Constitutional; Amendment of Constitution Nov. 8 Settles It," *Des Moines Register and Leader*, Dec. 2, 1908, at 1.

[107] *1857 Debates, supra* note 3, vol. 1, p. 64.

[108] *1857 Debates, supra* note 3, vol. 1, pp. 126–27.

[109] *1857 Debates, supra* note 3, vol. 1, p. 202. In several places, the convention records indicate that the proposed (and ultimately approved) phrase was "secured to be paid," not "secured to be made." *Id.* at pp. 202, 205; *1857 Journal, supra* note 3, p. 113. By the end of the convention, however, the phrase had changed to "secured to be made." *1857 Debates, supra* note 3, vol. 2, p. 1007.

injustices committed under an Iowa statute that permitted government officials to take private property for the purpose of building county roads while reducing the compensation paid to the property owners by the value of any benefits that the owners received as a result of the road's construction—a formula that sometimes resulted in property owners receiving no compensation whatsoever.[110] A road often benefits many people, Harris said, and yet those whose land is taken to build it might find themselves having to pay for the road with their land, while their neighbors receive the road's benefits for free. To illustrate his point, Harris cited a case involving "a poor widow woman, with a large family of children to support," as well as cases from his prior home state of Ohio. Some contended that the Iowa Supreme Court already interpreted the existing constitution to yield the results that Harris's amendment would secure, but Davis County's David Palmer argued that "[w]e do not want to go to the supreme court to ascertain what our Constitution means; we want to see it in the Constitution itself." Alpheus Scott—a real-estate agent from Clayton County—resisted Harris's amendment, saying that many desirable roads would never be built if property owners were entitled to full compensation for the value of the taken land.[111] By the exceptionally close vote of 17 to 16, the delegates approved Harris's amendment.[112]

Takings.

Ever since its 1897 ruling in *Chicago, Burlington & Quincy Railroad Co. v. Chicago*, the U.S. Supreme Court has regarded the requirements of the Fifth Amendment's Takings Clause as essential elements of due process that bind the states under the Fourteenth Amendment. Noting the federal Takings Clause's textual similarity to Section 18's takings provision, the Iowa Supreme Court has said that it generally will follow federal Fifth Amendment precedent unless a party or the court can identify a good reason to depart from that path (*Harms v. City of Sibley*, 2005).

In some instances—such as when acquiring land to build roads—the government launches formal, statutorily prescribed condemnation proceedings pursuant to its power of eminent domain.[113] Any constitutional disputes between the government and property owners in these cases are likely to concern either the amount of compensation owed or whether the government is taking the property "for public use." If the government has not initiated formal condemnation proceedings but a property owner believes that he or she has nevertheless suffered a

[110] Code of Iowa (1851), § 538.

[111] *1857 Debates, supra* note 3, vol. 1, pp. 202–05.

[112] *1857 Journal, supra* note 3, pp. 113–14.

[113] *See generally* Iowa Code chs. 6A, 6B.

taking, the owner can file an "inverse condemnation" claim to try to recover the compensation that he or she believes the government owes.[114] In these cases, the constitutional focus is chiefly on (1) whether there is a constitutionally protected property interest at stake, (2) whether the government has taken that property interest for public use, and (3) whether the government owes more compensation than the amount, if any, it has already paid (*Bormann v. Board of Supervisors*, 1998). We briefly examine each of those three focal points, in turn.

As a general matter, the property interests protected by American constitutional law "are created and their dimensions are defined by existing rules or understandings that stem from an independent source such as state law—rules or understandings that secure certain benefits and that support claims of entitlement to those benefits" (*Board of Regents v. Roth*, 1972).[115] Under Iowa law, a person's property interests in a given instance may include a wide range of prerogatives, including possessing, accessing, using, enjoying, and disposing of the property and excluding others from it (*Bormann v. Board of Supervisors*, 1998; *Simkins v. City of Davenport*, 1975; *Liddick v. City of Council Bluffs*, 1942). An additional property interest that landowners possess is the right to bring legal action against neighbors who maintain nuisances that interfere with the landowners' use and enjoyment of their property. The Iowa Supreme Court has said, for example, that the government has taken an easement in a person's land—and thus must pay compensation—if the law grants immunity to those who send noxious agricultural odors adrift over that land to a degree rising to the level of a nuisance (*Gacke v. Pork Xtra, L.L.C.*, 2004; *Bormann v. Board of Supervisors*, 1998). A person does not have a property interest, however, if he or she has nothing more than a unilateral expectation of some type of benefit. In *Crippen v. City of Cedar Rapids* (2000), for example, the Iowa Supreme Court held that a private recycling business had not suffered the loss of a property interest when municipalities launched their own curbside recycling operations and thereby diminished the private business's economic prospects.

A "taking" occurs when the government either (1) physically appropriates or invades private property or its low-altitude airspace or (2) regulates private property in an "onerous" manner that "goes too far" (*Harms v. City of Sibley*, 2005).[116] Takings of the physical-appropriation variety are commonly

---

[114] A property owner seeking compensation on an inverse-condemnation claim may file an action for a writ of mandamus to compel condemnation proceedings (*Schaller v. State ex rel. Iowa Department of Natural Resources*, 1995; *Phelps v. Board of Supervisors*, 1973).

[115] *Roth* was a U.S. Supreme Court case concerning the meaning of the term "property" in the Fourteenth Amendment's Due Process Clause. The Court has deployed that same definition when discussing the Fifth Amendment's Takings Clause. *See, e.g.*, *Webb's Fabulous Pharmacies, Inc. v. Beckwith* (1980).

[116] The "goes too far" language traces its roots to the U.S. Supreme Court's landmark ruling in *Pennsylvania Coal Co. v. Mahon* (1922).

called "per se" takings—the government's obligation to pay compensation is triggered no matter how minimal the appropriation and no matter how strong the underlying public purposes (*Kingsway Cathedral v. Iowa Department of Transportation,* 2006; *Fitzgarrald v. City of Iowa City,* 1992; *Lucas v. South Carolina Coastal Council,* 1992). As an example of this type of taking, the *Kingsway Cathedral* court pointed to the U.S. Supreme Court's ruling in *United States v. Causby* (1946), in which the federal government directed its own airplanes to fly low over a property owner's land, thereby diminishing the property's value.

Takings of the onerous-regulation variety are commonly called "regulatory" takings. Just as under federal law, Iowa recognizes two types of regulatory takings: those that are "per se" and those that are not. A "per se" regulatory taking occurs when the government either authorizes a third party to invade an owner's property or the property's low-altitude airspace, or deprives an owner of "all economically beneficial or productive use" of the property (*Bormann v. Board of Supervisors,* 1998; *Loretto v. Teleprompter Manhattan CATV Corp.,* 1982). In *Loretto,* for example—a U.S. Supreme Court case that the Iowa Supreme Court has approvingly cited—a city authorized a television-services company to install cables on the owner's apartment building. The Court found a taking because "[t]he installation involved a direct physical attachment of plates, boxes, wires, bolts, and screws to the building, completely occupying space immediately above and upon the roof and along the building's exterior wall." In *Bormann,* the Iowa Supreme Court found another kind of physical-invasion taking when government officials granted immunity from private nuisance suits to agricultural operations that produced noxious odors. For a compensable physical invasion to occur, the *Bormann* court explained, there need not necessarily be an invasion of "the surface of the land." Governmentally authorized third-party physical invasions have the same legal consequences as physical invasions by the government itself (*Bormann v. Board of Supervisors,* 1998; *Loretto v. Teleprompter Manhattan CATV Corp.,* 1982).

Determining whether a regulatory taking of the non–per se variety has occurred is often more difficult. As a general matter, courts try to distinguish on a case-by-case basis between regulations that unreasonably deprive owners of the use or enjoyment of their property in some substantial way, and reasonable property-regulating exercises of the state's police power that do not constitute takings and thus do not require the payment of compensation (*Kelley v. Story County Sheriff,* 2000). The *Kelley* opinion usefully cites numerous examples of the distinction. To determine on which side of the line a given governmental action falls, a court will conduct a balancing analysis, focusing chiefly on "the collective benefits of the regulatory action," the regulation's economic impact upon the property, the degree to which the regulation interferes with the owner's "investment-backed expectations," and the manner in which the regulation affects the owner's property interests (*Kelley v. Story County Sheriff,* 2000;

Bormann v. Board of Supervisors, 1998).[117] The court has explained that—so long as there has been no permanent physical invasion and no deprivation of all economically beneficial or productive use of the property—a property-affecting regulation will not be deemed a taking requiring compensation if it "substantially advances a legitimate state interest" (*Board of Water Works Trustees v. Sac County Board of Supervisors,* 2017; *Hunziker v. State,* 1994).

No taking of any sort has occurred within the meaning of Section 18 unless the contested governmental action is permanent, continual, or recurring in nature. When a city's construction work damaged a nearby church building, for example, the Iowa Supreme Court held that there had been no taking—and that the church's only remedy lay in a tort claim—because the construction work was temporary in nature (*Kingsway Cathedral v. Iowa Department of Transportation,* 2006). In *Phelps v. Board of Supervisors* (1973), on the other hand, the court held that property owners had a viable takings claim when the presence of a newly installed bridge caused the owners' land to flood on an "intermittent but inevitably recurring" basis. What if the contested government action—such as a physical invasion of the property or a deprivation of the property's economic benefits—is not permanent in nature but is scheduled to continue for a period of years? In *Brakke v. Iowa Department of Natural Resources* (2017)—a case concerning a five-year quarantine imposed upon private property where diseased deer had been found—the court said that such an action will not be deemed a *per se* taking, but will be a compensable taking if the case-by-case factors identified in *Kelley* and similar rulings indicate that a taking has occurred.

With respect to Section 18's "public use" requirement, the Iowa Supreme Court has said that "[c]ourts should not substitute their judgment for the legislature's judgment as to what constitutes a public use unless the use is palpably without reasonable foundation" (*CMC Real Estate Corp. v. Iowa Department of Transportation,* 1991). After the U.S. Supreme Court handed down its controversial ruling in *Kelo v. City of New London* (2005), for example—finding that a city's use of its eminent domain power to acquire private property for private economic development was a valid public use under the Fifth Amendment—it was the General Assembly, not the Iowa Supreme Court, that led the effort to give Iowa's landowners greater protection.[118]

When determining the amount of compensation that is "just," the decision-maker is to set a monetary value on what the property owner has lost as a result of the taking, rather than on what the government or others have gained (*Aladdin, Inc. v. Black Hawk County,* 1997). When the government has acquired full ownership of a given piece of property, it usually is required to pay compensation in

[117] *Kelley, Bormann,* and similar cases rely heavily upon the U.S. Supreme Court's 1978 ruling in *Penn Central Transportation Co. v. New York City* for the factors that courts should consider when determining on a case-by-case basis whether a regulatory taking has occurred.

[118] Iowa Code §§ 6A.21, 6A.22, 6A.24.

an amount equal to that property's fair market value, taking into account such things as the future uses to which the property could be put and any other features of the property that a seller might bring to a prospective buyer's attention (*Kurth v. Iowa Department of Transportation*, 2001). If there is no market for the unique property at issue, then the decision-maker is to ascertain the property's actual or intrinsic value (*Comstock v. Iowa State Highway Commission*, 1963). As Section 18 explicitly declares by virtue of Amos Harris's amendment at the 1857 convention, the amount of compensation owed cannot be reduced by the value of any benefits that the property owner receives as a result of the uses to which the government puts the taken land (*Britton v. D. M., O. & S. R. Co.*, 1882).

As one would expect, Section 18 does not bar the state from collecting taxes for public purposes (*McLeland v. Marshall County*, 1925).

Drains, ditches, and levees.

The General Assembly has exercised the power described in Section 18's second paragraph. Chapter 468 of the Iowa Code, for example, contains many of the state's statutory provisions concerning drainage districts and levees. For a discussion of the history and purposes of drainage districts, as well as a discussion of the law pertaining to those districts' operation and scope of liability, see *Board of Water Works Trustees v. Sac County Board of Supervisors* (2017). The court in that case explained, for example, that "a century's worth of precedent . . . precludes any remedy against drainage districts other than mandamus."

Section 19.
Imprisonment for debt.

No person shall be imprisoned for debt in any civil action, on mesne or final process, unless in case of fraud; and no person shall be imprisoned for a militia fine in time of peace.

Section 19 condemns the practice of jailing individuals for failing to pay their private debts. With only a couple of inconsequential typographical differences, Section 19 still stands today in the same form that the delegates to the Territory of Iowa's 1844 convention placed it. The only documented, significant discussion of the provision at any of Iowa's three constitutional conventions occurred in 1857, when Davis County's David Palmer suggested striking the phrase "unless in case of fraud." Section 19 bars imprisonment for debts in *civil* actions, Palmer said, and so—even without the text's fraud provision—the General Assembly retains the power to authorize imprisonment for those who commit the *crime* of fraud. Palmer said that, as he understood the law, "[i]n civil suits we never charge fraud." Contrary to Palmer's belief, however, Iowa did recognize the civil tort of fraud.[119] Perhaps recognizing Palmer's error and wishing to permit imprisonment for debt in civil fraud actions, the delegates rejected Palmer's proposed change without recorded discussion.[120]

The Iowa Supreme Court's leading ruling on Section 19 came in 1983's *In re Marriage of Lenger*. In that case, a man allegedly failed to pay his former wife the money he owed her under a property-settlement provision of the court decree dissolving their marriage. In response to the man's failure to pay, the woman launched contempt proceedings—proceedings that presented her former husband with the threat of jail time. The trial court dismissed the contempt action, finding it inconsistent with Section 19, but the Iowa Supreme Court reversed. Citing alimony and child-support cases from half a century earlier (*Roach v. Oliver*, 1933; *Roberts v. Fuller*, 1930), the court said that the contempt action here was aimed, at least in part, at punishing the man's alleged failure to obey a court order. The man's obligation to obey the financial provisions of the court's dissolution decree, the court said, was not a "debt" within the meaning of Section 19. As the court put it in *Roberts* and reiterated in *Lenger*, the word "debt" in Section 19 contemplates "an obligation growing out of a business transaction."

The woman in *Lenger* had alleged that her former husband was financially capable of obeying the court's order but had willfully refused to pay what he owed. Notwithstanding the court's narrow interpretation of the term "debt," the outcome in that case might have been different if the man had been indigent and unable to pay. In 1971's *State v. Hopp*, for example, the Iowa court stressed the difference between a parent who willfully refuses to pay court-ordered child support—and thus can face jail time for contempt—and a parent who lacks the financial resources necessary to obey the court's order and whose jail time thus would be the result of his or her indigence. That distinction was also evident in the court's 1938 ruling in *State ex rel. Bissell v. DeVore*, finding a violation of Section 19 when a trial court jailed a man for failing to financially support a child born out of wedlock. The father in that case had no demonstrated ability to pay the amount ordered, he had not yet even had an opportunity to comply with the court's order at the time he was jailed, and no contempt charges had ever been brought against him.

Federal law reinforces those cases' distinction between people who have the financial resources necessary to honor their court-ordered financial obligations and those who do not. The U.S. Supreme Court has said that federal due process and equal protection principles bar a court from deeming a fine the appropriate punishment in a given criminal case but then imprisoning the individual when he fails to pay the government what he owes, unless there is evidence that

---

[119] *Holmes v. Clark* (1860) (stating that the "test of what constitutes fraud in *fact* has been so long and well established that we do not feel it necessary to enter upon the discussion again").

[120] *1857 Debates*, *supra* note 3, vol. 1, p. 129.

he has the necessary financial resources but willfully refuses to surrender them (*Bearden v. Georgia*, 1983). If pressed on the point today, the Iowa Supreme Court might similarly say that it is the state constitution's due process and equal protection provisions—and not Section 19—that require the distinction drawn in cases like *Hopp* and *Bissell*.

One of the Iowa Supreme Court's older Section 19 cases appears difficult to defend under the law as we understand it today. In 1910, the court ruled in *Hubbell v. Higgins* that Section 19 barred jailing hotel owners who committed the misdemeanor of refusing to pay a governmental inspection fee. The hotel owners did not argue that they lacked the financial resources necessary to pay the fee, so let us assume that indigence was not an issue. So long as they were being jailed for committing a criminal offense, it is not easy to see how Section 19 posed any obstacle. Indeed, the court has even said that Section 19 does not bar jailing a person who, after being convicted of a crime, refuses to obey a court order to pay some of the costs of the criminal proceeding, on top of any fine that is levied as part of his or her punishment (*Boyer v. Kinnick*, 1894). In 1958's *City of Fort Madison v. Bergthold*, the court suggested that it decided *Hubbell* as it did because that case concerned the crime of failing to pay an inspection fee, rather than the crime of failing to pay a tax or license fee. Although it is clear that Section 19 does not forbid imprisonment for the latter, it is far less clear why one should conclude that Section 19 forbids imprisonment for the former. The *Bergthold* court itself did not try to explain the distinction. The better view may be simply that *Hubbell* was wrongly decided.

Section 19's provision regarding "militia fine[s] in time of peace" has never been the subject of reported appellate litigation.

Section 20.
Right of assemblage—petition.

The people have the right freely to assemble together to counsel for the common good; to make known their opinions to their representatives and to petition for a redress of grievances.

Echoing the U.S. Constitution's First Amendment, Section 20 protects rights that are central to full engagement in the political process. With the exception of using the word "counsel" rather than "consult"—a change that was made at the 1846 convention—Section 20 still stands in the same form that the delegates to the Territory of Iowa's 1844 convention placed it. Without any documented debate, the delegates to the 1857 convention declined William Penn Clarke's suggestion that they return to using the term "consult" and that they declare that people have the right to assemble only "in a peaceable manner."[121]

[121] *1857 Debates, supra* note 3, vol. 1, pp. 129, 208.

The latter change would have brought the text of Section 20 more fully into line with the First Amendment, which protects "the right of the people peaceably to assemble."

Although the rights it protects are vital to the democratic process, Section 20 has been the focus of very little appellate litigation. (At least in part, that might be due to the fact that, through the Fourteenth Amendment's Due Process Clause, the First Amendment's provisions concerning speech, assembly, and petition all apply to state officials.[122]) In 1925's *Kemble v. Weaver*, the Iowa Supreme Court held that Section 20's Petition Clause does not bar an entity from paying attorneys to lobby the General Assembly on its behalf. In 1939's *Carey v. District Court of Jasper County*, the Iowa court held that Section 20 does not entitle union members to use force and intimidation when picketing an employer.

In a third case—1968's *State v. Elliston*—the court rejected a facial attack on a criminal statute barring three or more people from gathering together to do an act "in a violent or tumultuous manner." It is not clear, however, whether the court regarded the defendant's claim as arising under the First Amendment or under Section 20; the majority opinion suggests that the justices were focused on the First Amendment, though the dissenting opinion (albeit only in passing) quotes comments made in the proceedings below indicating that the defendant's facial attack was grounded in both the federal and state constitutions. The ruling's lack of precision on this point is a hallmark of an era in which state constitutions were commonly ignored altogether when the U.S. Constitution contained comparable language.

Section 21.
Attainder—ex post facto law—obligation of contract.

No bill of attainder, ex post facto law, or law impairing the obligation of contracts, shall ever be passed.

Section 21's three clauses restrict the government's ability to punish individuals without judicial proceedings, to increase the criminal consequences of conduct after that conduct has already occurred, or to interfere with existing contractual relationships. The text of Section 21 carefully tracks that of the U.S. Constitution, which declares in Article I, Section 10, that "[n]o State shall . . . pass any Bill of Attainder, ex post facto Law, or Law impairing the Obligation of Contracts." With the inconsequential exception of using the plural form of the word "contract," Section 21 still stands in the same form in which it appeared in the draft constitution produced by the Territory of Iowa's 1844 convention. At the 1857 convention, Des Moines County's Jonathan Hall

---

122 *Gitlow v. New York* (1925) (speech); *De Jonge v. Oregon* (1937) (assembly); *Edwards v. South Carolina* (1963) (petition).

suggested inserting the phrase "or right of property" after the word "contracts." When making that suggestion, he accurately anticipated one of the angles of attack his opponents would take—namely, that the addition would undesirably bar the General Assembly from providing for the confiscation of intoxicating beverages that were produced or sold in violation of state law. Under Iowa law at that time, the sale of liquor was sharply restricted; illegally sold liquor was subject to confiscation, together with "the vessels, furniture, and other goods found" in the establishments where the violations occurred.[123] Hall said that he hoped delegates would not vote against the amendment "because they imagine they smell something in it intended to affect the prohibitory liquor law," but Muscatine County's John Parvin and Henry County's Rufus Clarke promptly rose to say they would vote against Hall's amendment for precisely that reason. Jefferson County's James Wilson added that the amendment would prevent the government from eliminating all nuisances that take the form of property and might even bar the government from imposing fines for criminal offenses. The delegates decisively rejected Hall's proposal by a vote of 7 to 26.[124]

Bills of attainder.

Drawing no perceptible distinction between the state and federal constitutions' bans on bills of attainder, the Iowa Supreme Court routinely invokes federal precedent when adjudicating Section 21 claims. Citing the U.S. Supreme Court, the Iowa court has said that "[a] bill of attainder is a legislative determination that metes out punishment to a particular individual or a designated group of persons without a judicial trial" (*State v. Swartz,* 1999). A legislative enactment constitutes a bill of attainder if three elements are present: "specificity as to the target of the legislation, imposition of punishment, and the lack of a judicial trial" (*State v. Phillips,* 2000). With respect to the second of those three elements, the court's inquiry focuses on the General Assembly's intentions. In *Atwood v. Vilsack* (2006), for example, the Iowa Supreme Court found that the legislature had not intended to punish—and thus did not put Section 21's ban on bills of attainder into play—when it denied bail to persons in custody awaiting a determination of whether they should be civilly committed as sexually violent predators. Similarly, the court ruled in *State v. Swartz* (1999) that Section 21 did not bar the General Assembly from making it a crime for previously convicted felons to possess firearms. Relying on federal precedent, the court said that the firearms ban was not enacted for the purpose of punishing convicted felons.

The *Swartz* ruling can also be justified by the absence of the third feature of bills of attainder—a lack of judicial process. The convicted felons in that case had obtained the benefits of judicial process when they were first convicted of

---

[123] Code of Iowa (1851), §§ 924–936.

[124] *1857 Debates, supra* note 3, vol. 1, pp. 208–09; *1857 Journal, supra* note 3, p. 115.

committing felonies, and would receive those benefits again if prosecuted for illegally possessing firearms. The court made this very point in *Wright v. Iowa Department of Corrections* (2008), citing *Swartz* on its way to upholding residency restrictions on those who previously had been convicted of sex offenses. The court upheld those same residency restrictions against subsequent attacks in *State v. Willard* (2008) and *Formaro v. Polk County* (2009). In *Willard*, the court noted the absence of both the second and third elements—the challenger received the benefits of judicial process when he was prosecuted for violating the residency restrictions, and, in any event, those restrictions were not imposed for the purpose of punishment. In *Formaro*, the court declined to reach the challenger's claim that juvenile adjudications do not provide sufficient judicial process to satisfy Section 21. Instead, the court rejected the challenge on the ground that the residency restrictions were not intended to be punitive.

Ex post facto laws.

To date, the Iowa Supreme Court has treated the state and federal constitutions' bans on ex post facto laws interchangeably, routinely citing both Iowa and federal precedent for the meaning of each. Citing the U.S. Supreme Court and Iowa's own precedent, the Iowa court explained in 2009's *State v. Iowa District Court* that both constitutional texts forbid

> any statute which punishes as a crime an act previously committed, which was innocent when done, which makes more burdensome the punishment for a crime, after its commission, or which deprives one charged with crime of any defense available according to law at the time when the act was committed.

The common denominators in all three of those scenarios are (1) the enactment of a punitive law that works to offenders' disadvantage and (2) retroactive application of that law to conduct that occurred prior to the law's enactment. In the *Iowa District Court* case, for example, a prisoner complained about the fact that, after he had been convicted of a sexual offense, the General Assembly passed a statute barring sex offenders from reducing their periods of incarceration by earning good-time credits unless they satisfactorily participated in a sex-offender treatment program. The court found a violation of the state and federal constitutions because the statute applied retroactively and made the prisoner's punishment "more onerous." In 2010's *State v. Lathrop*, the court similarly found a violation of Section 21 when a defendant was sentenced to lifetime parole for sex offenses that he committed prior to the sentencing statute's enactment. In 2003's *State v. Piper* and 2000's *State v. Corwin*, the court held that Section 21 did not allow the state to enforce a newly adopted victim-restitution statute against convicted felons whose crimes predated the statute.

In a number of cases, the Iowa Supreme Court has found no violation of Section 21 because the challenged laws at issue were not punitive in either purpose or effect, and thus did not bring the Ex Post Facto Clause into play. In *Formaro v. Polk County* (2009), for example, the court upheld newly imposed residency restrictions on previously convicted sex offenders; in *Schreiber v. State* (2003), the court upheld mandatory DNA sampling for those who had previously been convicted of specified felonies; in *State v. Oliver* (1998), the court upheld the retroactive application of a statute requiring certain classes of convicted criminals to pay a $100 parole-enrollment fee; and in *State v. Pickens* (1997), the court upheld a newly adopted statute requiring previously convicted sex offenders to register as such. In each of those cases, the court found that the purpose and effect of the challenged laws were to achieve societal purposes other than punishment.

One particularly instructive pair of cases concerned the revocation of licenses to drive. In 1998's *State v. Flam,* the court upheld the revocation of a driver's license based upon the defendant's repeated convictions for operating a motor vehicle while intoxicated. Those convictions had occurred during a time when a more lenient statutory regime was in place, but the court found no violation of Section 21 because the purpose of the revocation was to protect the public, rather than to punish a repeatedly intoxicated driver. In 1995's *Hills v. Iowa Department of Transportation,* however, the court found a violation of the Ex Post Facto Clause when the government revoked the driver's license of a person who, prior to the revocation statute's enactment, was convicted of possessing marijuana. The *Hills* court concluded that the revocation in that case was punitive because the connection between traffic safety and mere drug possession was "at most indirect."

Impairing the obligation of contracts.

As with Section 21's other two clauses, the Iowa Supreme Court regards the Impairment of Contracts Clause and its federal counterpart as coextensive. Emphasizing that Section 21's "prohibition . . . is not absolute and must yield to a reasonable exercise of the police power for the public good," the court has identified three focal points for adjudicating claims under this provision: "(1) [I]f the state law operates as a substantial impairment of a contractual relationship, (2) the state must have a significant and legitimate public purpose behind the regulation, which (3) adjusts the contracting parties' rights and responsibilities based on reasonable conditions appropriate to the public purpose" (*In re Estate of Serovy,* 2006). Because the court's standard of review is notably deferential to the General Assembly, persons challenging legislation under this provision rarely prevail. In *Adair Benevolent Society v. Iowa Insurance Division* (1992), for example, the court upheld a statute barring the operation of benevolent societies that failed to incorporate prior to July 1, 1988. The Adair Benevolent Society—which had operated in Iowa since 1941 and counted approximately 1,500 Iowans among its members—had challenged the statute, saying that it interfered with the contractual relationships into which the Society had entered with its members prior to the statute's adoption in 1967. The court rejected that argument, finding that the statute served the valuable purpose of protecting the public from financially unstable entities. Before the deferential standards recited in *Adair* were firmly in place, successful claims under the Impairment of Contracts Clause were only marginally more common. Appearing to regard the clause's requirements as more rigid than the court perceives them to be today, for example, the court in 1967's *Davenport Osteopathic Hospital Association v. Hospital Service, Inc.*, struck down state-approved changes in the reimbursement rates that a hospital had previously negotiated with Blue Cross.

Section 22.
Resident aliens.

Foreigners who are, or may hereafter become residents of this State, shall enjoy the same rights in respect to the possession, enjoyment and descent of property, as native born citizens.

By promising that Iowa would protect an array of property rights, Section 22 served as part of the young state's effort to entice immigrants to settle within Iowa's borders. At the Territory of Iowa's 1844 convention, the delegates unanimously approved the motion by Lee County's Henry Salmon that they include a provision in the Bill of Rights reading as one sees Section 22 here, but without the phrase "or may hereafter become."[125] That omitted phrase was added at the convention of 1846. The records from that convention do not explicitly state the reason for the addition, though the delegates presumably simply wished to make clear that a person did not have to be an Iowa resident at the time of the constitution's ratification in order to obtain Section 22's benefits.[126]

At the 1857 convention, Section 22's existing text was not controversial. What *was* controversial—and what sparked a remarkable exchange—was Rufus Clarke's ultimately unsuccessful motion to insert the phrase "and other persons" after the opening word "foreigners," in order to help secure the rights of racial minorities who were born in the United States but were not legally regarded as full-fledged citizens.[127] The delegates' discussion of Clarke's proposal is chronicled in Part I.

In the years that followed, Section 22 was largely uncontroversial. The only modern case to touch upon Section 22 at any length is 2005's *Sanchez v. State*, in which illegal aliens challenged Iowa's refusal to allow them to obtain drivers' licenses. The challengers obliquely argued that drivers' licenses are property

[125] *1844 and 1846 Fragments, supra* note 3, p. 41.

[126] *1846 Journal, supra* note 3, p. 35.

[127] *1857 Debates, supra* note 3, vol. 1, pp. 129–38.

within the meaning of Section 22, but the court found that they had waived that argument by failing to develop it more fully in their court filings.

There are only a few older Section 22 cases. In 1852, the Iowa Supreme Court ruled in *Stemple v. Herminghouser* that Section 22 did not entitle noncitizens who lived in Prussia to inherit property from their father who died in Iowa, because Section 22's inheritance benefits only extend to noncitizens who reside in Iowa at the time of the testator's death. In 1866's *Purczell v. Smidt*, the Iowa court unsurprisingly held that Section 22 does not limit the General Assembly's power to grant property rights to nonresident aliens; the court accordingly upheld legislation that the General Assembly had enacted in *Stemple*'s wake. In 1922, the court ruled in *Breuer v. Beery* that, under Section 22, a German citizen who resided in Iowa was entitled to inherit from his deceased American wife, even though the United States was at war with Germany at the time.

Section 23.
Slavery—penal servitude.

There shall be no slavery in this State; nor shall there be involuntary servitude, unless for the punishment of crime.

In language that the U.S. Constitution's Thirteenth Amendment would largely echo upon its ratification in 1865, Section 23 categorically bans slavery, in keeping with Iowa's entry into the Union as a free state (discussed in Part I). Section 23 also bans involuntary servitude, except as a means of punishing convicted criminals. The text produced by the conventions of 1844 and 1846 stated that "[n]either slavery nor involuntary servitude, unless for the punishment of crimes, shall ever be tolerated in this State." At the 1857 convention, Jefferson County's James Wilson pointed out that, under that phrasing, slavery was permissible so long as it was imposed upon convicted criminals. (Wilson was a young lawyer who later would serve terms in the state legislature, the United States House of Representatives, and the United States Senate, and would co-author the Thirteenth Amendment.) Wilson proposed redrafting the provision in the form that Section 23 takes today, declaring that slavery is categorically banned. The delegates accepted Wilson's proposal without any documented debate.[128]

With the ratification of the Thirteenth Amendment, Section 23 has not often been the focus of appellate litigation. In 1886, the Iowa Supreme Court ruled in *Martin v. Blattner* that imprisoning a person for disobeying a court's injunction—and for thereby committing contempt of court—would not amount to an unconstitutional "servitude" within the meaning of Section 23. Distinguishing *Blattner* half a century later, the court held in *Flannagan v. Jepson* (1916) that Section 23 *does* prohibit sentencing such a person to hard labor, because contempt of that

[128] *1857 Debates, supra* note 3, vol. 1, p. 209.

sort is not itself a crime and thus does not fall within the narrow realm in which Section 23 permits involuntary servitude.

The circumstances were quite different in 2008's *State v. McKinney.* In that case, the state had confined Nathanial McKinney for fifty-three days as a material witness in a murder investigation; prosecutors had feared McKinney would flee to a place beyond the reach of the state's subpoena power, and so held him until the court finally ordered his release. The state compensated McKinney at the statutory material-witness rate of $40 for each day he had been confined. McKinney argued that he was entitled to be paid at the minimum-wage rate for each hour he was held, and that paying him only $40 per day amounted to involuntary servitude in violation of Section 23 and the Thirteenth Amendment. Observing that McKinney had not proposed any reason why the court should interpret those two constitutional texts differently, the court proceeded on the assumption that they are coextensive. Citing federal precedent, the court found that providing testimony in court proceedings is an essential public duty that each person owes to the larger community, and that compelling a person to perform that duty, "even under threat of contempt or criminal sanctions, does not violate the prohibition against involuntary servitude."

Section 24.
Agricultural leases.

No lease or grant of agricultural lands, reserving any rent, or service of any kind, shall be valid for a longer period than twenty years.

Added to the Iowa Constitution by the delegates to the state's 1857 convention, Section 24 limits the period in which land may be leased or granted for agricultural purposes. Henry County's Rufus Clarke proposed the addition, saying simply that New York had adopted a similar provision in response to "the anti-rent difficulties in that State" and that "the provision must commend itself to the mind of every member of this body."[129] The delegates accepted Clarke's proposal without documented debate, presumably in an effort to ensure the productive use of farmland and to avoid the kinds of violent disputes that had beset regions of New York.[130]

The Iowa Supreme Court has decided a handful of Section 24 cases. A few of those rulings concern the meaning of the phrase "agricultural lands." In 1961's *Trustees of Green Bay Levee & Drainage District No. 2 v. Alexander*, the court held that an agreement falls within Section 24's reach only if it is "a contract for the

---

129 *1857 Debates, supra* note 3, vol. 1, p. 213. *See* N.Y. Const. of 1846, art. I, § 14.

130 *Stephens v. Reynolds* (N.Y. 1852) (discussing New York's reasons for adopting the provision); Note, "Iowa Constitution—Twenty-Year Limitation on Agricultural Leases," 39 *Iowa Law Review* 486, 486–88 (1954) (discussing the anti-rent eruptions that set the stage for New York's provision).

possession and profits of [agricultural] land." The court held that the provision thus did not limit the permissible length of a contract setting the maximum rate at which land could be assessed for drainage-district purposes. In 1995's *Howard v. Schildberg Construction Co.*, the court held that a lease of land is not subject to Section 24's time limitation if the lease is entirely for nonagricultural purposes (such as for mining, as in this case), even if the land is suitable for farming or other agricultural uses. The court thereby aligned itself with rulings in Michigan, Montana, South Dakota, and North Dakota. In 2016's *Iowa Arboretum, Inc. v. Iowa 4-H Foundation*, the court was asked to determine "whether incidental agricultural use of land leased for a nonagricultural purpose makes land agricultural for [Section 24] purposes." That case concerned a ninety-nine-year lease of three hundred acres of land, most of which were devoted to the nonagricultural purpose of maintaining an arboretum in accordance with the intention of the parties, but a few of which were farmed. The court concluded that Section 24 did not apply to the lease because the parties had entered the lease for a nonagricultural purpose.

Other cases concern the contours of Section 24's twenty-year limitation. In 1979's *Casey v. Lupkes*, the constitutional debate concerned whether a lease of farmland was categorically invalid or was instead valid for twenty years, where the parties had contractually agreed that the lease would last forty-five years or until the death or disability of the tenants, whichever came first. Seizing upon textual differences between New York's and Iowa's constitutional provisions, the court found that the lease was not categorically invalid, but was instead constitutionally limited to a twenty-year period. In 2016's *Gansen v. Gansen*, the court confronted an agricultural lease that initially ran for five years and then automatically renewed for additional five-year terms unless the tenant opted out. The court held that the lease was valid at its inception but was invalid once the twenty-year mark was reached, and that both lessors and lessees are entitled to enforce Section 24's limitation.

Section 25.
Rights reserved.

This enumeration of rights shall not be construed to impair or deny others, retained by the people.

Unmistakably echoing the U.S. Constitution's Ninth Amendment, Section 24 was not controversial at any of Iowa's constitutional conventions; it still stands in the same form that the delegates to the Territory of Iowa's 1844 convention placed it.

Like its counterpart in the U.S. Constitution, Section 25 sits at the intersection of opposing forces. On the one hand, drafters of constitutional rights naturally worry that, by specifically listing a collection of rights, a future court will say that people have no rights other than those explicitly named, and that important rights will thus fall through the system's cracks. On the other hand, if courts take provisions like Section 25 as a license to vindicate any rights they please, then the balance of power in our constitutional system will swing heavily toward the courts and away from the people's elected political leaders. That shift of power would be especially troubling as a matter of state constitutional law, given the fact that the General Assembly—unlike Congress—possesses *all* legislative power, and not merely those powers that the constitution specifically enumerates (see the discussion of Article III, Section 1 (Legislative Department)).

The Iowa Supreme Court has resolved this quandary by invoking Section 25 only sparingly. If one were to read no further than the court's 1862 ruling in *State ex rel. Burlington & Missouri River Railroad Co. v. County of Wapello*, one might find that fact surprising. The court in that early case appeared willing to put Section 25 to energetic use, stating that the judiciary plays the important role of protecting unenumerated rights that are "founded . . . upon natural justice and common reason." Under the court's modern analytic framework, however, Section 25 plays only a peripheral role in constitutional litigation. The court's 2006 ruling in *Atwood v. Vilsack* nicely illustrates the point. In that case, the General Assembly had denied bail to persons in custody awaiting a determination of whether they should be civilly committed as sexually violent predators. The court held that the denial of bail did not violate Section 25. The court explained that, like Section 1's provision concerning "inalienable rights," Section 25 protects only those "common law rights that pre-existed Iowa's Constitution," and that it protects those rights only by prohibiting "unreasonable" legislative action. Applying that deferential standard of review, the court concluded that "[b]ecause of the State's interests in rehabilitating sexually violent predators and protecting the public, . . . pre-trial detention . . . is a reasonable, and thus constitutional, exercise of legislative power."

Article II

Right of Suffrage

Section 1.
Electors.

Every citizen of the United States of the age of twenty-one years, who shall have been a resident of this state for such period of time as shall be provided by law and of the county in which he claims his vote for such period of time as shall be provided by law, shall be entitled to vote at all elections which are now or hereafter may be authorized by law. The general assembly may provide by law for different periods of residence in order to vote for various officers or in order to vote in various elections. The required periods of residence shall not exceed six months in this state and sixty days in the county.

Subject to various restrictions imposed by federal law,[1] states are free to decide for themselves who may vote in their elections. Responding to that circumscribed flexibility, Section 1 establishes voter-eligibility requirements

[1] *See*, e.g., U.S. Const. amend. XV (stating that the right to vote cannot be denied based on "race, color, or previous condition of servitude"); *id.* amend. XIX (stating that the right to vote cannot be denied "on account of sex"); *id.* amend. XXIV (stating that the right to vote in presidential and congressional elections cannot be denied "by reason of failure to pay any poll tax or other tax"); *id.* amend. XXVI (stating that the right to vote cannot be denied "on account of age" to any citizen eighteen years of age or older); *Harper v. Virginia State Board of Elections* (1966) (holding that the Fourteenth Amendment's Equal Protection Clause bars conditioning the right to vote in state elections upon "wealth or affluence or payment of a fee").

concerning citizenship, age, and residence.[2] Under the state's first constitution, ratified in 1846, the franchise was limited to white males twenty-one years of age and older who had been Iowa residents for at least six months and who had resided in the county where they wished to vote for at least twenty days.[3] The constitution of 1857 extended the required period of county residence to sixty days, but otherwise retained the 1846 requirements. Iowa voters expanded the franchise to non-white males in 1868, the same year that Iowa and the nation ratified the Fourteenth Amendment to the U.S. Constitution and thereby limited states' ability to make racial distinctions among people within their jurisdictions.[4] Women in Iowa did not obtain the right to vote until the U.S. Constitution's Nineteenth Amendment was ratified in 1920. It was not until 1970—in an amendment aimed primarily at giving the General Assembly greater power to establish residency requirements—that Iowans removed the word "male" from Section 1, even though the Nineteenth Amendment had rendered that sex-based restriction inoperative half a century earlier.[5]

Many of the Iowa Supreme Court's Section 1 cases have concerned disputes about residence. In early cases, the court equated residence with domicile, saying that both terms referred to the most recent place where two things coincided: one's physical location and one's intent to make that place one's "fixed" home (*Vanderpoel v. O'Hanlon*, 1880).[6] The General Assembly subsequently declared that, for voting purposes, a person's residence "is the place which the

---

[2] For an early-twentieth-century discussion of the history of voting rights in Iowa, see Carl H. Erbe, "Constitutional Provisions for the Suffrage in Iowa," 22 *Iowa Journal of History & Politics* 163 (1924).

[3] Iowa Const. of 1846, art. III, § 1.

[4] U.S. Const. amend. XIV, § 1.

[5] For a discussion of the lengthy battle in Iowa to secure women's right to vote, see Part I.

[6] *Vanderpoel* concerned the residence of a student at the University of Iowa. The court held that, because the student did not affirmatively intend to remain in Johnson County after he graduated, he had not become a resident of that county. The General Assembly subsequently adopted a standard that is more favorable to college students, allowing them to choose between voting in the county where their college is located and voting in the Iowa county of their more permanent residence. Iowa Code § 48A.5A(5). There is evidence that this legislation is in accord with the preferences of the delegates to the 1844 convention. Those delegates rejected James Gower's motion to include a provision barring college students from voting in the county where their college was located if that county was not the same as the one in which they had previously established their residence. *1844 Journal, supra* Article I, note 3, pp. 59–60. This was apparently a subject of some interest in the Gower family. James's son Robert served as a delegate at the 1857 convention, where he proposed declaring that a person who comes to Iowa for the purpose of attending "any seminary or institution of learning" be unable to acquire an Iowa residence for voting purposes "in consequence of being such student." He said that his proposal was inspired by experiences in his prior home state of Maine—a state that had adopted a constitutional provision aimed at preventing out-of-state students from wielding a dominant influence in local elections. *See* Maine Const. of 1820, art. II, § 1. The delegates narrowly rejected Gower's proposal. *1857 Debates, supra* Article I, note 3, vol. 2, p. 869.

person declares is the person's home with the intent to remain there permanently or for a definite, or indefinite or indeterminable length of time."[7] With its use of the term "definite," the legislature thereby expanded the definition of residence beyond the limits of domicile, to include circumstances in which a person temporarily makes a given place his or her home, but firmly intends to leave at a fixed time in the future, such as upon completing a college degree or fulfilling a contractual obligation at work (*Paulson v. Forest City Community School District*, 1976). The court has never indicated that the legislature's broadened definition violates Section 1, and—given the court's overall orientation, described below—it is unlikely ever to do so.

The Iowa Supreme Court has not provided a precise definition of the term "elections" as it is used here in Section 1, though the court has said that it may include more than the selection of public officials. In *Taylor v. Independent School District* (1917), for example, the court held that the term encompassed a decision by voters about whether to create a consolidated school district. The court has also indicated, however, that citizens do not have a right to vote for *all* public officials; some officials may be appointed, so long as those wielding the appointment power are themselves electorally chosen (*State ex rel. Jones v. Sargent*, 1910). The Iowa court has further held that primary elections—that is, elections to determine political parties' nominees for an upcoming general election—are not "elections" within the meaning of Section 1 (*State ex rel. Hatfield v. Carrington*, 1922).[8] The General Assembly has taken advantage of the resulting flexibility, such as by permitting a person to vote in a primary election even if he or she will not satisfy Section 1's residence requirements until shortly before the upcoming general election.[9]

This section—together with Section 2 of Article I—gives voters the right to write in the names of their preferred candidates if those candidates' names do not already appear on voters' ballots (*Barr v. Cardell*, 1915).[10]

Although the General Assembly cannot alter the age, citizenship, and residence qualifications prescribed by Section 1, it can establish mechanisms—such as a system for requiring would-be voters to register—aimed at ensuring that an individual meets those qualifications (*Edmonds v. Banbury*, 1869). The Iowa Supreme Court's attitude toward such legislation is heavily influenced by the court's recognition that the right to vote, protected by Section 1 and other legal texts, is fundamental:

> Statutory regulation of voting and election procedure is permissible so long as the statutes are calculated to facilitate and secure, rather than subvert or impede, the

[7] Iowa Code § 48A.5(2)(b).

[8] Chapter 43 of the Iowa Code defines and regulates primary elections.

[9] Iowa Code § 43.91.

[10] *See also* Iowa Code §§ 49.31(5), 49.99 (making arrangements for write-in votes).

> right to vote. Among legitimate statutory objects are shielding the elector from the influence of coercion and corruption, protecting the integrity of the ballot, and insuring the orderly conduct of elections. However, because the right to vote is so highly prized, these statutes must be construed liberally in favor of giving effect to the voter's choice, and every vote cast enjoys a presumption of validity (*Devine v. Wonderlich*, 1978).

That orientation was already on display in 1863's *Morrison v. Springer*, in which the court held that Section 1's phrase "county in which he claims his vote" does not require that a person be physically present in his or her home county when voting, and that the legislature thus may devise ways in which Iowans serving in the military may cast their ballots while stationed in other jurisdictions.

When the General Assembly uses the term "elector" or "qualified elector" in legislation, courts presume that the legislation refers to those who possess the qualifications described in Section 1, regardless of whether those individuals have registered to vote (*Piuser v. City of Sioux City*, 1935). When the General Assembly uses the term "voter," however, courts typically say that the legislation refers only to those who have successfully registered (*Buchmeier v. Pickett*, 1966). In at least one instance, legislation made clear that the term "qualified voter" referred to those who met Section 1's requirements, even if they had not registered to vote (*Piuser v. City of Sioux City*, 1935).

Section 2.
Privileged from arrest.

Electors shall, in all cases except treason, felony, or breach of the peace, be privileged from arrest on the days of election, during their attendance at such election, going to and returning therefrom.

Aside from some inconsequential changes in the wording of its final clause, Section 2 continues to stand in the same form that the delegates to the Territory of Iowa's 1844 convention placed it. The provision gives voters the same kind of protection that U.S. Senators and Representatives enjoy under Article I, Section 6, of the U.S. Constitution, which declares that Senators and Representatives "shall in all Cases, except Treason, Felony and Breach of the Peace, be privileged from Arrest during their Attendance at the Session of their respective Houses, and in going to and returning from the same." Section 2 has never been the subject of reported appellate litigation.

Section 3.
From military duty.

No elector shall be obliged to perform military duty on the day of election, except in time of war, or public danger.

Like Section 2 before it, Section 3 reflects the high value placed on individuals' right to vote. The provision's text was borrowed almost verbatim from other states' constitutions.[11] It has never been the focus of reported appellate litigation.

Section 4.
Persons in military service.

No person in the military, naval, or marine service of the United States shall be considered a resident of this State by being stationed in any garrison, barrack, or military or naval place, or station within this State.

Section 4 has not been substantively altered since its initial drafting at the Territory of Iowa's 1844 constitutional convention. In 1928's *Harris v. Harris*—a divorce case in which Section 4 made a peripheral appearance—the Iowa Supreme Court explained that this provision is premised upon the fact that individuals serving in the military often have no control over where they live and thus often cannot meaningfully intend to establish their residency in Iowa. Although Section 4 has never been the focus of reported appellate litigation, it has been the focus of opinions issued by the Office of the Attorney General. That office has sensibly concluded that members of the military may vote while stationed in Iowa, so long as they meet the constitutional and statutory requirements that everyone else wishing to vote must meet.[12] As Attorney General Richard Turner and Attorney General Lawrence Scalise both acknowledged on the occasions just cited, reading Section 4 as an outright ban on voting by those stationed in Iowa would bring the provision into conflict with the Fourteenth Amendment's Equal Protection Clause as interpreted by the U.S. Supreme Court in *Carrington v. Rash* (1965). Section 4 merely declares that being stationed in Iowa is not itself sufficient to establish the Iowa residency that Section 1 of this article requires for would-be voters.

Section 5.
Disqualified persons.

A person adjudged mentally incompetent to vote or a person convicted of any infamous crime shall not be entitled to the privilege of an elector.

Iowa's first constitution, ratified in 1846, denied the franchise to those convicted of "infamous crime[s]," as well as to "idiot[s]" and "insane person[s]." The constitution of 1857 repeated that same formulation. Iowans amended Section 5 in 2008, striking the anachronistic language used to describe those with certain mental disorders and replacing it with a clause that speaks instead about persons "adjudged mentally incompetent."

---

[11] *See, e.g.*, Maine Const. of 1820, art. II, § 3; Mich. Const. of 1835, art. II, § 4.

[12] *See, e.g.*, Op. Iowa Att'y Gen., 1972 WL 262447 (Sept. 27, 1972) (replying to Richard Kemming); Op. Iowa Att'y Gen., 1966 WL 155331 (Apr. 12, 1966) (replying to Edward Samore).

The provision concerning mental incompetence—both as currently framed and as written prior to 2008—has not been the subject of reported appellate litigation. With respect to what Iowans might have had in mind when first placing the terms "idiot" and "insane person" in Section 4, one finds a clue (albeit not a terribly helpful one) in the Iowa Code of 1851. The General Assembly there declared that, when used in any Iowa statute, the term "insane person" included "idiots, non-compotes, lunatics, and distracted persons."[13]

Notice that, as written today, Section 5 speaks only to circumstances in which a person has been "*adjudged* mentally incompetent to vote." A bare assertion by a medical professional, uttered outside the context of a legal proceeding, is not a sufficient basis for stripping a person (on mental-health grounds) of his or her right to vote. The adjudication requirement is consistent with the guidance that the Office of the Attorney General provided in 1985 when asked to explain what the now-abandoned terms "idiot" and "insane person" denoted. The office concluded that those terms "are not commonly understood with sufficient precision to articulate reliable criteria" and that adjudications should thus be central to the process of removing individuals' voting rights.[14] The General Assembly has declared that a court should find a person "incompetent to vote only upon determining that the person lacks sufficient mental capacity to comprehend and exercise the right to vote."[15]

With respect to Section 5's latter clause, the Iowa Supreme Court held in 1916 that an infamous crime was "[a]ny crime punishable by imprisonment in the penitentiary" (*Blodgett v. Clarke*). In more recent years, the court has focused on whether the crime at issue in a given case is a felony, although the court has wavered a bit along the way. Two cases dominate the field. The first, *Chiodo v. Section 43.24 Panel* (2014), featured a battle between Ned Chiodo and Anthony Bisignano to become the Democratic nominee for a seat in the state senate. Chiodo objected to Bisignano's candidacy on the ground that Bisignano had been convicted for the second time of operating a motor vehicle while intoxicated, a crime carrying a possible punishment of up to two years in prison. Because Iowa law states that a person is eligible to hold public office only if he or she is eligible to vote,[16] Chiodo argued that Bisignano was disqualified. Taking a fresh look at the phrase "infamous crime," a plurality of the court rejected *Blodgett*, finding that it swept too broadly. The plurality declined to provide a precise definition of the phrase "infamous crime," but said that "the crime must be classified as particularly serious, and it must be a crime that reveals that voters who commit the crime would tend to undermine

---

[13] Iowa Code § 26 (1851).

[14] Op. Iowa Att'y Gen., 1985 WL 549204 (June 19, 1985) (replying to Louise Whitcome).

[15] Iowa Code § 633.556(1).

[16] Iowa Code §§ 39.26, 39.3(6).

the process of democratic governance through elections." Focusing on the first of those two features, the plurality found that only felonies are sufficiently serious to fall within Section 5's scope, and that Bisignano's crime—an aggravated misdemeanor—thus was not infamous. Concurring in the judgment, Justices Mansfield and Waterman argued that a crime is infamous if and only if it is classified as a felony. Two years later, in *Griffin v. Pate* (2016)—a case asking whether a felony drug offense was an infamous crime—the Mansfield-Waterman view became law. With Justice Zager, those two justices joined an opinion authored by Chief Justice Cady (who also had authored the plurality opinion in *Chiodo*), placing heavy weight on the fact that, in 1994, the General Assembly enacted a statute defining an infamous crime as any crime classified as a felony by state or federal law.[17] The court held that, while the constitutional meaning of the phrase "infamous crime" might evolve in a different direction in the future, there was not yet sufficient evidence of a community standard contrary to the legislature's judgment that all felonies should be deemed infamous crimes.

In 1976, Attorney General Richard Turner concluded that—together with Article III, Section 1 (which ensures the separation of powers) and Article IV, Section 16 (which gives the governor, rather than the legislature, the power to issue pardons)—Section 5 bars the legislature from reinstating the electoral rights of those who have been convicted of infamous crimes.[18]

Section 6.
Ballot.

All elections by the people shall be by ballot.

Section 6 prescribes the means by which state authorities are to solicit voters' choices at elections, although, as we shall see, the provision's requirements are not as rigid as they might first appear. At the Territory of Iowa's 1844 convention, the Committee on Suffrage and Citizenship proposed that all elections be by ballot. Francis Gehon suggested that elections instead be held "viva voce" (by voice), but the delegates rejected that idea by a vote of 24 to 44. By roughly the same margins, they rejected John Taylor's proposal that the General Assembly be given the power to prescribe the manner of voting (25 to 45) and William Galbraith's proposal that Section 6 be deleted entirely (20 to 49).[19] At the 1846 convention, Mahaska County's Stephen Shelleday (who also had served at the 1844 convention) revived the proposal that Gehon had made two years earlier,

---

[17] Act of May 16, 1994, ch. 1180, § 1, 1994 Iowa Acts 538 (codified at Iowa Code § 39.3(8)); Act of May 11, 1994, ch. 1169, § 7, 1994 Iowa Acts 418 (codified at Iowa Code § 48A.6).

[18] Op. Iowa Att'y Gen., 1976 WL 375888 (Mar. 11, 1976) (replying to Clay Spear).

[19] *1844 Journal*, *supra* Article I, note 3, pp. 57–58.

but the delegates rejected it by a vote of 7 to 22.[20] At the 1857 convention, Dubuque County's John Emerson revived Gehon's proposal once again—and the delegates rejected it once again, this time by an unrecorded margin.[21]

Does Section 6 require the use of ballots whenever voters' preferences are officially solicited, or does the term "elections" here have some narrower meaning? In 1891's *Seaman v. Baughman*, the Iowa Supreme Court held that Section 6 did not apply—and that casting votes by raising hands or rising to a standing position was thus permissible—when the residents of a district township gathered to vote on whether to impose a property tax for building a new schoolhouse. The court found that, as used in Section 6, the term "elections" ordinarily refers to "a choice of persons for public offices." In its brief ensuing discussion of legislative intent, however, the court appeared to indicate that the General Assembly may create ballot-necessitating Section 6 elections concerning a broader range of matters.

When Section 6 does apply, the provision's use of the term "ballot" does not compel state authorities to solicit voters' choices using the same balloting techniques that were used when Iowans ratified the constitution in the mid-nineteenth century. Finding that a county could deploy voting machines on Election Day, the court explained in 1906's *United States Standard Voting Machine Co. v. Hobson* that Section 6 "was intended to require and protect the secrecy of the ballot with the general purpose of guarding against intimidation, securing freedom in the exercise of the elective franchise, and reducing to a minimum the incentives to bribery." So long as a voting machine protects voters' privacy, therefore, Section 6 does not bar its use. Section 6 permits government officials to deploy voting machines at general and special elections alike (*McLeland v. Marshall County*, 1925). Attorney General Milton Remley similarly concluded in 1900 that the central purpose of this provision is to ensure that "all elections by the people shall be by that system which enables the voter to express his choice without it being known for whom or what he has voted."[22]

Section 7.
General election.

The general election for state, district, county and township officers in the year 1916 shall be held in the same month and on the same day as that fixed by the laws of the United States for the election of presidential electors, or of president and vice-president of the United States; and thereafter such election shall be held at such time as the general assembly may by law provide.

---

[20] *1846 Journal, supra* Article I, note 3, p. 52. Some sources spell his last name "Shelleday," while others spell it "Shelledy." I follow here the spelling used in the *1844 Journal* and the *1846 Journal*.

[21] *1857 Debates, supra* Article I, note 3, vol. 2, p. 869.

[22] Op. Iowa Att'y Gen., 1900 WL 165748 (Mar. 21, 1900) (replying to William Hawk).

Section 7 has appeared in the Iowa Constitution in two different iterations. The first came in 1884, when Iowa voters declared that state and local elections "shall be held on the Tuesday next after the first Monday in November." In 1916, Iowans amended the provision by placing it in the form it takes today. The provision has not been the focus of reported appellate litigation.

Article III

Of the Distribution of Powers

Section 1.
Departments of government.

The powers of the government of Iowa shall be divided into three separate departments—the Legislative, the Executive, and the Judicial: and no person charged with the exercise of powers properly belonging to one of these departments shall exercise any function appertaining to either of the others, except in cases hereinafter expressly directed or permitted.

Although Montesquieu-inspired separation-of-powers principles "lie[] at the very foundation of [the American] constitutional system" (*State ex rel. White v. Barker*, 1902), the text of the U.S. Constitution never plainly declares that, as a general matter, the three branches of the federal government must remain confined to their respective domains of power. Like many other states before it,[1] Iowa made its commitment to the separation of powers explicit. Section 1 declares that—except as provided elsewhere in the state's constitution—none of the government's three departments may exercise any of the other departments' functions. That formulation was not altered during the course of any of the state's constitutional conventions.[2]

[1] *See*, e.g., Fla. Const. of 1838, art. II, §§ 1, 2; Ky. Const. of 1799, art. I, §§ 1, 2; Mich. Const. of 1835, art. III, § 1; Mo. Const. of 1820, art. II; Tenn. Const. of 1835, art. II, §§ 1, 2.

[2] *See*, e.g., *1857 Debates, supra* Article I, note 3, vol. 1, pp. 37, 510.

The Iowa Supreme Court has explained that Section 1 "is violated if one branch of government purports to use powers that are clearly forbidden, or attempts to use powers granted by the constitution to another branch" (*State v. Phillips*, 2000). Although, as we shall see, things get fuzzier once one moves into the details, the three branches' core powers are easily summarized:

> The legislative power lodged in the general assembly is the power to make, alter or repeal laws. The executive power is the power to execute the laws, and is vested in the governor and the administrative officers of the state and of the several subdivisions thereof. The judicial power is ordinarily defined to be the power to construe and interpret the Constitution and laws, and to apply them and to decide controversies, and is vested in courts (*Hutchins v. City of Des Moines*, 1916).

In numerous cases, the Iowa Supreme Court has held that governmental arrangements violate Section 1.[3] In 1902's *State ex rel. White v. Barker*, for example, the court struck down a statute that gave a district court the power to appoint "trustees to manage and control a system of waterworks belonging to a municipal corporation in advance of litigation or of any dispute concerning their management or control." In *In re Community School District of Malvern* (1959), the court held that Section 1 bars the courts from drawing school districts' boundaries; that responsibility rests with legislative bodies. In *Slater v. Olson* (1941), the court held that the legislature had unconstitutionally intruded upon the executive's power by invoking prior felony convictions as the basis for imposing adverse consequences upon individuals whom the governor had pardoned. In *Klouda v. Sixth Judicial District Department of Correctional Services* (2002), the court held that legislation had impermissibly authorized administrative law judges employed by the executive branch to conduct probation-revocation hearings and to perform other sentencing tasks.[4] In *In the Interest of D.C.V.* (1997), the court struck down a statute that called upon juvenile courts to help devise group-foster-care plans that would not exceed specified cost constraints. In *State ex rel. Klise v. Town of Riverdale* (1953), the court held that legislative bodies—not courts—must be chiefly responsible for determining whether it would be desirable for a city to annex additional land.

Separation-of-powers principles influence the care that courts take when exercising their own power to determine whether legislation is unconstitutional and thus unenforceable. Recognizing that "[i]t is not [judges'] province to pass upon the policy, wisdom, advisability or justice of a statute" and that "[t]he remedy

[3] The Office of the Attorney General has also weighed in on Section 1's requirements, concluding, for example, that sitting state senators and representatives cannot hold positions in agencies that perform executive functions. Op. Iowa Att'y Gen., 1993 WL 122655 (Jan. 27. 1993) (replying to John H. Connors) (citing several prior opinions).

[4] Because of the differences between probation and parole, administrative law judges employed by the executive branch may conduct hearings concerning the latter's revocation (*State v. Wade*, 2008).

for unwise or oppressive legislation within constitutional bounds is not to be found in the courts but by appeal to the legislators" (*Dickinson v. Porter*, 1948), Iowa's courts are reluctant to invalidate lawfully enacted legislation. As the court explained in 1957's *De Berg v. County Board of Education*, the courts' job is "to interpret legislative enactments, but not to establish new legislative provisions by judicial procedure, nor to nullify the clear intention of such enactments." The court has cautioned that the judiciary "should never give construction to a statute which will render it unconstitutional, or which may even create serious doubts as to constitutionality, if any other construction be possible, within the bounds of reason" (*Hunter v. Colfax Consolidated Coal Company*, 1916). In the early case of *Santo v. State* (1855), for example, the Iowa Supreme Court explained that the judiciary's power to strike down statutes "is considered of the most delicate and responsible nature, and is not resorted to, unless the case be clear, decisive, and unavoidable." Presenting another commonly cited formulation, the court said in 1863's *Morrison v. Springer* that it will invalidate legislation only when the constitutional violation is "clear" and "palpable." In a more recent case involving a constitutional claim brought under Section 1 itself, the court said that "[a] party who challenges a statute must negate every reasonable basis upon which we could hold the statute constitutional" and "must show beyond a reasonable doubt that a statute violates the constitution" (*Klouda v. Sixth Judicial District Department of Correctional Services*, 2002). As a matter of constitutional power, however, it is indeed "for the judicial department to determine whether any department has exceeded its constitutional functions" (*Webster County Board of Supervisors v. Flattery*, 1978).

When the General Assembly enacts legislation that purports to affect the outcome of pending or completed litigation, the Iowa Supreme Court draws a line between statutes that are invalid because they constitute "a direct legislative assertion of judicial power" (such as by declaring that courts lack subject-matter jurisdiction in specified pending cases) and statutes that merely constitute "a belated assertion of a power inherently possessed by the legislature" (*Schwarzkopf v. Sac County Board of Supervisors*, 1983). The court's rulings in *Frink v. Clark* (1939) and *McSurely v. McGrew* (1908) provide examples of the legislature unconstitutionally attempting to deprive the courts of jurisdiction in pending cases. One finds an example of a related but different breed of unconstitutional legislation in *City of Sioux City v. Young* (1959), where the facts of the case prompted the court to explain that the General Assembly may not "by a later enactment direct the courts to give an interpretation to a statute different from the one which they have already applied to the same law in a case involving the same claim, the same state of facts and the same parties."

The boundaries between the three branches are not as clear and inflexible as Section 1's insistently separationist language might lead one to believe. The Iowa Supreme Court has said that Section 1 does not draw "rigid boundaries" between the government's three departments (*State v. Hoegh*, 2001), that "the functions of the different departments shade into each other, as do the colors of the rainbow" (*Hutchins v. Des Moines*, 1916), and that "harmonious cooperation among the three branches of government is fundamental to our system of government" (*Webster County Board of Supervisors v. Flattery*, 1978). The court elaborated on this flexibility in *State ex rel. Keasling v. Keasling* (1989):

> In cases where activities of coordinate branches of government rub shoulder-to-shoulder, as they do in child support cases, we must view the concept of separation of powers with a certain amount of pragmatism and cooperation. In areas of concern mutual to separate branches of government, the boundaries of respective authority are not always clearly circumscribed. In those cases, it is permissible, often even desirable, to view the constitutional allocation of authority with an eye toward the common goal.

This flexibility manifests itself in varying ways. It appears in Iowa's articulation and application of the nondelegation doctrine, for example, as discussed in the commentary on the next section of this article. In addition, there are areas of governmental activity in which two or more branches play roles that are closely intertwined. Ensuring the prompt collection of child support—a task involving the efforts of executive and judicial officials—provides one example, as the court explained in *State ex rel. Allee v. Gocha* (1996). Similarly, because the judicial and executive branches share responsibility for deciding whether a child's best interests would be served by terminating parental rights, a juvenile court may direct county attorneys to initiate termination proceedings; such orders, the court has said, pose no real threat that the judicial branch will aggrandize itself at the expense of executive officials (*In the Interest of K.C.*, 2003).

One finds flexibility in other ways, as well. In addition to carrying out acts that are, by their very essence, of the sort that a given branch is chiefly responsible for performing—acts that are legislative in nature if one is talking about the General Assembly, acts that are executive in nature if one is talking about the governor and his or her agencies, and acts that are judicial in nature if one is talking about the courts—a branch may also perform acts that bear the hallmarks of one or both of the other two branches, so long as those acts are necessary to carry out the acting branch's core functions. In *Webster County Board of Supervisors v. Flattery* (1978), for example, the court acknowledged that legislative bodies are usually responsible for deciding how taxpayer funds will be spent, but said that courts possess at least a modicum of inherent power to hire the personnel needed to perform essential judicial functions. Courts similarly possess "the inherent power to prescribe such rules of practice and rules to regulate their proceedings, in order to expedite the trial of cases, and to keep their dockets clear, and to facilitate the administration of justice" (*Hammon v. Gilson*, 1940). Courts also inherently have the power to punish individuals for contempt of court, though the legislature may place limits on the punishments' severity (*Wilson v. Fenton*, 1981; *Eicher v. Tinley*, 1936).

Finally, one should not forget Section 1's closing clause: the constitution itself may prescribe ways in which one branch may exercise powers that ordinarily might be deemed to lie within another branch's domain. Section 16 of Article IV, for example, authorizes the governor "to grant reprieves, commutations, and pardons," but authorizes the General Assembly to pardon individuals who have been convicted of treason.

LEGISLATIVE DEPARTMENT

Section 1.
General assembly.

The Legislative authority of this State shall be vested in a General Assembly, which shall consist of a Senate and House of Representatives; and the style of every law shall be, "Be it enacted by the General Assembly of the State of Iowa."

It first bears noting that Article III contains two provisions denominated as "Section 1"—the first to appear under Article III declares the state's commitment to the separation of powers, while the second appears under the heading "Legislative Department" and initiates a series of provisions concerning the General Assembly. Attorneys frequently cite both provisions as "Article III, Section 1," raising the risk that—absent a quotation of the provision to which one is referring or some other form of clarification—one's audience will not know which of the two provisions one is talking about. The Iowa Supreme Court's usual practice is to include the words "Legislative Department" when citing the second of the two provisions.

The Section 1 being discussed here declares the fundamental proposition that a bicameral General Assembly possesses the state's lawmaking power, and it also provides the verbal formulation that the General Assembly must use when promulgating laws. The substance of the provision remains the same as it was under the state's first constitution (ratified in 1846), though the delegates to the 1857 convention adjusted the provision's phrasing in nonsubstantive ways.[5] Those adjustments were made off the floor of the convention between the provision's second and third readings and were not the subject of documented discussion.[6]

Unlike Congress, which possesses only those powers that are delegated to it by the U.S. Constitution, the General Assembly possesses *all* legislative power, except as restricted by the Iowa Constitution or by federal law. The Iowa

---

[5] Under the 1846 constitution, the provision stated: "The Legislative authority of this State shall be vested in a Senate and House of Representatives, which shall be designated the General Assembly of the State of Iowa, and the style of their laws shall commence in the following manner: 'Be it enacted by the General Assembly of the State of Iowa.'" Iowa Const. of 1846, art. IV, § 1 (Legislative Department).

[6] *1857 Debates, supra* Article I, note 3, vol. 1, pp. 509–10 (presenting the unaltered version in the second reading); *id.* at vol. 2, p. 1008 (presenting the new version in the third reading).

Constitution, in other words, "is a limitation, and not a grant of power. Hence the courts look not at what the instrument authorizes, but at what is prohibited" (*Eckerson v. City of Des Moines*, 1908). Pursuant to its police powers, the General Assembly has the "broad, inherent power to pass laws that promote the public health, safety, and welfare" (*Gravert v. Nebergall*, 1995). The General Assembly's powers with respect to property taxes and common-law causes of action provide two illustrations. With respect to taxation, the Iowa Supreme Court ruled early in the state's history that, absent limitations imposed by the state's constitution or by federal law, "the General Assembly possesses the power, derived from its general legislative authority, to subject all kinds and classes of property to taxation for all proper purposes" (*City of Davenport v. Chicago, Rock Island & Pacific Railroad Co.*, 1874). With respect to the common law, the court has said that the General Assembly may alter or eliminate common-law causes of action, so long as it clearly reveals its intent to do so (*Fabricius v. Montgomery Elevator Co.*, 1963).

Some of the most frequently litigated Section 1 issues appear under the banner of the nondelegation doctrine. Just as is the case with the U.S. Constitution's vesting of legislative power in Congress, the Iowa Constitution's vesting of legislative power in the General Assembly raises questions about the degree to which the legislature can delegate rulemaking tasks to others. Readers interested in the historical evolution of Iowa's nondelegation doctrine will find a useful discussion in *Warren County v. Judges of the Fifth Judicial District* (1976). Under the law as it stands today, the General Assembly enjoys substantial latitude to delegate rulemaking tasks to its sister branches. That latitude, however, is not unlimited. In *In the Interest of C.S.* (1994) and *In the Interest of D.C.V.* (1997), the Iowa Supreme Court explained that, when delegating rulemaking power to another branch, the General Assembly must either provide substantive standards to guide the other branch's policymaking discretion or provide procedural safeguards that will ensure the other branch does not perform in an arbitrary, capricious, or illegal manner. *C.S.* and *D.C.V.* both provide examples of those standards not being met: *C.S.* concerned a statute giving the executive and judicial branches responsibility for deciding which children in need of assistance would receive funds for placement in out-of-state facilities, while *D.C.V.* concerned a statute giving the executive and judicial branches responsibility for developing a plan to restrict the number of children placed in group foster care. The court's ruling in *Lewis Consolidated School District v. Johnston* (1964) provides another example: without providing any decision-making standards, the General Assembly unconstitutionally authorized an executive official to determine whether a school district was eligible to receive state funds.

Delegations of legislative power to *private* individuals and entities raise constitutional concerns, as well. In *Gamel v. Veterans Auditorium Memorial Commission* (1978), for example, the Iowa Supreme Court struck down a statute that empowered private individuals to appoint commissioners responsible for deciding how best to spend public funds. The court reserved judgment on whether "delegation of other powers [to private individuals or entities] might survive scrutiny if proper safeguards or special qualifications are present."

Delegations of legislative power to local governmental entities (such as municipalities), however, are generally permitted. The court explained in *Koelling v. Board of Trustees* (1966) that "[i]t is a well settled rule, supported with practical unanimity by the authorities, that the general doctrine prohibiting the delegation of legislative authority has no application to the vesting in political subdivisions of powers to govern matters which are local in scope."

Section 2.
Annual sessions of general assembly—special sessions.

The General Assembly shall meet in session on the second Monday of January of each year. Upon written request to the presiding officer of each House of the General Assembly by two-thirds of the members of each House, the General Assembly shall convene in special session. The Governor of the state may convene the General Assembly by proclamation in the interim.

Under the original text of the 1857 constitution, the General Assembly met every two years, unless the governor issued a proclamation calling for a special session. At the 1857 convention, Davis County's David Palmer had proposed requiring annual sessions, but his fellow delegates resisted, citing financial costs, a perceived lack of necessity, and a fear that—as Lucas County's John Edwards put it—legislators would fill their time by governing the people "too much."[7] In 1968, Iowans finally came around to Palmer's view, amending Section 2 to require the General Assembly to meet annually. Iowa voters put Section 2 into the form it takes today when they amended the provision once again in 1974, authorizing a supermajority of the legislature to call for a special session.

The Iowa Supreme Court's only noteworthy ruling concerning Section 2 came in 1859's *Morford v. Unger*, when the justices ruled that the General Assembly's powers at a special session are just as broad as they are at a regularly scheduled session, and are not constrained by the exigencies or objectives that prompted the special session to be convened.

Section 3.
Representatives.

The members of the House of Representatives shall be chosen every second year, by the qualified electors of their respective districts; and their term of office shall

[7] *1857 Debates, supra* Article I, note 3, vol. 1, pp. 510–13. Johnson County's William Penn Clarke subsequently proposed holding annual sessions for the first five years following the new constitution's ratification and biennial sessions thereafter. The delegates rejected Clarke's proposal by the narrow vote of 15 to 17. *Id.* at pp. 558–67.

commence on the first day of January next after their election, and continue two years, and until their successors are elected and qualified.

Section 3 still reads as it did in the original text of the 1857 constitution, with one exception. The constitution originally stated that, in years lacking a presidential election, Iowans would select their representatives in elections held the second Tuesday in October. That language has twice been rendered irrelevant (and thus has been removed from the codified constitution that the state publishes from time to time, and has been removed from the quotation that appears above). In 1904, Iowa voters added Section 16 of Article XII to the constitution, moving the state's biennial elections to November. That provision was then trumped in 1916, when Iowa voters amended Section 7 of Article II, aligning the state's general elections with the federal election calendar unless the General Assembly decides to do otherwise.

Section 3 has not been the subject of reported appellate litigation, but the Office of the Attorney General has occasionally been called upon to help discern its requirements. In 1926, for example, Attorney General Ben Gibson issued an opinion stating that, if a representative is elected but then dies before taking office, there is no "vacancy" to be filled within the meaning of Article III, Section 12; rather, the prior officeholder serves for the upcoming term pursuant to Section 3's closing clause.[8]

Section 4.
Qualifications.

No person shall be a member of the House of Representatives who shall not have attained the age of[9] twenty-one years, be a citizen of the United States, and shall have been an inhabitant of this State one year next preceding his election, and at the time of his election shall have had an actual residence of sixty days in the County, or District he may have been chosen to represent.

Section 4 still reads as it did in the original 1857 constitution,[10] with two exceptions. In 1880, Iowa voters removed the words "free white," which had appeared before the phrase "citizen of the United States." In 1926, Iowans struck the word "male," which had appeared in that same location. With those two amendments, Iowa removed the race and sex qualifications that the delegates

[8] Op. Iowa Att'y Gen., 1926 WL 64048 (Dec. 7, 1926) (replying to Governor John Hammill).

[9] The signed, handwritten text of the 1857 constitution contains two "of"s here. *See* State Library of Iowa, "Constitutions," http://www.statelibraryofiowa.org/services/collections/law-library/iacon/iacons (presenting the handwritten copy and other iterations of the Iowa Constitution).

[10] At the Territory of Iowa's 1844 convention, the delegates settled upon requiring one year of inhabitancy as a compromise between those who wished to require two years of inhabitancy and those who did not want to impose any inhabitancy requirement at all. *1844 and 1846 Fragments, supra* Article I, note 3, pp. 56–57. The one-year requirement was then carried forward to the 1846 and 1857 constitutions.

to the 1857 convention—like the delegates to the 1844 and 1846 conventions before them—had placed there.

Attorneys General Richard Turner (in 1974) and Thomas Miller (in 1979) both concluded that Section 4's residency requirements only apply to the period preceding a representative's election; once a district's representative has been lawfully elected, he or she remains eligible to represent that district even if he or she moves elsewhere.[11]

Section 4 has not been the subject of reported appellate litigation, in part because Section 7 of this article gives the house of representatives—not the courts—the leading role in determining whether candidates possess Section 4's qualifications.

Section 5.
Senators—qualifications.

Senators shall be chosen for the term of four years, at the same time and place as Representatives; they shall be twenty-five years of age, and possess the qualifications of Representatives as to residence and citizenship.

Section 5 still reads as it did when it left the delegates' hands at the 1857 convention.[12] George Gillaspy, a farmer from Wapello County, had urged his fellow delegates to reduce the age required for senate membership to twenty-one, thereby equalizing the age requirements for senators and representatives, but his proposal was defeated with little documented debate.[13] Like Article I of the federal Constitution, the Iowa Constitution thus sets a higher minimum age for senators than it does for representatives. Note that, unlike Section 4 concerning the requirements for membership in the house of representatives, Section 5 does not clearly impose an inhabitancy requirement for membership in the senate, a matter discussed in *State ex rel. Turner v. Scott* (1978).

Section 5 has not been frequently litigated. One of the Iowa Supreme Court's two noteworthy Section 5 rulings (*State ex rel. Turner v. Scott*, 1978) also concerned Article III, Section 7, and is discussed in this book's commentary on that section. The court's other Section 5 ruling came in *Selzer v. Synhorst* (1962).

---

[11] Op. Iowa Att'y Gen., 1974 WL 353736 (Apr. 1, 1974) (replying to Richard Drake and Andrew Varley); Op. Iowa Att'y Gen., 1979 WL 21035 (Aug. 2, 1979) (replying to Roger A. Halvorson).

[12] At the Territory of Iowa's 1844 convention, the delegates rejected the suggestion that they grant senators two-year terms. Dubuque County's Edward Langworthy had made that proposal, arguing that "[t]his was an age of progression" and that allowing senators to serve longer terms would undesirably slow down the process of legal change. Johnson County's Robert Lucas spoke against Langworthy's proposal, arguing that it "would destroy the object of that branch of the Legislature, which was that there should always be some who had the experience of former sessions." *1844 and 1846 Fragments, supra* Article I, note 3, pp. 57–58.

[13] *1857 Debates, supra* Article I, note 3, vol. 1, pp. 516, 567.

When reapportioning Iowa's senatorial districts in response to the 1960 census, the General Assembly had identified three districts in which the senators elected in 1964 would serve two-year terms. Section 5 states that senators will serve four-year terms, but the legislature determined that a brief departure from that requirement was necessary in order to place the state on a trajectory that—in keeping with the requirements of Article III, Section 6—would bring roughly half of the senate's members up for election every two years. The *Selzer* court ruled that the temporary departure from Section 5's requirements was permissible:

> No candidate for office has in advance of his election any basic right to be elected for a specified term of years. Elections for short terms to fill vacancies are common in our law. The voters in the [three] districts in 1964 will be in the same position as if a vacancy through resignation or death existed. They will elect for a short term. No basic or fundamental rights are denied.

The Office of the Attorney General has issued several opinions concerning Section 5. In 1972, for example, Attorney General Richard Turner determined that a senatorial candidate need not be at least twenty-five years of age on Election Day, so long as the candidate reaches that age by the date of his or her induction into office.[14]

Section 6.
Senators—number and classification.

The number of senators shall total not more than one-half the membership of the house of representatives. Senators shall be classified so that as nearly as possible one-half of the members of the senate shall be elected every two years.

In the 1846 and 1857 constitutions, Section 6 required that the number of senators never be fewer than one-third the number of members of the house of representatives, and required that the senate's seats be divided "by lot" into two groups, to try to ensure that approximately half of the senate's seats could be contested every two years.[15] Iowa voters amended Section 6 in 1968, putting it into its current form.

The Iowa Supreme Court's only ruling on the provision came in 1962's *Selzer v. Synhorst*, discussed in the commentary on Section 5 of this article.

---

[14] Op. Iowa Att'y Gen., 1972 WL 262417 (Aug. 23, 1972) (replying to Melvin D. Synhorst).

[15] For the delegates' debate about Section 6 at the 1857 convention—a debate that centered mostly around short-term concerns regarding the future status of currently sitting legislators—see *1857 Debates, supra* Article I, note 3, vol. 1, pp. 516–24.

Section 7.
Officers—elections determined.

Each house shall choose its own officers, and judge of the qualification, election, and return of its own members. A contested election shall be determined in such manner as shall be directed by law.

Modeled on portions of Sections 2, 3, and 5 of Article I of the U.S. Constitution, Section 7 places the senate and house of representatives in charge of choosing their own officers and resolving controversies concerning the qualifications, elections, and returns of their own members. The provision continues to read just as it did under the state's first constitution, ratified in 1846. The delegates to the 1857 convention carried the provision's text forward without recorded debate.[16] Chapter 59 of the Iowa Code prescribes some of the procedures that apply when there is a contested election.

In its 1894 ruling in *Cliff v. Parsons*, the Iowa Supreme Court confirmed that Section 7 gives each house of the General Assembly the power "to choose, in such way as it pleases, its own officers," as well as the power to "remove its own officers at pleasure." Section 7 also gives each house the leading role in resolving disputes concerning members' qualifications, elections, and returns. In 1978's *State ex rel. Turner v. Scott*, for example, the court dismissed an effort by the attorney general to enforce what he perceived to be Section 5's inhabitancy requirement. The senate's credentials committee had concluded that Section 5 did not impose such a requirement, so had seated previously peripatetic John Richard Scott as a senator. The attorney general challenged the senate's actions, but to no avail. Citing Section 7, the court ruled that the attorney general's lawsuit presented a nonjusticiable political question. Absent a claim that Scott's seating violated someone's constitutional rights, the court said, Scott's eligibility was a matter for the senate to resolve.

As the preceding paragraph's final sentence suggests, Section 7 does not push the courts entirely to the sidelines in disputes about house and senate elections. In *Luse v. Wray* (1977), the Iowa Supreme Court held that "Iowa courts have power to adjudicate substantial claims of deprivation of federal or Iowa constitutional rights by the houses of the Iowa General Assembly in the exercise of the houses' election contest powers under § 7." The *Luse* court emphasized that the courts' power in these cases extends only to claims involving constitutional rights; it does not extend to lesser matters, such as questions of statutory interpretation.

---

[16] *1857 Debates, supra* Article I, note 3, vol. 1, p. 524.

Section 8.
Quorum.

A majority of each house shall constitute a quorum to transact business; but a smaller number may adjourn from day to day, and may compel the attendance of absent members in such manner and under such penalties as each house may provide.

Strongly echoing portions of Article I, Section 5, of the U.S. Constitution, Section 8 still stands in substantively the same form as it appeared in Iowa's first constitution. The provision permits a chamber to conduct ordinary business if a majority of its members are present, and permits smaller fractions of a chamber's members to adjourn a day's business or to round up absent members according to that house's rules. Each chamber has adopted rules giving each of its members the power to inquire whether the necessary quorum is present, and specifying the means by which absent members' presence may be secured.[17]

Section 8 has never been the focus of reported appellate litigation. In response to an inquiry from the house of representatives in 1924, Attorney General Ben Gibson concluded that a quorum is required in order to vote on a motion to adjourn *sine die* (that is, to adjourn—typically at the end of an annual session—without specifying the date when the General Assembly's activities will resume).[18]

Section 9.
Authority of the houses.

Each house shall sit upon its own adjournments, keep a journal of its proceedings, and publish the same; determine its rules of proceedings, punish members for disorderly behavior, and, with the consent of two-thirds, expel a member, but not a second time for the same offense; and shall have all other powers necessary for a branch of the General Assembly of a free and independent State.

Echoing portions of Article I, Section 5, of the U.S. Constitution, Section 9 still stands in substantively the same form as it appeared in Iowa's first constitution, ratified in 1846. The provision gives each chamber an array of powers to govern its own proceedings, and requires each to keep an official journal.

The chambers' journals have been the subject of litigation in a small handful of cases. In *Miller v. City of Oelwein* (1912), for example, the Iowa Supreme Court stated that "enrolled bills duly signed and deposited with the Secretary of State constitute the ultimate proof of their regular enactment," and that "[m]ere

[17] *See* House Rule 2 ("Quorum Call and Time of Convening"); House Rule 77 ("Call of the House"); House Rule 78 ("Method of Calling the House"); House Rule 80 ("Quorum and Record Roll Call Votes"); Senate Rule 1 ("Quorum"); Senate Rule 18 ("Call of the Senate"). Each chamber's rules are available at https://www.legis.iowa.gov/chambers/rules.

[18] Op. Iowa Att'y Gen., 1924 WL 60460 (July 29, 1924) (replying to the House of Representatives).

failure of the journals to show compliance with the requirements as to the method of enacting a law will not be conclusive that such requirements were not complied with." In *Carlton v. Grimes* (1946), the court explained that "[t]here is no constitutional mandate as to just how, or in what manner, the journal of the proceedings shall be kept," that the chambers are not required to record the text of proposed or approved bills in their journals, and that "the best and the only recorded legislative evidence of the text and content of any bill enacted is the enrolled bill authenticated by the signatures of the presiding officers, signed and approved by the governor, and deposited in the office of the secretary of state." The chambers' broad constitutional leeway to decide what to record in their journals is constrained, of course, when another constitutional provision—of the sort one finds in Article III, Sections 10 and 17, for example—requires that certain information be memorialized there.

In *Des Moines Register & Tribune Co. v. Dwyer* (1996), the Iowa Supreme Court turned its attention to each chamber's power to craft its own procedural rules. The case concerned the senate's refusal to give the *Register* detailed records of its members' incoming and outgoing telephone calls; after the senate's secretary refused to provide those records, the senate adopted a rule ratifying the secretary's actions. The *Register* sued to obtain the records, but the Iowa Supreme Court held that—in light of Section 9's declaration that each chamber may "determine its rules of proceedings"—the suit presented a nonjusticiable political question. The court explained that the judiciary has the power "to review the senate's rules for constitutionality and to ensure they do not violate individual fundamental rights," but that, absent such constitutional concerns, "[i]t is entirely the prerogative of the legislature . . . to make, interpret, and enforce its own procedural rules."

The Office of the Attorney General has also weighed in on each chamber's right to govern its own proceedings. In 1973, for example, Attorney General Richard Turner issued an opinion stating that the senate could bar individuals from the chamber if they were not attired in compliance with the senate's unwritten dress code.[19] In 1964, Attorney General Evan Hultman concluded that the senate even has the power to adopt rules aimed at barring individual members from filing bills or joint resolutions.[20]

Section 10.
Protest—record of vote.

Every member of the General Assembly shall have the liberty to dissent from, or protest against any act or resolution which he may think injurious to the public, or an individual, and have the reasons for his dissent entered on the journals;

---

[19] Op. Iowa Att'y Gen., 1973 WL 324489 (Apr. 5, 1973) (replying to Adrian Brinck).

[20] Op. Iowa Att'y Gen., 1964 WL 121092 (Mar. 5, 1964) (replying to Eugene M. Hill).

and the yeas and nays of the members of either house, on any question, shall, at the desire of any two members present, be entered on the journals.

At the 1857 convention, the delegates carried forward Section 10's text, unaltered, from the 1846 constitution. The provision gives dissenting members of the General Assembly the opportunity to memorialize the reasons for their displeasure and thereby to lay the groundwork for later arguing that they had warned of proposed legislation's dangers. Section 10 also empowers any two members present in a chamber to demand that all present members' votes on a given matter be recorded in that chamber's journal. By implication, Section 10's last clause reinforces the Iowa Supreme Court's finding under Section 9 of this article that each chamber ordinarily has the power to decide what to include—and what not to include—in its journal. Section 17 of this article requires that "the yeas and nays" on the question of a bill's "final passage" be entered on a chamber's journal; Section 10 is thus referring to other matters when it authorizes two members of either house to demand that members' "yeas and nays" be recorded (*Carlton v. Grimes*, 1946).

In 1935, Attorney General Edward O'Connor issued an opinion stating that, under Section 10, a chamber may require all present members to vote on a given matter, and may punish those who refuse "for disorderly or contemptuous conduct."[21]

Section 11.
Privileged from arrest.

Senators and Representatives, in all cases, except treason, felony, or breach of the peace, shall be privileged from arrest during the session of the General Assembly, and in going to and returning from the same.

The delegates to the 1857 convention carried Section 11's text forward, unchanged, from the 1846 constitution. By protecting members of the General Assembly from being arrested under the specified circumstances, the provision provides protections that are similar to those enjoyed by members of Congress under Article I, Section 6, of the U.S. Constitution.

Section 11 has not been the subject of reported appellate litigation. In 1975, however, the Office of the Attorney General issued an opinion concerning Section 11's scope in response to an inquiry from a senator who had received a speeding ticket on a day when he believed the senate was in session. The senator wished to know whether his traffic stop and citation were lawful. Citing federal law and rulings in other states, and finding that the exceptions listed in Section 11 are framed in language broad enough to cover all crimes, Attorney General Richard Turner replied that the privilege afforded by Section 11 applies only to

[21] Op. Iowa Att'y Gen., 1935 WL 60686 (Apr. 8, 1935) (replying to the House of Representatives).

arrests for civil offenses. Even if the senator was traveling to or from a legislative session when he was stopped, Turner said, Section 11 provided him with no protection from arrest for a criminal offense.[22]

Section 12.
Vacancies.

When vacancies occur in either house, the Governor or the person exercising the functions of Governor, shall issue writs of election to fill such vacancies.

Section 12 continues to read just as it did in the state's first constitution, ratified in 1846. The provision provides an electoral mechanism for filling vacancies in either chamber of the General Assembly.

Section 12 has never been the subject of reported appellate litigation, but the Office of the Attorney General has been asked on a number of occasions to provide guidance concerning its meaning. In 1933, for example, Attorney General Edward O'Connor advised the governor that, if a state senator dies while the General Assembly is in session, the governor has a duty under Section 12 to call for a special election to fill the seat.[23] In 1926, Attorney General Ben Gibson issued an opinion stating that, if a representative is elected but then dies before taking office, there is no "vacancy" to be filled within the meaning of Section 12; rather, the prior officeholder serves for the upcoming term pursuant to the closing clause of Article III, Section 3.[24] In response to a subsequent inquiry concerning that same deceased individual, Attorney General John Fletcher stated that he agreed with Gibson's analysis, but that—exercising its powers under Article III, Section 7—the house of representatives could declare that there was indeed a vacancy, thereby triggering the governor's Section 12 duty to call an election to fill the seat.[25]

Section 13.
Doors open.

The doors of each house shall be open, except on such occasions, as, in the opinion of the house, may require secrecy.

The delegates to the 1857 convention carried Section 13's text forward, unchanged, from the 1846 constitution. The provision embraces public transparency as a general norm for the General Assembly's proceedings, but gives

---

[22] Op. Iowa Att'y Gen., 1975 WL 368781 (July 18, 1975) (replying to Richard J. Norpel, Sr.). For more on the scope of legislators' immunity, see Op. Iowa Att'y Gen., 1979 WL 20966 (May 21, 1979) (replying to Lowell Junkins).

[23] Op. Iowa Att'y Gen., 1933 WL 66241 (Mar. 13, 1933) (replying to Governor Clyde Herring).

[24] Op. Iowa Att'y Gen., 1926 WL 64048 (Dec. 7, 1926) (replying to Governor John Hammill).

[25] Op. Iowa Att'y Gen., 1927 WL 63270 (Jan. 10, 1927) (replying to L.B. Forsling).

the two chambers broad authority to operate in secret when they deem it appropriate.[26] The provision has never been the subject of reported appellate litigation or of opinions published by the Office of the Attorney General.

Section 14.
Adjournments.

Neither house shall, without the consent of the other, adjourn for more than three days, nor to any other place than that in which they may be sitting.

Closely tracking portions of Article I, Section 5, of the U.S. Constitution, Section 14 continues to read just as it did in the state's 1846 constitution. By requiring the chambers' mutual consent for adjournments of more than three days and for adjournments to different locations, Section 14 ensures that the two chambers will remain available to one another while the General Assembly is in session.

Section 14 has never been the subject of reported appellate litigation, but on at least one occasion the Office of the Attorney General has provided guidance concerning its meaning. In response to an inquiry from a senator in 1978, Attorney General Richard Turner concluded that the word "days" in Section 14 refers to calendar days, including Saturdays and Sundays, and that a chamber's lengthy adjournment without the other chamber's consent does not have the effect of terminating the General Assembly's session.[27]

Section 15.
Bills.

Bills may originate in either house, and may be amended, altered, or rejected by the other; and every bill having passed both houses, shall be signed by the Speaker and President of their respective houses.

Section 15 describes some of the basic steps by which proposed legislation becomes law. Under the state's first constitution, ratified in 1846, revenue-raising bills had to originate in the house of representatives, just as they must in Congress under Article I, Section 7, of the U.S. Constitution. When the Committee on Distribution of Powers and Legislative Department presented its draft of Article III at the 1857 convention, that requirement had been dropped, putting Section 15 into the form one sees above.[28]

Section 15 has been litigated in only a small number of cases. The Iowa Supreme Court's two most noteworthy rulings on the provision both concerned

---

[26] *See generally* Jonathan Roos, "'65 Changes Reduced Legislative Secrecy," *Des Moines Register*, Jan. 11, 2004, at 18A (discussing a shift in 1965 away from closed-door committee meetings).

[27] Op. Iowa Att'y Gen., 1978 WL 17432 (July 11, 1978) (replying to James M. Redmond).

[28] *1857 Debates, supra* Article I, note 3, vol. 1, p. 83. The change did not provoke any documented debate on the convention floor. *See, e.g., id.* at p. 525.

its signing requirement. In *Miller v. City of Oelwein* (1912), the court found that a bill had become law even though the president of the senate had evidently not signed the bill in the senate's presence; a joint rule of the General Assembly required the president to be in the senate's presence when he signed the measure, but the court held that Section 15 does not impose any such locational requirement. In *State ex rel. Hammond v. Lynch* (1915), the court held that an anti-prostitution statute was invalid because it had not been signed by the speaker of the house. Section 15 requires the speaker's and president's signatures, the court explained, in order to certify that the given measure has successfully passed through both chambers.

The Office of the Attorney General has issued a handful of opinions concerning Section 15's requirements. In 1939, for example, Attorney General John Rankin reiterated the fundamental proposition that a bill does not become law under Section 15 unless identical versions of it are approved by the General Assembly's two chambers.[29] (For more on that requirement, see Article III, Section 17.) In 1896, Attorney General Milton Remley stated that, if the governor signs a bill that has not yet been signed by the speaker and the president, the bill does not become law until those other two signatures have been obtained.[30]

Section 16.
Executive approval—veto—item veto by governor.

Every bill which shall have passed the General Assembly, shall, before it becomes a law, be presented to the Governor. If he approve, he shall sign it; but if not, he shall return it with his objections, to the house in which it originated, which shall enter the same upon their journal, and proceed to re-consider it; if, after such re-consideration, it again pass both houses, by yeas and nays, by a majority of two thirds of the members of each house, it shall become a law, notwithstanding the Governor's objections. If any bill shall not be returned within three days after it shall have been presented to him, Sunday excepted, the same shall be a law in like manner as if he had signed it, unless the General Assembly, by adjournment, prevent such return. Any bill submitted to the Governor for his approval during the last three days of a session of the General Assembly, shall be deposited by him in the office of the Secretary of State, within thirty days after the adjournment, with his approval, if approved by him, and with his objections, if he disapproves thereof.

The governor may approve appropriation bills in whole or in part, and may disapprove any item of an appropriation bill; and the part approved shall become a law. Any item of an appropriation bill disapproved by the governor shall be returned, with his objections, to the house in which it originated, or shall be deposited by him in the office of the secretary of state in the case of an appropriation bill submitted to the governor for his approval during the last three days of

[29] Op. Iowa Att'y Gen., 1939 WL 77272 (Aug. 4, 1939) (replying to C. Fred Porter).

[30] Op. Iowa Att'y Gen., 1896 WL 38019 (Apr. 22, 1896) (replying to Governor Francis Drake).

a session of the general assembly, and the procedure in each case shall be the same as provided for other bills. Any such item of an appropriation bill may be enacted into law notwithstanding the governor's objections, in the same manner as provided for other bills.

Section 16 describes the governor's constitutional role in the lawmaking process, as well as the General Assembly's power to override gubernatorial vetoes by a two-thirds vote. In the state's first constitution, ratified in 1846, Section 16 consisted only of the first paragraph one sees above, minus that paragraph's final sentence. That 1846 text was the product of a debate in the Territory of Iowa's 1844 constitutional convention, in which at least one delegate argued that the governor should not have any veto power at all, at least one believed the governor should have a veto power but that a majority of the General Assembly should be able to overcome it, and some believed a strong veto power was necessary "to prevent hasty and ill-advised legislation" and to "defend the people's rights."[31] The delegates to the 1857 convention added the first paragraph's final sentence after Jefferson County's James Wilson pointed out that a large volume of legislation is often finalized in a session's closing days and that a governor might thus need more than just three days to work his or her way through the stack.[32] That sentence is often described as giving the governor a "pocket veto"—without overtly vetoing a bill, the governor can kill it simply by holding it for more than thirty days. Iowans added Section 16's second paragraph in 1968, giving the governor the power to single out particular portions of spending bills for disapproval, subject to the General Assembly's power to override such "item vetoes" by a two-thirds vote. Taking Section 16 as a whole, one thus finds that the governor possesses three different varieties of veto power: the power to explicitly veto an entire bill, the power to veto a late-submitted bill merely by taking no action on it, and the power to veto items of an appropriation bill.[33]

Both the Iowa Supreme Court and the Office of the Attorney General have addressed the mechanics described in Section 16's first paragraph. The court has confirmed that, as a general rule, if the governor does not either sign or return a bill within three days of receiving it (not counting Sundays), the bill automatically becomes law (*Collins v. Laucier*, 1877). There is an exception: a bill that has been passed by the General Assembly does not become law if both (1) the

---

[31] *1844 and 1846 Fragments, supra* Article I, note 3, pp. 58–63.

[32] *1857 Debates, supra* Article I, note 3, vol. 2, p. 1012. The delegates to the 1857 convention also rejected proposals to give the General Assembly the power to override vetoes by the vote of either a majority or seven-twelfths. The debate on those proposals focused on whether the governor was a reliable protector of the people's interests and on whether recent vetoes were laudable. *Id.* at vol. 1, pp. 525–27, 567.

[33] For an early history of the governor's veto power, see Jacob A. Swisher, "The Executive Veto in Iowa," 15 *Iowa Journal of History & Politics* 155 (1917).

General Assembly adjourns *sine die*[34] or otherwise "terminates the organized existence of the legislature" prior to the expiration of the governor's three-day review period, thereby preventing the governor from being able to promptly return the bill to the house in which it originated, and (2) the governor does not sign the bill within thirty days of the adjournment (*Redmond v. Ray*, 1978; *Darling v. Boesch*, 1888). In *Redmond*, the court explained that, in its references to three-day periods, Section 16 refers to calendar days (rather than to days when legislators are actually meeting) and that, when calculating a three-day period, one does not count the day when the governor received the bill. In 1978, Attorney General Richard Turner advised a state senator that, upon receiving a vetoed bill, the chamber in which the bill originated is constitutionally obliged either to table it or to vote on the measure again prior to adjourning *sine die*.[35]

Many of the Section 16 opinions issued by the Iowa Supreme Court and the Office of the Attorney General have concerned the item-veto provision, added in 1968. The governor may exercise the item-veto power only when presented with an appropriation bill. Iowa's high court has identified two types of appropriation bills, both of which are susceptible to item vetoes:

> a traditional form which contains at least one allocation of a monetary amount on the face of the bill, and a specialized type . . . which allocates funds by either directly ordering an expenditure or commanding alterations to standing allocations within sections of the Iowa Code resulting in the expenditure of funds absent subsequent legislation to stop the expenditure or somehow redirect it (*Rants v. Vilsack*, 2004).

The governor's item-veto power is limited to those portions of an appropriation bill that constitute "items" within the meaning of the first sentence of Section 16's second paragraph. The court has identified three different types of veto-eligible items: provisions that allocate funds, provisions (often called "riders") that are unrelated to the bill's funding provisions, and provisions that place conditions or limitations upon the uses to which appropriated funds may be put (*Rants v. Vilsack*, 2004).[36] With respect to the third of those three types of items, the court has held that Section 16 does not allow the governor to veto

---

[34] The General Assembly adjourns *sine die* when it adjourns—typically at the end of an annual session—without specifying the date when its activities will resume.

[35] Op. Iowa Att'y Gen., 1978 WL 17435 (July 13, 1978) (replying to James M. Redmond).

[36] That three-part typology flows in part from the court's early embrace of the "scar tissue" test. Under that test, a provision in an appropriation bill constitutes an "item" if it "may be taken out of [the] bill without affecting its other purposes and provisions. It is something that can be lifted bodily from it rather than cut out. No damage can be done to the surrounding legislative tissue, nor should any scar tissue result therefrom" (*Welsh v. Branstad*, 1991). In 2006, the Office of the Attorney General used the "scar tissue" language to summarize the law in this area. Op. Iowa Att'y Gen., 2006 WL 6337824 (Oct. 20, 2006) (replying to Paul McKinley).

a condition- or limitation-imposing provision unless he or she also vetoes the appropriation itself (*Welden v. Ray*, 1975).[37] In other words, if the legislature appropriates funds with strings attached, the governor may not "cut the strings and spend the money differently" (*Homan v. Branstad*, 2012). The Office of the Attorney General has taken the position that, just as it must when the governor vetoes a non-appropriation bill, "the house of origin . . . must proceed to reconsider" any items of an appropriation bill that the governor has vetoed.[38]

When the governor attempts to item veto portions of a bill in an unconstitutional manner, determining the result can be a bit complicated—a point demonstrated by the remainder of this paragraph. If the governor deploys his or her item-veto power in an impermissible manner on an appropriation bill that he or she otherwise approves during the thirty-day review period that applies for all bills submitted in a session's final three days—for example, if the governor attempts to veto a spending condition but not the spending itself—then all of the provisions constituting that disputed appropriation item are deemed invalid, but the balance of the bill becomes law (*Homan v. Branstad*, 2012). If, during that thirty-day review period, the governor impermissibly attempts to item veto a provision of a *non*-appropriation bill, then the entire bill fails because non-appropriation bills must be approved or vetoed in their entirety (*Rants v. Vilsack*, 2004). If the governor deploys the item-veto power impermissibly on either an appropriation bill or a non-appropriation bill when the thirty-day review period does *not* apply—that is, if the governor wields that power impermissibly during a time when a bill automatically becomes law unless the governor lawfully acts within three days—then the entire bill becomes law (*Rants v. Vilsack*, 2004; *State ex rel. Turner v. Iowa State Highway Commission*, 1971).

Section 17.
Passage of bills.

No bill shall be passed unless by the assent of a majority of all the members elected to each branch of the General Assembly, and the question upon the final passage shall be taken immediately upon its last reading, and the yeas and nays entered on the journal.

Section 17 declares that a bill may become law only if it is approved by a majority of all the members of both chambers (and not, say, merely by a majority of those present on a given day[39]), and it requires that the final votes on each bill

---

[37] *Cf. Homan v. Branstad* (2012) (explaining that "the item veto cannot be used to strike a provision that is 'inextricably linked' to or an 'integral part' of an appropriation").

[38] Op. Iowa Att'y Gen., 1978 WL 17468 (Sept. 6, 1978) (replying to James M. Redmond).

[39] When a chamber is voting on a *non-legislative* matter—such as whether to confirm a gubernatorial appointment—the approval of a mere majority of those present is required, unless a constitutional or statutory provision requires more. Op. Iowa Att'y Gen., 1978 WL 17575 (Dec. 29, 1978) (replying to Arthur A. Neu).

be recorded in each chamber's journal. Section 17 was added to the constitution at the suggestion of the 1857 convention's Committee on Distribution of Powers and Legislative Department,[40] and it was not the subject of documented debate.[41] The provision's inspiration undoubtedly came from Article III, Section 15, of the New York Constitution of 1846, which—with the exception of referring to the "General Assembly" rather than the "legislature"—Section 17 tracks verbatim.

Nearly all of the Iowa Supreme Court's Section 17 cases come from the first half of the twentieth century. Many of those cases were provoked by the court's inconsistent rulings concerning the degree to which courts could dig into the legislative record to ensure that both chambers of the General Assembly had approved identical versions of bills. In *State ex rel. Hammond v. Lynch* (1915) and *Davidson Building Co. v. Mulock* (1931), for example, the court had resisted such a power, finding that—as the *Davidson Building* court put it—

> a bill which has been enrolled, properly authenticated by the presiding officers of both Houses of the Legislative body, and approved by the Executive, is *conclusively presumed* to have been regularly and legally enacted, and . . . the courts have no power to go behind it and look at the legislative journals, or other records, for the purpose of determining whether constitutional requirements as to form and procedure were observed.

In *Dayton v. Pacific Mutual Life Insurance Co.* (1926) and *Smith v. Thompson* (1934), however, the court said that a properly signed and enrolled bill was *not* conclusive evidence that the bill was properly enacted, and that courts could indeed turn to the chambers' journals and other extrinsic evidence to determine whether the General Assembly had followed the constitution's requirements.

The court put an end to that uncertainty—and did so in a manner that largely put an end to Section 17 litigation—with its ruling in 1946's *Carlton v. Grimes*. The *Carlton* court observed that each chamber has a duty under Section 17 to enter on its journal the votes on a bill's "final passage," but the court also made it clear that the chambers' journals do not play an essential role in proving that a bill has been passed by both chambers. Expressly overruling the portions of *Dayton* and *Smith* noted above, the court held that "the final, conclusive, ultimate, and only evidence of the passage of a bill by both houses of the legislature is the enrolled bill, signed by both the president of the senate and the speaker of the house, approved by the governor, and filed in the office of the secretary of state." (For more about those signatures, see the commentary on Section 15 of this article.) The *Carlton* court also noted that the Iowa Constitution does not require a specified number of readings of each bill (with the result that—so far as Section 17 is concerned—a bill's first reading may also

---

[40] *1857 Debates, supra* Article I, note 3, vol. 1, p. 83.

[41] *See, e.g.*, *1857 Debates, supra* Article I, note 3, vol. 1, p. 527.

be its last) and suggested that Section 17 does not even require a full reading of each bill, since all legislators now have ready access to copies of proposed legislation. Indeed, full readings are now largely a thing of the past.[42] Rule 30 of the house's current rules, for example, states that all readings of a bill "shall consist of a reading of the title and enacting clause."[43]

Section 18.
Receipts and expenditures.

An accurate statement of the receipts and expenditures of the public money shall be attached to and published with the laws, at every regular session of the General Assembly.

Without documented debate,[44] the delegates to the 1857 convention carried Section 18 forward, unchanged, from the state's 1846 constitution. Modeled loosely on the final portion of Article I, Section 9, Clause 7, of the U.S. Constitution, the provision has not been the focus of reported appellate litigation or of opinions published by the Office of the Attorney General.[45] In Section 2B.10.4 of the Iowa Code, the General Assembly has directed the Department of Administrative Services and the Legislative Services Agency to satisfy this annual constitutional requirement.

Section 19.
Impeachment.

The House of Representatives shall have the sole power of impeachment, and all impeachments shall be tried by the Senate. When sitting for that purpose, the senators shall be upon oath or affirmation; and no person shall be convicted without the concurrence of two thirds of the members present.

Together with Section 20, Section 19 provides a mechanism by which—upon impeachment by the house of representatives—a supermajority of the senate may remove from office the governor, a judge, or another state officer for certain kinds of bad behavior. Section 19 continues to read just as it did in the state's 1846 constitution.[46] Its provisions closely track the impeachment provisions

---

[42] In earlier cases, such as 1936's *Witmer v. Polk County*, the court had indicated that a full reading of each bill's text was required upon the conclusion of debate, to "let every member of the legislature know exactly what he is voting upon."

[43] Each chamber's rules are available at https://www.legis.iowa.gov/chambers/rules.

[44] *See, e.g., 1857 Debates, supra* Article I, note 3, vol. 1, p. 527.

[45] In 1969, however, Attorney General Richard Turner did note in passing that this provision's requirements do not apply at special sessions of the General Assembly. Op. Iowa Att'y Gen., 1969 WL 181544 (Mar. 24, 1969) (replying to Floyd Millen).

[46] The provision was uncontroversial at the 1857 convention. *See, e.g., 1857 Debates, supra* Article I, note 3, vol. 1, p. 527.

of Article I, Sections 2 and 3, of the U.S. Constitution. Chapter 68 of the Iowa Code prescribes a variety of procedures to be followed in impeachment proceedings. The Iowa Supreme Court and the Office of the Attorney General have had few opportunities to address impeachment matters; those opportunities are discussed next, in the commentary on Section 20.

Section 20.
Officers subject to impeachment—judgment.

The Governor, Judges of the Supreme and District Courts, and other State officers, shall be liable to impeachment for any misdemeanor or malfeasance in office: but judgment in such cases shall extend only to removal from office, and disqualification to hold any office of honor, trust, or profit, under this State; but the party convicted or acquitted shall nevertheless be liable to indictment, trial, and punishment, according to law. All other civil officers shall be tried for misdemeanors and malfeasance in office, in such manner as the General Assembly may provide.

Section 20 identifies the state employees who, through impeachment, may be removed from office and barred from holding certain kinds of state positions in the future. It also authorizes the General Assembly to provide for the trial of "[a]ll other civil officers" for in-office bad behavior. The provision makes clear that, regardless of the outcome of a person's impeachment proceedings, he or she may be the target of civil or criminal litigation concerning the conduct that provoked the impeachment effort.

Section 20 continues to read as it did in the state's first constitution (ratified in 1846), with two exceptions. First, the only individuals subject to impeachment under the 1846 constitution were the governor, the secretary of state, and the state's auditor, treasurer, and judges. Second, both in the 1846 provision's opening clause and in its final sentence, the text referred only to "misdemeanors," and not to "malfeasance." At the 1857 convention, Hardin County's Sheldon Winchester recommended deleting the references to the secretary of state, the auditor, and the treasurer, and inserting an overarching reference to "other state officers." The delegates accepted that suggestion without documented debate.[47] Henry County's Rufus Clarke recommended adding the term "malfeasance" in the two locations noted above. He argued that the term "misdemeanor" captured only low-level wrongdoings that did not rise to the level of criminal conduct, while the term "malfeasance" would more expansively permit impeachment for any "injurious act which the party had contracted not to do,

[47] *1857 Journal, supra* Article I, note 3, p. 194; *1857 Debates, supra* Article I, note 3, vol. 1, p. 551. Mahaska County's James Young and Des Moines County's Jonathan Hall had earlier urged the delegates in a comparable direction. *1857 Debates, supra* Article I, note 3, vol. 1, p. 527.

or had no right to do." The delegates accepted Clarke's proposal without documented debate.[48]

The Iowa Supreme Court's leading impeachment ruling—now more than three-quarters of a century old—came in *Clark v. Herring* (1935). One of the issues in that case was whether the Commissioner of Insurance—an executive-branch official whose position had been created by statute—was subject to impeachment. The court ruled that the phrase "other state officers" in Section 20's opening clause did not include the commissioner, whom the court described as "an appointive head of a mere ministerial agency." To rule otherwise, the court explained, would risk burdening legislators with impeachment proceedings concerning all sorts of low-level government officials, thereby blunting legislators' ability to carry out their lawmaking function. Nearly two decades earlier, Attorney General Howard Byers had comparably advised Governor Beryl Carroll that Section 20 authorizes impeachment only for individuals holding offices created by the constitution, and not for individuals holding offices created by statute.[49]

In Chapter 66 of the Iowa Code, the General Assembly has created a statutory framework for removing non-impeachable state and local officeholders. Chapter 67 provides a framework for suspending state officers. Section 67.7 speaks directly to the issue of officers' compensation during the pendency of their suspension, an issue that the Iowa Supreme Court and the Office of the Attorney General addressed in the late nineteenth and earlier twentieth centuries, respectively. Both the court (*Brown v. Duffus*, 1885) and the attorney general[50] concluded that a loss of compensation is appropriate for those who have been convicted on articles of impeachment, but is not appropriate for those who have merely been suspended.

---

[48] *1857 Debates, supra* Article I, note 3, vol. 1, pp. 574–75. One day earlier, Mahaska County's James Young had—perhaps inadvertently—proposed the same addition. Moments after the Committee on Distribution of Powers and Legislative Department read for a second time its proposed framing of Section 20, Young proposed tinkering with the list of officers who would be subject to impeachment—and when he quoted how the provision would read under his amendment, he included the word "malfeasance" in both of the locations one sees above in Section 20. The delegates approved Young's suggested text. *Id.* at p. 527. Later that same day, when the text of Section 20 was read once again for the delegates' consideration—the occasion when Sheldon Winchester proposed what would become the final formulation of Section 20's description of the officers subject to impeachment—the word "malfeasance" was omitted from Section 20's opening clause but included in its final sentence. *Id.* at p. 551. Many days later, the delegates were still having difficulty keeping Section 20's language straight. When the Committee on Revision, Engrossment, and Enrollment presented Section 20 and the rest of Article III for a final vote on March 4, the malfeasance language was included in Section 20's opening clause but omitted from its final sentence. *Id.* at vol. 2, p. 1009. When the delegates sent out the entire constitution for Iowans' approval, however, the word appeared in both locations. *Id.* at p. 1074.

[49] Op. Iowa Att'y Gen., 1909 WL 60263 (Mar. 24, 1909) (replying to Governor Beryl Carroll).

[50] Op. Iowa Att'y Gen., 1932 WL 71554 (Apr. 30, 1932) (replying to the Auditor of State).

Section 21.
Members not appointed to office.

No senator or representative shall, during the time for which he shall have been elected, be appointed to any civil office of profit under this State, which shall have been created, or the emoluments of which shall have been increased during such term, except such offices as may be filled by elections by the people.

Modeled on Article I, Section 6, Clause 2, of the U.S. Constitution, Section 21 stands as an obstacle to a particular form of self-dealing by Iowa's senators and representatives. The provision bars a sitting state legislator from holding a "civil office of profit" during the term for which he or she was elected if both (1) the office was created—or its financial benefits were increased—during that same term and (2) the office is filled by appointment rather than by election. The provision continues to read precisely as it did under the state's first constitution, ratified in 1846; it was not the subject of documented debate at the 1857 convention.[51]

The Iowa Supreme Court's only Section 21 ruling came more than three-quarters of a century ago, in *Clark v. Murtagh* (1934). Unfortunately, it provides no interpretive guidance. Governor Daniel Turner had appointed a sitting state senator, E.W. Clark, to serve as Commissioner of Insurance. (This is the same commissioner who would later be the subject of the impeachment proceedings at issue in *Clark v. Herring* (1935); see the commentary on Section 20 of this article.) The General Assembly had increased the salary for that position while Clark was a sitting legislator. When the state's comptroller refused to pay him a portion of his salary, Clark sought a writ of mandamus to force the comptroller to make the payment. In defense, the comptroller argued that, under Section 21, Clark was ineligible to hold the commissioner position. The court refused to reach the merits of that argument, ruling that it was not procedurally permissible to raise such a defense in a mandamus lawsuit. It bears noting that, eight months before the court's opinion came down, Attorney General Edward O'Connor had issued an opinion finding that Section 21 rendered Clark ineligible to hold the position of commissioner, and that barring him from office—rather than merely stripping him of the salary increase for which he had voted as a senator—was what Section 21 required.[52] O'Connor then represented the comptroller in the ensuing *Clark* litigation.

The Office of the Attorney General has issued numerous additional opinions concerning Section 21. In 1993, for example, the office advised the speaker of the house that sitting representatives may serve on local school boards, because those board positions are uncompensated and thus do not constitute "office[s] of profit."[53] In 1977, Attorney General Richard Turner similarly advised a member

[51] *See, e.g., 1857 Debates, supra* Article I, note 3, vol. 1, p. 527.

[52] Op. Iowa Att'y Gen., 1933 WL 66062 (Aug. 10, 1933) (replying to the State Comptroller).

[53] Op. Iowa Att'y Gen., 1993 WL 122649 (Jan. 8, 1993) (replying to Robert Arnould).

of the governor's staff that an "office of profit" is not one for which "expenses are merely reimbursed."[54] In 1975, Turner issued an opinion stating that a post within an entity does not amount to an "office" if the entity's functions are limited to making mere recommendations.[55] In 1934, Attorney General Edward O'Connor determined that Section 21 bars members of the General Assembly from holding offices of profit that were created while they were serving in that body, even if they voted against the offices' creation.[56] In 1925, Attorney General Ben Gibson issued an opinion focusing on Section 21's closing clause; he concluded that a sitting member of the General Assembly could serve as a compensated Presidential Elector because the latter positions were filled by election, rather than by appointment.[57]

Section 22.
Disqualification.

No person holding any lucrative office under the United States, or this State, or any other power, shall be eligible to hold a seat in the General Assembly; but offices in the militia, to which there is attached no annual salary, or the office of justice of the peace, or postmaster whose compensation does not exceed one hundred dollars per anum, or notary public, shall not be deemed lucrative.

With narrow specified exceptions, Section 22 bars sitting legislators from holding other public offices for which compensation is paid. Modeled loosely on the final portion of Article I, Section 6, Clause 2, of the U.S. Constitution, the provision still stands in substantively the same form that it did in Iowa's first constitution (ratified in 1846), with two exceptions. First, without recorded debate, the delegates to the 1857 convention added the phrase "or notary public," as proposed by the Committee on Distribution of Powers and Legislative Department.[58] Second, the 1857 delegates added the phrase "hold a seat in." Henry County's Rufus Clarke unsuccessfully proposed that addition on two occasions, arguing that the 1846 language—stating that no person holding a lucrative public office "shall be eligible to the General Assembly"—arguably barred a person from being able to hold a lucrative public position, run for a seat in the General Assembly, and then (if victorious in that election) resign

[54] Op. Iowa Att'y Gen., 1977 WL 18980 (Sept. 27, 1977) (replying to Susan Mickelsen).

[55] Op. Iowa Att'y Gen., 1975 WL 368865 (Dec. 5, 1975) (replying to James V. Gallagher and William P. Winkelman). That same year, Turner also determined that the term "civil" excludes military offices. Op. Iowa Att'y Gen., 1975 WL 368687 (Jan. 16, 1975) (replying to William N. Plymat).

[56] Op. Iowa Att'y Gen., 1934 WL 63071 (Mar. 29, 1934) (replying to the Iowa Liquor Control Commission).

[57] Op. Iowa Att'y Gen., 1925 WL 66113 (Mar. 2, 1925) (replying to the Auditor of State).

[58] *1857 Debates, supra* Article I, note 3, vol. 1, p. 84 (indicating that the addition had already been made by the time the committee took its draft of Article III to the floor of the convention for the first time).

his current public position in order to take the seat that he had won.[59] On both of those occasions, the delegates rejected Clarke's proposal. Because he served as one of three members of the Committee on Revision, Engrossment, and Enrollment,[60] however, Clarke was in an unusually good position to make a third attempt. When he later presented the revision committee's draft of Article III, the phrase "hold a seat in" appeared in Section 22's text.[61] The addition did not provoke any documented discussion.

Section 22 has never been the focus of any decision handed down by the Iowa Supreme Court. The Office of the Attorney General, however, has been called upon many times to help discern its meaning. Representatives of that office have found, for example, that a public office is "lucrative" within the meaning of Section 22 if it is one for which compensation is attached, even if that compensation is "meager"[62] and even if the legislator declares that he or she is willing to serve in that office without pay.[63] (An office is not lucrative, however, if its holder is merely reimbursed for expenses incurred while carrying out the office's functions.[64]) The Office of the Attorney General has thus determined that a sitting legislator cannot simultaneously hold such positions as city mayor[65] or member of the Natural Resources Council.[66] In 1957, the office also concluded that Section 22's $100 limitation applies only to postmasters, and not to justices of the peace, such that individuals holding the latter position are categorically exempt from Section 22's eligibility bar.[67] (The General Assembly statutorily abolished the position of justice of the peace in 1972, as discussed in the commentary on Article XI, Section 1.)

Attorney General Richard Turner concluded in 1968 that a person holding a lucrative public office is eligible to run for a seat in the General Assembly, but must step down from that office before being sworn in as a legislator.[68] In 1975, Turner further determined that sequencing is important when determining how Section 22 problems should be resolved. If a newly elected legislator does not voluntarily step down from a lucrative public office that he or she holds, Turner said, he or she will automatically vacate that previously held office upon taking his or her oath as a legislator; but if a sitting legislator begins work as the

---

[59] *1857 Debates, supra* Article I, note 3, vol. 1, pp. 527–28, 576–77.

[60] *1857 Debates, supra* Article I, note 3, vol. 1, p. 524.

[61] *1857 Debates, supra* Article I, note 3, vol. 2, pp. 1008–09.

[62] Op. Iowa Att'y Gen., 1966 WL 157012 (Aug. 26, 1966) (replying to Clark Rasmussen).

[63] Op. Iowa Att'y Gen., 1976 WL 376041 (Sept. 23, 1976) (replying to Louis P. Culver).

[64] Op. Iowa Att'y Gen., 1992 WL 470378 (Oct. 14, 1992) (replying to Paul L. Martin and others).

[65] Op. Iowa Att'y Gen., 1909 WL 60311 (Mar. 24, 1909) (replying to C.J. Fulton).

[66] Op. Iowa Att'y Gen., 1959 WL 109283 (Jan. 1, 1959) (replying to Herschel C. Loveless).

[67] Op. Iowa Att'y Gen., 1957 WL 95203 (Jan. 18, 1957) (replying to A.C. Hanson).

[68] Op. Iowa Att'y Gen., 1968 WL 172592 (May 21, 1968) (replying to Jean M. Kleve).

holder of a lawfully created lucrative public office, he or she thereby automatically vacates his or her seat in the General Assembly.[69]

Many questions concerning Section 22 concern the definition of the word "office." It took some time for that definition to take shape. In 1924, for example, Attorney General Ben Gibson determined that a sitting representative could serve as a proofreader for the state, simply because that was a "clerical" position.[70] Over the course of the following half century—drawing heavily upon a definition that the Iowa Supreme Court had developed in other contexts—the Office of the Attorney General adopted a more nuanced understanding of the term, finding that, to be an "office,"

> (1) the position must be created by constitution or statute; (2) a portion of the sovereign power of government must be delegated to that position; (3) the duties and powers must be defined directly or impliedly by the legislature or through legislative authority; (4) the duties must be performed independently and without control of a superior power other than the law; and (5) the position must have some permanency and continuity and not be only temporary and occasional.[71]

A person who serves as an assistant police chief, for example, is not a public officer, because the General Assembly did not create that position.[72]

Even when an office is not compensated and thus is not lucrative, the Office of the Attorney General has sometimes determined that common-law principles of incompatibility bar sitting legislators from holding it. In 1966, for example, Attorney General Lawrence Scalise concluded that a state senator could not simultaneously serve as a board member for a community college or vocational school, because such schools are "subordinate" to the General Assembly and are "subject to [the General Assembly's] revisory power."[73] In more recent years, the Office of the Attorney General has cautioned that the common-law doctrine of incompatibility should be applied "narrowly" and "cautiously."[74] The General Assembly has itself narrowed the doctrine's application in some circumstances.[75]

---

[69] Op. Iowa Att'y Gen.,1975 WL 368687 (Jan. 16, 1975) (replying to William N. Plymat) (citing *State ex rel. LeBuhn v. White* (1965) for common-law principles of incompatibility).

[70] Op. Iowa Att'y Gen., 1924 WL 60481 (Apr. 12, 1924) (replying to the Code Editor).

[71] Op. Iowa Att'y Gen., 1975 WL 368687 (Jan. 16, 1975) (replying to William N. Plymat). For an example of the Iowa Supreme Court influentially applying that definition in a different context, see *Hutton v. State* (1944).

[72] Op. Iowa Att'y Gen., 1976 WL 376078 (Nov. 30, 1976) (replying to Calvin O. Hultman).

[73] Op. Iowa Att'y Gen., 1966 WL 155365 (Apr. 15, 1966) (replying to W.T. Edgren) (citing *State ex rel. Crawford v. Anderson* (1912), which held that the offices of mayor and justice of the peace were incompatible and that a person thus could not hold them simultaneously). The Office of the Attorney General has expressed views in numerous incompatibility cases.

[74] Op. Iowa Att'y Gen., 1993 WL 122649 (Jan. 8, 1993) (replying to Robert Arnould).

[75] *See, e.g.*, Iowa Code § 331.216 (concerning county supervisors).

Section 23.
Failure to account.

No person who may hereafter be a collector or holder of public monies, shall have a seat in either House of the General Assembly, or be eligible to hold any office of trust or profit in this State, until he shall have accounted for and paid into the treasury all sums for which he may be liable.

Section 23 ensures that no one who has been responsible for collecting or holding public funds can fill a sensitive state position unless he or she has accounted for and released all of the public funds that he or she is not lawfully entitled to keep. With the exception of its use of the term "hold" before the phrase "any office"—a term added by the delegates to the 1857 convention[76]—the provision still reads as it did under the state's first constitution. Section 23 has never been the focus of reported appellate litigation or of opinions published by the Office of the Attorney General.

Section 24.
Appropriations.

No money shall be drawn from the treasury but in consequence of appropriations made by law.

Section 24 ensures that the General Assembly retains primary control over how the state's revenues are spent. Tracking the opening clause of Article I, Section 9, Clause 7, of the U.S. Constitution, the provision still reads precisely as it did under the state's first constitution, ratified in 1846. It was not the subject of documented debate at any of the state's constitutional conventions.

The Iowa Supreme Court has decided only a small handful of Section 24 cases. The most broadly applicable is *Prime v. McCarthy* (1894), in which the court said that legislative intent is of paramount importance in Section 24 disputes; that, when trying to determine whether the General Assembly made an "appropriation," the central inquiry is whether the legislature lawfully authorized money to be drawn from the treasury for a specified purpose; that the legislature need not use the word "appropriation" when authorizing spending, so long as it otherwise makes its intentions clear; and that the General Assembly's past practices can help to illuminate its intentions in a given instance.

In *AFSCME/Iowa Council 61 v. State* (1992), the court held that the absence of an appropriation under Section 24 did not release the state from its contractual obligation to pay increased wages to unionized state employees in accordance with arbitrators' decisions. In *Graham v. Worthington* (1966), the court

---

[76] The Committee on Revision, Engrossment, and Enrollment evidently proposed that addition. *Compare 1857 Debates, supra* Article I, note 3, vol. 1, p. 528 (omitting that term), *with id.* at vol. 2, p. 1009 (using that term).

explained that the General Assembly may make an appropriation in general terms; it need not authorize the spending "of a sum certain out of some 'ear marked' fund." In *O'Connor v. Murtagh* (1938)—a case concerning payment of the attorney general's salary—the court determined that it should resolve any statutory ambiguities against finding that the General Assembly intended to authorize a continuing appropriation that would carry over from one legislative session to the next.

The Office of the Attorney General has issued numerous opinions concerning Section 24. In 1986, for example, the office concluded that, even when funds are received through federal consent decrees and may be spent only for purposes specified by federal law, action by the General Assembly is still required before those funds may be expended.[77] In 1979, the office determined that, absent an appropriation of the necessary funds, a court could not order the state to pay the hazardous-waste clean-up costs for which the state was liable under state law.[78] In another opinion issued that same year, the office explained that Section 24's appropriation requirement typically applies only to the state's general fund, and not to money that the state collects "to finance a governmental agency to which no general fund appropriation is made by the state."[79] In 1906, the office reiterated its earlier determination that a mere joint resolution cannot function as an appropriation-making "law" within the meaning of Section 24.[80]

Section 25.
Compensation and expenses of general assembly.

Each member of the General Assembly shall receive such compensation and allowances for expenses as shall be fixed by law but no General Assembly shall have the power to increase compensation and allowances effective prior to the convening of the next General Assembly following the session in which any increase is adopted.

Section 25 gives the General Assembly the power to establish legislators' rates of compensation and reimbursement through properly enacted legislation, but bars legislators from granting themselves mid-session increases. The provision has undergone several revisions. Under the state's 1846 constitution, legislators were authorized to set their own compensation, up to a maximum of $2 per day for a session's first fifty days and up to a maximum of $1 per day for a session's remaining days. The 1846 constitution also stated that legislators would

[77] Op. Iowa Att'y Gen., 1986 WL 1226204 (Oct. 22, 1986) (replying to Larry L. Bean).

[78] Op. Iowa Att'y Gen., 1979 WL 21155 (Dec. 31, 1979) (replying to Larry Crane).

[79] Op. Iowa Att'y Gen., 1979 WL 21164 (Apr. 30, 1979) (replying to Bob Rush and Robert Anderson).

[80] Op. Iowa Att'y Gen., 1906 WL 52813 (Jan. 4, 1906) (replying to the Executive Council).

be reimbursed $2 for every twenty miles they traveled to and from the General Assembly's meetings, and that, for extra sessions, legislators would be paid "such sum as shall be fixed for the first fifty days of the ordinary session."

At the 1857 convention, some of the delegates expressed unhappiness about the fact that, after a recently concluded extra session, legislators had granted themselves added compensation equal to what they were paid for a full regular session.[81] At the urging of Johnson County's William Penn Clarke and others, the delegates altered Section 25's text in several ways. Legislators were to be compensated at the rate of $3 per day while the General Assembly was in session (and reimbursed $3 for every twenty miles they traveled to and from the General Assembly's meetings), "after which they [would] receive such compensation as shall be fixed by law." The delegates also revised Section 25 to declare that "no General Assembly shall have power to increase the compensation of its own members" and that, for extra sessions, legislators would receive "the same mileage and per diem compensation, as fixed by law for the regular session, and none other." Noting the delegates' emphasis on a per diem compensation system, the Iowa Supreme Court later ruled in *Gallarno v. Long* (1932) that legislators' compensation for regular and extra sessions had to be fixed on a per diem—rather than a salary—basis.[82]

In 1968, Iowans placed Section 25 in the form it takes today, removing the constitutional mandate that legislators be compensated on a per diem basis, while continuing to bar legislators from granting themselves mid-session increases in pay or in expense allowances.[83] Section 2.10 of the Iowa Code establishes Iowa legislators' current rates of compensation and reimbursement.

The current version of Section 25 has never been the subject of reported appellate litigation, but has been the subject of a handful of opinions issued by the Office of the Attorney General. In 1981, for example, the office advised a pair of legislators that Section 25 does not limit the General Assembly's ability to reduce compensation and reimbursement rates for future legislative sessions.[84]

---

[81] *1857 Debates, supra* Article I, note 3, vol. 1, p. 529.

[82] The *Gallarno* court also distinguished between "legislative" and "personal" expenses, finding that reimbursement for the latter amounted to compensation and thus was subject to Section 25's constraints.

[83] Immediately prior to the 1968 amendment, the General Assembly had provided its members (other than the speaker) with compensation of $40 per day. Iowa Code § 2.11 (1966). Immediately after the amendment, the General Assembly shifted to a salary basis of compensation. Iowa Code § 2.10 (1971).

[84] Op. Iowa Att'y Gen., 1981 WL 37093 (Mar. 6, 1981) (replying to Darrell Hanson and Rod Halvorson).

Section 26.
Time laws to take effect.

An act of the general assembly passed at a regular session of a general assembly shall take effect on July 1 following its passage unless a different effective date is stated in an act of the general assembly. An act passed at a special session of a general assembly shall take effect ninety days after adjournment of the special session unless a different effective date is stated in an act of the general assembly. The general assembly may establish by law a procedure for giving notice of the contents of acts of immediate importance which become law.

Section 26 establishes default rules for determining when newly enacted statutes take effect. Those rules have gone through several iterations over the course of the state's history. Under the state's 1846 constitution, new statutes took effect once they had been "published and circulated in the several counties of this State, by authority." If it regarded a law as being "of immediate importance," the legislature was authorized to "provide that [the law] shall take effect by publication in the newspapers in the state." Under the original text of the 1857 constitution, laws passed during a regular session took effect on the following July 4, laws passed at a special session took effect ninety days after the special session adjourned, and the legislature continued to have the authority to make especially important laws effective upon publication in the state's newspapers. The delegates' brief discussion of these matters at the 1857 convention focused on how much time was needed to give the public notice of recently enacted laws.[85] In 1966, Iowans amended Section 26, changing the July date from the fourth to the first. Iowans put Section 26 into its current form in 1986, authorizing the General Assembly to designate effective dates different from those that would be set under Section 26's default rules.[86] In Section 3.7 of the Iowa Code, the General Assembly has adopted various provisions concerning statutes' and resolutions' effective dates.

On most of the occasions when the Iowa Supreme Court and the Office of the Attorney General have been presented with questions regarding statutes' effective dates, they have been able to respond simply by applying Section 26's plain terms. There have been a few exceptions, however, all of them concerning earlier versions of Section 26 but articulating principles that undoubtedly still have vitality today. In *Butters v. City of Des Moines* (1926), for example, the court

---

[85] *1857 Debates, supra* Article I, note 3, vol. 1, p. 551.

[86] Prior to that amendment, the Office of the Attorney General had concluded that the General Assembly could not establish effective dates any *earlier* than those specified in Section 26 absent special publication of those laws' contents, but could establish effective dates that extended well beyond those constitutional minimums. *See*, e.g., Op. Iowa Att'y Gen., 1973 WL 324523 (June 5, 1973) (replying to John C. Mendenhall). The office had approved making laws retroactively applicable, so long as the laws' contents and retroactivity were adequately publicized. *See*, e.g., Op. Iowa Att'y Gen., 1970 WL 207624 (Mar. 13, 1970) (replying to Wayne A. Faupell).

explained that, "[u]ntil the time arrives when a law is to take effect and be in force, a statute which is passed by both houses of the legislature and approved by the executive has no force whatever, for any purpose." In *Santo v. State* (1855), the court observed that the General Assembly may make part of a statute effective on one date and another part of the statute effective on another.

Section 27.
Divorce.

No divorce shall be granted by the General Assembly.

Section 27's ban on legislatively granted divorces continues to read precisely as it did in the state's 1846 constitution. The provision was modeled on several other states' comparable constitutional bans.[87] It was not the subject of recorded debate at any of the state's constitutional conventions, nor has it been the focus of reported appellate litigation or of opinions published by the Office of the Attorney General.

Section 28.
Lotteries.

[Repealed.]

Like the 1846 constitution before it, the constitution of 1857 stated, "No lottery shall be authorized by this State; nor shall the sale of lottery tickets be allowed." Several other early state constitutions contained similar bans.[88] Iowans repealed Section 28 in 1972.

Section 29.
Acts—one subject—expressed in title.

Every act shall embrace but one subject, and matters properly connected therewith; which subject shall be expressed in the title. But if any subject shall be embraced in an act which shall not be expressed in the title, such act shall be void only as to so much thereof as shall not be expressed in the title.

Section 29 imposes two requirements upon the General Assembly, one concerning the number of subjects that a single bill may address and the other concerning the descriptive accuracy of a bill's title. The state's first constitution, ratified in 1846, simply stated, "Every law shall embrace but one object, which shall be expressed in the title." By the time the 1857 convention's Committee

---

[87] *See,* e.g., N.J. Const. of 1844, art. IV, § 7; N.C. Const. of 1835, art. I, § 4; Tenn. Const. of 1835, art. XI, § 4.

[88] *See,* e.g., Ark. Const. of 1836, art. VII, § 6; N.J. Const. of 1844, art. IV, § 7; Tenn. Const. of 1835, art. XI, § 5.

on Distribution of Powers and Legislative Department presented its initial draft of Article III, the committee had largely put Section 29 into the form one sees here, giving the General Assembly somewhat greater latitude in the provision's opening clause and addressing the consequences of faulty titles in the provision's second sentence.[89] Apart from a short conversation about whether the word "subject" should be changed to "object" in each place it appeared in the provision,[90] the delegates regarded the committee's draft as uncontroversial.

The Iowa Supreme Court has explained that Section 29's chief purposes are threefold. First, by requiring that a bill's subject be stated in its title, the provision prevents "the evils of . . . surreptitious legislation" by ensuring that—right up front—a new bill fairly notifies legislators and citizens of its subject matter (*State v. Hutchinson Ice Cream Co.*, 1914). As the court put it in its frequently cited ruling in *State v. Talerico* (1940), Section 29 "was designed to prevent surprise in legislation, by having matter of one nature embraced in a bill whose title expressed another." Second, by requiring that each bill concern no more than "one subject, and matters properly connected therewith," Section 29 prevents "'log-rolling' in the enactment of laws, the practice of several minorities combining their several proposals as different provisions of a single bill, and thus consolidating their votes so that a majority is obtained for the omnibus bill where perhaps no single proposal of each minority could have obtained majority approval separately" (*Long v. Board of Supervisors*, 1966). Third, and relatedly, Section 29's one-subject rule "was designed to prevent riders from being attached to bills that are popular and so certain of adoption that the riders will secure adoption, not on their own merits, but on the merits of the measure to which they are attached" (*Long v. Board of Supervisors*, 1966).

The court has found significant flexibility in both of Section 29's requirements. The court has long said, for example, that an act's title need not contain "an index of the details of the act" (*Fevold v. Board of Supervisors*, 1926) and that "[a] title is sufficient, even though it is broad, if it gives fair notice of" what the act contains (*Western International v. Kirkpatrick*, 1986). The court also has explained that a single bill may "embrace all matters reasonably connected with the subject expressed in the title and not utterly incongruous thereto" (*Motor Club of Iowa v. Department of Transportation*, 1978; *Independent School District v. Iowa Employment Security Commission*, 1946). Section 29 is satisfied so long as there is "a 'unity of object' in [the act's] various provisions, and that

---

[89] The only difference between the committee's draft and the ultimately adopted text was that the former did not include the word "properly" in the opening clause. *1857 Debates*, *supra* Article I, note 3, vol. 1, p. 84. The committee added that word, without any recorded explanation, before they presented Section 29 to the delegates for discussion two and a half weeks later. *Id.* at p. 530.

[90] *1857 Debates*, *supra* Article I, note 3, vol. 1, pp. 530–31.

general object is indicated by the title" (*Cook v. Marshall County*, 1903). As the court stated in 1966's *Long v. Board of Supervisors*, "it is the general rule that all matters, however diverse they may be, which have a logical or natural connection with or are germane to the general subject, may properly be included in one statute." The more that a bill presses against the boundaries of the one-subject rule, the greater the descriptive burden that the bill's title must carry. "[A]s an act's provisions become more disjointed and less obviously related to each other," the court explained in *State v. Iowa District Court* (1987), "the legislature's obligation to provide greater specificity in the act's title necessarily increases."

Even though the court has rejected most of the Section 29 attacks it has faced, the provision—particularly its requirement concerning titles' descriptive accuracy—does have teeth. In *State v. Nickelson* (1969), for example, the court struck down a criminal provision of the Uniform Commercial Code, finding that "[n]o one reading the title to the Act would be alerted or be led to think that on the 151st page there was a recitation and prohibition of acts that might lead to five years in the penitentiary." In 1987's *State v. Iowa District Court*—a case involving a bill containing a broad range of provisions on the transportation, sale, and use of alcohol—the court found the bill's title defective because "[n]o legislator or citizen reading the title could anticipate a provision dealing with first offense drunk driving, much less a provision dealing with magistrates' jurisdiction over such offenses, would be included in the act." In 1986's *Western International v. Kirkpatrick*, the court found a bill's title insufficient because it provided readers with no indication that, "buried in the middle of a sixty-one section enactment which could fairly be said to make otherwise lexicographical changes," the enactment made "a drastic change in the workers' compensation law." The court's ruling in *State v. Taylor* (1996) presented a rare instance in which legislation violated both of Section 29's requirements. In a bill titled "Juvenile Justice," the legislature created a weapons-trafficking offense that was insufficiently related to the other subjects covered by the bill and was insufficiently described by the bill's title.

In 1990's *State v. Mabry*, the Iowa Supreme Court adopted an important timing requirement for those wishing to argue that legislation violates Section 29. Finding that "codification of the challenged legislation cures a constitutional defect in title or subject matter," the court held that there is "a window of time measured from the date legislation is passed until such legislation is codified." It is only during that time period that a Section 29 challenge may succeed. The court has acknowledged that "this limitation means that the window of opportunity for challenging a statute on this ground is entirely fortuitous because persons are not motivated to challenge a statute until they are placed in a position in which the statute adversely affects them" (*State v. Kolbet*, 2001).

Section 30.
Local or special laws—general and uniform—boundaries of counties.

The General Assembly shall not pass local or special laws in the following cases:

For the assessment and collection of taxes for State, County, or road purposes;

For laying out, opening, and working roads or highways;

For changing the names of persons;

For the incorporation of cities and towns;

For vacating roads, town plats, streets, alleys, or public squares;

For locating or changing county seats.

In all the cases above enumerated, and in all other cases where a general law can be made applicable, all laws shall be general, and of uniform operation throughout the State; and no law changing the boundary lines of any county shall have effect until upon being submitted to the people of the counties affected by the change, at a general election, it shall be approved by a majority of the votes in each county, cast for and against it.

At its heart, Section 30 rests on principles of equality, separation of powers, and the rule of law. The provision expresses Iowans' judgment that, to the extent possible, the General Assembly should be in the business of prescribing rules and standards governing all within the state who are actors in a given realm, rather than enacting laws aimed at delivering victories and losses to particular locales, entities, or individuals. In 1865's *Town of McGregor v. Baylies*, the Iowa Supreme Court catalogued some of the "evils" that Section 30 was crafted to prevent:

> the granting of exclusive privileges to certain persons to the prejudice of others; the inequality of the laws and want of uniformity in their operation resulting in confusion, and often in injustice; and, among others, the possibility of improper motives in legislators, who, to secure the passage of a law of supposed advantage to a part or all of their immediate constituency, might readily unite with others having like special schemes, and thus, by a system of combination which has been denominated "log rolling," secure the passage of many laws, not only of doubtful propriety, but some of absolute prejudice to the best interests of the State.

Prior to Section 30's adoption in 1857, for example, the General Assembly had frequently handed out charters that incorporated municipalities, sometimes with notable disparities in those charters' provisions (*Eckerson v. City of Des Moines*, 1908). In response to lobbying by individuals wishing to increase their own political power or the value of their land, the General Assembly also had frequently adopted legislation dictating which town would be a county's seat or where a county's boundary lines would be drawn.[91]

---

[91] *1857 Debates, supra* Article I, note 3, vol. 1, pp. 532–39, 556–57.

Modeled loosely on provisions of the Indiana Constitution of 1851, Section 30 was aimed at eliminating such practices.[92] It expresses a strong preference for "general" laws. A law is "general" within the meaning of Section 30 "if it operates upon all within a proper classification" (*State ex rel. Wright v. Iowa State Board of Health*, 1943). A law is "local or special" if, instead of regulating all members of a class, it limits its reach to a particular locale or to particular entities or individuals.[93] In the six specific instances that the first half of Section 30 describes, the ban on local or special legislation—and the corresponding demand for general legislation, if there is to be any legislation at all—is absolute; in all other instances, local or special legislation is forbidden only if the General Assembly could readily achieve its aims through general legislation (*State Board of Regents v. Lindquist*, 1971).

Consider, for example, *Davis & Bro. v. Woolnough* (1859). In that case, the General Assembly had repealed a portion of the City of Dubuque's charter. Because the General Assembly could have created a general law to address such matters—such as a law empowering each of the state's cities and towns to modify their own charters—the court found that the Dubuque-specific legislation was impermissible. The court had reached the same conclusion one year earlier concerning legislation aimed at amending the City of Davenport's charter (*Ex parte Pritz*, 1858).

The fact that a statute affects only a tiny number of actors does not necessarily raise Section 30 problems (*Frost v. State*, 1969; *McAunich v. Mississippi & Missouri R.R. Co.*, 1866). If, at the time of enactment, only one entity meets the statute's qualifications for receiving legislative treatment of a particular kind, Section 30 is not violated so long as it is "possible for other [entities] to attain to such qualifications" and thereby secure the right to the same treatment "without the aid of further legislation" (*Eckerson v. City of Des Moines*, 1908).[94] Moreover, there are instances in which general legislation is not essential. In 1971's *State Board of Regents v. Lindquist*, for example, the General Assembly had enacted legislation approving revenue bonds specifically for the University of Iowa Hospitals, the only major system of hospitals at a state-run university in Iowa. Iowa's justices explained that, when determining whether a "general law can be made applicable" within the meaning of Section 30, a court must "consider the nature and

---

[92] *1857 Debates, supra* Article I, note 3, vol. 1, p. 531 (referencing the Indiana Constitution); Indiana Const. of 1851, art. IV, §§ 22, 23. This is not the only constitutional provision adopted with that objective at least partially in mind. *See* Iowa Const. art. VIII, § 1 (barring the General Assembly from creating corporations "by special laws").

[93] *Cf. Dickinson v. Porter* (1948) ("The terms local, special, or private, when applied to the purpose of legislation are practically synonymous.").

[94] The court elaborated on this point in *State ex rel. West v. City of Des Moines* (1896) and *Knudson v. Linstrum* (1943).

purpose of the legislation and the conditions and circumstances under which it was enacted," bearing in mind that "the usual presumption in favor of constitutionality attends a legislative act of this kind." Finding that "the schools of higher learning possess but a single major institution like this hospital and that this hospital, which needs enlargement, has peculiar revenue-producing capabilities making revenue bonds feasible," the court held that special legislation was permissible.

When legislation is curative in nature and thus adjusts preexisting legislation in ways that particularly affect certain individuals or entities, the court is likely to find the changes "valid as against the uniformity clauses of our constitution if they would have been within the authority of the legislature to enact originally" (*Fleur de Lis Motor Inns, Inc. v. Bair,* 1981).[95]

Section 30's preference for "general" and "uniform" laws overlaps substantially with the equality provision of Article I, Section 6 ("All laws of a general nature shall have a uniform operation; the General Assembly shall not grant to any citizen, or class of citizens, privileges or immunities, which, upon the same terms shall not equally belong to all citizens."). The Iowa Supreme Court has "generally viewed these provisions of the Iowa Constitution as being similar in scope, import, and purpose to the equal protection provision of the Fourteenth Amendment to the federal Constitution" (*City of Coralville v. Iowa Utilities Board,* 2008). When legislation is challenged under Section 30 for lacking uniformity, for example, the court usually applies mere rational-basis review, just as it usually does when evaluating challenges brought under Article I, Section 6 (*Heritage Cablevision v. Marion County Board of Supervisors,* 1989). That is the approach the court took in 1943's *State ex rel. Wright v. Iowa State Board of Health,* holding that the General Assembly may adopt legislation that treats cities differently based upon the size of their populations, so long as the classification "bears a reasonable relation to the objects of the legislation." This constitutional flexibility is not, however, without limits. For example, "the systematic and intentional valuation of a particular kind of property at a higher percentage of its actual value than that at which other kinds of property are valued, or the systematic and intentional assessment of taxes on a particular kind of property at a higher rate than that imposed on property of the same kind cannot be upheld" (*Hanselman v. Humboldt County,* 1969). For more on the court's equal-protection jurisprudence, see the commentary on Article I, Section 6.

95 For an example and discussion of curative legislation concerning taxation, see *Zaber v. City of Dubuque* (2010).

Section 31.
Extra compensation—payment of claims—appropriations for local or private purposes.

No extra compensation shall be made to any officer, public agent, or contractor, after the service shall have been rendered, or the contract entered into; nor, shall any money be paid on any claim, the subject matter of which shall not have been provided for by pre-existing laws, and no public money or property shall be appropriated for local, or private purposes, unless such appropriation, compensation, or claim, be allowed by two-thirds of the members elected to each branch of the General Assembly.

To help ensure that the state's money and property are not used in unwise or inappropriate ways, Section 31 imposes three separate requirements—one on the payment of extra compensation, one on the payment of claims, and one on the appropriation of public assets for local or private purposes. The provision was added by the delegates to the 1857 convention and was not the subject of documented debate.[96] Its language closely tracks Article II, Section 29, of the Ohio Constitution of 1851.

Most of the litigation concerning Section 31 has focused on the provision's third restriction, which—absent the General Assembly's supermajority approval—bars the use of public assets for local or private purposes.[97] In *Dickinson v. Porter* (1948), the Iowa Supreme Court made it clear that the restriction is not particularly powerful. The court explained that an appropriation is not for a private purpose if it furthers some "public purpose" or "principle of public policy," that "[t]he term 'public purpose' is not to be construed narrowly," that "the legislature has the broadest discretion as to what is a public purpose," that "[a] law may serve the public interest although it benefits certain individuals or classes more than others," and that legislation violates this portion of Section 31 only if there is "an absence of all possible public interest in the purposes for which the appropriation . . . is used." Even if a public expenditure will benefit a private developer, for example, the expenditure is permissible if it serves such purposes as "preventing economic decline and promoting economic growth" (*McMurray v. City Council*, 2002).

Citing *Dickinson* and other authorities, the Office of the Attorney General has stated that government money or property is used for public purposes if the funded activity "serve[s] as a benefit to the community as a whole and, at the same time, directly relate[s] to the functions of government."[98] Emphasizing the

---

[96] *1857 Debates, supra* Article I, note 3, vol. 1, pp. 84, 539–40.

[97] In a pair of cases handed down in 1975, the Iowa Supreme Court assumed, without deciding, that this requirement applies to cities. *See Richards v. City of Muscatine* (1975); *Sampson v. City of Cedar Falls* (1975). In *Love v. City of Des Moines* (1930), however, the court stated without qualification that Section 31 places restrictions on "every city council in the state."

[98] Op. Iowa Att'y Gen., 1978 WL 17555 (Dec. 21, 1978) (replying to Norman C. Jesse).

latitude that elected officials enjoy when determining how to spend public assets, the office has said that legislation violates Section 31's public-purpose requirement only if the challenger makes "a showing of [the expenditure's] unconstitutionality beyond a reasonable doubt and a negation of every conceivable basis in its support."[99] In 1977, for example, the office determined that the state could give $1.2 million to a private educational institution in exchange for the institution's promise that at least thirty percent of its admitted students would be Iowa residents.[100] The office has nevertheless sometimes found Section 31's line crossed, as when it issued an opinion in 1976 stating that a city could not pay subsidies to private employers that hired recently laid-off workers.[101]

Section 31's other two restrictions have been examined less frequently. The provision's first restriction states that, unless a supermajority of the General Assembly approves, extra compensation cannot be paid to officers, contractors, or public agents "after the service shall have been rendered, or the contract entered into." In *Busch v. Joint Drainage District* (1924), the court held that Section 31 did not bar the payment of extra compensation to a contractor who, after launching a drainage project, encountered substantial construction difficulties that none of the parties to the contract had anticipated. In 1946, the Office of the Attorney General concluded that teachers are employees, rather than "officer[s], public agent[s], or contractor[s]," and that Section 31 thus does not bar them from receiving more compensation than the amount specified in their existing contracts.[102]

Section 31's second restriction states that, unless a supermajority of the General Assembly approves, no "money [may] be paid on any claim, the subject matter of which shall not have been provided for by pre-existing laws." In *Graham v. Worthington* (1966), the Iowa Supreme Court held that it was permissible for the Iowa Tort Claims Act to authorize payment for claims arising during the two-year period prior to the statute's enactment. Even though those torts occurred prior to the statute's adoption, the court explained, the claims would not be "paid" until thereafter.

In *Love v. City of Des Moines* (1930), the court examined Section 31's last clause, which authorizes the General Assembly to permit—with a two-thirds vote—compensation, claims, and appropriations that Section 31 would otherwise bar. The issue in *Love* was whether the City of Des Moines could pay extra compensation to a contractor in the absence of any public benefit received in exchange. Spurred on by problems caused during wartime conditions, the General Assembly had enacted legislation that purported to authorize such

---

[99] Op. Iowa Att'y Gen., 1998 WL 541522 (Jan. 6, 1998) (replying to Michael J. Moreland).

[100] Op. Iowa Att'y Gen., 1977 WL 18883 (Feb. 25, 1977) (replying to John Pelton).

[101] Op. Iowa Att'y Gen., 1976 WL 376050 (Oct. 14, 1976) (replying to Lloyd R. Smith).

[102] Op. Iowa Att'y Gen., 1946 WL 65473 (Dec. 4, 1946) (replying to M.J. Carey).

payments as a blanket matter, but the court found the statute unconstitutional. The court explained that Section 31's closing clause does not empower the legislature to enact general legislation broadly authorizing uses of public funds that would otherwise violate Section 31. Rather, it empowers the legislature to approve particular, specifically identified uses of public funds on a case-by-case basis, such as the payment that Des Moines wished to make to the contractor here. In *Grout v. Kendall* (1923), for example, the court upheld legislation that—by the vote of a legislative supermajority—approved the retroactive payment of funds to Iowans who had served in the armed services during World War I.

Section 32.
Oath of members.

Members of the General Assembly shall, before they enter upon the duties of their respective offices, take and subscribe the following oath or affirmation: "I do solemnly swear, or affirm, (as the case may be,) that I will support the Constitution of the United States, and the Constitution of the State of Iowa, and that I will faithfully discharge the duties of Senator, (or Representative, as the case may be,) according to the best of my ability." And members of the General Assembly are hereby empowered to administer to each other the said oath or affirmation.

Section 32, prescribing the oath or affirmation that the members of the General Assembly must recite before taking office, continues to read just as it did under the state's 1846 constitution. The provision has not been the focus of reported appellate litigation. In 1955, Attorney General Dayton Countryman advised a legislator that if—as the legislator feared—many sitting members of the General Assembly had not satisfied Section 32's requirement, that failure would not "operate to deny legal qualification of a member of the Legislature." Countryman determined that Section 32 is merely "directory," imposing a duty on legislators but not specifying any consequences that flow from failing to fulfil that duty.[103]

Section 33.
Census.

[Repealed.]

Section 33 of the 1857 constitution declared that, in specified years, the General Assembly was required to take a census of the state's "white inhabitants." Iowans struck the word "white" from the provision in 1868 (the same year that the nation added the Fourteenth Amendment to the U.S. Constitution and thereby limited states' ability to make racial distinctions among people within their jurisdictions[104]) and then repealed the provision altogether in 1936.

---

[103] Op. Iowa Att'y Gen., 1955 WL 78400 (Mar. 22, 1955) (replying to Howard C. Reppert, Jr.).

[104] U.S. Const. amend. XIV, § 1.

Section 34.
Senate and house of representatives—limitation.

The senate shall be composed of not more than fifty and the house of representatives of not more than one hundred members. Senators and representatives shall be elected from districts established by law. Each district so established shall be of compact and contiguous territory. The state shall be apportioned into senatorial and representative districts on the basis of population. The general assembly may provide by law for factors in addition to population, not in conflict with the Constitution of the United States, which may be considered in the apportioning of senatorial districts. No law so adopted shall permit the establishment of senatorial districts whereby a majority of the members of the senate shall represent less than forty percent of the population of the state as shown by the most recent United States decennial census.

Section 34 places a cap on the size of the senate's and house of representatives' membership; it requires that districts be compact and contiguous and sets population as the primary basis for allocating representation among the state's various communities, but otherwise leaves the district-drawing task to the lawmaking process; and it declares that a majority of the senate's members must represent at least forty percent of the state's population. Added to the constitution in 1968, Section 34 differs in a number of ways from the corresponding provisions of the 1857 constitution. Under the original 1857 text, for example, apportionment was to be determined by counting white inhabitants (that racial restriction was lifted in 1868); compactness and contiguity were not required; and there was no minimally acceptable percentage of the state's population that a majority of the senate was required to represent.[105] The 1857 text also relied upon county lines, as did constitutional amendments that Iowans adopted in 1904 and 1928. Under the current version of Section 34, county lines need not play any role at all in the state's apportionment scheme for senatorial and representative districts. Part I of this book tells the story of Iowa's apportionment battles leading to the adoption of this and other provisions.

Section 41.1 of the Iowa Code divides the state into one hundred representative districts, while Section 41.2 divides the state into fifty senatorial districts. Section 42.4 states that, when redistricting, population must be the basis for drawing district lines; it also lays out additional requirements, as well as standards by which to evaluate a district's compactness.

Citing the U.S. Supreme Court's ruling in *Reynolds v. Sims* (1964) and the Equal Protection Clause of the U.S. Constitution's Fourteenth Amendment, the Iowa Supreme Court stated in 1970's *In re Legislative Districting of General Assembly* that, "[w]hatever the means of accomplishment, the overriding

---

[105] For the delegates' debates about apportionment and closely related matters at the 1857 convention, see *1857 Debates, supra* Article I, note 3, vol. 1, pp. 540–49, 552–55, 576–78; *id.* at vol. 2, pp. 1011–17.

objective [when apportioning representation] must be substantial equality of population among the various districts, so that the vote of any citizen is approximately equal in weight to that of any other citizen in the state." Legislative districts must be drawn in such a way, the court said, that their populations are equal "as nearly as is practicable." In subsequent litigation of the same name (*In re Legislative Districting of General Assembly*), the court explained in 1972 that, to satisfy the "as nearly as is practicable" standard, the state must make a good faith effort to achieve precise mathematical equality in the districts' populations, rather than decide at the outset that a certain degree of variation will be acceptable. The court further stated that, while it is constitutionally permissible for the state to draw district lines with an eye toward helping certain incumbents retain their seats or ensuring that certain incumbents will not have to face one another in electoral battles, those objectives cannot justify population variances from district to district or a particular district's lack of compactness.[106] With respect to compactness, the court explained that Section 34 requires that each district be "as compact as practicable, having proper regard for equality of population between the several districts." If a district has a "strange shape," the court will determine whether that shape was "necessitated by considerations of population equality or result[ed] from unfeasibility." As explained in Part I of this book, the court found in both the 1970 litigation and the 1972 litigation that apportionment plans failed to meet the constitution's requirements.

Section 35.
Senators and representatives—number and districts.

The General Assembly shall in 1971 and in each year immediately following the United States decennial census determine the number of senators and representatives to be elected to the General Assembly and establish senatorial and representative districts. The General Assembly shall complete the apportionment prior to September 1 of the year so required. If the apportionment fails to become law prior to September 15 of such year, the Supreme Court shall cause the state to be apportioned into senatorial and representative districts to comply with the requirements of the Constitution prior to December 31 of such year. The reapportioning authority shall, where necessary in establishing senatorial districts, shorten the term of any senator prior to completion of the term. Any senator whose term is so terminated shall not be compensated for the uncompleted part of the term.

Iowans added Section 35 (together with Sections 34 and 36) to the constitution in 1968. The commentary on Article III, Section 34, describes some of the Iowa Supreme Court's key holdings concerning apportionment of representation in the General Assembly, and identifies sections of the Iowa Code that are

[106] Section 42.4(5) of the Iowa Code now states that "[n]o district shall be drawn for the purpose of favoring a political party, incumbent legislator or member of Congress, or other person or group. . . ."

central to Iowa's current apportionment scheme. For the story of Iowa's apportionment battles leading to the adoption of this and other provisions, see Part I of this book.

In a 1981 opinion, Attorney General Thomas Miller explained that Section 35 was aimed, in part, at putting an end to the kinds of lengthy volleys that had occurred between the courts and the General Assembly in the 1960s when questions were raised about the state's legislative apportionment. Miller predicted that, absent significant delays in receiving the federal census data in a given reapportionment cycle, the Iowa Supreme Court would strictly enforce Section 35's September deadlines, such that, if the General Assembly failed to meet those deadlines, it would "irretrievably surrender jurisdiction to the Iowa Supreme Court" according to Section 35's terms.[107]

Section 36.
Review by supreme court.

Upon verified application by any qualified elector, the Supreme Court shall review an apportionment plan adopted by the General Assembly which has been enacted into law. Should the Supreme Court determine such plan does not comply with the requirements of the constitution, the court shall within ninety days adopt or cause to be adopted an apportionment plan which shall so comply. The Supreme Court shall have original jurisdiction of all litigation questioning the apportionment of the General Assembly or any apportionment plan adopted by the General Assembly.

As Part I of this book explains in greater detail, Iowans added Section 36 (together with Sections 34 and 35) to the constitution in 1968. Under the provision's terms, the Iowa Supreme Court resolves disputes about whether the state's apportionment plans conform to the constitution's requirements, and is charged with putting a permissible apportionment plan into place when it has determined that an existing plan is unconstitutional. Iowa voters have twice brought actions in the Iowa Supreme Court alleging that the General Assembly had adopted unconstitutional apportionment plans (*In re Legislative Districting of General Assembly*, 1970 and 1972). The court agreed with the voters on both occasions, as described in Part I and in the commentary on Article III, Section 34.

Section 37.
Congressional districts.

When a congressional district is composed of two or more counties it shall not be entirely separated by a county belonging to another district and no county shall be divided in forming a congressional district.

---

[107] Op. Iowa Att'y Gen., 1981 WL 37094 (Mar. 7, 1981) (replying to Roger Halvorson).

Section 37 still reads as it did in the original text of the 1857 constitution, with one exception: under the 1857 constitution, Section 37's requirements applied to congressional districts, senatorial districts, and representative districts alike. Iowa voters removed the latter two sets of districts from the provision in 1968, the same year they adopted the current version of Article III, Section 34. As explained above, Section 34 places population (rather than county lines) at the heart of the state's apportionment system for senatorial and representative districts, and requires that those districts be compact. Section 37 has never been the focus of reported appellate litigation or of opinions published by the Office of the Attorney General.

Section 40.1 of the Iowa Code divides the state's ninety-nine counties into congressional districts.

Section 38.
Elections by general assembly.

In all elections by the General Assembly, the members thereof shall vote viva voce and the votes shall be entered on the journal.

Section 38 continues to read just as it did in the original text of the 1857 constitution. Carried over from Article II, Section 33, of the state's first constitution (ratified in 1846), the provision did not provoke any recorded discussion at the 1857 convention.[108] Nor has it been the focus of appellate litigation.

By requiring legislators to cast their votes "viva voce"—that is, orally—Section 38 would appear to preclude the use of modern voting technologies in the General Assembly. Both chambers, however, do make regular use of voting machines.[109] The key to understanding why that practice does not violate Section 38 lies in understanding the provision's purpose. Recall that Article II, Section 6, states that "[a]ll elections by the people shall be by ballot." In 1900, Attorney General Milton Remley was asked whether Section 6 bars the use of voting machines on Election Day. Remley replied that machines are indeed permissible. His explanation is illuminating:

> [I]f we consider the original meaning of the word "ballot" as "a ball," and limit the manner of election to that used originally when the ball was in use, it will be seen that since the constitution was adopted there has never been a constitutional election, for never have balls been used in the state of Iowa. The Greeks use shells, ostrakon, for their method of conducting a secret ballot, hence the word "ostracial." In this growth of language, ballot has come to mean, and did so mean, in my judgment, at the time our constitution was adopted, a method of conducting a secret ballot.

---

[108] *See, e.g., 1857 Debates, supra* Article I, note 3, vol. 1, p. 549.

[109] *See* Senate Rule 22 ("Manner of Voting"); House Rule 74 ("Manner of Voting"). Both chambers' rules are available at https://www.legis.iowa.gov/chambers/rules.

> [Article II, Section 6], therefore, means that all elections by the people shall be by that system which enables the voter to express his choice without it being known for whom or what he has voted. It is used in contradistinction to a viva voce vote, as had been formerly used in England. Any system, then, which preserves that secrecy of the ballot or vote of the elector, in my judgment fulfills the constitutional requirement.[110]

Under Remley's logic—logic that the Iowa Supreme Court subsequently echoed, as explained in the commentary on Article II, Section 6—legislators' use of voting machines does not violate Article III, Section 38, so long as the content of legislators' votes is not concealed.

Section 38A.
Municipal home rule.

Municipal corporations are granted home rule power and authority, not inconsistent with the laws of the General Assembly, to determine their local affairs and government, except that they shall not have power to levy any tax unless expressly authorized by the General Assembly.

The rule or proposition of law that a municipal corporation possesses and can exercise only those powers granted in express words is not a part of the law of this state.

In the mid-nineteenth century, the Iowa Supreme Court's Chief Justice John Forrest Dillon influentially authored a ruling declaring that municipalities possess only those powers that the state legislature has expressly conferred upon them, that are "necessarily implied" by expressly conferred powers, and that are "absolutely essential to the declared objects and purposes of the [municipal] corporation" (*Merriam v. Moody's Executors*, 1868).[111] In 1968, Iowans ratified Section 38A—commonly called the Home Rule Amendment—and thereby decisively rejected the Dillon Rule.[112] Section 38 gives cities and towns significant control over their own local affairs, so long as they stay within the overarching boundaries set by the General Assembly and so long as they secure the General Assembly's express permission before levying taxes. Persons studying municipal home-rule issues will also want to consult various portions of the Iowa Code, including Chapter 364 ("Powers and Duties of Cities") and Chapter 372 ("Organization of City Government").

---

[110] Op. Iowa Att'y Gen., 1900 WL 165748 (Mar. 21, 1900) (replying to William W. Hawk).

[111] In another ruling issued that same year, Chief Justice Dillon wrote that "[m]unicipal corporations owe their origin to, and derive their powers and rights wholly from, the legislature. It breathes into them the breath of life, without which they cannot exist. As it creates, so it may destroy. If it may destroy, it may abridge and control" (*City of Clinton v. Cedar Rapids & Missouri River Railroad Co.*, 1868).

[112] For background information on the Home Rule Amendment, the Iowa Supreme Court has frequently cited Sam F. Scheidler, "Implementation of Constitutional Home Rule in Iowa," 22 *Drake Law Review* 294 (1973).

In its first significant ruling on Section 38A, the Iowa Supreme Court held that the phrase "not inconsistent with the laws of the general assembly" refers to all laws that the legislature may enact from time to time, rather than merely to those laws that were in existence on the date of Section 38A's adoption (*Bechtel v. City of Des Moines*, 1975). The General Assembly is thus free to adopt, amend, or repeal statutes concerning towns and cities. As the court observed in 2010's *Hensler v. City of Davenport*, the legislature "retain[s] the unfettered power to forbid a municipality from exercising police powers, even over those matters traditionally thought to involve local matters." Absent the General Assembly's decision to bar municipal regulation in a given area, however, towns and cities today enjoy far greater regulatory power than they did when the Dillon Rule was in effect.

When determining whether a municipality has regulated in a manner "inconsistent" with a state statute, the court asks whether the General Assembly has "preempted" the local regulation. State law preempts local regulation if "the legislature has explicitly prohibited local action in a given area" (express preemption), if "a local ordinance prohibits an act permitted by a statute or permits an act prohibited by a statute" and thus stands in "irreconcilable" conflict with state law (implied conflict preemption), or if "the legislature has so covered a subject by statute as to demonstrate a legislative intent that regulation in the field is preempted by state law" (implied field preemption) (*Hensler v. City of Davenport*, 2010). In 2012's *Mall Real Estate, LLC v. City of Hamburg*, for example, the court ruled that the General Assembly had preempted a city's ability to regulate live nude dancing. The court's 2008 ruling in *Baker v. City of Iowa City* provides another example: the court ruled that Iowa City's extension of liability for unfair employment practices to very small employers could not be reconciled with the General Assembly's decision to exempt employers with fewer than four employees from liability.

For reasons that the court explained in *Goodell v. Humboldt County* (1998), implied field preemption is rare in Iowa. Unlike courts in a number of other states, Iowa courts will not try to determine whether, as a matter of public policy, uniform state regulation of a given matter is more desirable than a regime in which localities are allowed to tailor laws to their own liking. When confronted with a field-preemption claim, Iowa courts focus instead on whether the General Assembly has itself clearly indicated that it desires uniform regulation and has thus preempted the field. The *Goodell* court explained that "extensive regulation of an area is not sufficient [for implied field preemption] in the absence of a clear expression of legislative intent to preempt regulation of a field by local authorities, or a clear expression of the legislature's desire to have uniform regulations statewide." On this and other matters concerning home-rule preemption, *Goodell*'s extensive and frequently cited discussion is a profitable starting point for anyone wishing to obtain detailed information about the Iowa Supreme Court's analytic framework.

In Section 364.3(3) of the Iowa Code, the General Assembly has authorized municipalities to "set standards and requirements which are higher or more stringent than those imposed by state law, unless a state law provides otherwise." The court has tried to square this statute with the commonly declared proposition that an ordinance is irreconcilable with a statute—and is thus invalid under Section 38A—if it bans conduct that a statute permits. As the court's ruling in *BeeRite Tire Disposal/Recycling v. City of Rhodes* (2002) illustrates, the justices try to discern whether it is possible to conclude that, despite its greater demands, the challenged ordinance is "in harmony with the statutory scheme." On the facts of the case before it, for example, the *BeeRite* court concluded that the ordinance was valid because it "promot[ed] the underlying policy of th[e tire-disposal] statute, but with greater force," such as by requiring "a permit for storing a minimum of 100 plus tires, rather than a minimum of 500 plus tires" and by requiring "a solid metal fence rather than a chain link fence." In *Goodell v. Humboldt County* (1998), the court observed that "[a]ny distinction between a local ordinance that is inconsistent with state law and one that merely sets a higher standard or requirement is at best subtle," but stated that courts are nevertheless obliged to reconcile a challenged ordinance with state law whenever it is possible to do so. Citing *Sioux City Police Officers' Association v. City of Sioux City* (1993), for example, the *Goodell* court explained that "[w]hen a state law merely sets a standard, a local law setting a higher standard would not conflict with the state law," as when a locality determines that job applicants for civil-service positions must possess qualifications that go beyond merely passing a state-prescribed civil-service examination.

Numerous matters are "local affairs" within the meaning of Section 38A and thus are appropriate subjects of municipal regulation. In *Green v. City of Cascade* (1975), for example, the court held that a municipality enjoys broad authority to adopt regulations governing the construction and repair of streets and sewage facilities. Of course, not everything is a local concern. In *Molitor v. City of Cedar Rapids* (1985), for example, the court ruled that municipalities cannot help to define the jurisdiction of state courts. Litigation concerning what is and is not a local affair is rare, because the General Assembly has broadly declared in Section 364.1 of the Iowa Code that, unless forbidden by state law, a municipality may "exercise any power and perform any function it deems appropriate to protect and preserve the rights, privileges, and property of the city or of its residents, and to preserve and improve the peace, safety, health, welfare, comfort, and convenience of its residents."

The final clause of Section 38A's first paragraph states that municipalities need the General Assembly's express permission if they wish to "levy any tax." A tax is a charge that a government imposes for the primary purpose of raising revenue to support the government's operations, rather than a charge imposed in exchange for conferring "special benefits" upon the person or entity making the payment (*Home Builders Association v. City of West Des Moines*, 2002). When a municipality does charge a fee in exchange for conferring a special benefit, that fee "is not a tax so long as it is the fair and reasonable cost of providing that" benefit (*City of Asbury v. Iowa City Development Board*, 2006). In *Kragnes v. City of Des Moines* (2006), the court similarly explained that "a license fee, permit fee, or franchise fee is not a tax so long as it is related to the reasonable costs of inspecting, licensing, supervising, or otherwise regulating the activity that is being licensed, permitted, or franchised." In *City of Asbury*, for example, the court ruled that a municipality had not levied a tax when it charged property owners a portion of the cost of extending water and sewer lines to their properties, while in *City of Hawarden v. US West Communications* (1999), the court ruled that a city had impermissibly levied a tax when it excessively charged a telephone utility for using public property.

Section 39.
Legislative districts.

In establishing senatorial and representative districts, the state shall be divided into as many senatorial districts as there are members of the senate and into as many representative districts as there are members of the house of representatives. One senator shall be elected from each senatorial district and one representative shall be elected from each representative district.

Iowans added Section 39 to the constitution in 1970. The provision ensures that the residents of each senatorial and representative district will be represented by no more than one senator and one representative. Prior to 1968—when the state's apportionment system was overhauled by the addition of retooled versions of Article III, Sections 34, 35, and 36—some populous counties were allocated more than one senator and representative, elected at large. For voters in those heavily populated counties, that system worked both to their advantage (such as by allowing them to vote for a greater fraction of each chamber's members) and to their disadvantage (such as by minimizing the voting influence of minority groups). Citing the "one person, one vote" principle that the U.S. Supreme Court had recently adopted, the Iowa Supreme Court declared in 1966's *Kruidenier v. McCulloch* that, absent unusual circumstances, "[a]ny scheme of legislative apportionment in which there are multimember districts and single-member districts in the same house impairs the right of a resident of a single-member district to have the laws operate uniformly as guaranteed by section 6, Article I, of the Constitution of Iowa." The General Assembly initially responded to *Kruidenier* by dividing those populous counties into subdistricts, but that system was quickly replaced by the regime required by Section 39 and the 1968 amendments.[113]

[113] Attorney General Richard Turner described these developments in Op. Iowa Att'y Gen., 1969 WL 181546 (Mar. 27, 1969) (replying to Charles P. Miller).

Section 39A.
Counties home rule.

Counties or joint county-municipal corporation governments are granted home rule power and authority, not inconsistent with the laws of the general assembly, to determine their local affairs and government, except that they shall not have power to levy any tax unless expressly authorized by the general assembly. The general assembly may provide for the creation and dissolution of joint county-municipal corporation governments. The general assembly may provide for the establishment of charters in county or joint-municipal corporation governments.

If the power or authority of a county conflicts with the power and authority of a municipal corporation, the power and authority exercised by a municipal corporation shall prevail within its jurisdiction.

The proposition or rule of law that a county or joint county-municipal corporation government possesses and can exercise only those powers granted in express words is not a part of the law of this state.

Iowans ratified Section 39A in 1978, thereby placing counties and county-municipal governments on the same footing that municipalities enjoy under Section 38A of this article. As *Decatur County v. Public Employment Relations Board* (1997) and *Hensler v. City of Davenport* (2010) respectively illustrate, the Iowa Supreme Court routinely relies upon cases decided under Section 38A when adjudicating cases arising under Section 39A, and vice versa. The commentary on Section 38A explains the Dillon Rule that Section 38A and Section 39A both reject. It also provides an overview of the analytic frameworks that the Iowa Supreme Court uses when determining whether a local law is "inconsistent with the laws of the general assembly" and when determining whether a governmental charge constitutes a "tax" requiring the General Assembly's authorization.

In *Smith v. Board of Supervisors* (1982), the court ruled that Section 39A does not unconstitutionally subordinate the constitution to the will of the legislature or unlawfully permit constitutional amendments by means other than those specified in Article X. Rather, the court said, Section 39A simply gives the General Assembly "reasonable and appropriate control to override the counties' home-rule power in certain instances."

Persons studying county home-rule issues will want to consult various portions of the Iowa Code, including Chapter 331 ("County Home Rule Implementation"). For example, Section 331.301(1) declares that, unless forbidden by state law, a county may "exercise any power and perform any function it deems appropriate to protect and preserve the rights, privileges, and property of the county or of its residents, and to preserve and improve the peace, safety, health, welfare, comfort, and convenience of its residents." As the court noted in *Worth County Friends of Agriculture v. Worth County* (2004), that definition renders "almost anything . . . a local affair," thereby largely obviating the need for judicial determinations of what is and is not a "local affair" within the meaning of Section 39A.

Section 40.
Nullification of administrative rules.

The general assembly may nullify an adopted administrative rule of a state agency by the passage of a resolution by a majority of all of the members of each house of the general assembly.

Iowans added Section 40 to the constitution in 1984, giving the General Assembly the unilateral power to reject administrative rules that the state's administrative agencies have promulgated. The argument for the provision's necessity runs as follows. Just like Congress in the federal system, the General Assembly will sometimes enact a statute that sketches the broad outlines of a regulatory regime on a given matter and that tasks an administrative agency with fleshing out the regime's details through the agency's rulemaking process. If the General Assembly believes that the agency has subsequently adopted a rule that takes the law in an undesirable direction, it might wish to nullify the rule. Absent Section 40, however, the General Assembly could run into trouble. The agency is almost certain to be an arm of the executive branch of government, and the governor might wish to keep the rule in place. Under the separation-of-powers doctrine described in Article III, Section 1, the General Assembly could not unilaterally compel the agency to abandon the rule. Moreover, any bill rejecting the rule would be susceptible to the governor's veto under Article III, Section 16.[114] Section 40 resolves that standoff in favor of the General Assembly, giving it the power to nullify an administrative rule—even over the governor's objection—so long as both chambers pass resolutions expressing their desire to do so.

In *Iowa Federation of Labor, AFL-CIO v. Iowa Department of Job Service* (1988), the Iowa Supreme Court recited the above rationales for Section 40, then rejected a state agency's contention that Section 40 was intended "to be a transfer of agency rule review power from the judiciary to the legislature, thereby depriving the courts of jurisdiction to review agency rules." Without elaborating on Section 40's justification or requirements, the court enforced a Section 40 nullification in 1988's *Alexander v. Employment Appeal Board*.

Under Section 17A.8(9) of the Iowa Code, a committee of legislators is authorized to "delay the effective date of a rule until the adjournment of the next regular session of the general assembly," thereby giving the legislature time to decide whether to adopt a joint resolution nullifying the rule. Section 17A.4(7) similarly gives the committee the power to delay a rule's implementation for seventy days, when necessary to give the committee more time to study the rule. There is reason to question those provisions' constitutionality under the

[114] Attorney General Richard Turner provided this same analysis in 1967. Op. Iowa Att'y Gen., 1967 WL 167056 (May 10, 1967) (replying to Ray Bailey). For one of the U.S. Supreme Court's leading rulings on the subject of congressional efforts to control the actions of federal executive agencies, see *INS v. Chadha* (1983).

separation-of-powers doctrine. Section 40 gave the General Assembly the power to nullify rules, but it did not explicitly give the legislature the power to suspend an executive agency's lawfully promulgated rules while deciding whether to exercise the nullification power.[115]

---

[115] For a discussion of these and related issues, see Jerry L. Anderson & Christopher Poynor, "A Constitutional and Empirical Analysis of Iowa's Administrative Rules Committee Procedure," 61 *Drake Law Review* 1 (2012).

Article IV

Executive Department

Section 1.
Governor.

The Supreme Executive power of this State shall be vested in a Chief Magistrate, who shall be styled the Governor of the State of Iowa.

Section 1, which introduces the Iowa Constitution's treatment of the executive branch by giving the governor the "Supreme" authority to put the state's laws into action, continues to stand in precisely the same form that it took in the state's first constitution, ratified in 1846.[1] By vesting the "Supreme" executive power in the governor, Section 1's language differs from that of the U.S. Constitution, which vests "[t]he Executive Power"—unmodified by adjectives—in the nation's president.[2] Because Section 1 was not the subject of documented debate at any of the state's three constitutional conventions, we cannot be sure what particular baggage the Iowa Constitution's framers intended the word "supreme" to carry. They certainly did not invent the phrase; numerous other states had already used

---

[1] The delegates to the Territory of Iowa's 1844 constitutional convention had proposed stating that "[t]he supreme executive power shall be vested in a governor." *1844 Journal, supra* Article I, note 3, p. 24. When Cedar County's Samuel Bissell presented the Committee on the Executive Department's draft of Section 1 for discussion at the 1846 convention, the provision already had been reframed in the language that it uses today. *1846 Journal, supra* Article I, note 3, p. 54.

[2] U.S Const. art. II, § 1.

the same formulation when vesting their states' executive powers in their respective governors.[3]

Section 1 has done little freestanding work in the opinions issued by the Iowa Supreme Court and the Office of the Attorney General. Ordinarily, Section 1 either is cited in conjunction with an explanation of the separation of powers—an important topic discussed in this book's commentary on Article III, Section 1—or is cited in conjunction with other, more particularized constitutional texts. In 1941's *Ryan v. Wilson*, for example, Section 1 was among the constitutional provisions on which the Iowa Supreme Court relied when ruling that the governor was protected by an absolute privilege in a lawsuit alleging that defamatory statements had been made in an auditing report that the governor had lawfully commissioned. In 1988, the Office of the Attorney General issued an opinion in which it briefly noted that Section 1 gives the governor "such powers as will secure efficient execution of the laws, as distinguished from the power to make or judge laws."[4]

Section 2.
Election and term.

The governor and the lieutenant governor shall be elected by the qualified electors at the time and place of voting for members of the general assembly. Each of them shall hold office for four years from the time of installation in office and until a successor is elected and qualifies.

When the Committee on the Executive Department first presented its draft of Section 2 at the 1846 convention, it proposed that governors serve two-year terms.[5] On the motion of Stephen Shelleday, a farmer from Mahaska County, the delegates extended the governor's term to four years.[6] By the time of the 1857 convention eleven years later, the four-year term had become highly controversial. As Part I explains in greater detail, the delegates to that convention opted to reduce the governor's term to two years.[7] Thus it remained for more

---

[3] *See*, e.g., Ala. Const. of 1819, art. IV, § 1; Ark. Const. of 1836, art. V, § 1; Conn. Const. of 1818, art. IV, § 1; Del. Const. of 1792, art. III, § 1; Me. Const. of 1820, art. V, part 1, § 1; Ohio Const. of 1803, art. II, § 1; Tex. Const. of 1845, art. V, § 1. These early state constitutions may owe a debt to Blackstone. *See* William Blackstone, *Commentaries on the Laws of England* (1765), vol. 1, p. 183 ("The supreme executive power of these kingdoms is vested by our laws in a single person, the king or queen. . . ."). Litigation involving such provisions has sometimes featured battles between governors and attorneys general regarding the litigation course that a state ought to take. *See*, e.g., *Riley v. Cornerstone Community Outreach, Inc.* (Ala. 2010); *State ex rel. Stubbs v. Dawson* (Kan. 1911).

[4] Op. Iowa Att'y Gen., 1988 WL 247768 (Jan. 20, 1988) (replying to Thomas J. Jochum).

[5] *1846 Journal, supra* Article I, note 3, p. 54.

[6] *1846 Journal, supra* Article I, note 3, p. 82. Some sources spell his name "Shelledy." I follow here the spelling used in the *1844 Journal* and the *1846 Journal*.

[7] *1857 Journal, supra* Article I, note 3, p. 216.

than a century, until Iowa voters in 1972 extended the governor's term back to four years.[8] Iowans amended Section 2 once again in 1988, adding the reference to the lieutenant governor (and thereby transplanting a provision that in 1972 had been placed in Section 3).

Perhaps because Section 2 is not beset by ambiguities, neither the Iowa Supreme Court nor the Office of the Attorney General has been called upon to interpret its meaning.

Section 3.
Governor and lieutenant governor elected jointly—returns of elections.

The electors shall designate their selections for governor and lieutenant governor as if these two offices were one and the same. The names of nominees for the governor and the lieutenant governor shall be grouped together in a set on the ballot according to which nominee for governor is seeking office with which nominee for lieutenant governor, as prescribed by law. An elector shall cast only one vote for both a nominee for governor and a nominee for lieutenant governor. The returns of every election for governor and lieutenant governor shall be sealed and transmitted to the seat of government of the state, and directed to the speaker of the house of representatives who shall open and publish them in the presence of both houses of the general assembly.

Iowa's first constitution, ratified in 1846, did not establish the position of lieutenant governor.[9] If the governor died, resigned, was removed from office, or was "absen[t] from the state," for example, "the powers and duties of the office [were to] devolve upon the Secretary of State."[10] As Part I explains in greater detail, the delegates to the 1857 convention concluded that Iowa would be better off having a lieutenant governor elected to serve as the senate's president and to stand first in the line of gubernatorial succession.[11] Moreover, under the scheme that the delegates established, the governor and lieutenant governor were elected separately,[12] such that political antagonists could find themselves contemporaneously holding the state's two highest executive positions.

Iowans altered that state of affairs in two separate amendments to Section 3. In 1972, they lengthened the governor's and lieutenant governor's terms to four years. Then, in 1988, Iowa voters took steps to ensure that the persons serving

[8] For contemporaneous coverage of Iowans' decision, see Richard Doak, "Iowa Voters Face Issues of Lottery, Judges, Office Term," *Des Moines Register*, Oct. 8, 1972, at 1B; Editorial, "For Improved Iowa Government," *Des Moines Register*, Oct. 15, 1972, at 10C.

[9] In the Territory of Iowa's first proposed constitution, however, the office of lieutenant governor was part of the delegates' plan. *1844 Journal, supra* Article I, note 3, pp. 25–27.

[10] Iowa Const. of 1846, art. V, § 18.

[11] Iowa Const. of 1857, art. IV, §§ 17, 18.

[12] Iowa Const. of 1857, art. IV, § 3.

together as governor and lieutenant governor would be political allies.[13] In an amendment approved that year, Iowans repealed the prior version of Section 3 in its entirety and replaced it with the text that appears above. Pursuant to Section 3's first three sentences, a candidate for either governor or lieutenant governor must run as a team with an individual seeking the other office, and voters are not allowed to split their ballots between members of two competing teams. Section 3's final sentence, setting forth the process by which each gubernatorial election's returns are to be delivered to the speaker of the house and then opened and published in the presence of the General Assembly, carries forward procedures that are substantively identical to those that the 1857 constitution prescribed.[14]

Like those of Section 2, Section 3's requirements are reasonably straightforward, and so it is not surprising that neither the Iowa Supreme Court nor the Office of the Attorney General has elaborated upon their meaning.

Section 4.
Election by general assembly in case of tie—succession by lieutenant governor.

The nominees for governor and lieutenant governor jointly having the highest number of votes cast for them shall be declared duly elected. If two or more sets of nominees for governor and lieutenant governor have an equal and the highest number of votes for the offices jointly, the general assembly shall by joint vote proceed, as soon as possible, to elect one set of nominees for governor and lieutenant governor. If, upon the completion by the general assembly of the canvass of votes for governor and lieutenant governor, it appears that the nominee for governor in the set of nominees for governor and lieutenant governor receiving the highest number of votes has since died or resigned, is unable to qualify, fails to qualify, or is for any other reason unable to assume the duties of the office of governor for the ensuing term, the powers and duties shall devolve to the nominee for lieutenant governor of the same set of nominees for governor and lieutenant governor, who shall assume the powers and duties of governor upon inauguration and until the disability is removed. If both nominees for governor and lieutenant governor are unable to assume the duties of the office of governor, the person next in succession shall act as governor.

Iowa added the position of lieutenant governor to the state's slate of executive officers in 1857. As explained in Part I and in the commentary on Section 3 of this article, the 1857 constitution required candidates for governor and lieutenant governor to run for office separately from one another, such that individuals with sharply conflicting political views might find themselves elected to serve concurrently. The General Assembly was given the task of breaking

---

[13] For contemporaneous coverage of Iowans' decision, see Linda Lantor, "Lieutenant Governor Amendments Big Winners," *Des Moines Register*, Nov. 9, 1988, at 8M.

[14] That procedure is reinforced by Iowa Code § 50.35.

ties in races for those two positions. In 1952, Iowa voters amended Section 4 by adding a provision stating that if, "upon the completion of the canvass of votes for Governor and Lieutenant Governor by the General Assembly," the governor-elect had become unable to serve, the governor's powers and duties would fall to the person who had received the highest number of votes for the position of lieutenant governor. In 1988, in conjunction with the 1988 amendment described in the commentary on Section 3 of this article, Iowa voters replaced the entirety of Section 4 with the text that one sees above. A candidate for the governorship now runs as a team with a candidate for the position of lieutenant governor. As under the prior constitutional text, the General Assembly breaks ties in gubernatorial races and the governor's duties fall to the newly elected lieutenant governor if the governor-elect is unable to serve. If both the governor-elect and the lieutenant governor-elect are unable to serve, then the duties of the governor's office are assigned to "the person next in succession."

Iowa Code Sections 2.27 and 2.28 provide for the General Assembly's canvass of votes cast for the positions of governor and lieutenant governor. The line of succession for vacancies in those two offices is established by Section 19 of this article.

Neither the Iowa Supreme Court nor the Office of the Attorney General has had occasion to elaborate upon Section 4's requirements. For a discussion of important issues concerning the line of gubernatorial succession, see the commentary on Sections 17 and 19 of this article.

Section 5.
Contested elections.

Contested elections for the offices of governor and lieutenant governor shall be determined by the general assembly as prescribed by law.

Disputes about the rightful winners of races for the positions of governor and lieutenant governor are to be resolved by the General Assembly. Apart from a minor adjustment in 1988 to account for Iowans' decision to begin electing its governors and lieutenant governors jointly (see Sections 3 and 4 of this article), Section 5 remains substantively identical to the original 1857 text. The procedural framework for resolving contested gubernatorial elections is established by Chapter 58 of the Iowa Code.

Neither the Iowa Supreme Court nor the Office of the Attorney General has had an opportunity to address Section 5's requirements.

Section 6.
Eligibility.

No person shall be eligible to the office of Governor, or Lieutenant Governor, who shall not have been a citizen of the United States, and a resident of the

State, two years next preceding the election, and attained the age of thirty years at the time of said election.

Section 6 describes the criteria one must meet in order to serve as governor or lieutenant governor. The provision is substantively identical to the corresponding passage of the constitution proposed by the delegates to the Territory of Iowa's 1844 convention, with one exception: the 1844 draft would have required that one be a United States citizen, but would not have required that this citizenship be of any particular duration.[15] The two-year federal citizenship requirement was added in the state's first constitution, ratified in 1846.[16] At the 1857 convention, Mills County's Daniel Solomon (a twenty-seven-year-old lawyer) and Clayton County's Alpheus Scott (a thirty-two-year-old real-estate agent) proposed that the age requirement be eliminated, arguing that the world provided plenty of examples of successful leaders younger than thirty, and that there was little evidence that people become more thoughtful or talented as they grow older. Henry County's Rufus Clarke and Wapello County's George Gillaspy agreed that—contrary to the tenets of what they called "fogyism"—there was no need to distrust voters' ability to decide whether a given candidate was up to the job. By a vote of 13 to 16, however, the convention rejected those arguments.[17] They also rejected Gillaspy's proposal that the required age be reduced to twenty-one[18] and the suggestion by Benton County's James Traer that the required age be reduced to twenty-five.[19]

The Iowa Supreme Court has not issued any rulings concerning Section 6. In 1974, Attorney General Richard Turner stated (in an opinion principally focused on legislators' eligibility) that Section 6 does not require the governor or lieutenant governor to remain a resident of Iowa after he or she has been elected.[20]

Section 7.
Commander in chief.

The Governor shall be commander in chief of the militia, the army, and navy of this State.

---

[15] *1844 Journal, supra* Article I, note 3, p. 24.

[16] Iowa Const. of 1846, art. V, § 3. The change was evidently made by the Committee on Revision, late in the convention's proceedings. *See 1846 Journal, supra* Article I, note 3, p. 82 (noting an amendment to Section 6, without the two-year federal citizenship requirement having yet been proposed or approved); *id.* at pp. 104–05 (summarily indicating that the article on the Executive Department was among a slate of texts that the Committee on Revision had amended and that the delegates approved).

[17] *1857 Debates, supra* Article I, note 3, vol. 1, pp. 580–82.

[18] *1857 Journal, supra* Article I, note 3, p. 217.

[19] *1857 Debates, supra* Article I, note 3, vol. 1, p. 583.

[20] Op. Iowa Att'y Gen., 1974 WL 353736 (Apr. 1, 1974) (replying to Richard Drake and Andrew Varley).

By declaring that the governor shall serve as the head of Iowa's military forces, Section 7 works in conjunction with Section 1 of Article VI, which establishes the state's militia. Section 7 closely echoes language found in the U.S. Constitution, which states that the president is the "Commander in Chief of the Army and Navy of the United States, and of the Militia of the several States, when called into actual Service of the United States."[21] Section 7 remains identical to the corresponding provision of the state's 1846 constitution.[22] It was not the focus of documented debate at any of the state's three constitutional conventions. Provisions substantively similar to Section 7 appear in state constitutions across the country, and were prevalent in constitutions that Iowa's framers had available as models.[23]

The Iowa Supreme Court has not yet had an opportunity to interpret Section 7's meaning, although in 1935's *State ex rel. O'Connor v. District Court in Shelby County* the court described the circumstances in which Governor Clyde Herring—acting as the state's commander in chief—briefly declared martial law in Iowa's Crawford County and adjacent areas. In 1997, Section 7 was among the many texts that the Office of the Attorney General cited in support of its conclusion that, when the governor uses the Iowa Army National Guard to help enforce the state's drug laws, the Guard is acting as a "state law enforcement agency" within the meaning of federal forfeiture law and is thus eligible to receive forfeited assets.[24] In 1980, the office indicated that, as the state's commander in chief, the governor may call out the National Guard while awaiting completion of any statutory prerequisites for such a deployment, if he or she "determines that a public disorder or disaster presents a significant problem of law enforcement or threats to life and property."[25] In 1977, Attorney General Richard Turner concluded that Section 7 is not self-executing and that the General Assembly may constrain the governor's ability to remove the state's adjutant general.[26] (The statute was subsequently amended; the adjutant general now "serve[s] at the pleasure of the governor."[27])

Iowa Code § 29A.7 elaborates upon the governor's powers and duties as Iowa's commander in chief.

---

[21] U.S. Const. art. II, § 2.

[22] Iowa Const. of 1846, art. V, § 5.

[23] *See*, e.g., Me. Const. of 1820, art. V, pt. 1, § 7; Miss. Const. of 1832, art. V, § 5; Ohio Const. of 1803, art. II, § 10; Penn. Const. of 1838, art. II, § 7.

[24] Op. Iowa Att'y Gen., 1997 WL 988719 (Aug. 12, 1997) (replying to Warren Lawson).

[25] Op. Iowa Att'y Gen., 1980 WL 25903 (Jan. 2, 1980) (replying to Bob Rush).

[26] Op. Iowa Att'y Gen., 1977 WL 18976 (Sept. 13, 1977) (replying to William Hargrave).

[27] Iowa Code § 29A.11.

Section 8.
Duties of governor.

He shall transact all executive business with the officers of government, civil and military, and may require information in writing from the officers of the executive department upon any subject relating to the duties of their respective offices.

Section 8 gives the governor the power both to do business with all of the state's civil and military officers and to require written information from any of the state's executive officers concerning matters within their job responsibilities. The provision remains virtually identical to the corresponding provision of the first constitution presented to the Territory of Iowa's voters,[28] and was not the subject of recorded debate at any of the state's constitutional conventions. Section 8's latter provision—empowering the governor to obtain written responses to inquiries—is modeled closely upon the clause of the U.S. Constitution that authorizes the president to "require the Opinion, in writing, of the principal Officer in each of the executive Departments, upon any Subject relating to the Duties of their respective Offices."[29] Language to that same effect appeared in many of the other state constitutions that the Iowa delegates had at hand.[30]

Section 8 was among the authorities that the Iowa Supreme Court cited in *Ryan v. Wilson* (1941), discussed briefly in the commentary on Section 1 of this article. The Office of the Attorney General peripherally cited Section 8 a couple of times roughly a century ago, but not in ways aimed at illuminating its meaning.[31]

Section 9.
Execution of laws.

He shall take care that the laws are faithfully executed.

The U.S. Constitution states that the president "shall take Care that the Laws be faithfully executed."[32] Section 9 imposes a comparable responsibility upon Iowa's governor. The state's first constitution, ratified in 1846, stated that the governor "shall *see* that the laws are faithfully executed."[33] When the 1857 convention's Committee on the Executive initially presented a draft of Section 9, the provision's phrasing already had been brought into line with its federal

---

[28] *1844 Journal, supra* Article I, note 3, pp. 24–25.

[29] U.S. Const. art. II, § 2, cl. 1.

[30] *See,* e.g., Fla. Const. of 1838, art. III, § 7; Ind. Const. of 1816, art. IV, § 11; Ohio Const. of 1803, art. II, § 7.

[31] Op. Iowa Att'y Gen., 1936 WL 68694 (July 13, 1936) (replying to the Board of Control); Op. Iowa Att'y Gen., 1909 WL 60263 (Mar. 24, 1909) (replying to Governor Beryl Carroll).

[32] U.S. Const. art. II, § 3.

[33] Iowa Const. of 1846, art. V, § 7 (emphasis added).

counterpart.[34] Section 9 was not the subject of documented debate at any of the state's constitutional conventions.

The Iowa Supreme Court's opportunities to interpret Section 9 have been scarce. In *Homan v. Branstad* (2016), a group of state legislators and the leader of a public-employee union argued that Section 9 restricted the governor's ability to item veto appropriations for certain mental-health institutes. The court declined to reach that issue, concluding that the plaintiffs' claim was based upon a mistaken interpretation of previously enacted legislation. In a case of that same name decided in 2012, a group of state legislators and the leader of a public-employee union alleged that the governor's failure to spend money that had been appropriated for a juvenile home violated his duty to execute the law. Rather than address the merits of that claim, the Iowa Supreme Court held that the case was moot. Section 9 was among the authorities that the court cited in *Ryan v. Wilson* (1941), discussed briefly in the commentary on Section 1 of this article.

The Office of the Attorney General has issued numerous opinions concerning Section 9, several of them emphasizing the distinction between making and executing the law. (For more on that distinction, see the commentary on Article III, Section 1.) In 1974, for example, Attorney General Richard Turner advised Governor Robert Ray that Ray did not have the independent authority to set the speed limit for the state's highways.[35] The office has further explained that Section 9 gives the governor the authority to issue executive orders,[36] but only if those orders do not violate a constitutional or statutory provision or intrude upon the judicial power.[37] In 1980, the office found that Section 9 does not give the governor the unrestricted authority to refuse to spend lawfully appropriated funds, but it does allow the governor to act upon "a reasonable determination that the full legislative purpose can be accomplished by spending less than the legislative forecast or estimate represented by an appropriation."[38]

Several of the office's opinions have concerned issues relating to appointments. In 1985, for example, the office concluded that, although the Iowa Constitution does not bar the senate from reserving for itself the power to decide whether to confirm the governor's executive-branch appointees, Section 9 likely bars the General Assembly from "attempt[ing] generally to strip the Governor of the power to appoint key policy makers in state government."[39] In 1979, the office found that Section 9 authorizes the governor to unilaterally

---

[34] *1857 Debates, supra* Article I, note 3, vol. 1, p. 77.

[35] Op. Iowa Att'y Gen., 1974 WL 353678 (Jan. 3, 1974) (replying to Governor Robert Ray).

[36] Op. Iowa Att'y Gen., 1993 WL 546195 (Nov. 18, 1993) (replying to John Sarcone and Ted Stilwill).

[37] Op. Iowa Att'y Gen., 1991 WL 495692 (Dec. 30, 1991) (replying to Ralph Rosenberg).

[38] Op. Iowa Att'y Gen., 1980 WL 26040 (Aug. 11, 1980) (replying to Bob Rush); *accord* Op. Iowa Att'y Gen., 1989 WL 264979 (June 30, 1989) (replying to Jack Hatch and Richard Varn).

[39] Op. Iowa Att'y Gen., 1985 WL 68966 (Jan. 30, 1985) (replying to Douglas Ritsema).

appoint an "acting" officer to fill a vacancy that can statutorily be filled only with the senate's confirmation, but the governor may wield this power "only for a period reasonably necessary to locate a person to be nominated for a permanent appointment."[40] The office also has said that Section 9 provides sufficient authority for the governor to make appointments to fill executive-branch vacancies, but only when neither the constitution nor a statute specifies the process by which those vacancies are to be filled.[41] Section 10, addressed next, has more to say about filling vacancies.

Section 10.
Vacancies.

When any office shall, from any cause, become vacant, and no mode is provided by the Constitution and laws for filling such vacancy, the Governor shall have power to fill such vacancy, by granting a commission, which shall expire at the end of the next session of the General Assembly, or at the next election by the people.

Section 10, which authorizes the governor to fill vacancies in "any office" when existing law does not provide otherwise, remains identical to the corresponding provision of Iowa's first constitution, ratified in 1846.[42] It was not the subject of historically preserved debate at any of the state's constitutional conventions. The U.S. Constitution gives the president the authority to temporarily fill only those vacancies "that may happen during the Recess of the Senate."[43] The Iowa Constitution does not similarly limit the governor's vacancy-filling power to periods when the state's senate (or the state's house of representatives) is in recess—a fact that is not surprising, given that neither chamber of the General Assembly has a constitutionally assigned "advice and consent" power akin to what the U.S. Senate possesses.[44]

When neither the constitution nor a statute provides a "mode" for filling a vacancy, the governor may appoint someone to temporarily fill it. In 1967, for example, Attorney General Richard Turner concluded that Section 10 authorized

---

[40] Op. Iowa Att'y Gen., 1979 WL 21037 (Aug. 6, 1979) (replying to Bill Hutchins).

[41] Op. Iowa Att'y Gen., 2006 WL 6337824 (Oct. 20, 2006) (replying to Paul McKinley).

[42] Iowa Const. of 1846, art. V, § 8. Those interested in issues concerning vacancies should also consult Article XI, § 6, of the present-day constitution.

[43] U.S. Const. art. II, § 2, cl. 3. For the leading interpretation of that clause, see *NLRB v. Noel Canning* (2014).

[44] U.S. Const. art. II, § 2, cl. 2. *Cf.* Op. Iowa Att'y Gen., 1985 WL 68966 (Jan. 30, 1985) (replying to Douglas Ritsema) (concluding that "statutes conditioning gubernatorial appointments to positions within the executive branch of government on senate confirmation and statutes providing procedures for senate confirmation would be upheld as constitutional if these statutes were challenged in court as violative of the separation of powers doctrine").

the governor to temporarily fill a vacancy within a sanitary district's office of trustees, since no constitutional or statutory provision stated how such vacancies were to be filled.[45] But when the constitution or a statute *does* describe the means for filling a vacancy, Section 10 is inapplicable.[46] In 1953's *City of Nevada v. Slemmons*, for example, the Iowa Supreme Court held that the governor did not have the power under Section 10 to fill a vacancy on a city council, because a statute stated that the city council's remaining members held that power.[47]

Section 11.
Convening general assembly.

He may, on extraordinary occasions, convene the General Assembly by proclamation, and shall state to both Houses, when assembled, the purpose for which they shall have been convened.

Section 11, which authorizes the governor to call the General Assembly into session "on extraordinary occasions," remains identical to the corresponding passage in Iowa's first constitution.[48] It resembles the provision of the U.S. Constitution that authorizes the president, "on extraordinary Occasions, [to] convene both Houses, or either of them."[49] Perhaps inspired by provisions akin to what one finds in the Tennessee Constitution of 1835,[50] the 1857 convention's Committee on the Executive proposed adding a passage at the end of the text that appears above, stating: "and when so convened, they shall have no power to legislate upon any subject save that suggested in the message of the Governor."[51] Daniel Solomon, a young lawyer from Mills County, endorsed that addition, arguing that it would spare Iowans "from a great deal of unnecessary and improper legislation." Others were unpersuaded. Jasper County's Harvey Skiff and Henry County's Rufus Clarke argued, for example, that the committee's proposal would give the governor too much power over the legislative branch and that the General Assembly ought to be able to consider any matter it deems appropriate when in session, while Des Moines County's Jonathan Hall worried that a new level of complexity would be imposed on the legislative

---

45 Op. Iowa Att'y Gen., 1967 WL 167109 (July 11, 1967) (replying to William Faches).

46 Op. Iowa Att'y Gen., 1979 WL 21037 (Aug. 6, 1979) (replying to Bill Hutchins).

47 To the extent the statute was ambiguous, the *Slemmons* court said that it should be interpreted as giving the city council the vacancy-filling power because (1) absent clear statutory language to the contrary, it appeared "inconceivable" that the legislature would have wished to burden the governor with involvement in such local affairs, and (2) the council's remaining members were "better able to know and select replacements in their community than the Governor of the state far removed from the concerned community."

48 Iowa Const. of 1846, art. V, § 9.

49 U.S. Const. art. II, § 3.

50 Tenn. Const. of 1835, art. III, § 9.

51 *1857 Debates, supra* Article I, note 3, vol. 1, p. 77.

process if legislators had to consider whether a given matter fell within the scope of the governor's message.[52] By an unrecorded margin, the delegates approved Skiff's motion that the committee's proposed additional language be rejected.[53] The text that emerged from the convention was thus substantively identical to the corresponding provisions of a handful of other states' constitutions.[54]

The significance of the 1857 convention's drafting decision was not lost on the Iowa Supreme Court. Two years later, in 1859's *Morford v. Unger*, the court confirmed that, when the governor has called it into a special session, the General Assembly possesses "the full and exclusive legislative authority of the state." Because the legislature does not derive its lawmaking power from the governor's proclamation, the court explained, it is "not confined to the special purpose for which it may have been convened by him." Consistently with that view, Attorney General Edward O'Connor issued an opinion in 1933 stating that the General Assembly has as much power to initiate and pass a resolution amending the constitution during a special session as it does during a regular session.[55] In 1924, Attorney General Ben Gibson similarly concluded that the General Assembly's "powers at a special session are as broad and comprehensive as it may exercise at a regular session," and legislators thus may take action during a special session on a proposed amendment to the U.S. Constitution.[56]

Section 12. Message.

He shall communicate, by message, to the General Assembly, at every regular session, the condition of the State, and recommend such matters as he shall deem expedient.

With the exception of the word "regular"—an addition made by the Committee on the Executive at the 1857 convention,[57] presumably to make clear that the governor need not deliver condition-of-the-state messages at special sessions[58]—Section 12 still reads as it did under Iowa's 1846 constitution. Section 12 plainly echoes the provision of the U.S. Constitution that directs the president "from time to time [to] give to the Congress Information of the State of the Union, and recommend to their consideration such Measures as he shall judge necessary and

[52] *1857 Debates, supra* Article I, note 3, vol. 1, pp. 583–84.

[53] *1857 Journal, supra* Article I, note 3, p. 214.

[54] *See, e.g.*, Ill. Const. of 1818, art. III, § 9; Ohio Const. of 1803, art. II, § 9.

[55] Op. Iowa Att'y Gen., 1933 WL 66203 (Feb. 17, 1933) (replying to the Senate Chamber).

[56] Op. Iowa Att'y Gen., 1924 WL 60458 (July 5, 1924) (replying to Governor Nathan Kendall).

[57] *1857 Debates, supra* Article I, note 3, vol. 1, p. 77.

[58] Today, the governor may call a special session pursuant to Section 11 of this article, and a supermajority of the General Assembly may call a special session pursuant to Article III, Section 2.

expedient."[59] Neither the Iowa Supreme Court nor the Office of the Attorney General has had occasion to discuss Section 12's requirement.

Section 13.
Adjournment.

In case of disagreement between the two Houses with respect to the time of adjournment, the Governor shall have power to adjourn the General Assembly to such time as he may think proper; but no such adjournment shall be beyond the time fixed for the regular meeting of the next General Assembly.

Providing an authority akin to what the president possesses under the U.S. Constitution,[60] Section 13 empowers the governor to resolve stalemates between the legislature's two houses concerning when to adjourn. Such stalemates between the two houses may indeed occur, by virtue of the fact that, under Article III, Section 14, neither house may adjourn for more than three days without the other's consent. Stylistic differences aside, the provision remains substantively identical to the corresponding text in Iowa's 1846 constitution.[61]

In 1978, Attorney General Richard Turner concluded that Section 13 gives the governor the power to determine in a given instance whether there is, in fact, a disagreement between the General Assembly's two houses about when to adjourn.[62] Iowa's appellate courts have not yet had an opportunity to discuss issues arising under Section 13, such as whether a court may review the governor's determination that there is or is not a disagreement between the house and the senate on a given occasion. In his 1978 opinion, Turner indicated that, in his view, courts do not possess that power.

Section 14.
Disqualification.

No person shall, while holding any office under the authority of the United States, or this State, execute the office of Governor, or Lieutenant Governor, except as hereinafter expressly provided.

---

[59] U.S. Const. art. II, § 3.

[60] U.S. Const. art. II, § 3 ("[I]n Case of Disagreement between [Congress's two chambers], with Respect to the Time of Adjournment, [the President] may adjourn them to such Time as he shall think proper. . . .").

[61] Iowa Const. of 1846, art. V, § 11. The stylistic changes were made on the 1857 convention's penultimate day at the suggestion of Jefferson County's James Wilson. *1857 Debates, supra* Article I, note 3, vol. 2, p. 1018. At the Territory of Iowa's 1844 convention, the delegates decisively rejected—by a vote of 7 to 58—a motion by Des Moines County's Andrew Hooten to strike the provision in its entirety. *1844 Journal, supra* Article I, note 3, p. 62. (Andrew's last name sometimes appears in the records as "Hooton.")

[62] Op. Iowa Att'y Gen., 1978 WL 17432 (July 11, 1978) (replying to James Redmond).

Section 14 ensures that neither the governor nor the lieutenant governor will be afflicted by the distractions and conflicts of interest that would come with simultaneously holding other state or federal offices. The state's first constitution, ratified in 1846, contained a differently worded but substantively comparable provision, applicable only to the governor.[63] As explained in the commentary on Section 3 of this article, the lieutenant governorship was not created until 1857. Section 14 was not the subject of documented debate at any of the state's constitutional conventions, except to the extent it got swept up in the 1857 debate about whether to establish the position of lieutenant governor.[64]

The Iowa Supreme Court has not yet discussed the restrictions that Section 14 imposes. In 1980, the Office of the Attorney General determined that Section 14 would bar the governor "from acting as a federal official by exercising powers conferred on him solely by a delegation from the federal government under the Emergency Energy Conservation Act."[65]

Section 15.
Terms—compensation.

The official terms of the governor and lieutenant governor shall commence on the Tuesday after the second Monday of January next after their election and shall continue until their successors are elected and qualify. The governor and lieutenant governor shall be paid compensation and expenses as provided by law. The lieutenant governor, while acting as governor, shall be paid the compensation and expenses prescribed for the governor.

Section 15 sets the date on which Iowa's governors and lieutenant governors begin their terms in office. Also, apart from requiring that, when acting as governor, the lieutenant governor be paid as much as is required for the governor, Section 15 places the General Assembly in the driver's seat for determining how much the state's two leading executive officials will be compensated and for setting the terms on which their expenses will be reimbursed. The state's 1846 constitution was silent regarding when the governor's term would begin. With respect to compensation, the 1846 text largely tracked the federal Constitution's language concerning the president, declaring that "[t]he Governor shall, at stated times, receive for his services a compensation which shall neither be increased nor diminished during the time for which he shall have been elected."[66] That

[63] Iowa Const. of 1846, art. V, § 12.

[64] During a stretch of the 1857 convention when the tide was flowing against establishing the lieutenant governorship, Hardin County's Sheldon Winchester successfully moved to strike Section 14's reference to that position. *1857 Debates*, *supra* Article I, note 3, vol. 1, p. 586. In the end, the movement against the lieutenant governorship failed.

[65] Op. Iowa Att'y Gen., 1980 WL 25972 (Apr. 25, 1980) (replying to Edward Stanek).

[66] Iowa Const. of 1846, art. V, § 14; *cf.* U.S. Const., art. II, § 1, cl. 7 ("The President shall, at stated Times, receive for his Services, a Compensation, which shall neither be increased nor diminished during the Period for which he shall have been elected. . . .").

pattern of silence and speaking was initially flipped at the 1857 convention: in its first public draft of Article IV, the Committee on the Executive proposed saying nothing on the subject of executive compensation, while specifying when the governor's and lieutenant governor's terms would officially begin.[67] At the suggestion of Henry County's Rufus Clarke and Davis County's David Palmer, the delegates opted to specify benchmarks for determining the lieutenant governor's compensation, based on whether he was acting as governor or as the senate's presiding officer.[68] Iowa voters amended Section 15 in 1972, giving the General Assembly greater power to set the lieutenant governor's compensation for those periods when he or she was not acting as governor. Iowans put Section 15 into its current form in 1988,[69] giving the legislature the power to establish the governor's and lieutenant governor's rates of pay and reimbursement, with the sole constraint that, when he or she is acting as the governor, the lieutenant governor must receive the same "compensation and expenses" that are statutorily prescribed for the governor. Section 7.8 of the Iowa Code similarly states that the General Assembly shall determine the governor's and lieutenant governor's salaries.

Neither the Iowa Supreme Court nor the Office of the Attorney General has fielded questions concerning the requirements of Section 15 in its current form.[70]

Section 16.
Pardons—reprieves—commutations.

The Governor shall have power to grant reprieves, commutations and pardons, after conviction, for all offenses except treason and cases of impeachment, subject to such regulations as may be provided by law. Upon conviction for treason, he shall have power to suspend the execution of the sentence until the case shall be reported to the General Assembly at its next meeting, when the General Assembly shall either grant a pardon, commute the sentence, direct the execution of the sentence, or grant a further reprieve. He shall have power to remit fines and forfeitures, under such regulations as may be prescribed by law; and shall report to the General Assembly, at its next meeting, each case of reprieve, commutation, or pardon granted, and the reasons therefor; and also all persons

---

[67] *1857 Debates, supra* Article I, note 3, vol. 1, p. 77. The delegates debated when those terms should begin and whether it was even necessary for Section 15 to speak to the matter. *Id.* at pp. 586, 596.

[68] *1857 Debates, supra* Article I, note 3, vol. 1, pp. 597–98; *1857 Journal, supra* Article I, note 3, pp. 217–18.

[69] As explained in the commentary on Section 18 of this article, the year 1988 was when Iowans decided that the lieutenant governor need no longer serve as the senate's president.

[70] Both the Iowa Supreme Court and the Office of the Attorney General did, however, field at least one inquiry each concerning payment of the lieutenant governor's expenses under a prior version of Section 15. *Gallarno v. Long* (1932); Op. Iowa Att'y Gen., 1959 WL 107724 (Mar. 4, 1959) (replying to Glenn Sarsfield).

in whose favor remission of fines and forfeitures shall have been made, and the several amounts remitted.

Section 16 sets the terms on which the governor may come to the aid of those who have been convicted of crimes. Iowa's first constitution stated simply that "[t]he Governor shall have power to grant reprieves and pardons, and commute punishments after conviction, except in cases of impeachment."[71] With only one notable exception, the 1857 convention's Committee on the Executive proposed the lengthier text that one sees above. The exception is the phrase "and the reasons therefor" in Section 16's closing lines: Johnson County's William Penn Clarke proposed that addition, explaining that Governor James Grimes had told him that such a provision would help "to prevent the improper exercise of this pardoning power."[72] Iowa's framers did not build Section 16 from scratch. Close stylistic similarities suggest that the Indiana Constitution of 1851, in particular, may have provided the 1857 text's drafters with their starting point.[73]

Section 16 divides convictions into three categories: impeachment, treason, and all other criminal offenses. With respect to impeachment, Article III, Section 19, gives the house of representatives the power to impeach and the senate the power to decide whether to convict. If the senate opts to convict, the provision now under discussion bars the governor from intervening on the defendant's behalf. The governor's power with respect to treason convictions is only marginally greater: the governor may suspend the execution of the sentence until the General Assembly next meets, but it is the General Assembly that then decides whether a pardon, commutation, or further reprieve is appropriate. For all other convictions, the governor has the power to grant pardons, commutations, and reprieves, and the power to cancel fines and forfeitures,[74] though he or she must report all such actions to the General Assembly. The legislature may adopt regulations governing these gubernatorial actions.

A reprieve is a postponement in carrying out a criminal sentence. The closest the Iowa Supreme Court has come to focusing on reprieves, in particular, is in its rulings stating that a sentencing court violates Section 16 if it purports to suspend a sentence that it has already imposed (*State ex rel. Preston v. Hamilton*, 1928; *Miller v. Evans*, 1901). Most of the Section 16 opinions issued by Iowa's appellate courts, as well as by the Office of the Attorney General, have focused on commutations and pardons.

---

[71] Iowa Const. of 1846, art. V, § 13. The 1846 constitution drew inspiration from the U.S. Constitution, which states that the president "shall have Power to grant Reprieves and Pardons for Offences against the United States, except in Cases of Impeachment." U.S. Const. art. II, § 2, cl. 1.

[72] *1857 Debates, supra* Article I, note 3, vol. 1, p. 587.

[73] Ind. Const. of 1851, art. V, § 17.

[74] *Cf.* Iowa Code § 914.1 ("The power of the Governor . . . to grant a reprieve, pardon, commutation of sentence, [or] remission of fines and forfeitures . . . shall not be impaired.").

A commutation "is the executive's substitution in a particular case of a less severe punishment for a more severe one that has already been judicially imposed on the defendant" (*State v. Ragland*, 2013). The lesser sentence that the governor selects may itself be judicially reviewed for statutory and constitutional defects. In *Ragland*, for example, the court determined that the sentence the governor had chosen for a juvenile offender—life imprisonment with no possibility of parole for the first sixty years—amounted to an unconstitutional form of cruel and unusual punishment.

When the governor issues a pardon, he or she thereby "absolves a party from all legal consequences for his crime" (*Slater v. Olson*, 1941). In *Slater*, for example, the court held that, if the governor has fully pardoned a convicted felon, a city cannot deny that person a job on the ground that he or she had indeed been convicted of a felony. Pursuant to the pardoning power, the governor may restore citizenship rights (such as the right to vote or to hold public office) that a person has lost pursuant to Iowa law as a result of a criminal conviction, even if that conviction was for a federal offense (*State ex rel. Dean v. Haubrich*, 1957) or for a crime in another state.[75] The governor may not, however, relieve a pardon recipient of his or her legal obligation to pay costs and attorneys' fees relating to the earlier legal proceeding (*State v. Beebee*, 1893). The governor may issue a conditional pardon, and the defendant is free to decide whether to accept or reject it on any lawful terms that the governor has set (*Arthur v. Craig*, 1878). If one of the governor's conditions is violated—such as a condition that the pardon recipient not engage in any further criminal conduct—the governor cannot then force the person to suffer a stiffer penalty than he or she would have received if the pardon had never been issued (*State ex rel. Davis v. Hunter*, 1904).

With the exception of convictions for treason, the pardoning power belongs exclusively to the governor; neither the General Assembly nor the courts may issue pardons (*Slater v. Olson*, 1941).[76] The General Assembly does not intrude upon the governor's Section 16 powers when it declares that those convicted of particular crimes are eligible or ineligible for parole or work release (*State v. Phillips*, 2000; *State v. Duff*, 1909). Section 16 does not prevent the General Assembly or a lesser lawmaking body (such as a municipality) from imposing bars to proceedings that, if played out, might result in a person's conviction. The Iowa Supreme Court has explained that such bars are not pardons within the meaning of Section 16, because, by its terms, Section 16 triggers the governor's pardoning power only after a conviction has been secured (*State ex rel. Witter v. Forkner*, 1895).

A sentencing court does not intrude upon the governor's Section 16 powers when it imposes a stiff sentence (such as consecutive life terms) in part to

[75] Op. Iowa Att'y Gen., 1964 WL 121187 (June 9, 1964) (replying to Governor Harold Hughes).

[76] *See also* Op. Iowa Att'y Gen., 1976 WL 375888 (Mar. 11, 1976) (replying to Clay Spear).

send a message to the governor that any subsequent application for commutation "should not be taken seriously" (*State v. Bentley*, 2008). The *Bentley* court explained that such a message "does not bind or limit the board of parole or the governor in any future consideration of commutation of the sentences."

Section 16 states that the governor's power to issue reprieves, commutations, and pardons is "subject to such regulations as may be provided by law." In 1939, Attorney General John Rankin concluded that this provision does not permit the legislature to restrict the governor's ability to issue pardons and commutations.[77] Drawing a distinction between "regulations" (Section 16's term) and restrictions, Rankin said that the legislature cannot require the governor to obtain another body's approval before issuing a pardon or commutation, but it can require the governor to publicize his or her decision in the county in which the sentence was imposed. In 1933, Attorney General Edward O'Connor tried to mark that same line when he advised Governor Clyde Herring that the General Assembly could require him to obtain the *advice* of a parole board before issuing a pardon, but could not require him to obtain the parole board's *consent*.[78]

The legislature has exercised some of the regulatory power that it possesses under Section 16.[79] It is interesting to ponder whether, in some instances, the General Assembly has gone too far. Section 914.7 of the Iowa Code states, for example, that a person who has been convicted of specified felonies "shall not have the person's rights of citizenship restored to the extent of allowing the person to receive, transport, or possess firearms." Might that provision unconstitutionally restrict the governor's pardoning power, given that—as noted above—a pardon ordinarily "absolves a party from all legal consequences for his crime" (*Slater v. Olson*, 1941)? Or is it instead a permissible regulation of the sort that Section 16's opening sentence contemplates? Section 902.2 of the Iowa Code, meanwhile, specifies the commutation procedure for "class A" felons, and states that such individuals may apply for commutation "no more frequently than once every ten years," while the director of the department of corrections may initiate a commutation application on a prisoner's behalf "at any time." Suppose a prisoner applies for commutation once and then wishes to apply again a few years later, and suppose further that the corrections director declines to file a commutation application on the prisoner's behalf. Might the statute's ten-year restriction unconstitutionally intrude upon the governor's power to issue commutations, or is it instead a permissible regulation?[80] If it is a permissible

[77] Op. Iowa Att'y Gen., 1939 WL 77080 (Mar. 11, 1939) (replying to G.R. Hill).

[78] Op. Iowa Att'y Gen., 1933 WL 66113 (Sept. 20, 1933) (replying to Governor Clyde Herring).

[79] *See, e.g.*, Iowa Code ch. 904A (concerning the board of parole); *id.* ch. 914 (concerning reprieves, pardons, commutations, remissions, and restorations of rights).

[80] The Iowa Court of Appeals considered a variety of challenges to Section 902.2 in *Shearon v. Iowa Board of Parole* (2015), but this particular issue was not among them.

regulation, would that answer change if the required interval between applications were significantly expanded? Or is the answer instead that Section 902.2 merely regulates the frequency with which certain felons may file applications, but does not purport to limit the governor's power to grant a commutation in the absence of an application?[81]

Section 17.
Lieutenant governor to act as governor.

In case of the death, impeachment, resignation, removal from office, or other disability of the Governor, the powers and duties of the office for the residue of the term, or until he shall be acquitted, or the disability removed, shall devolve upon the Lieutenant Governor.

Under Iowa's 1846 constitution, the secretary of state was the first in line to succeed the governor if the governor became unable to serve.[82] As explained in Part I and in the commentary on Section 3 of this article, the delegates to the 1857 constitution created the lieutenant governorship for the principal purpose of allowing Iowa voters to choose the person who—without detracting from the secretary of state's performance of his or her own duties—would be waiting in the governorship's wings. Section 17 puts that purpose into action. One additional difference between the 1846 and 1857 texts bears mention: under the first constitution, but not under the second, the devolution of gubernatorial duties occurred upon the governor's "absence from the state." Today, the governor's departure from the state does not bring Section 17 into play.[83]

In 1923, Governor Nathan Kendall advised Attorney General Ben Gibson that, for reasons relating to physical health, Kendall needed to take two or three months off work; he asked Gibson whether Lieutenant Governor John Hammill could carry out the governor's duties during that time. Gibson answered in the affirmative, and added that "[i]n cases of physical disability, there is no doubt but that the governor is to determine the time when such disability begins and the time when it ends."[84] For a discussion of Attorney General Tom Miller's response in 2017 to a high-profile issue concerning gubernatorial succession, see the commentary on Section 19 of this article.

Iowa's appellate courts have not yet had occasion to interpret Section 17. Iowa Code Section 7.14 specifies various procedures to be followed when gubernatorial succession issues arise by virtue of an apparent disability.

---

[81] In a concurring opinion in *State v. Ragland* (2013), Justice Edward Mansfield indicated that he likely would read the statute this way.

[82] Iowa Const. of 1846, art. V, § 18.

[83] Op. Iowa Att'y Gen., 1980 WL 25903 (Jan. 2, 1980) (replying to Bob Rush).

[84] Op. Iowa Att'y Gen., 1923 WL 54991 (Aug. 23, 1923) (replying to Governor Nathan Kendall).

Section 18.
Duties of lieutenant governor.

The lieutenant governor shall have the duties provided by law and those duties of the governor assigned to the lieutenant governor by the governor.

Under the original text of the 1857 constitution, the lieutenant governor served as the president of the senate and cast votes in the senate only when necessary to break deadlocks; in addition, the senate was to select a president pro tempore to serve as that chamber's presiding officer if the lieutenant governor ever became unable to carry out his or her duties. In 1988, Iowa voters replaced that text with what one sees above, implicitly removing the lieutenant governor from the senate's presidency and explicitly giving both the General Assembly and the governor the power to assign responsibilities to the lieutenant governor. Today, pursuant to Senate Rules 52 and 53, the senate elects its own president and president pro tempore.[85]

Neither the courts nor the Office of the Attorney General has issued an opinion concerning the current version of Section 18.

Section 19.
Succession to office of governor and lieutenant governor.

If there be a vacancy in the office of the governor and the lieutenant governor shall by reason of death, impeachment, resignation, removal from office, or other disability become incapable of performing the duties pertaining to the office of governor, the president of the senate shall act as governor until the vacancy is filled or the disability removed; and if the president of the senate, for any of the above causes, shall be incapable of performing the duties pertaining to the office of governor the same shall devolve upon the speaker of the house of representatives; and if the speaker of the house of representatives, for any of the above causes, shall be incapable of performing the duties of the office of governor, the justices of the supreme court shall convene the general assembly by proclamation and the general assembly shall organize by the election of a president by the senate and a speaker by the house of representatives. The general assembly shall thereupon immediately proceed to the election of a governor and lieutenant governor in joint convention.

Under the original text of the 1857 constitution, the senate's president pro tempore stood in the gubernatorial line of succession immediately behind the lieutenant governor, followed by the speaker of the house of representatives. (As explained in the commentary on Section 18 of this article, the lieutenant governor himself served as the president of the senate until 1988.) In 1952, Iowa voters modestly altered the 1857 text, while also specifying how the state's two leading executive offices are to be filled if the speaker of the house is unable to

[85] The senate's rules are available at https://www.legis.iowa.gov/docs/publications/SR/644148.pdf.

serve. In 1988—the same year that Iowans opted to allow the senate to elect its own president—Iowans amended Section 19 once again, declaring that it is the president of the senate—not the president pro tempore—who stands in line immediately behind the lieutenant governor.

In 2017, President Donald Trump appointed Governor Terry Branstad to serve as the United States Ambassador to China. Lieutenant Governor Kim Reynolds announced that, upon assuming the duties of the governorship, she would want to appoint a new lieutenant governor. Could she do that? Attorney General Tom Miller concluded she could not.[86] Miller determined that, upon Branstad's departure, Reynolds would become Iowa's governor *and* would continue to be the state's lieutenant governor, and that there thus would be no vacancy to fill in the latter position. Miller also found that allowing Reynolds to appoint a new lieutenant governor would undercut Section 19's assurance that everyone who stands in the line of gubernatorial succession is someone whom Iowans have elected to office. Reluctantly accepting Miller's decision, Reynolds appointed Adam Gregg to hold the title of lieutenant governor and to carry out that office's day-to-day functions without standing in the constitutional line of succession.[87]

Section 20.
Seal of state.

There shall be a seal of this State, which shall be kept by the Governor, and used by him officially, and shall be called the Great Seal of the State of Iowa.

Section 20, which provides for the creation and use of a state seal, still stands in the same form that it took in the corresponding provision of Iowa's first constitution, ratified in 1846.[88] The provision was not the subject of meaningful recorded discussion at any of the state's constitutional conventions. Numerous other early state constitutions contained comparable provisions.[89] Under Section 21 of this article, the seal is to be used on "[a]ll grants and commissions."

In 1963, Attorney General Evan Hultman advised Governor Harold Hughes that Section 20 permits only the governor to use the seal, and that even the governor can use it only for official purposes.[90] Other governmental bodies, Hultman said, should not be allowed to use or display it.

---

86 Op. Iowa Att'y Gen. (May 1, 2017) (replying to David Johnson), available at https://www.iowaattorneygeneral.gov/media/cms/Johnson_opinion_1741_D8D94636D652C.pdf.

87 *See* Jason Noble, "Reynolds Chooses Gregg as Lieutenant Governor; He Won't Take Over if Top Office Is Vacant," *Des Moines Register*, May 26, 2017, at 1A.

88 Iowa Const. of 1846, art. V, § 15.

89 *See*, e.g., Ark. Const. of 1836, art. V, § 12; N.C. Const. of 1776, art. XVII; Tenn. Const. of 1835, art. III, § 15.

90 Op. Iowa Att'y Gen., 1963 WL 113693 (Feb. 28, 1963) (replying to Governor Harold Hughes).

Iowa's appellate courts have not been called upon to resolve disputes concerning Section 20. The contents of Iowa's seal are prescribed by Section 1A.1 of the Iowa Code.

Section 21.
Grants and commissions.

All grants and commissions shall be in the name and by the authority of the people of the State of Iowa, sealed with the Great Seal of the State, signed by the Governor, and countersigned by the Secretary of State.

Section 21, which designates some of the uses for the seal whose creation is mandated by Section 20 of this article, still stands in the same form that it took in the corresponding provision of Iowa's 1846 constitution.[91] It was not the subject of documented debate at any of Iowa's constitutional conventions.[92]

The provision has not been the subject of any appellate-court rulings, and has received only scant attention from the Office of the Attorney General. In 1937, Attorney General John Mitchell said that neither the constitution nor the Iowa Code clearly specified the scope of the governor's authority to issue commissions to appointed officers, and he indicated that he believed it would be inappropriate for the governor to issue a commission to the state librarian because that position was not filled by executive appointment.[93] In 1907, Attorney General Howard Byers indicated that the governor was obliged to follow Section 21's formalities when issuing a land patent.[94]

Section 22.
Secretary—auditor—treasurer.

A Secretary of State, an Auditor of State and a Treasurer of State shall be elected by the qualified electors at the same time that the Governor is elected and for a four-year term commencing on the first day of January next after their election, and they shall perform such duties as may be provided by law.

Iowa's first constitution established the offices of "secretary of state, auditor of public accounts, and treasurer" and slated them for two-year terms.[95] With minor alterations to the latter two job titles, the delegates to the 1857 constitution

[91] Iowa Const. of 1846, art. V, § 16.

[92] At the 1857 convention, Jasper County's Harvey Skiff asked for clarification of the provision's meaning, but the historical record provides no indication that he received a response. *1857 Debates, supra* Article I, note 3, vol. 1, p. 588.

[93] Op. Iowa Att'y Gen., 1937 WL 67730 (Apr. 3, 1937) (replying to G.W. Kirtley).

[94] Op. Iowa Att'y Gen., 1907 WL 58227 (Mar. 8, 1907) (replying to Governor Albert Cummins).

[95] Iowa Const. of 1846, art. V, § 17.

preserved that arrangement.[96] Iowans amended the provision in 1972, giving the holders of the specified positions four-year terms. (That same year, as explained in the commentary on Section 2 of this article, Iowa voters similarly extended governors' terms from two years to four.) The provision mandates the maintenance of the three named positions and authorizes lawmakers to assign duties to the individuals who hold them.

Because Section 22's language is straightforward, it is not surprising that neither Iowa's appellate courts nor the Office of the Attorney General has resolved disputes about its meaning.

---

[96] For the 1857 delegates' brief discussion of the provision, see *1857 Debates, supra* Article I, note 3, vol. 1, pp. 588–89, 596; *id.* at vol. 2, pp. 1018–19.

Article V

Judicial Department

Section 1.
Courts.

The Judicial power shall be vested in a Supreme Court, District Courts, and such other Courts, inferior to the Supreme Court, as the General Assembly may, from time to time, establish.

Section 1, which vests the State of Iowa's judicial power in a network of courts, continues to read largely as it did in Iowa's 1846 constitution. At the 1857 convention, a majority of the Committee on the Judiciary Department proposed creating "superior courts" to serve within each of the state's judicial districts as intermediate tribunals with appellate jurisdiction, but a minority of the committee objected to that plan.[1] The disagreement between the two camps provoked a lengthy debate, during which the precise contents of the competing proposals changed many times.[2] Led by Henry County's Rufus Clarke and Des Moines

[1] *1857 Debates, supra* Article I, note 3, vol. 1, pp. 115–17, 227. For part of the story on why the committee produced two competing proposals—an outcome that evidently frustrated the entire committee, with neither proposal commanding the full assent of any individual member—see *id.* at pp. 254–58.

[2] *1857 Debates, supra* Article I, note 3, vol. 1, pp. 227–60, 430–46, 467–71. After the first round of debate, for example, the majority submitted a revamped draft of Article V, which would have vested the state's judicial power "in a supreme court, district courts, circuit courts, and such other inferior courts as

County's Jonathan Hall, proponents of the superior courts argued that these intermediate appellate courts would reduce the burden on the Iowa Supreme Court, make appellate litigation more geographically convenient, help the growing state manage its burgeoning caseload, and increase the quality of judicial decision-making. Led by Johnson County's William Penn Clarke, opponents contended that the added appellate layer would unjustifiably increase costs for the state and litigants alike. By a vote of 15 to 10, the delegates opted to leave the General Assembly free to decide for itself whether intermediate appellate courts should be created.[3] Albeit on a model different from what Rufus Clarke and Jonathan Hall envisioned, the General Assembly established the Iowa Court of Appeals in 1976 to serve as an intermediate appellate court, adjudicating appeals referred to it by the Iowa Supreme Court.[4]

The historical record suggests that the delegates to the 1846 and 1857 conventions did not publicly debate the contours of "[t]he judicial power" that the state's courts would wield. As the Iowa Supreme Court observed in 1916's *Hutchins v. City of Des Moines*, "[w]hile the Constitution created the courts, it has not undertaken to specify in detail their functions nor to define their power, save plainly to indicate that the entire judicial power has been conferred on them." The court subsequently explained that the "[j]udicial power vested in the courts by the Iowa Constitution is the power to decide and pronounce a judgment and carry it into effect" (*Klouda v. Sixth Judicial District Department of Correctional Services*, 2002). The *Klouda* court concluded that, although the legislature has the power to define crimes and to prescribe the penalties for those who commit them, sentencing functions "are clearly reserved to the judiciary" because they are the means by which courts implement their judgments. This component of the judicial power also underlay a portion of the court's ruling in *Cedar Rapids Human Rights Commission v. Cedar Rapids Community School District* (1974), in which the justices ruled that a municipal human rights commission was an administrative entity—and not a court exercising the judicial power—because the commission could not enforce its own orders, but instead had to invoke the aid of a district court.

Section 1 helps to explain why the state's "supreme" court figures so prominently in a book of this kind: sitting atop the state's judicial hierarchy, the

---

the General Assembly may establish" and which would have divided the state into three judicial districts, with each district itself then divided into four circuits. *See id.* at p. 259. Once the convention had become clogged with numerous competing drafts of Article V, the delegates opted to abandon the committee's drafting work altogether and proceed simply by using the 1846 constitution's text as their starting point. *See id.* at pp. 441–42.

[3] *1857 Debates, supra* Article I, note 3, vol. 1, p. 438; *see also id.* at p. 462 (presenting Section 1 in the form that it takes today).

[4] Iowa Code §§ 602.4102, 602.5101, 602.5103. *See generally* Rosemary Shaw Sackett & Richard H. Doyle, "History of the Iowa Court of Appeals," 60 *Drake Law Review* 1 (2011).

Iowa Supreme Court is "the final arbiter" of the Iowa Constitution's meaning (*Kruidenier v. McColloch*, 1966). Section 1 also gives the Iowa Supreme Court the authority to license and regulate those who practice law in the state (*Rowen v. Le Mars Mutual Insurance Co.*, 1975). In *Rowen*, for example, the court held that it had the power to adjudicate a motion to disqualify (on conflict-of-interest grounds) two attorneys representing the defendants in an appeal pending before the court.

When interpreting Section 1, the court has focused most of its attention on the judiciary's relationship with the legislative and executive branches. This book's commentary on Article III, Section 1, discusses separation-of-powers principles in greater detail—principles that are not repeated here but are nevertheless important for anyone studying the scope of the judicial power.

Section 2.
Supreme court.

The Supreme Court shall consist of three Judges, two of whom shall constitute a quorum to hold Court.

Iowa's 1846 constitution stated that the supreme court would "consist of a Chief Justice and two Associates, two of whom shall be a quorum to hold court."[5] The delegates to the 1857 convention changed the language to what one sees above. Under proposals initially submitted by members of that convention's Committee on the Judiciary Department, the court was to have four members, with one justice elected in each of four judicial districts.[6] The convention nevertheless settled upon a court of three members, reasoning that the existing supreme court rarely produced dissenting opinions (and that there thus was no reason to believe the court needed additional perspectives or wisdom) and that, when there *was* a dissent in a given case, it was better to have a precedent-setting ruling by a 2–1 majority than to risk having a non-precedent-setting 2–2 tie.[7] In Section 10 of this article, however, the delegates opted to allow the General Assembly to increase or decrease the total number of justices. Today, by virtue of legislation, seven justices sit on the Iowa Supreme Court.[8]

---

[5] Iowa Const. of 1846, art. VI, § 2.

[6] *1857 Debates, supra* Article I, note 3, vol. 1, pp. 115–17.

[7] *1857 Debates, supra* Article I, note 3, vol. 1, pp. 446–49, 462–67.

[8] Iowa Code § 602.4101. The state maintains an online report titled "Chronological Chart and Tables of the Iowa Supreme Court: 1938 to Present," which nicely illustrates the historic fluctuations in the court's size and identifies each justice and his or her term of service. *See* http://www.iowacourts.gov/wfData/files/SupremeCourt/ChronologicalchartoftheIowaSupremeCourt.pdf.

Section 3.
Election of judges—term.

[Repealed.]

In 1962, Iowa voters made substantial changes to Article V. Prior to 1962, Section 3 provided for the selection of supreme court justices, each of whom served a six-year term; Section 5 provided for the selection of district court judges, each of whom served a four-year term; Section 9 set the salaries of both categories of judges up to the year 1860, after which the General Assembly was authorized to establish new rates of compensation; and Section 11 declared that both categories of judges would be "chosen at the general election" and would take office on the first day of the ensuing January. In 1962, Iowans repealed all four of those sections and replaced them with Sections 15, 16, 17, and 18 of this article.

As background to the changes that Iowans made in 1962, a brief word is in order regarding the ways in which the state selected its judges prior to that time. Under the state's first constitution, ratified in 1846, the General Assembly chose the members of the state's highest court, while voters within each judicial district chose their district court judges.[9] By the time of the 1857 constitutional convention, the tide had turned against allowing the legislature to select the Iowa Supreme Court's members. So far as one can discern from the historical record, no one at the 1857 convention pushed hard for leaving this portion of the 1846 constitution unchanged. Instead, the delegates debated whether supreme court justices should be chosen in statewide elections or by voters within each judicial district. Johnson County's William Penn Clarke argued in favor of electing justices on a district-by-district basis, reasoning that this would increase the likelihood that voters could make their decisions based upon firsthand knowledge of the candidates rather than upon the candidates' partisan affiliations. Jefferson County's James Wilson and Scott County's George Ells urged the delegates to embrace statewide elections, so that each voter could play a role in selecting all of the state's justices and so that the state would not lose the services of any extraordinarily well-qualified candidate who happened to live in the same district as an equally well-qualified candidate. The proponents of statewide elections prevailed.[10] That is where matters stood until 1962. The changes implemented that year are chronicled in Part I of this book.

---

[9] Iowa Const. of 1846, art. VI, §§ 3, 4. The delegates to the 1846 convention thereby adopted the scheme proposed by the delegates to the Territory of Iowa's first constitutional convention, held in 1844. At the 1844 convention, the scheme was the result of a compromise struck among delegates who disagreed about whether popular elections or legislative appointments were most likely to result in high-quality, unbiased judging. *See 1844 and 1846 Fragments, supra* Article I, note 3, pp. 103–07, 111–22.

[10] *1857 Debates, supra* Article I, note 3, vol. 1, pp. 449–55; *see also* Iowa Const. of 1857, art. V, § 3.

Section 4.
Jurisdiction of supreme court.

The Supreme Court shall have appellate jurisdiction only in cases in chancery, and shall constitute a Court for the correction of errors at law, under such restrictions as the General Assembly may, by law, prescribe; and shall have power to issue all writs and process necessary to secure justice to parties, and shall exercise a supervisory and administrative control over all inferior judicial tribunals throughout the state.

Section 4, which outlines the Iowa Supreme Court's core powers, generally tracks the corresponding text of Iowa's 1846 constitution,[11] with one exception: today, Section 4 gives the supreme court "supervisory *and administrative* control over" the state's lower courts. Iowa voters made that addition in 1962. So far as one can discern from the convention records, the delegates to the 1846 and 1857 conventions did not significantly debate the jurisdiction and powers of the Iowa Supreme Court. As this book discusses in its commentary on Sections 2 and 3 of this article, the delegates focused instead on how the court's members should be chosen and how many members there should be.

The opening lines of Section 4 indicate that, as a general matter, the Iowa Supreme Court is not a court of original jurisdiction—that is, it is not a court in which one can launch a new lawsuit (*Lampson v. Platt*, 1855; *McGregor v. Gardner*, 1864). Rather, it is a court to which one turns when one believes a lower court has made a mistake affecting the outcome of one's litigation. As we shall see, however, the court does sometimes take jurisdiction of original petitions asking the court to wield its Section 4 power to supervise the state's lower courts. Also, Section 36 of Article III gives the court original jurisdiction for all litigation regarding the apportionment of the General Assembly.

Chancery and law.

The first half of Section 4 distinguishes between equity ("chancery") and law. The reference to chancery points toward principles and practices that trace their roots to England's Court of Chancery—a court that endeavored to fill some of the justice-hindering gaps in the English common-law system. The jurisdiction conferred by the chancery provision "is that possessed by chancery courts at the time of the adoption of the constitution" (*Lessenich v. Sellers*, 1903).

Like England, some of the Union's early states maintained separate equity and law courts. By the late 1860s, however, most states—like Iowa—had unified judiciaries, though some of them—again, like Iowa—continued to maintain law

[11] Iowa Const. of 1846, art. VI, § 3.

and equity as separate jurisdictional categories.[12] In 1937's *Ontjes v. McNider*, the Iowa Supreme Court explained:

> Prior to the adoption of our Constitution and the enactment of statutes authorizing appeals to this court, there were many differences between obtaining a review in an appellate court in an action in equity, and a correction of errors in an action at law. Under the old English system, courts of law and courts of equity were entirely distinct, and a review in an equity case was by a different tribunal than that in which a review could be had in an action at law. Now [in Iowa] the same tribunal, the supreme court, entertains appeals from and reviews both actions in equity and those at law. The procedure followed in removing actions from the trial court to an appellate court was likewise different, actions at law being removed by a writ of error, and actions in equity by appeal. Writs of error are now dispensed with and the same method, notice of appeal, is pursued in transferring cases to the supreme court in both actions in equity and those at law.

Although some of the institutional differences between law and equity have thus been discarded, the law-equity distinction remains meaningful in Iowa today.[13] In law cases, the "court can only act as a court for the correction of such errors as are specifically pointed out" (*Ontjes v. McNider*, 1937) and the court is bound by the lower court's factual findings if those findings are supported by substantial evidence (*Midwest Recovery Services v. Wolfe*, 1990). Equity cases are different. As the Iowa Supreme Court explained early in the state's history, "[u]nder the appellate jurisdiction of a chancery case, that court is authorized to investigate it in all its merits and equities, while, in an action at law, that court can only correct errors which are patent of record" (*Claussen v. Lafrenz*, 1854). When taking an appeal in equity, the supreme court may review both the law *and* the facts de novo (*In re Marriage of Smiley*, 1994; *Gibson v. Deuth*, 1978), although the court does give some "weight" to the district court's factual findings (*Hyler v. Garner*, 1996; *Hayne v. Cook*, 1961) and is "especially deferential to the [district] court's assessment of the credibility of witnesses" (*Wellmark, Inc. v. Polk County Board of Review*, 2016).[14] Nevertheless, the supreme court in equity cases does not venture off in a freewheeling search for matters requiring adjustment; rather, the scope of the court's review is typically limited to the specific factual and legal issues raised by the appellant (*Richardson v. Neppl*, 1970).

---

[12] Samuel L. Bray, "The Supreme Court and the New Equity," 68 *Vanderbilt Law Review* 997, 1017–18, & nn. 112–13 (2015).

[13] *See*, e.g., Iowa Const. art. V, § 6 ("The district court shall be a court of law and equity, which shall be distinct and separate jurisdictions. . . ."); Iowa Code § 602.4102(1) ("The supreme court has appellate jurisdiction only in cases in chancery, and constitutes a court for the correction of errors at law.").

[14] If the appeal in an equity case is from summary judgment, however, the court will not find the facts de novo; rather, its review is limited to correction of errors at law (*Iowa Arboretum, Inc. v. Iowa 4-H Foundation*, 2016; *Lyon v. Willie*, 1980).

Because the law-equity distinction remains significant, Section 4 requires those appearing before the Iowa Supreme Court to know on which side of the line their cases fall. Examples of equity actions include (among many others) actions for injunctive relief (*State ex rel. Miller v. Midwest Pork, L.C.*, 2001),[15] specific performance of contractual obligations (*Janssen v. North Iowa Conference Pensions, Inc.*, 1969), and dissolution of marriage (*In re Marriage of Geil*, 1993). Examples of law actions include (among many others) actions for money damages (*Mosebach v. Blythe*, 1979), breach of contract (*Knudsen v. Andreasen*, 1990), and garnishment (*Ellefson v. Centech Corp.*, 2000).[16] As a general matter, the supreme court's practice is to follow the trial court's lead when deciding whether to treat a case as legal or equitable in nature (*Citizens Savings Bank v. Sac City State Bank*, 1982). When determining how an action for declaratory judgment was tried below, the court pays particular attention to "[t]he pleadings, relief sought, and nature of the case" (*Nelson v. Agro Globe Engineering*, 1998). If there are doubts about how to treat a case in any given instance, the supreme court might resolve its uncertainty by determining whether the trial court excluded evidence in response to evidentiary objections. If evidence was indeed excluded in the proceedings below, the case might best be treated as legal in nature, since the exclusion could frustrate the justices' effort to conduct the de novo review that is appropriate in equity proceedings (*Sille v. Shaffer*, 1980).

Under such restrictions as the general assembly may, by law, prescribe.

Under Section 4's "restrictions" clause, the General Assembly can "set terms and conditions for appeal[s]" and restrict the Iowa Supreme Court's jurisdiction, but it cannot enlarge that jurisdiction beyond the boundaries that the constitution sets (*Western International v. Kirkpatrick*, 1986). In *Western International*, for example, the court reiterated that "the original jurisdiction of this court is limited to the supervision of inferior judicial tribunals"—and because administrative agencies are not such tribunals, legislation that authorized the court to hear appeals directly from an agency amounted to an unconstitutional expansion of the court's original jurisdiction. Parties to a case cannot themselves confer jurisdiction on the court by mutually agreeing to appear there (*Rosmann v. Lawler*, 1965).

---

[15] The equitable prerequisites for obtaining injunctive relief are pushed aside, however, if the General Assembly "impose[s] a duty to grant an injunction by specifying conditions in a statute" (*Max 100 L.C. v. Iowa Realty Co.*, 2001).

[16] For a lengthier list of equity and law actions, see the Iowa State Bar Association's *Appellate Practice Manual* (2004), pp. 32–38.

Power to issue all writs and process necessary to secure justice to parties.

Section 4 authorizes the Iowa Supreme Court "to issue all the common-law writs" (*State ex rel. O'Connor v. District Court in Shelby County,* 1935). In *State ex rel. O'Connor,* for example, the court stated that—if it were justified by the merits—it could issue a writ of prohibition barring a district court from proceeding with a case that challenged the governor's power to temporarily declare martial law in an Iowa county. The writ of certiorari is among those that the court may issue when justice so requires (*Hadjis v. Iowa District Court,* 1979), especially as a device for "avoid[ing] unnecessary and costly litigation" (*Steinbeck v. Iowa District Court,* 1974). Certiorari may be warranted when the lower court "is alleged to have exceeded its jurisdiction or to have acted illegally" (*State Public Defender v. Iowa District Court,* 1999). The court has "interpreted this standard liberally, stating that illegality exists when the [lower] court's ruling lacks substantial evidentiary support or when the court has not applied the proper rule of law" (*Bousman v. Iowa District Court,* 2001). In *City of Okoboji v. Iowa District Court* (2008), for example, the court used certiorari as the vehicle for correcting a district court's failure to issue an injunction in accordance with the supreme court's prior mandate in the case. The court's use of the writ in *City of Okoboji* is closely tied to the court's power to supervise the state's lower courts, considered next.

Supervisory and administrative control over inferior judicial tribunals.

Section 4 grants the Iowa Supreme Court broad power to supervise and administer the state's judicial system. As the court observed in both *Warren County v. Judges of the Fifth Judicial District* (1976) and *Welty v. McMahon* (1982),

> [t]he superintending control is hampered by no specific rules or means for its exercise. It is so general and comprehensive that its complete and full extent and use have practically hitherto not been fully and completely known and exemplified. It is unlimited, being bounded only by the exigencies which call for its exercise. As new instances of these occur it will be found able to cope with them.

The provision empowers the court to admonish or censure judges, for example, when they commit ethical infractions (*In re Howes,* 2016). In 2017, the court invoked its Section 4 powers to "prohibit[] all weapons from courtrooms, court-controlled spaces, and public areas of courthouses and other justice centers," except those weapons carried by "peace officers . . . while performing law enforcement duties."[17] The supervisory powers granted by Section 4 are not,

[17] Iowa Supreme Court, Supervisory Order (June 19, 2017), *available at* http://www.iowacourts.gov/wfdata/frame10109-1263/File303.pdf.

however, wholly unrestricted. In 2013's *Root v. Toney*, for example, the court concluded that Section 4 authorized the court "to set the office hours of the clerks of court" (such as by reducing those hours in order to reduce the judiciary's annual operating costs), but not—absent legislative authorization—to "reduce the time allowed to file a notice of appeal." In 1971's *In re Municipal Court of Cedar Rapids*, the court stated that Section 4 did not authorize the court to remove judges from office. (That particular shortcoming was remedied in 1972, when Iowans amended Article V by adding Section 19.[18])

The writ of certiorari provides the Iowa Supreme Court with an important (but not the exclusive[19]) means of exercising these powers.[20] Although the court has said that it possesses "original jurisdiction" to adjudicate certiorari petitions (*Western International v. Kirkpatrick*, 1986), it often is jurisdiction of a derivative sort. The court explained in 1935's *Independent School District v. Samuelson*:

> Applications to this court for writs of certiorari are sometimes referred to as original proceedings, but that is not the equivalent of saying that in the granting of said writs the court exercises original jurisdiction. The granting of writs of certiorari by this court are original proceedings only in a very limited sense inasmuch as the function of the writ is to bring before this court for review in a particular manner a limited class of errors alleged to have been committed by inferior judicial tribunals, namely, those which result from such tribunals exceeding their jurisdiction or otherwise acting illegally. The only purpose which the writ serves is to annul proceedings of such inferior judicial tribunals. No other relief can be granted. What is accomplished, therefore, by means of the writ is the correction of a particular class of errors at law committed by inferior judicial tribunals. Moreover, this court has power to issue the writ only to carry out the constitutional mandate of exercising "a supervisory control over inferior judicial tribunals." To afford a means of exercising such supervisory control is one of the chief offices of the writ.

In *Samuelson* itself, the court held that, because the State Superintendent of Public Instruction was not a judicial officer under the court's supervision, the

---

[18] The *Des Moines Register*'s editorial board cited the Cedar Rapids case as a prime illustration of the need for giving the Iowa Supreme Court the authority to remove judges from office for good cause. Editorial, "Judges Rebuked," *Des Moines Register*, June 20, 1971, at 12-T.

[19] In *Redmond v. Carter* (1976), for example, the court took original jurisdiction of a "petition for supervisory review" challenging the eligibility of three district court judges to accept appointments to serve on the Iowa Court of Appeals.

[20] *See generally Hohl v. Board of Education* (1959) ("Certiorari is the method of bringing the record of an inferior tribunal before the court for the purpose of ascertaining whether the inferior tribunal or body had jurisdiction and whether its proceedings were authorized. . . . The writ of certiorari is distinguishable from appeal in that certiorari prevents the body performing or exercising a judicial or quasi-judicial function from violating principle[s] of jurisdiction or exceeding the scope of its authority, while appeal is aimed to relieve the individual litigant substantively or from mistake in applying adjective law.").

writ of certiorari could not be used as a vehicle for reviewing that official's alleged illegal behavior.[21]

Although Section 4 does impose upon the Iowa Supreme Court the task of supervising the state's lower courts (*In re Judges of the Cedar Rapids Municipal Court,* 1964), it does not require the court to entertain all original petitions asking the court to wield that power. The court has explained that, if a district court is empowered to provide a suitable remedy, the supreme court's usual preference is to require the complainant to file its petition there, deferring any review until an appeal has been filed (*Iowa Civil Liberties Union v. Critelli,* 1976; *Warren County v. Judges of the Fifth Judicial District,* 1976). Nevertheless, in *In re Judges of the Cedar Rapids Municipal Court, Iowa Civil Liberties Union,* and *Warren County,* as well as in *Welty v. McMahon* (1982), the court took jurisdiction of original petitions due to the public importance of the issues they presented. In *Judges of Cedar Rapids,* for example, two municipal court judges had appeared to run their courts "according to their personal whims and predilections," such as by unduly delaying their rulings and by dismissing criminal and civil cases without giving the initiating parties an opportunity to be heard.

This same clause also empowers the court to "implement protocols to protect the rights of criminal defendants" (*State v. Dahl,* 2016). In *Dahl,* the court fashioned "a protocol to balance the statutory right of an indigent defendant to the appointment of a private investigator . . . against his or her burden to present sufficient information to the trial court to support the granting of an application for appointment of a private investigator at state expense."

Section 5.
District court and judge.

[Repealed.]

For a brief explanation of Section 5 and its repeal, see the commentary on Article V, Section 3.

Section 6.
Jurisdiction of district court.

The District Court shall be a court of law and equity, which shall be distinct and separate jurisdictions, and have jurisdiction in civil and criminal matters arising in their respective districts, in such manner as shall be prescribed by law.

Section 6, which sketches the expansive jurisdictional boundaries of Iowa's district courts, continues to be framed in the language adopted by the delegates

---

[21] The court has stated more broadly that administrative agencies are not "inferior judicial tribunal[s]" from which appeals can be taken directly to the state's high court (*Western International v. Kirkpatrick,* 1986).

to the state's 1857 constitutional convention. That text differs in two notable ways from the corresponding passage of the state's first constitution, ratified in 1846. First, the 1846 text declared that the district courts had "jurisdiction in *all* civil and criminal matters arising in their respective districts."[22] The delegates in 1857 opted to strike the word "all" after Des Moines County's Jonathan Hall pointed out that the Iowa Supreme Court had concluded that the 1846 text did not allow the General Assembly to place limits on the district courts' jurisdiction.[23] In a pair of separate cases concerning a horse and a debt—*Hutton v. Drebilbis* (1850) and *Nelson v. Gray* (1850), respectively—the court had indeed held that, due to the breadth of the district courts' constitutional authority under the 1846 text, the state's justices of the peace could not be given the exclusive power to hear civil suits for small sums. The 1857 delegates believed the General Assembly should have greater power to tailor the judicial system to particular circumstances.

Second, the delegates in 1857 added the phrase "which shall be distinct and separate jurisdictions." Three years earlier—in a case in which the plaintiff had "so blended and confounded" the principles of law and equity that the case could not "be designated as belonging to either"—the Iowa Supreme Court had insisted that the distinction between law and equity is as significant as the distinction between civil and criminal proceedings (*Claussen v. Lafrenz*, 1854).[24] Johnson County's William Penn Clarke proposed adding the "distinct and separate" language in order to ensure "that law and equity could not be mixed up together" in a single case.[25] With that same objective evidently in mind, the General Assembly soon enacted legislation barring litigants from joining legal and equitable causes of action in the same petition.[26] That is where matters stood until 1943, when—in keeping with a national movement toward easing the law-equity divide—Iowa adopted a rule of civil procedure permitting a plaintiff to "join in the same petition as many causes of action, legal or equitable," as he or she has against a given defendant.[27] Without explanatory discussion, the Iowa Supreme Court has concluded that Section 6 does not bar such joinders (*First National Bank v. Curran*, 1973). If a plaintiff separates his or her legal and equitable claims

---

[22] Iowa Const. of 1846, art. VI, § 4 (emphasis added).

[23] *1857 Debates, supra* Article I, note 3, vol. 1, pp. 459–60.

[24] *Cf. Cooper v. Armstrong* (1851) ("[S]o far as this court is concerned, it is clear that the constitution does not authorize legal and equitable claims to be blended together in one suit.").

[25] *1857 Debates, supra* Article I, note 3, vol. 1, p. 460.

[26] Revised Code of Iowa (1860), § 2844 ("Causes of action of whatever kind, *where each may be prosecuted by the same kind of proceedings*, . . . may be joined in the same petition. . . .") (emphasis added); *see also Cooper v. Erickson* (1931) (holding that this statute bars a party from joining legal and equitable actions in a single petition).

[27] Iowa R. Civ. Proc. 1.231 (originally adopted as Iowa R. Civ. Proc. 22 (1943)). For discussions of the rule's enactment, see *Johanik v. Des Moines Drug Co.* (1945) and Dan C. Dutcher, "Joinder of Parties and Actions," 29 *Iowa Law Review* 3, 9–10 (1943).

into two separate proceedings, the two proceedings may be consolidated (for an example, see *Knigge v. Dencker*, 1955). For further discussion of the distinction between law and equity, see the commentary on Article V, Section 4.

Iowa's district courts are courts of general jurisdiction, authorized to hear all matters of law and equity arising within their respective districts (*Schott v. Schott*, 2008).[28] Even if a district court's judges opt to split the cases between them along law-equity lines, any judge on that court retains jurisdiction to adjudicate any case falling within Section 6's broad description (*Foley v. Utterback*, 1923). The provision's geographic restriction is reminiscent of the Vicinage Clause in the Sixth Amendment to the U.S. Constitution, which states that a criminal defendant is entitled to trial "by an impartial jury of the State and district wherein the crime shall have been committed." In *State v. Rimmer* (2016), noting that the defendants had not sought to distinguish between the requirements of the Vicinage Clause and Section 6, the Iowa Supreme Court held that Section 6's "arising in" requirement was satisfied so long as at least part of the charged crime was committed in the district where the prosecution had been brought.

The General Assembly cannot strip district courts of their broad jurisdictional reach, but it can regulate the manner in which the courts' jurisdiction is exercised (*In re Guardianship of Matejski*, 1988; *Laird Bros. v. Dickerson*, 1875). In *Schrier v. State* (1997), for example, the court noted that the General Assembly may impose statutes of limitations on petitions for postconviction relief; such statutes restrict a district court's authority to act, but they do not unconstitutionally strip the court of jurisdiction. The distinction between authority and jurisdiction is important more generally because "a defect in the court's authority to hear a particular case may be waived, whereas any defect in its subject matter jurisdiction is not subject to waiver" (*State v. Emery*, 2001).

Section 7.
Conservators of the peace.

The Judges of the Supreme and District Courts shall be conservators of the peace throughout the State.

This rarely noted provision imposes upon Iowa judges the duty to help preserve public peace. When framing the text that one sees here, the delegates to the 1857 constitutional convention pulled together provisions that had appeared in two separate sections of the 1846 constitution.[29] The records of Iowa's 1846 and 1857 conventions do not contain any indication that these provisions were

---

[28] *Accord* Iowa Code § 602.6101 ("The district court has all the power usually possessed and exercised by trial courts of general jurisdiction. . . .").

[29] Iowa Const. of 1846, art. VI, §§ 3, 4.

publicly debated. Rather, they appear simply to have been copied from a handful of other states' constitutions.[30]

The Iowa Supreme Court's only significant ruling on Section 7 is half a century old. In *Newby v. District Court of Woodbury County* (1967), a state judge had heard four young men carousing on the street near the judge's house. The judge went outside, identified himself as a judge, and told the troublemakers that he was ordering them to disperse. After some of the youths physically assaulted him, the judge initiated contempt proceedings against them, arguing that he had a judicial duty under Section 7 to conserve the peace and that the young men had interfered with his exercise of that duty. The Iowa Supreme Court agreed with the judge, observing that Section 7 does not "specif[y] the manner in which judges of this court or of the district courts shall discharge their duties as conservators of the peace," but that the judge was plainly trying to put an end to a public disturbance. That outcome is consistent with the court's brief observation in *Reed v. Murphy* (1850) that when judges act as conservators of the peace, they may be acting individually as judges, rather than as a court.

Section 8.
Style of process.

The style of all process shall be, "The State of Iowa," and all prosecutions shall be conducted in the name and by the authority of the same.

Section 8 requires that all "process" be denominated as coming from the State of Iowa and that all prosecutions be conducted under the State of Iowa's name and authority. The term "process" refers to any document (such as a warrant or a summons) that the state uses to notify a person that he or she is required to appear in court (*City of Davenport v. Bird,* 1872). Section 8 still reads as it did in the corresponding provision of Iowa's 1846 constitution.[31] The historical record does not provide any indication that the provision was publicly debated at any of the state's constitutional conventions.

The Iowa Supreme Court first encountered this provision's requirements during the period between the state's 1846 and 1857 constitutions. In *Rogers v. Alexander* (1850), the treasurer of Van Buren County had commenced a criminal prosecution in his own name for the defendant's alleged violation of certain liquor laws. A statute had appeared to direct the treasurer to style the action in this way, but the court vacated the conviction, ruling that the prosecution was fatally defective because it had not been designated as proceeding in the name and by the authority of the State of Iowa. In 1855's *Wrocklege v. State,* however,

---

[30] *See,* e.g., Ala. Const. of 1819, art. V, § 16; Mo. Const. of 1820, art. V, § 4.

[31] Iowa Const. of 1846, art. VI, § 6.

the court explained that papers launching a prosecution need not recite Section 8's precise language. The court held that it was permissible for the indictment to say merely that the prosecution was being brought "in behalf of" the state.

After the 1857 constitution's ratification, the court continued to develop the flexible interpretation of Section 8 that *Wrocklege* had signaled. In *State v. Gurlock* (1863), for example, the court held that a criminal indictment was not rendered ineffective by being brought in the name of the State of "Sowa," rather than the State of Iowa. In *City of Davenport v. Bird* (1872), the court concluded that Section 8's requirements do not apply to criminal prosecutions brought by municipalities for violations of city ordinances. And if the city in such a case *does* provide the name of the state in addition to the name of the city, the paperwork does not violate Section 8 (*City of Des Moines v. Pugh*, 1942; *State v. Wilson*, 1899; *State v. Smouse*, 1878).

Section 9.
Salaries.

[Repealed.]

For a brief explanation of Section 9 and its repeal, see the commentary on Article V, Section 3.

Section 10.
Judicial districts.

The General Assembly may re-organize the Judicial Districts and increase or diminish the number of Districts, or the number of Judges of the said Court, and may increase the number of Judges of the Supreme Court; but such increase or diminution shall not be more than one District, or one Judge of either Court, at any one session; and no re-organization of the Districts, or diminution of the number of Judges, shall have the effect of removing a Judge from office. Such re-organization of the districts, or any change in the boundaries thereof, or increase or diminution of the number of Judges, shall take place every four years thereafter, if necessary, and at no other time.

At any regular session of the general assembly, the state may be divided into the necessary judicial districts for district court purposes, or the said districts may be reorganized and the number of the districts and the judges of said courts increased or diminished; but no reorganization of the districts or diminution of the judges shall have the effect of removing a judge from office.

Section 10 gives the General Assembly broad (but not limitless) freedom to change the judicial districts' boundaries and to adjust the number of the state's judges and district courts. It is this provision, for example, that gives the legislature the power to enlarge the Iowa Supreme Court beyond the three-member tribunal that Section 2 of this article would otherwise prescribe. Iowa's first constitution directed the General Assembly to divide the state into four judicial districts and authorized it to create additional districts as it saw fit.[32] In a now-outdated passage that is commonly omitted from recitations of Section 10 (just as it is omitted here), the delegates to the 1857 convention chose to expand the minimum number of districts to eleven and authorized the General Assembly to create additional districts after 1860.[33] In the first paragraph that one sees above, the delegates also restricted the legislature's power to restructure the state's district courts (such as by barring the legislature from removing a judge from office through the district-altering process). During the delegates' discussion of Section 10 at the 1857 convention, Davis County's David Palmer explained that the reason for limiting the number of districts or judges that could be added in a single session was to make sure that "they shall not be increased five or six at a time, as was done this winter." The delegates also briefly debated whether reorganizations should be permitted every five years or every four, ultimately settling upon the latter.[34]

Iowans added Section 10's second paragraph in 1884. Read superficially, it might appear simply to repeat what the first paragraph already said. As the Iowa Supreme Court explained in *State v. Emmons* (1887), however, the amendment was significant: it empowered the General Assembly to restructure the state's district courts without abiding by the restrictions imposed by the passages that appear in the middle and at the end of Section 10's first paragraph, so long as no sitting judge is removed from office. Shortly after that amendment was ratified, the legislature abolished a circuit court that it had established less than two decades earlier and significantly expanded the number of Iowa's judicial districts (*State v. Emmons*, 1887). The *Emmons* court pointed out that the constitution leaves the legislature free to place more than one judge within a given district.

In 1970, Attorney General Richard Turner expressed the view that the General Assembly may delegate much of the district-drawing task to the Iowa Supreme Court, so long as the legislature provides the court with guidelines.[35] In 1971, he determined that Section 10 authorizes the legislature to cut short the terms of judicial nominating commissioners when reducing the total number of the state's districts.[36] In 1975, Turner concluded that Section 10 and separation-of-powers principles bar the legislature from delegating to a district's chief judge

---

[32] Iowa Const. of 1846, art. VI, § 4.

[33] For the delegates' debate about the number of districts the state should have prior to 1860, see *1857 Debates, supra* Article I, note 3, vol. 1, pp. 456, 475, 507–09, 628–35. One of the central issues in that debate concerned whether judges, lawyers, and litigants would face undue difficulties if required to travel within large districts, especially in the less-populated western portion of the state.

[34] *1857 Debates, supra* Article I, note 3, vol. 1, pp. 460, 472–75.

[35] Op. Iowa Att'y Gen., 1970 WL 207598 (Mar. 3, 1970) (replying to Lucas DeKoster).

[36] Op. Iowa Att'y Gen., 1971 WL 240842 (Oct. 19, 1971) (replying to John Mowry). For more on Iowa's judicial nominating commissions, see Article V, § 16.

the power to reduce the number of the district's judges by swapping three part-time magistrate judges for one full-time magistrate judge.[37]

Section 11.
Judges—when chosen.

[Repealed.]

For a brief explanation of Section 11 and its repeal, see the commentary on Article V, Section 3.

Section 12.
Attorney general.

The General Assembly shall provide, by law, for the election of an Attorney General by the people, whose term of office shall be four years, and until his successor is elected and qualifies.

Iowa's first constitution, adopted in 1846, directed the voters within each county to elect a prosecuting attorney,[38] but it did not create the position of attorney general. In 1853, the General Assembly established the position of attorney general as a statutory matter.[39] At the 1857 constitutional convention, Johnson County's William Penn Clarke proposed going one step further by raising the position to constitutional stature. Appanoose County's Amos Harris resisted Clarke's suggestion, saying that he "was always of the opinion that the attorney general was a sort of fifth wheel to the wagon, and of no account. The legislature created this officer, and if it be deemed necessary, they can provide for him." The delegates nevertheless accepted Clarke's proposal by a vote of 18 to 13.[40]

As ratified in 1857, the attorney general's term was set at two years. Iowans extended that term to four years in 1972, the same year they extended the governor's term of office from two years to four (as described in the commentary on Article IV, Section 2).

Section 13.2 of the Iowa Code lays out the attorney general's core duties. Those duties render the officeholder far more important than Harris's "fifth wheel."

---

[37] Op. Iowa Att'y Gen., 1975 WL 368757 (June 4, 1975) (replying to James Middleswart).

[38] Iowa Const. of 1846, art. VI, § 5.

[39] Act of Jan. 24, 1853, ch. 107, 1852 Iowa Acts 186.

[40] *1857 Debates*, *supra* Article I, note 3, vol. 1, p. 478. In an ill-fated subsequent attempt to strike the position from the constitution, Wapello County's George Gillaspy said that he "consider[ed] it a perfect sinecure, and an office of no benefit to the State." *Id.* at p. 588.

Section 13.
District attorney.

[Repealed.]

Under the original text of Iowa's 1857 constitution, voters in each judicial district were to elect a district attorney to serve a four-year term.[41] Iowa voters altered that scheme in 1884, shifting to an arrangement in which voters in each county elected a county attorney to serve a two-year term. In 1970, Iowans repealed Section 13 altogether, thereby maximizing the General Assembly's freedom to make whatever arrangements it sees fit for local public attorneys.[42] Today, the position of county attorney is established by legislation.[43] With Section 13 no longer standing in the way, the legislature has authorized counties that wish to do so to share the services of a single county attorney.[44]

Section 14.
System of court practice.

It shall be the duty of the General Assembly to provide for the carrying into effect of this article, and to provide for a general system of practice in all the Courts of this State.

Section 14, which directs the legislature to ensure that Article V's requirements are implemented and to develop a "system of practice" for the state's courts, was proposed without recorded explanation at the state's 1857 constitutional convention by Henry County's Rufus Clarke.[45] The convention records contain no evidence that the provision was controversial.

The Iowa Supreme Court's leading Section 14 ruling is *Iowa Civil Liberties Union v. Critelli* (1976). In that case, judges in the Fifth Judicial District had adopted a local rule imposing various time restrictions on pretrial procedures in criminal cases. The Iowa Civil Liberties Union and other petitioners argued that the judges had intruded upon the General Assembly's Section 14 domain, but the court concluded otherwise. The court explained that Section 14 does not give the legislature the *exclusive* power to prescribe court rules, and that the supreme court had "consistently recognized the inherent common-law power of the courts to adopt rules for the management of cases on their dockets in the

---

[41] For a portion of the delegates' debate at the 1857 convention about whether to constitutionally mandate a prosecutorial position and whether such prosecutors should be elected on a district or county basis, see *1857 Debates, supra* Article I, note 3, vol. 1, pp. 456–57, 475–77.

[42] For an articulation of reasons for discarding Section 13, see Editorial, "County Attorney Reform," *Des Moines Register*, Sept. 23, 1968, at 6.

[43] Iowa Code §§ 331.751–59.

[44] Iowa Code § 331.753.

[45] *1857 Debates, supra* Article I, note 3, vol. 1, pp. 460–61, 477.

absence of [a] statute." "Where the legislature has not acted," the court wrote, "courts possess a residuum of inherent common-law power to adopt rules to enable them to meet their independent constitutional and statutory responsibilities." In *Eicher v. Tinley* (1936), the court determined that the General Assembly had not exceeded its power under this section when it limited the fines and jail time that a judge may impose for contempt of court.

Section 15.
Vacancies in courts.

Vacancies in the Supreme Court and District Court shall be filled by appointment by the Governor from lists of nominees submitted by the appropriate judicial nominating commission. Three nominees shall be submitted for each Supreme Court vacancy, and two nominees shall be submitted for each District Court vacancy. If the Governor fails for thirty days to make the appointment, it shall be made from such nominees by the Chief Justice of the Supreme Court.

As described in Part I and in the commentary on Article V, Section 3, Iowa voters in 1962 substantially altered the means by which judicial vacancies are filled. Prior to that year, the Iowa Supreme Court's members were chosen in statewide elections and district court judges were chosen in district elections. The changes in 1962 were part of a movement in portions of the country away from choosing judges through elections—a method that many believed led to real or perceived corruption—and toward a merit-based selection process.[46] Section 15 empowers the governor to select the members of the state's supreme and district courts, but the eligible candidates are limited to those whose names appear on slates supplied by the appropriate judicial nominating commission (as described in Section 16 of this article). Because Section 15 was adopted in 1962, fourteen years prior to the creation of the Iowa Court of Appeals, the provision says nothing about filling vacancies on that intermediate appellate tribunal. The General Assembly has filled that void by enacting legislation charging the state judicial nominating commission with giving the governor a slate of three names when vacancies on that court occur.[47]

The Iowa Supreme Court's chief justice is tasked with selecting from the commission's slate in the unlikely event that the governor opts not to make a decision within thirty days. By giving the chief justice that power, Section 15 helps to ensure that the judiciary remains fully staffed even if a governor concludes that

[46] *See* "Iowa Adopts Society's Judicial Selection and Tenure Plan for All State Judges," 46 *Journal of American Judicature Society* 1, 1 (1962) ("Iowa became the first state in the nation to amend its constitution to provide for nonpolitical selection of all of its state court judges on June 4, 1962."). As Part I of this book explains, the movement toward merit selection traces its roots to Albert Kales, the co-founder of the American Judicature Society. *See generally* Todd E. Pettys, "Judicial Retention Elections, the Rule of Law, and the Rhetorical Weaknesses of Consequentialism," 60 *Buffalo Law Review* 69, 74–75 (2012).

[47] Iowa Code §§ 46.14A, 46.15.

he or she would rather have a diminished judiciary than appoint any of the people whose names appear on the slate of options that he or she has been given.

The selection process introduced by Section 15 does not apply to every state employee who performs judicial functions. In *Warren County v. Judges of the Fifth Judicial District* (1976), the court held that judicial magistrates are not district court judges and thus need not be selected by the means that Section 15 prescribes.

Section 16.
State and district nominating commissions.

There shall be a State Judicial Nominating Commission. Such commission shall make nominations to fill vacancies in the Supreme Court. Until July 4, 1973, and thereafter unless otherwise provided by law, the State Judicial Nominating Commission shall be composed and selected as follows: There shall be not less than three nor more than eight appointive members, as provided by law, and an equal number of elective members on such Commission, all of whom shall be electors of the state. The appointive members shall be appointed by the Governor subject to confirmation by the Senate. The elective members shall be elected by the resident members of the bar of the state. The judge of the Supreme Court who is senior in length of service on said Court, other than the Chief Justice, shall also be a member of such Commission and shall be its chairman.

There shall be a District Judicial Nominating Commission in each judicial district of the state. Such commissions shall make nominations to fill vacancies in the District Court within their respective districts. Until July 4, 1973, and thereafter unless otherwise provided by law, District Judicial Nominating Commissions shall be composed and selected as follows: There shall be not less than three nor more than six appointive members, as provided by law, and an equal number of elective members on each such commission, all of whom shall be electors of the district. The appointive members shall be appointed by the Governor. The elective members shall be elected by the resident members of the bar of the district. The district judge of such district who is senior in length of service shall also be a member of such commission and shall be its chairman.

Due consideration shall be given to area representation in the appointment and election of Judicial Nominating Commission members. Appointive and elective members of Judicial Nominating Commissions shall serve for six year terms, shall be ineligible for a second six year term on the same commission, shall hold no office of profit of the United States or of the state during their terms, shall be chosen without reference to political affiliation, and shall have such other qualifications as may be prescribed by law. As near as may be, the terms of one-third of such members shall expire every two years.

Section 16 establishes a state judicial nominating commission to identify candidates for filling vacancies on the Iowa Supreme Court and establishes district judicial nominating commissions to identify candidates for filling vacancies on the state's district courts. Section 16 should be read in conjunction with Sections 15, 17, and 18, all of which were added to the Iowa Constitution in 1962 as part of an overhaul of the means by which the state's judgeships are filled. Part

I of this book describes that overhaul. Regulations concerning the nominating commissions are located in Chapter 46 of the Iowa Code.[48] Section 46.14A, for example, gives the state judicial nominating commission the task of identifying candidates for filling vacancies on the Iowa Court of Appeals.

Note that a sizable number of seats on the nominating commissions must be held by individuals who have been elected by members of the Iowa Bar. Two points about that arrangement deserve special mention. First, in *Carlson v. Wiggins* (2012), the U.S. Court of Appeals for the Eighth Circuit held that Iowa's system of allowing only members of the Iowa Bar to select the commissions' elective members does not violate the Fourteenth Amendment's Equal Protection Clause. The court held that the arrangement is rationally related to Iowa's legitimate interest in ensuring that only highly qualified individuals serve as state judges. Second, the Office of the Attorney General concluded in 1996 that Section 16 does not require the commissioners elected by the Iowa Bar to themselves be attorneys.[49]

In *Welty v. McMahon* (1982), the Iowa Supreme Court confronted an unusual circumstance. Two individuals had served terms on their respective districts' judicial nominating commissions. Because the election for those seats had been delayed for a period of months, however, the two commissioners ultimately held those positions for five and a half years, rather than for the full six years authorized by Section 16. The two men sought re-election, arguing that Section 16's restriction on second terms did not apply to them because they had not served a full first term. The court rejected that argument, reasoning that although the men's "tenure" in office had indeed been less than six years, they nevertheless had completed six-year "terms."

Section 17.
Terms—judicial elections.

Members of all courts shall have such tenure in office as may be fixed by law, but terms of Supreme Court Judges shall be not less than eight years and terms of District Court Judges shall be not less than six years. Judges shall serve for one year after appointment and until the first day of January following the next judicial election after the expiration of such year. They shall at such judicial election stand for retention in office on a separate ballot which shall submit the question of whether such judge shall be retained in office for the tenure prescribed for

[48] The Office of the Attorney General has issued numerous opinions concerning these statutory regulations. *See*, e.g., Op. Iowa Att'y Gen., 1994 WL 328333 (June 20, 1994) (replying to Clark E. McNeal) ("[W]e conclude that a member of a judicial nominating commission who resigns prior to the expiration of his or her term is not eligible for nomination to fill a vacancy during the remainder of the unexpired term, even if the vacancy occurred after the commissioner's resignation.") (interpreting Iowa Code § 46.14).

[49] Op. Iowa Att'y Gen., 1996 WL 769291 (Dec. 18, 1996) (replying to R. Keith Richardson).

such office and when such tenure is a term of years, on their request, they shall, at the judicial election next before the end of each term, stand again for retention on such ballot. Present Supreme Court and District Court Judges, at the expiration of their respective terms, may be retained in office in like manner for the tenure prescribed for such office. The General Assembly shall prescribe the time for holding judicial elections.

Adopted in 1962 with Sections 15, 16, and 18 of this article, Section 17 sets the minimum length of judges' terms and requires judges periodically to appear before Iowa voters in retention elections. The most widely noted judicial retention election to date occurred in 2010, when Iowa voters removed three members of the Iowa Supreme Court who had joined the court's unanimous ruling in *Varnum v. Brien* (2009), striking down the state's ban on same-sex marriage.[50]

Subject to the minima that it establishes, Section 17 charges the General Assembly with establishing the length of judicial terms. The legislature has carried out that responsibility in Section 46.16 of the Iowa Code. Section 17's last sentence instructs the General Assembly to set the time for holding judicial elections. In Section 46.17 of the Iowa Code, the legislature has said that judicial elections "shall be held at the time of the general election."

In a 1969 opinion largely focused on other matters, Attorney General Richard Turner stated that Section 17's requirement that judicial retention elections be conducted "on a separate ballot" is not violated when election officials opt to use voting machines to present voters with all questions before them.[51] The General Assembly shares that view: Section 46.22 of the Iowa Code permits judicial elections to be held "by separate paper ballot or optical scan ballot" and states that, "[i]f optical scan ballots are used, either a separate ballot or a distinct heading may be used to distinguish the judicial ballot."

Section 18.
Salaries—qualifications—retirement.

Judges of the Supreme Court and District Court shall receive salaries from the state, shall be members of the bar of the state and shall have such other qualifications as may be prescribed by law. Judges of the Supreme Court and District Court shall be ineligible to any other office of the state while serving on said court and for two years thereafter, except that District Judges shall be eligible to the office of Supreme Court Judge. Other judicial officers shall be selected in such manner and shall have such tenure, compensation and other qualification as may be fixed by law. The General Assembly shall prescribe mandatory retirement for Judges of the Supreme Court and District Court at a specified age

---

[50] For a history of the 2010 retention election, see Todd E. Pettys, "Letter from Iowa: Same-Sex Marriage and the Ouster of Three Justices," 59 *Kansas Law Review* 715 (2011). For a history of the retention election of 2012, in which a fourth *Varnum* justice was retained, see Todd E. Pettys, "Retention Redux: Iowa 2012," 14 *Journal of Appellate Practice & Process* 47 (2013).

[51] Op. Iowa Att'y Gen., 1969 WL 181592 (May 29, 1969) (replying to Donald E. Voorhees).

and shall provide for adequate retirement compensation. Retired judges may be subject to special assignment to temporary judicial duties by the Supreme Court, as provided by law.

Together with Sections 15, 16, and 17, Section 18 was included in the package of constitutional amendments that Iowa voters approved in 1962 in order to overhaul the state's system of selecting and retaining judges. Part I describes that overhaul. Section 18's first sentence requires all state judges to be licensed Iowa attorneys, and invites the General Assembly to prescribe additional qualifications. Section 46.14 of the Iowa Code states that, in addition to being members of the Iowa Bar, nominees for judicial vacancies "shall be residents of the state or district of the court to which they are nominated, and shall be of such age that they will be able to serve an initial and one regular term of office to which they are nominated before reaching the age of seventy-two years."

By not allowing judges to hold other state offices while on the bench and for two years thereafter, Section 18's second sentence helps to maintain the separation of powers, prevent corruption and conflicts of interest, and ensure that judges are able to devote their professional energies to their judicial tasks. Because Section 18 was adopted in 1962, fourteen years prior to the creation of the Iowa Court of Appeals, the provision makes no reference to that tribunal. That silence created complications in 1976, when Governor Robert Ray appointed three sitting district court judges to the state's newly created intermediate appellate court. Strictly read, Section 18's second sentence would have appeared to render those three judges ineligible for elevation to any Iowa tribunal other than the Iowa Supreme Court. Attorney General Richard Turner interpreted the provision this way, alerting Governor Ray that the appointments were "clearly void."[52] In *Redmond v. Carter* (1976), the court resolved the difficulty by concluding that, even if Section 18 rigidly purported to make the three judges ineligible (a matter about which a majority of the court declined to reach a conclusion), barring the three appointees from elevation on those grounds would violate their rights under the Equal Protection Clause of the U.S. Constitution's Fourteenth Amendment.[53]

Section 18's third sentence follows from the declaration in Article V, Section 1, that the General Assembly may establish tribunals beyond those that the Iowa Constitution itself mandates. If the legislature does create such tribunals, it must

[52] Op. Iowa Att'y Gen., 1976 WL 376052 (Oct. 18, 1976) (issuing the opinion on his own initiative to alert Governor Ray of "a grave problem"). Fielding an unrelated inquiry two years later, Turner concluded that Section 18 renders judges ineligible to serve on the board of directors of the Judicial District Department of Correctional Services. Op. Iowa Att'y Gen., 1978 WL 17392 (Apr. 3, 1978) (replying to Roland McCauley).

[53] Concurring specially in the judgment, another group of justices said that, rather than decide the case on federal constitutional grounds, the court simply should have rejected the rigid interpretation of Section 18.

establish the judicial officers' required qualifications, manner of selection, compensation, and tenure in office.

Section 18's fourth sentence requires an age-based system of mandatory retirement for all state judges. Section 602.1610 of the Iowa Code sets the mandatory retirement age at seventy-two years. This same sentence of Section 18 requires the legislature to provide retired judges with "adequate retirement compensation."[54] Sections 602.9101–9116 of the Iowa Code establish and regulate the state's "Judicial Retirement System."

Section 18's final sentence allows the Iowa Supreme Court to assign temporary judicial tasks to retired judges, under such regulations as the General Assembly adopts. Section 602.1612 of the Iowa Code broadly authorizes a retired judge to be assigned "temporary judicial duties on a court in this state," so long as the supreme court has "deemed [the assignment] necessary . . . to expedite the administration of justice" and so long as the judge has not elected to practice law.

Section 19.
Retirement and discipline of judges.

In addition to the legislative power of impeachment of judges as set forth in Article three (III), sections nineteen (19) and twenty (20) of the Constitution, the Supreme Court shall have power to retire judges for disability and to discipline or remove them for good cause, upon application by a commission on judicial qualifications. The General Assembly shall provide by law for the implementation of this section.

Iowa voters added Section 19 to the constitution in 1972, providing for the creation of a commission on judicial qualifications, authorizing the Iowa Supreme Court to discipline, retire, or remove state judges upon receiving a meritorious application from the commission, and instructing the General Assembly to adopt appropriate implementing legislation.[55] The legislature responded by

[54] For an opinion from Attorney General Richard Turner regarding this requirement, see Op. Iowa Att'y Gen., 1967 WL 167234 (Nov. 21, 1967) (replying to Eugene M. Hill) ("The State cannot fulfill th[is] duty by a system which requires contribution by the judiciary in order to obtain retirement compensation, whether that system is optional on the part of the judges or is enacted before or after the effective date of the constitutional amendment.").

[55] In 1971's *In re Municipal Court of Cedar Rapids*, the Iowa Supreme Court had held that Article V, Section 4, did not give the court the power to remove judges for good cause. The *Des Moines Register*'s editorial board cited that case as a prime illustration of the need for strengthening the supreme court's hand. Editorial, "Judges Rebuked," *Des Moines Register*, June 20, 1971, at 12-T. In an editorial appearing shortly before Iowans went to the polls to decide whether to adopt Section 19, the *Register*'s editorial board cited California's Commission on Judicial Qualifications as a model for Iowa to follow. Editorial, "Power to Discipline Judges," *Des Moines Register*, Sept. 2, 1972, at 4.

establishing a seven-member Commission on Judicial Qualifications and prescribing various procedures for its operations.[56]

In *In re Carstensen* (1982), the Iowa Supreme Court fielded its first disciplinary application from the commission. The case concerned a district judge who, in "blatant" violation of a rule promulgated by the supreme court, had not been filing timely and accurate reports regarding his judicial activities. A majority of the commission recommended that the judge be suspended without pay for thirty days, but a minority of the commissioners believed the commission lacked the authority to specify the particular sanctions that it believed were appropriate. The court concluded that Section 19 and its implementing legislation do implicitly authorize the commission to recommend particular sanctions, though the court emphasized that the court itself makes the final decision on its de novo review.

[56] Iowa Code §§ 602.2101–2107.

Article VI

Militia

Section 1.
Composition—training.

The militia of this State shall be composed of all able-bodied male citizens, between the ages of eighteen and forty five years, except such as are or may hereafter be exempt by the laws of the United States, or of this State, and shall be armed, equipped, and trained, as the General Assembly may provide by law.

Section 1, which establishes Iowa's militia and grants the General Assembly broad power to provide for its supplies and training, continues to read precisely as it did in the corresponding provision of the state's 1846 constitution, with one exception: the 1846 text limited militia membership to men who were "white."[1] Iowa voters removed that racial restriction in 1868, the same year that the nation added the Fourteenth Amendment to the U.S. Constitution and thereby limited states' ability to make racial distinctions among people within their jurisdictions.[2] Section 1 works in harness with Section 7 of Article IV, which declares that the governor shall be the commander in chief of the state's military forces.

---

[1] Iowa Const. of 1846, art. VII, § 1. Under the draft of Section 1 that was initially circulated at the 1846 convention, militia duty would have been imposed upon all "able-bodied white male *persons*." *1846 Journal, supra* Article I, note 3, p. 70 (emphasis added). Late in the convention's proceedings, Linn County's Socrates Tryon successfully moved to replace "persons" with "citizens." *Id.* at pp. 101–02.

[2] U.S. Const. amend. XIV, § 1.

These provisions, together with the remainder of Article VI, do not merely give the state a certain degree of military power; they also help constitute Iowa's contribution to the forces that the federal government may deploy in suitable circumstances.[3] Section 1's reference to arming and training Iowa's militia must be read in deference to the U.S. Constitution, which gives Congress the power "[t]o provide for organizing, arming, and disciplining the Militia" and the power to prescribe "the discipline" for training the militia's members.[4] The General Assembly's extensive regulations of the state's military forces are located in chapters 29, 29A, 29B, and 29C of the Iowa Code.[5]

At the 1857 constitutional convention, Benton County's James Traer proposed that the minimum age required for compelled militia membership be increased from eighteen to twenty-one, explaining that he was "opposed to compelling a man to serve in a military capacity until he is allowed the right to vote." Jasper County's Harvey Skiff, who was serving as the chair of the Committee on the Militia, opposed Traer's suggestion, arguing that it was commonplace among the states to require young men to serve in the militia once they reached eighteen, and that the country needed their services.[6] Evidently on the strength of that argument, the delegates sided with Skiff by an unrecorded margin. The delegates to the 1857 convention also rejected the suggestion made by Clayton County's Alpheus Scott that they remove the racial restriction that then existed for militia duty.[7]

Neither the Iowa Supreme Court nor the Office of the Attorney General has had much occasion to interpret Section 1. To date, the court's only brush with the provision came in *Morrison v. State* (1970), when the justices concluded that, under statutes then in effect, a pilot was a state employee at the time he crashed a National Guard plane. In 2001, the Office of the Attorney General observed that Section 1 "does not expressly recognize an individual right to keep and bear arms."[8] In 1978, Attorney General Richard Turner concluded that the term "men" in the Iowa Constitution refers generically to all human beings, while the term "male"—including in its appearance in Section 1—is intended to exclude females.[9] In a 1947 opinion concerning the sources of funds that

---

[3] U.S. Const. art. I, § 8, cls. 15 and 16 (giving Congress certain powers regarding the states' militias); *id.* art. II, § 2 (stating that the president is the "Commander in Chief of... the Militia of the several States, when called into actual Service of the United States").

[4] U.S. Const. art. I, § 8, cl. 16.

[5] For an early-twentieth-century discussion of the Iowa militia, see Carl H. Erbe, "The Militia Under the Constitution of Iowa," 24 *Iowa Journal of History & Politics* 270 (1926).

[6] *1857 Debates, supra* Article I, note 3, vol. 1, p. 641.

[7] *1857 Journal, supra* Article I, note 3, p. 232. For more on the 1857 constitution's racial distinctions, see Part I of this book.

[8] Op. Iowa Att'y Gen., 2001 WL 1651437 (Oct. 2, 2001) (replying to Dan Boddicker).

[9] Op. Iowa Att'y Gen., 1978 WL 17349 (Jan. 30, 1978) (replying to Douglas Smalley).

could be used to pay the salary of a National Guard employee, Attorney General Robert Larson devoted several paragraphs to explaining the militia's historic status as an institution with both state and federal functions.[10]

Section 2. Exemption.

No person or persons conscientiously scrupulous of bearing arms shall be compelled to do military duty in time of peace: Provided, that such person or persons shall pay an equivalent for such exemption in the same manner as other citizens.

Section 2, which allows individuals with adverse conscientious scruples to refuse to serve in the state's militia "in time of peace," traces its roots to the Territory of Iowa's 1844 constitutional convention. The delegates to that assembly debated the criteria for exempting men from militia service. Henry County's Jonathan Hall initially argued that exemptions from militia duty should be narrowly granted only to those who were performing other varieties of public service. Henry County's Joseph Hawkins replied that he believed exemptions should not be available on any grounds during times of war, but that during times of peace exemptions should be granted to anyone "having religious scruples against bearing arms." Hall largely acquiesced, but successfully proposed reframing Hawkins's sentiments in the more secular language that remains in Section 2 today.[11] That language, as well as the provision requiring exempted individuals to reimburse society for their refusal to make a bodily contribution to the community's armed protection, closely echoes provisions found in a handful of other states' early constitutions.[12]

Neither the Iowa Supreme Court nor the Office of the Attorney General has issued opinions further illuminating Section 2's meaning.

Section 3. Officers.

All commissioned officers of the militia, (staff officers excepted,) shall be elected by the persons liable to perform military duty, and shall be commissioned by the Governor.

Section 3, which injects a democratic element into the selection of the militia's commissioned officers, was not the subject of debate at any of the state's

[10] Op. Iowa Att'y Gen., 1947 WL 58175 (Oct. 9, 1947) (replying to Charles Grahl).

[11] *1844 and 1846 Fragments, supra* Article I, note 3, pp. 66–67; *1844 Journal, supra* Article I, note 3, pp. 85–86.

[12] *See, e.g.,* Ky. Const. of 1799, art. III, § 28; Miss. Const. of 1817, art. IV, Militia, § 3; N.H. Const. of 1792, pt. I, art. 13; Penn. Const. of 1838, art. VI, § 2.

constitutional conventions. The provision still stands in the same form that it took in the draft constitution produced by the delegates to the Territory of Iowa's 1844 constitutional convention.[13]

Neither the Iowa Supreme Court nor the Office of the Attorney General has issued opinions concerning Section 3.

[13] *1844 Journal, supra* Article I, note 3, p. 199. The delegates to the 1846 convention rejected a more complicated selection scheme proposed by Jackson County's William Hubbell. *1846 Journal, supra* Article I, note 3, pp. 86–87.

Article VII

State Debts

Section 1.
Credit not to be loaned.

The credit of the State shall not, in any manner, be given or loaned to, or in aid of, any individual, association, or corporation; and the State shall never assume, or become responsible for, the debts or liabilities of any individual, association, or corporation, unless incurred in time of war for the benefit of the State.

Section 1 ensures that, outside the context of war, the state will not become secondarily liable for debts incurred by others.[1] When Jefferson County's James Wilson introduced Section 1 on behalf of the Committee on State Debts at Iowa's 1857 constitutional convention, he said that the provision had been so "universally" acclaimed within the committee that he saw no need to explain its rationale. The portion of Section 1 that appears before the semicolon was copied verbatim from the New York Constitution of 1846[2] and echoes provisions found in a handful of other states' constitutions.[3] The committee's draft stood precisely as one sees above, with the exception of the final clause permitting the state to

---

[1] For a historical discussion of the constitution's limitations on state debts, see Carl H. Erbe, "Constitutional Limitations on Indebtedness in Iowa," 22 *Iowa Journal of History & Politics* 363 (1924).

[2] N.Y. Const. of 1846, art. VII, § 9.

[3] *See*, e.g., N.J. Const. of 1844, art. IV, § VI; Ohio Const. of 1851, art. VIII, § 4.

assume state-benefiting wartime debts.[4] That closing language was added late in the convention's proceedings at the suggestion of Wilson and Johnson County's William Penn Clarke.[5]

The outcome of Section 1 litigation turns primarily on whether the state would be primarily or secondarily liable for the debt in question. If the state's liability would be primary, Section 1 poses no bar. If the state's liability would be secondary, such that the state is acting as a surety, Section 1 forbids the arrangement. The Iowa Supreme Court drew that fundamental distinction in *Grout v. Kendall* (1923), one of the court's first and most important Section 1 rulings. The court explained that this provision does not bar the state from itself borrowing money in order to benefit particular individuals or entities.[6] In *Grout,* for example, Section 1 did not prevent the state from incurring a sizable debt in order to make cash payments to Iowans who had served in the U.S. military during World War I. Rather, no matter how laudable the countervailing public purposes might appear to be in a given instance, Section 1 bars the state from becoming a surety for others' debts—and from thereby becoming secondarily liable if the original debtor fails to pay—and from assuming responsibility for others' non-wartime debts. The *Grout* court explained that other states had agreed to become sureties for railroads and others wishing to undertake ostensibly public-benefiting projects, only to find themselves burdened with millions of dollars of debt when the primary debtors defaulted on their obligations. "[F]or thousands of years," the court wrote, "gratuitous suretyship has been the bottomless pitfall of delusion into which men otherwise thrifty and frugal have persistently fallen." Reiterating *Grout*'s understanding of Section 1 nearly a century later in *Star Equipment, Ltd. v. State* (2014), the court held that the provision did not shield the state from financial liability for work that subcontractors had performed on state-owned highway-side rest areas. The state had been a direct beneficiary of the work financed by the debts that the state's general contractor had failed to pay, and so the state had not acted as a mere surety when it statutorily agreed to be liable for the subcontractors' claims. "[T]his case," the *Star Equipment* court explained, "is a far cry from the *privately* owned canals and railroads whose financial collapse saddled prior state governments with financial burdens."[7]

In *Graham v. Worthington* (1966), the Iowa Supreme Court held that the Iowa Tort Claims Act—legislation that renders the state financially liable for

[4] *1857 Debates, supra* Article I, note 3, vol. 1, pp. 260–61.

[5] *1857 Debates, supra* Article I, note 3, vol. 2, p. 1020.

[6] In an earlier, less elaborated ruling, the court had reached the same conclusion (*Merchants' Union Barb-Wire Co. v. Brown,* 1884).

[7] *Cf. State ex rel. Fletcher v. Executive Council of Iowa* (1929) (allowing the state to agree to pay debts incurred by Iowa counties for road construction, reasoning that, although counties are incorporated entities, they are "a component part of the state").

certain wrongs committed by its employees—does not violate Section 1. Under that statute, the court reasoned, both the state and its tort-committing employee are directly and primarily liable to the person whom the employee has injured, such that the state's liability is not secondary in nature.

The Office of the Attorney General has fielded numerous inquiries concerning Section 1. In 2002, for example, Solicitor General Dennis Johnson concluded that tax credits do not fall within Section 1's reach.[8] In 1983, the office found that Section 1 did not bar the state from agreeing to pay Medicaid recipients' travel costs for obtaining covered medical treatment.[9] In 1967, Attorney General Richard Turner determined that the state could not agree to indemnify the federal government for liabilities it incurred arising from injuries suffered at an Iowa National Guard training facility.[10]

The Iowa Supreme Court has assumed, without firmly deciding, that cities and counties—and not merely the State of Iowa—are bound by Section 1's constraints.[11] In an early opinion, the Office of the Attorney General concluded without elaboration that cities and counties are indeed bound.[12] More recently, noting the court's tentativeness on this point, the office has joined the court in merely assuming for the sake of argument that local governments must comply with Section 1.[13]

Section 2.
Limitation.

The State may contract debts to supply casual deficits or failures in revenues, or to meet expenses not otherwise provided for; but the aggregate amount of such debts, direct and contingent, whether contracted by virtue of one or more acts

[8] Op. Iowa Att'y Gen., 2002 WL 87016 (Jan. 18, 2002) (replying to Governor Tom Vilsack).

[9] Op. Iowa Att'y Gen., 1983 WL 856559 (Feb. 18, 1983) (replying to Joseph Royce); *accord* Op. Iowa Att'y Gen., 1980 WL 26095 (Dec. 5, 1980) (replying to W.C. Wellman) (concluding that the state could pay Iowa Library Commission members' annual dues for membership in the Western Council of State Librarians); Op. Iowa Att'y Gen., 1979 WL 21021 (July 12, 1979) (replying to Edgar Holden) (concluding that counties may pay employees' work-related travel expenses).

[10] Op. Iowa Att'y Gen., 1967 WL 167095 (June 19, 1967) (replying to Joseph May).

[11] *See, e.g., Richards v. City of Muscatine* (1975); *Sampson v. City of Cedar Falls* (1975). In a substantially overlapping provision, the constitution declares in Article VIII, Section 3, that the state cannot become liable for corporations' non-wartime debts. In *Green v. City of Mt. Pleasant* (1964), the court rejected a Section 3 attack on a municipal project. The court did not discuss the possibility that Section 3 might not constrain municipalities. Instead, the court rejected the attack on the merits of the court's internal Section 3 analysis. In a short paragraph in *Brady v. City of Dubuque* (1993)—again without discussing the possibility that the provision might not apply to municipalities—the court similarly rejected a Section 3 attack on a municipal funding plan. For more on related issues, see this volume's commentary on Article VIII, Sections 3 and 4, and on Article XI, Section 3.

[12] Op. Iowa Att'y Gen., 1937 WL 67673 (Feb. 25, 1937) (replying to Ralph Prichard).

[13] Op. Iowa Att'y Gen., 2002 WL 87016 (Jan. 18, 2002) (replying to Governor Tom Vilsack).

of the General Assembly, or at different periods of time, shall never exceed the sum of two hundred and fifty thousand dollars; and the money arising from the creation of such debts, shall be applied to the purpose for which it was obtained, or to repay the debts so contracted, and to no other purpose whatever.

Working in harness with this article's Sections 3 and 4 (which authorize additional debt for specified purposes) and Section 5 (which allows voters to authorize additional debt for specified purposes), Section 2 limits the aggregate amount of contractual debt that the State of Iowa may carry at any given moment in time.[14]

With the exception of the dollar figure it contains, Section 2 was copied verbatim from the Ohio Constitution of 1851[15] (the home state of James Wilson, the chair of the Committee on State Debts at Iowa's 1857 constitutional convention) and echoes provisions found in a small handful of other states' constitutions.[16] When introducing Section 2, the Committee on State Debts recommended that the cap be set at $100,000,[17] the same limit that the state's 1846 constitution had established in a differently worded provision.[18] Wilson said that he personally was "opposed to the principle of State indebtedness *in toto*," but was nevertheless willing to give the legislature flexibility up to the 1846 constitution's $100,000 limit. He pointed out that another 1846 provision that the committee was proposing to retain—the provision that appears today in revised form in Section 5 of this article—would allow Iowa voters to approve additional debt for specific projects. The committee's desire to retain the $100,000 cap sparked a lengthy debate among the delegates. Muscatine County's John Parvin, for example, said that he believed the 1846 limit had "been the salvation of our State" because it had prevented Iowa from getting caught up in "the mania for building railroads," but he said he nevertheless believed it would be appropriate to give legislators more financial freedom. George Gillaspy, a farmer from Wapello County, warned that the General Assembly would rapidly increase the state's debt to any higher limit that the new constitution set. James Traer, a banker from Benton County, said that the state's debt already exceeded $100,000, demonstrating that legislators needed greater flexibility to respond to the needs of the state's growing population. Agreeing that the cap should be at least modestly increased, John Edwards—a lawyer from Lucas County—said that he believed it would be a mistake to rely heavily upon the provision allowing voters to approve additional debt for specified projects; this, he said, would drag Iowa "back to the barbarous

[14] For a skeptical account of constitutionally imposed debt limits in Iowa and elsewhere, see Robert H. Bowmar, "The Anachronism Called Debt Limitation," 52 *Iowa Law Review* 863 (1967).

[15] Ohio Const. of 1851, art. VIII, § 1.

[16] *See*, e.g., N.Y. Const. of 1846, art. VII, § 10.

[17] *1857 Debates*, *supra* Article I, note 3, vol. 1, pp. 260–61.

[18] Iowa Const. of 1846, art. VIII, § 1. For the delegates' debate about this and other matters concerning state debts at the 1846 convention, see *1846 Journal*, *supra* Article I, note 3, pp. 79–82.

days of ancient Greece, when the whole people met for the purpose of making laws for their government." After the convention agreed by an 18-to-9 vote to extend the debt cap beyond $100,000, various delegates proposed new limits ranging as high as $500,000. Taking the proposals in order from highest to lowest, the favorable vote of a majority was not secured until they reached the figure of $250,000, the same limit that Section 2 continues to impose today.[19]

The Iowa Supreme Court has explained that a "debt" arises within the meaning of Article VII "only where the state itself is under a legally enforceable obligation" (*Train Unlimited Corp. v. Iowa Railway Finance Authority*, 1985; *John R. Grubb, Inc. v. Iowa Housing Finance Authority*, 1977).[20] Even when the state is indeed legally on the hook, however, its freedom to finance large operations is far greater than one might initially infer from a casual reading of Section 2. In *Rowley v. Clarke* (1913) and *Stanley v. Fitzgerald* (1998), the court held that the state does not incur a "debt" within the meaning of Section 2 when it issues notes that will be fully covered by anticipated tax revenues collected for the same fiscal period. Additional flexibility flows from the court's determination that, when the state finances a new facility using revenue bonds—bonds that will be retired using revenues generated by the newly constructed facility or by designated other revenue-producing state-owned facilities or operations—the state is not incurring a "debt" within the meaning of Section 2 (*State Board of Regents v. Lindquist*, 1971; *Brack v. Mossman*, 1969; *Iowa Hotel Association v. State Board of Regents*, 1962).[21] In *Lindquist*, for example, the court approved the use of such bonds to make millions of dollars' worth of improvements to the University of Iowa's revenue-producing hospital. The court has explained more generally that "the financing of public purpose projects by special funding [such as by using tuition and fees paid by students at Iowa's public universities to pay for improvements on those campuses], specifically exempting any tax obligation, does not create a state debt" (*Farrell v. State Board of Regents*, 1970).[22] For a rare example of legislation establishing a financial scheme that ran afoul of Section 2, see *Hubbell v. Herring* (1933).

Focusing on Section 2's use of the terms "contract" and "contracted," the Iowa Supreme Court held in *Graham v. Worthington* (1966) that Section 2 had no bearing on amounts owed by the state under the Iowa Tort Claims Act for injuries caused by the state's employees. The court explained that "judgments

[19] *1857 Debates, supra* Article I, note 3, vol. 1, pp. 261–73.

[20] Principles similar to those described here apply when determining whether a city or county has exceeded its constitutionally imposed debt limit. For those principles, see this volume's commentary on Article XI, § 3.

[21] Some of these are called "self-liquidating projects." *See, e.g., Brack v. Mossman* (1969).

[22] For a summation of these principles, see Op. Iowa Att'y Gen., 1991 WL 495691 (Dec. 23, 1991) (replying to Richard Johnson).

or awards entered upon tort claims are not *debts contracted* as the term is here employed."

In 1992, the Office of the Attorney General stated that the validity of a debt is to be "determined at the time the contract is made."[23] In 1976, Attorney General Richard Turner determined that the state would not be incurring a debt within the meaning of Section 2 if it received advances from the federal government for the state's unemployment insurance trust fund; the state, Turner explained, was not obliged under federal law to repay the amounts received.[24] Returning to that same topic in 1982, Attorney General Thomas Miller embraced Turner's 1976 reasoning and further concluded that interest owed to the federal government for such advances would not constitute a Section 2 "debt" because the interest payments would not be used to cover "casual deficits or failures in revenues, or to meet expenses not otherwise provided for."[25] In 1981, pointing to Section 2's use of the phrase "money arising" when discussing the debts that fall within its ambit, the Office of the Attorney General determined that interest owed on unpaid bills for goods and services does not create a "debt" because the state does not raise money when it merely fails to pay its bills in a timely fashion.[26]

Section 3.
Losses to school funds.

All losses to the permanent, School, or University fund of this State, which shall have been occasioned by the defalcation, mismanagement or fraud of the agents or officers controlling and managing the same, shall be audited by the proper authorities of the State. The amount so audited shall be a permanent funded debt against the State, in favor of the respective fund, sustaining the loss, upon which not less than six per cent. annual interest shall be paid. The amount of liability so created shall not be counted as a part of the indebtedness authorized by the second section of this article.

Working in tandem with Article IX (which should be consulted by anyone interested in issues concerning the state's educational funds), Section 3 is aimed at ensuring that Iowa's schoolchildren and university students will not suffer as a result of financial losses caused by the bad conduct of state officials or their agents. Jonathan Hall, a lawyer from Des Moines County, proposed the provision at the 1857 constitutional convention in nearly the same form that one sees above. Hall argued that educating children was "the most sacred of all trusts that can be confided to any people" and that the quality of children's schooling should not be placed at risk by the carelessness or wrongdoing of those responsible for managing the state's educational accounts. He reasoned that the state was unlikely

[23] Op. Iowa Att'y Gen., 1992 WL 470346 (Mar. 16, 1992) (replying to Richard Johnson).

[24] Op. Iowa Att'y Gen., 1976 WL 375883 (Mar. 3, 1976) (replying to Calvin Hultman).

[25] Op. Iowa Att'y Gen., 1982 WL 42725 (Mar. 2, 1982) (replying to Governor Robert Ray).

[26] Op. Iowa Att'y Gen., 1981 WL 315355 (July 7, 1981) (replying to Ned Chiodo).

to find itself having to restore lost funds pursuant to this provision, because the provision's very appearance in the Iowa Constitution would incentivize taxpayers "to see that this property is placed in safe hands."[27] Alamakee County's John Clark resisted Hall's suggestion, arguing that the protection of state funds should be left wholly to devices put in place by the General Assembly, but his arguments were unavailing. After a brief discussion of the amount of interest that the state ought to pay when Section 3 has been triggered, the delegates approved Hall's proposal by an unrecorded margin.[28]

Both to clarify Section 3's meaning and to warn those interpreting any portion of the Iowa Constitution against relying too hastily upon the location of punctuation marks,[29] the first comma to appear in Section 3 merits a brief discussion. On an isolated reading, the comma after the first appearance of the word "permanent" could be understood to suggest that Section 3 deals with losses to three different funds, the first of which might not have anything to do with education: the permanent fund, the school fund, and the university fund.[30] As just noted, however, Jonathan Hall made it clear when proposing the provision that his goal was to protect funds designated for education. When the provision was brought back to the delegates for further discussion the following day, Hall's opening language was initially reported in the *1857 Debates* in a manner wholly consistent with Hall's purposes: "[A]ll losses to the permanent school, or university funds of this State. . . ."[31] By omitting commas altogether, the convention's official journal initially reported the new provision in a manner that underscored the same purpose: "All losses to the permanent school or university fund of this State. . . ."[32] When later reporting the text that the delegates approved, however, the *1857 Debates* published the text's opening language in conflicting ways, one comma-free and one containing all of the commas one sees in Section 3 as it stands above.[33] The latter version was used when the constitution was published in its entirety in the closing pages of the convention's official journal.[34] Yet when the Iowa Supreme Court quoted the provision for the

[27] *1857 Debates, supra* Article I, note 3, vol. 1, pp. 272–73. Hall contended that the management of the state's school fund had already proved to be "intolerably defective; that it had been carelessly and indifferently managed, and that great losses had already accrued to the fund." *Id.* at p. 279.

[28] *1857 Debates, supra* Article I, note 3, vol. 1, pp. 277–79.

[29] For an example of a punctuation-centered debate, see the commentary on Article I, Section 8.

[30] When Hall first proposed Section 3, his recommended text was recorded in the *1857 Debates* as beginning this way: "[A]ll losses to the government, school, or university funds of this State. . . ." *1857 Debates, supra* Article I, note 3, vol. 1, p. 272.

[31] *1857 Debates, supra* Article I, note 3, vol. 1, p. 277.

[32] *1857 Journal, supra* Article I, note 3, p. 130.

[33] *1857 Debates, supra* Article I, note 3, vol. 2, pp. 1021 (with commas), 1084 (without commas). The handwritten text signed by the delegates contains all of the commas one sees above.

[34] *1857 Journal, supra* Article I, note 3, Appendix, p. 16.

first time nineteen years later, the commas were entirely absent (*Weary v. State University*, 1876). Despite this punctuational confusion, Section 3 has long been understood to concern only the state's educational funds, just as Hall intended and as the section's subsequently assigned title indicates.

The Iowa Supreme Court has invoked Section 3 in only a small handful of instances, and in none of those has the court significantly elaborated upon the provision's meaning. In *Monona County v. Waples* (1935), for example, the court cited Section 3 on its way to determining that a mortgage given to Monona County in exchange for a loan from the state's permanent school fund was superior to a competing mortgage. In *Johnson County v. O'Connor* (1942), the court similarly relied upon Section 3 and other authorities when determining that a county's effort to foreclose on an unrecorded school-fund mortgage was not statutorily time-barred. In *Weary v. State University* (1876), the court cited Section 3 in support of its conclusion that the University of Iowa was a state entity and thus was immune from suit.

Like the Iowa Supreme Court, the Office of the Attorney General has been called upon to speak to Section 3's significance on only a few occasions. In 1939, for example, Attorney General John Rankin advised a state senator that proposed legislation would violate Section 3 because it would permit county officials to disregard their duty to preserve the state's permanent school fund.[35] Attorney General John Mitchell had provided similar advice two years earlier.[36]

Section 4.
War debts.

> In addition to the above limited power to contract debts, the State may contract debts to repel invasion, suppress insurrection, or defend the State in war; but the money arising from the debts so contracted shall be applied to the purpose for which it was raised, or to repay such debts, and to no other purpose whatever.

Section 4 authorizes the state to incur contractual debts beyond the $250,000 cap imposed by Section 2 of this article, if those additional debts are incurred to enable the state to deal with invasion, insurrection, or war. Iowa's first constitution, ratified in 1846, similarly authorized the state to contract debts for war and warlike purposes without regard to the otherwise constitutionally imposed limit.[37] At the 1857 constitutional convention, the Committee on State Debts recommended framing the provision in a manner substantively identical to what

---

[35] Op. Iowa Att'y Gen., 1939 WL 77084 (Mar. 16, 1939) (replying to Hugh Lundy).

[36] Op. Iowa Att'y Gen., 1937 WL 67691 (Mar. 4, 1937) (replying to L.H. Doran).

[37] Iowa Const. of 1846, art. VIII, § 1.

one sees above.[38] The committee's proposal was not controversial among the delegates.[39]

Section 4 has not been the focus of any opinions issued by the Office of the Attorney General, and has been noted by the Iowa Supreme Court only infrequently. In *Grout v. Kendall* (1923), the court observed in passing that for debts incurred pursuant to this provision, "there is no maximum in *amount;* but the *object* for which an unlimited indebtedness may be created is limited and specific." In *Knorr v. Beardsley* (1949), the court similarly stated that the $250,000 cap imposed by Section 2 of this article plainly does not apply to debts incurred for the costly purposes identified here in Section 4.

Section 5.
Contracting debt—submission to the people.

Except the debts herein before specified in this article, no debt shall be hereafter contracted by, or on behalf of this State, unless such debt shall be authorized by some law for some single work or object, to be distinctly specified therein; and such law shall impose and provide for the collection of a direct annual tax, sufficient to pay the interest on such debt, as it falls due, and also to pay and discharge the principal of such debt, within twenty years from the time of the contracting thereof; but no such law shall take effect until at a general election it shall have been submitted to the people, and have received a majority of all the votes cast for and against it at such election; and all money raised by authority of such law, shall be applied only to the specific object therein stated, or to the payment of the debt created thereby; and such law shall be published in at least one newspaper in each County, if one is published therein, throughout the State, for three months preceding the election at which it is submitted to the people.

Section 5 allows the General Assembly to seek Iowa voters' approval for incurring project-specific debt beyond the $250,000 aggregate cap imposed by Section 2 of this article and for imposing a new tax sufficient to retire the added debt in no more than twenty years. The provision differs from its counterpart in the state's 1846 constitution in two notable ways: it requires a debt-incurring law to "provide for the collection of a direct annual tax" (as opposed to the 1846 requirement that the law "provide ways and means, exclusive of loans," for paying the debt), and it requires that notice of the ballot proposal be published in each county (as opposed to the 1846 requirement that it be published in each judicial district).[40] The Committee on State Debts had already adopted both of those changes when it first presented its draft of Article VII on the convention

[38] *1857 Journal, supra* Article I, note 3, p. 54.

[39] *1857 Debates, supra* Article I, note 3, vol. 1, pp. 273, 279; *id.* at vol. 2, p. 1021.

[40] *Cf.* Iowa Const. of 1846, art. VIII, § 1.

floor.[41] The text proposed by the committee was not controversial among the delegates.[42]

Section 5 describes the circumstances in which the General Assembly may add to Iowa's contractual "debt." That term is not as broadly encompassing as one might initially suppose. For an explanation of the kinds of financial obligations that do not constitute debts within the meaning of this and related constitutional provisions, see the commentary on Section 2 of this article.

In some of the Section 5 cases that it has adjudicated, the Iowa Supreme Court has easily found that the provision's requirements were met. For example, in *Grout v. Kendall* (1923)—a case concerning the Soldiers' Bonus Act, under which the state was to pay additional compensation to Iowans who had served in the U.S. military during World War I—the court recited Section 5's various requirements and quickly concluded that the statute met them. In *Knorr v. Beardsley* (1949), the court found no fatal shortcoming when notice of the pending ballot measure had been published at least once during three different months in 98 of Iowa's 99 counties but had been published during only two months in the remaining county. In *Faber v. Loveless* (1958)—a case in which the court rejected attacks on legislation aimed at providing cash bonuses to Iowans who had served in the Korean War—the court explained that a tax is a "direct" tax within the meaning of Section 5 if it is a property or ad valorem tax—that is, if it is a tax "imposed directly on property according to its value," regardless of whether the property is tangible or intangible.

But not all cases have afforded state officials such smooth sailing. In *Patterson v. Iowa Bonus Board* (1955), for example—a case concerning an amendment to the same veterans-benefiting legislation at issue in *Grout*—the court held that Section 5 barred the state from repurposing revenues raised by a tax that voters had specifically approved for providing World War I veterans with cash bonuses. (The state had wished to use some of those revenues to build a nursing home for veterans.) In *State ex rel. Fletcher v. Executive Council of Iowa* (1929), the General Assembly had secured Iowans' approval for incurring $100 million in new debt for road construction. Rather than sell all of the necessary bonds at the outset of the project, the legislature's plan was to sell a series of bonds over a period of years, with each new series payable within twenty years. The court found this arrangement unconstitutional, reasoning that Iowa's framers had wished to ensure that all voter-approved debt is retired by the same generation that authorized it, and that the General Assembly's scheme in this case allowed the debt to be extended well beyond one twenty-year generation. The court further held that, by relying upon gasoline taxes and license fees to pay an unspecified portion of the debt, the General Assembly had failed to impose—and voters had

[41] *1857 Journal, supra* Article I, note 3, pp. 54–55.

[42] *1857 Debates, supra* Article I, note 3, vol. 1, pp. 273, 279; *id.* at vol. 2, p. 1021.

failed to approve—a "direct annual tax" (as Section 5's text requires) sufficient to cover the bonds' principal and interest. The General Assembly also ran into trouble in *Hubbell v. Herring* (1933), in which the court held that legislation was poised to create a multi-million-dollar debt without Iowa voters' prior approval.

Section 6.
Legislature may repeal.

The Legislature may, at any time, after the approval of such law by the people, if no debt shall have been contracted in pursuance thereof, repeal the same; and may, at any time, forbid the contracting of any further debt, or liability, under such law; but the tax imposed by such law, in proportion to the debt or liability, which may have been contracted in pursuance thereof, shall remain in force and be irrepealable, and be annually collected, until the principal and interest are fully paid.

For those instances in which Iowa voters have authorized the state to contract additional debt pursuant to Section 5, Section 6 allows the General Assembly to change course and opt against entering some or all of the authorized debt contracts. Setting aside minor differences in phrasing, the provision that the Committee on State Debts proposed at the 1857 constitutional convention was almost substantively identical to what one sees above.[43]

The Iowa Supreme Court applied and briefly underscored Section 6's plain meaning in *Knorr v. Beardsley* (1949). The Office of the Attorney General's only noteworthy opinion on Section 6 dates back to 1939, when Attorney General John Rankin explained to the state comptroller that this provision gives the General Assembly significant freedom to scale back its debt plans.[44]

Section 7.
Tax imposed distinctly stated.

Every law which imposes, continues, or revives a tax, shall distinctly state the tax, and the object to which it is to be applied; and it shall not be sufficient to refer to any other law to fix such tax or object.

Section 7 imposes a pair of requirements upon the General Assembly when it enacts legislation that levies, maintains, or brings back a tax. Section 7 did not have a precursor in the state's 1846 constitution. At the 1857 constitutional convention, the Committee on State Debts proposed adding Section 7 in precisely

---

[43] *1857 Journal, supra* Article I, note 3, p. 55. The convention made one uncontroversial substantive change to the committee's draft of Section 6's closing language, in order to give the General Assembly greater freedom to pay down debt by the means of its choosing. *1857 Debates, supra* Article I, note 3, vol. 1, p. 280.

[44] Op. Iowa Att'y Gen., 1939 WL 77270 (Aug. 4, 1939) (replying to C. Fred Porter).

the form one sees here.[45] The committee copied the provision's language verbatim from the New York Constitution of 1846[46] and echoed provisions found in a small handful of other states' constitutions.[47] Section 7's text was not controversial among the delegates.[48]

When Section 7 applies to a given statute, it requires that the law "distinctly state" two related things: "the tax" and "the object to which [the tax] is to be applied." Legislation satisfies the first requirement if "the amount, rate or factors from which the rate is computed are included in the act" (*Motor Club of Iowa v. Department of Transportation*, 1978).[49] A law satisfies Section 7's second requirement if it identifies the governmental purpose to which the revenues will be put (*Kartridg Pak Co. v. Department of Revenue*, 1985). One of the provision's purposes is to ensure that, when it imposes a tax, the General Assembly has some greater objective in mind than satisfying a bare desire to obtain revenue (*C.C. Taft Co. v. Alber*, 1919). Although Section 7 bars the General Assembly from simply referring to other laws to establish a tax or its purpose, it does not bar the legislature from referring to federal law or other sources for the definitions of such operative terms as "taxable income" (*City National Bank v. Iowa State Tax Commission*, 1960) and "moneyed capital" (*Ballard-Hassett Co. v. Local Board of Review*, 1933).

Section 7 applies only to laws that impose taxes; it does not apply to laws that delegate a taxing power to other governmental entities (*Cook v. Hannah*, 1941; *Youngerman v. Murphy*, 1898). Even when a law does itself demand a payment of some sort to the government, Section 7 is not necessarily in play; there are a great many governmental exactions that do not fall within Section 7's reach. In some of its earliest Section 7 cases, for example, the Iowa Supreme Court held that the state was not levying a Section 7 tax when it demanded that a father reimburse the government for hospital services provided to his minor son (*Guthrie County v. Conrad*, 1907) or when it imposed a fee on the owners of real estate being used for certain kinds of illegal activity (*C.C. Taft Co. v. Alber*, 1919). The court held somewhat more recently that the state was not imposing a Section 7 tax when it sold bonds that would be retired using revenue generated by the University of Iowa's hospital (*State Board of Regents v. Lindquist*, 1971).

It is possible that Section 7 applies only to taxes levied on property. Citing an "unbroken line of authority" in jurisdictions across the country, the court so held in *Solberg v. Davenport* (1930). The exaction at issue in *Solberg* was a

[45] *1857 Journal, supra* Article I, note 3, p. 55.

[46] N.Y. Const. of 1846, art. VII, § 13.

[47] *See, e.g.*, Ohio Const. of 1851, art. XII, § 5.

[48] *See, e.g.*, *1857 Debates, supra* Article I, note 3, vol. 1, pp. 273, 280.

[49] *Cf. In re Estate of Kite* (1922) ("Under this constitutional provision, a tax is not to be implied against a class of property or a class of persons not within the provisions of the statute imposing the tax.").

fee imposed on trucks carrying heavy loads on public roads; the court held that Section 7 did not apply, reasoning in part that "it is no more than right and just" that those who place the heaviest burdens on the state's roads be required to pay an extra share to help cover the cost of road repairs. Citing *Solberg* in 1968's *Lee Enterprises, Inc. v. Iowa State Tax Commission*—a case concerning a sales tax on advertising—the court similarly brushed aside a Section 7 attack, observing that "[s]ales tax statutes by their nature are excise taxes and, as such, are not subject to the constitutional objections applicable to property taxes." It thus is not surprising to learn that, in 1985's *Kartridg Pak Co. v. Department of Revenue*, state officials argued that Section 7 does not apply to excise taxes imposed on raw materials used to make leased machinery. Rather than agree with that proposition under the authority of *Solberg* and *Lee Enterprises*, however, the court merely assumed for the sake of argument that Section 7 applied and concluded that the provision's requirements had been met. The court's decision not to unequivocally embrace *Solberg* and *Lee Enterprises* sends the signal that the court might be persuaded to further distance itself from those rulings in the future.

The Office of the Attorney General has issued a handful of opinions concerning Section 7. In 1962, for example, Attorney General Evan Hultman advised a state senator that legislation would violate this provision if it declared that the amount of state income tax that one owes is simply a percentage of one's federal income taxes.[50] Attorney General Richard Turner withdrew that opinion in 1969, however, pointing out that "[a]n income tax is an excise tax, not a property tax," and that the Iowa Supreme Court appeared inclined to hold that Section 7 applies only to the latter.[51] (Turner indicated that he was baffled by the court's decision to limit Section 7 in this way.) While acknowledging that *Kartridg Pak* precludes one from making caveat-free proclamations on the matter, the Office of the Attorney General again cited *Solberg* in 1991 for the proposition that Section 7 applies only to property taxes.[52]

Section 8.
Motor vehicle fees and fuel taxes.

All motor vehicle registration fees and all licenses and excise taxes on motor vehicle fuel, except cost of administration, shall be used exclusively for the construction, maintenance and supervision of the public highways exclusively within the state or for the payment of bonds issued or to be issued for the construction of such public highways and the payment of interest on such bonds.

---

[50] Op. Iowa Att'y Gen., 1962 WL 122962 (Oct. 18, 1962) (replying to C. Edwin Gilmour).

[51] Op. Iowa Att'y Gen., 1969 WL 181577 (Apr. 30, 1969) (replying to Chester Hougen, Elmer Den Herder, Michael Kennedy, and George Milligan).

[52] Op. Iowa Att'y Gen., 1991 WL 495646 (Mar. 27, 1991) (replying to Dennis Black, Leonard Boswell, and Dale Cochran).

Added to the constitution by Iowa voters in 1942, Section 8—sometimes called "the anti-diversion amendment"—ensures that revenues raised from the specified vehicle- and fuel-related sources will be devoted solely to building, maintaining, and supervising Iowa's roads. Examining Section 8's use of the term "construction," the Iowa Supreme Court held in *Edge v. Brice* (1962) that the specified revenues could be used to pay for "all things necessary to the completed accomplishment of a highway for all uses properly a part thereof," including the cost of relocating utility services. Zeroing in on the provision's reference to the "cost of administration," the court held in *Plank v. Grimes* (1947) that funds derived from the specified sources could be used to reward those who tip off the state about individuals who are evading their vehicle- or fuel-related taxes. Focusing on Section 8's use of the phrase "exclusively within the state," the court held in *Frost v. State* (1969) that vehicle- and fuel-derived funds could not be used to help build Illinois's portion of an interstate bridge connecting the two states.

The Office of the Attorney General has determined that funds from the sources described in Section 8 may be used for a broad range of purposes, including for (among other things) building bikeways,[53] building highway-side rest areas,[54] building barriers aimed at preventing high winds and soil erosion along roadways,[55] paying the salaries of the Iowa Highway Safety Patrol's employees,[56] building a garage for road-construction equipment,[57] building municipal traffic signals and painting municipal roadways,[58] building a daycare facility for the children of Department of Transportation employees,[59] and paying for tort judgments against the Department of Transportation.[60] Although Section 8's expenditure parameters are indeed broad, they are not unlimited. The office has said, for example, that these funds cannot be given or loaned to governmental accounts that serve unrelated purposes,[61] cannot be used by counties to pay

[53] Op. Iowa Att'y Gen., 1988 WL 247775 (Apr. 4, 1988) (replying to Ralph Rosenberg). Such rulings stand in some tension with the office's earlier determination that these funds cannot be used to build and maintain a vehicle ferry service. *See* Op. Iowa Att'y Gen., 1977 WL 18988 (Oct. 12, 1977) (replying to Robert Rigler).

[54] Op. Iowa Att'y Gen., 1968 WL 172451 (Jan. 16, 1968) (replying to Governor Harold Hughes).

[55] Op. Iowa Att'y Gen., 1979 WL 20936 (Apr. 26, 1979) (replying to John Scott).

[56] Op. Iowa Att'y Gen., 1971 WL 240746 (May 3, 1971) (replying to John Walsh).

[57] Op. Iowa Att'y Gen., 1969 WL 181593 (June 2, 1969) (replying to Ray Fenton).

[58] Op. Iowa Att'y Gen., 1976 WL 376019 (Sept. 7, 1976) (replying to William Monroe, Jr.).

[59] Op. Iowa Att'y Gen., 1985 WL 549226 (Oct. 29, 1985) (replying to Richard Welden).

[60] Op. Iowa Att'y Gen., 1984 WL 60027 (Sept. 26, 1984) (replying to Norman Rodgers).

[61] Op. Iowa Att'y Gen., 1995 WL 583921 (Sept. 12, 1995) (replying to Harold Van Maanen); Op. Iowa Att'y Gen., 1991 WL 495646 (Mar. 27, 1991) (replying to Dennis Black, Leonard Boswell, and Dale Cochran).

damages for adverse breach-of-contract and tort judgments,[62] and cannot be used to build screens shielding junkyard sites along Iowa's roadways.[63]

The office has distinguished between fees paid for registering a vehicle and fees paid to obtain a vehicular certificate of title, concluding that Section 8 does not reach the latter.[64] No matter what their origin, once funds that initially stand beyond Section 8's reach have been commingled with funds that *are* within Section 8's ambit, they may be used only for the limited purposes that Section 8 identifies.[65]

Section 9.
Fish and wildlife protection funds.

All revenue derived from state license fees for hunting, fishing, and trapping, and all state funds appropriated for, and federal or private funds received by the state for, the regulation or advancement of hunting, fishing, or trapping, or the protection, propagation, restoration, management, or harvest of fish or wildlife, shall be used exclusively for the performance and administration of activities related to those purposes.

Approved by Iowa voters in 1996 in response to some lawmakers' efforts to use these revenues for general budget-balancing purposes,[66] Section 9 ensures that certain funds associated with the state's wildlife and with hunting, fishing, and trapping will be used solely for corresponding state purposes. The provision has not yet been the focus of appellate rulings or of opinions issued by the Office of the Attorney General.

Section 10.
Natural resources.

A natural resources and outdoor recreation trust fund is created within the treasury for the purposes of protecting and enhancing water quality and natural areas in this State including parks, trails, and fish and wildlife habitat, and conserving agricultural soils in this State. Moneys in the fund shall be exclusively appropriated by law for these purposes.

The general assembly shall provide by law for the implementation of this section, including by providing for the administration of the fund and at least annual audits of the fund.

---

[62] Op. Iowa Att'y Gen., 1980 WL 26084 (Nov. 3, 1980) (replying to Kevin McGuire).

[63] Op. Iowa Att'y Gen., 1972 WL 262275 (Feb. 16, 1972) (replying to Edgar Holden).

[64] Op. Iowa Att'y Gen., 1971 WL 240723 (Apr. 13, 1971) (replying to Derby Thompson).

[65] Op. Iowa Att'y Gen., 1988 WL 247782 (May 12, 1988) (replying to William Harbor).

[66] *See* Larry Stone, "Fish, Wildlife Money Up for Vote Nov. 5," *Des Moines Register*, Oct. 27, 1996, at 12D.

Except as otherwise provided in this section, the fund shall be annually credited with an amount equal to the amount generated by a sales tax rate of three-eighths of one percent as may be imposed upon the retail sales price of tangible personal property and the furnishing of enumerated services sold in this State.

No revenues shall be credited to the fund until the tax rate for the sales tax imposed upon the retail sales price of tangible personal property and the furnishing of enumerated services sold in this State in effect on the effective date of this section is increased. After such an increased tax rate becomes effective, an amount equal to the amount generated by the increase in the tax rate shall be annually credited to the fund, not to exceed an amount equal to the amount generated by a tax rate of three-eighths of one percent imposed upon the retail sales price of tangible personal property and the furnishing of enumerated services sold in this State.

Approved by Iowa voters in 2010 (thereby making it the most recent amendment to the Iowa Constitution), Section 10 establishes a framework for funding environmental improvements within the state. At the present time, the most important of the provision's four paragraphs is the fourth, which states that the initiative will not be funded until the General Assembly approves an increase in the state's sales tax. At the time of this writing, the trust fund has yet to receive its first dollar.[67] Not surprisingly (given its youth and the General Assembly's refusal to fund the initiative), the provision has not yet been the focus of opinions issued by Iowa's appellate courts or by the Office of the Attorney General.

[67] The Iowa Department of Natural Resources maintains a webpage dedicated to issues relating to the trust fund: http://www.iowadnr.gov/About-DNR/Grants-Other-Funding/Natural-Resources-Rec-Trust. That website collects all of the DNR's annual reports on the fund, from 2011 to the present year. In its most recent report (dated January 15, 2017), the DNR states that, "since its inception and enactment occurring on January 1, 2011, the Natural Resources and Outdoor Recreation Trust Fund has not acquired any receipts."

Article VIII

Corporations

Section 1.
How created.

No corporation shall be created by special laws; but the General Assembly shall provide, by general laws, for the organization of all corporations hereafter to be created, except as hereinafter provided.

By requiring the General Assembly to establish "general laws" governing the organization of corporations, Section 1 constrains (but, as shall be explained, does not fully eliminate) the legislature's ability to decide on a case-by-case basis whether to charter proposed corporations. Iowa's 1846 constitution directed the General Assembly to "provide . . . for the organization" of non-banking corporations "by general laws," and barred it from creating corporations "by special laws" unless those entities were being created "for political or municipal purposes."[1] Pursuant to that latter exception, the legislature chartered numerous cities by special legislation, often giving those municipalities widely varying powers—a practice that drew the public's condemnation (*Eckerson v. City of Des Moines*, 1908).[2] By removing the exception for political and municipal corporations, the delegates to the 1857 constitutional convention broadened the ban on

[1] Iowa Const. of 1846, art. IX, § 2.

[2] For a survey of those special charters' features, see George F. Robeson, "Special Municipal Charters in Iowa, 1836–1858," 18 *Iowa Journal of History & Politics* 163 (1920).

creating corporations by special laws.[3] Section 1 was not controversial among the delegates.[4] Today, the General Assembly extensively regulates the organization of numerous different kinds of corporations.[5]

Section 1 has seldom been the focus of appellate litigation. In an early ruling on the provision, the court held in *Warren v. Henly* (1870) that city charters created by special legislation under the 1846 constitution remained valid. Although not by constitutional dictate, those charters were nevertheless steadily abandoned. Thirty-three years after Section 1's adoption, the Iowa Supreme Court was able to write that "no municipal corporation has been organized under a special charter by any act of the legislature since the adoption of the constitution, and many of those which were organized before that have since abandoned their special charters, and incorporated under the general law; so that there are now but three or four cities in the state acting under special charters" (*Ford v. Town of North Des Moines*, 1890). Section 1 does not apply to the creation of state governmental entities, such as the state's board of medical examiners (*Iowa Eclectic Medical College Association v. Schrader*, 1893).[6]

In 1985, in its most important opinion on Section 1 to date, the Office of the Attorney General sought to clarify the meaning of the phrase "special laws."[7] The office rejected the notion that a corporation is necessarily created by a special law if it is directly created by a legislative enactment, rather than created pursuant to a general incorporation statute. Based upon its assessment of the history of such provisions in state constitutions, the office determined that a law is not "special" within the meaning of Section 1 if (1) it is "intended to serve a particular need, in order to meet some special evil or to promote some public interest," and (2) it does not extend "special benefits not generally available to others similarly situated." Based upon those factors, the office gave its blessing to legislation creating the Iowa Venture Capital Fund, the Iowa Product Development Corporation, and the Iowa Development Commission Foundation. Citing "[t]he public purposes of the statute as well as its uniform application," the office concluded in

---

[3] *See also* Iowa Const. art. III, § 30 (stating that the General Assembly cannot enact "special laws . . . [f]or the incorporation of cities and towns").

[4] *1857 Debates, supra* Article I, note 3, vol. 1, pp. 96, 289, 414–15; *id.* at vol. 2, pp. 648, 773.

[5] *See, e.g.*, Iowa Code chapters 490 (business corporations), 491 (corporations for pecuniary profit), 496B (economic development corporations), 496C (professional corporations), and 504 (nonprofit corporations). For a history of corporate regulation in Iowa from 1846 until the end of the nineteenth century, see Frank Edward Horack, "Some Phases of Corporate Regulation in the State of Iowa," 2 *Iowa Journal of History & Politics* 485 (1904).

[6] *Accord* Op. Iowa Att'y Gen., 1977 WL 19018 (Dec. 22, 1977) (replying to Kenneth Miller) (approving of legislation creating the state's corn promotion board); Op. Iowa Att'y Gen., 1900 WL 165747 (Mar. 14, 1900) (replying to W.F. Harriman) (approving of legislation creating the state's department of agriculture).

[7] Op. Iowa Att'y Gen., 1985 WL 68970 (May 7, 1985) (replying to Richard Johnson).

1988 that legislation creating the Iowa Export Trading Company was not a forbidden special law.[8]

Section 2.
Taxation of corporations.

The property of all corporations for pecuniary profit, shall be subject to taxation, the same as that of individuals.

By making the property of individuals and for-profit corporations equally subject to taxation, Section 2 complements two other provisions of the Iowa Constitution: Article I, Section 6 (which states that "[a]ll laws of a general nature shall have a uniform operation; the general assembly shall not grant to any citizen, or class of citizens, privileges or immunities which, upon the same terms shall not equally belong to all citizens") and Article I, Section 30 (which states that "in all . . . cases where a general law can be made applicable, all laws shall be general, and of uniform operation throughout the state"). In its initial draft of this provision, the 1857 convention's Committee on Incorporations proposed that the property of *all* corporations be "liable to taxation in the same manner as natural persons."[9] At the suggestion of Des Moines County's Jonathan Hall, the delegates readily agreed to focus more narrowly on the property of corporations formed "for pecuniary profit."[10]

The Iowa Supreme Court's cases on Section 2 are now quite old. In *City of Davenport v. Chicago, Rock Island & Pacific Railroad Co.* (1874), the court explained that Section 2 bars the General Assembly from taxing a given kind of property held by individuals and for-profit corporations at differing rates or for differing purposes. If property of a given kind is taxed at *x* rate for *y* purpose when held by a corporation, then, as a general matter, it must be taxed at *x* rate for *y* purpose when held by a natural person, and vice versa.[11] Based upon those principles, the *City of Davenport* court struck down a statute that released railroad corporations—but not natural persons—from their property-tax obligations if they paid state income taxes. The court struck down a similarly designed law in *Hawkeye Insurance Co. v. French* (1899). Section 2 requires

---

[8] Op. Iowa Att'y Gen., 1988 WL 486116 (Feb. 12, 1988) (replying to Allan Thoms).

[9] *1857 Debates, supra* Article I, note 3, vol. 1, p. 96.

[10] *1857 Debates, supra* Article I, note 3, vol. 1, pp. 289, 415. For the provision's remaining drafting history, see *id.* at p. 430; *id.* at vol. 2, p. 648.

[11] *Accord City of Dubuque v. Chicago, Dubuque & Minnesota Railroad Co.* (1877) (stating that "all property, whether owned by corporations or individuals, shall be equally burdened with taxation, [though] the legislature may adopt different methods of ascertaining values, adapted to the various peculiarities of the property"); *United States Express Co. v. Ellyson* (1869) (stating that individuals' and for-profit corporations' property must be subject to taxation "in the same manner, and to the same extent").

that corporations and individuals be treated "the same," not only with respect to the rates and purposes of property taxation but also with respect to whether property will be taxed at its actual or some lesser value (*Pierce v. Green*, 1940). Section 2 does not apply if the tax at issue is not being levied on property (*Vilas v. Iowa State Board of Assessment & Review*, 1937; *Iowa Mutual Tornado Insurance Association v. Gilbertson*, 1906).

The Office of the Attorney General's dealings with Section 2 are of a similar vintage. Citing *Central Iowa Railway Co. v. Board of Supervisors* (1885), for example, Attorney General Charles Mullan issued an opinion in 1902, stating that the General Assembly does not violate Section 2 when it places property into different categories (such as railway property and non-railway property, in this instance) and taxes those categories at different times.[12]

Section 3.
State not to be a stockholder.

The State shall not become a stockholder in any corporation, nor shall it assume or pay the debt or liability of any corporation, unless incurred in time of war for the benefit of the State.

Section 3 bars the state from holding shares in any corporation and—outside the context of war—bars the state from taking responsibility for corporations' debts and liabilities. The ban on state ownership of corporate shares traces its roots to Iowa's 1846 constitution,[13] and (in the judgment of the Office of the Attorney General) reflects a desire to avoid "excessive government entanglement in the activities of private corporations," the risk of losing "public funds due to private corporate activity," and incurring "public debt for private activity."[14] At the 1857 constitutional convention, the Committee on Incorporations successfully proposed also banning the state from taking responsibility for corporations' non-wartime debts.[15] That ban echoes Article VII, Section 1, which declares that "the state shall never assume, or become responsible for, the debts or liabilities of any individual, association, or corporation, unless incurred in time of war for the benefit of the state."

The Iowa Supreme Court has resolved Section 3 disputes on only a handful of occasions. In *Merchants' Union Barb-Wire Co. v. Brown* (1884), the court upheld legislation that allocated funds to help the Farmers' Protective Association of Iowa defend against claims of infringing on others' barbed-wire patents. To

---

[12] Op. Iowa Att'y Gen., 1902 WL 48624 (Feb. 27, 1902) (replying to the Senate Committee on Ways and Means).

[13] Iowa Const. of 1846, art. IX, § 2.

[14] Op. Iowa Att'y Gen., 1994 WL 68689 (Jan. 11, 1994) (replying to Richard Johnson).

[15] *1857 Debates*, *supra* Article I, note 3, vol. 1, p. 96. The committee's proposal was not controversial. *See id.* at p. 289; *id.* at vol. 2, p. 773.

justify its ruling, the court emphasized that the litigation debts were anticipated, rather than already existing; that the state had frequently appropriated funds to agricultural and horticultural societies; and that the association was a nonprofit entity organized for the purpose of helping Iowa's farmers affordably enclose their properties. In *Edge v. Brice* (1962), the court clarified and embraced the rule applied in *Merchants' Union*: like Section 1 of Article VII, this provision bars the state from playing the role of a surety by agreeing to be secondarily liable for a corporation's future debts. If the General Assembly wishes to make the state *primarily* liable for a corporation's future debts—like the legislature's decision to make the state primarily liable for the Farmers' Protective Association's anticipated legal debts in *Merchants' Union*—it may do so. In *Edge*, the court sustained the legislature's prospective decision to reimburse utility corporations for the costs of relocating their service lines and pipes to accommodate highway construction. In *Brady v. City of Dubuque* (1993), the court brushed aside a Section 3 attack on a city's economic-development project, finding that the city had not agreed to serve as a surety. In *Green v. City of Mt. Pleasant* (1964), the court upheld a city's plan to reimburse a corporation for costs it had already incurred when it launched construction of an industrial facility (a facility that the city hoped would generate local jobs). The court's brief analysis appeared to turn on the fact that, when reimbursing the corporation, the city would be using the proceeds from revenue bonds,[16] rather than taxes.

The Office of the Attorney General has fielded a number of Section 3 queries. In 1994, for example, the office concluded that, as a unit of state government, the Iowa Product Development Corporation likely could not acquire corporate shares.[17] Based on its assessment of Section 3's original purposes, the office determined in 1993 that the provision likely does not bar the state from investing deferred compensation funds in corporate stock at the direction of the benefited employees.[18] In 1987, based in part on its observation that Section 4 of this article bars municipal corporations from holding stock in banking corporations but says nothing about holding stock in other kinds of incorporated entities, the office concluded that Section 3's opening clause does not bar cities and counties from owning shares in corporations, although the General Assembly may provide to the contrary.[19]

---

[16] For a discussion of revenue bonds, see the commentary on Article VII, Section 2.

[17] Op. Iowa Att'y Gen., 1994 WL 68689 (Jan. 11, 1994) (replying to Richard Johnson).

[18] Op. Iowa Att'y Gen., 1993 WL 546186 (Dec. 21, 1993) (replying to Michael Fitzgerald).

[19] Op. Iowa Att'y Gen., 1987 WL 119628 (Jan. 15, 1987) (replying to Kay Chapman); *see also* Op. Iowa Att'y Gen., 1987 WL 119607 (Mar. 19, 1987) (replying to Norman Goodwin) (reaching a comparable conclusion about certain retirement systems that cities create for their employees). In the January 15 opinion just cited, the office expressly overruled Attorney General Richard Turner's 1968 conclusion that Section 3 does bar municipalities from acquiring corporate stock. *See* Op. Iowa Att'y Gen., 1968 WL 172673 (Aug. 14, 1968) (replying to Albert Goeldner).

Section 4.
Municipal corporations.

No political or municipal corporation shall become a stockholder in any banking corporation, directly or indirectly.

While Section 3 of this article bars the state from holding shares in *any* corporation, Section 4 bars political and municipal corporations from holding shares in *banking* corporations. Iowa's 1846 constitution had altogether banned corporations and other entities from "exercising the privileges of banking" within the state and had declared that "[t]he State shall not directly or indirectly become a stockholder in any corporation,"[20] but it did not bar cities and counties from owning corporations' shares. At the 1857 convention, the Committee on Incorporations recommended precisely the language that one sees here,[21] but further proposed (1) that political and municipal corporations be barred from owning more than an aggregate of $200,000 in non-banking corporations' stock and (2) that an aggregate cap of $200,000 be placed on political and municipal corporations' ability to incur debt, loan credit, and pledge security.[22] The ban on city and county investments in banking corporations was not controversial among the delegates. The desire to limit cities' and counties' aggregate debt ultimately found expression in Article XI, Section 3.

The most controversial of the committee's recommendations for Section 4 was the proposed limit on cities' and counties' ability to invest in non-banking corporations.[23] Edward Johnston—a lawyer from Lee County—said that it was widely understood that the central purpose of the proposed $200,000 cap on corporate shareholding would be to limit cities' and counties' ability to finance railroad corporations. Using the latitude that the 1846 constitution had given them, local governments had collectively invested millions of dollars in railroads. Some were optimistic about those stock investments, but others feared that the corporations would fail and that local governments thus would find themselves saddled with substantial debt and with correspondingly high taxes. Noting that, with Governor James Grimes's prodding, this had become a matter of discussion across the state, Jasper County's Harvey Skiff proposed that the convention simply schedule a statewide vote on whether incorporated political entities should be allowed to hold shares in non-banking corporations. Marion County's Hiram Gibson spoke in favor of broadly allowing such investments (and of rejecting the committee's proposed $200,000 cap), arguing that cities

---

[20] Iowa Const. of 1846, art. IX, § 2.

[21] Iowa was not alone in taking its state constitution in this direction. In this same year (1857), for example, Pennsylvania similarly barred its local governments from becoming stockholders in corporations. Penn. Const. of 1838, art. XI, § 7 (amended 1857) (located today in revised form in art. IX, § 9).

[22] *1857 Debates, supra* Article I, note 3, vol. 1, p. 96.

[23] *1857 Debates, supra* Article I, note 3, vol. 1, pp. 289–344, 415–19; *id.* at vol. 2, pp. 775–79.

and counties should be left free to make their own decisions about whether and how to finance railroad lines and other local improvements.[24] Taking the contrary view, Dubuque County's John Emerson urged his colleagues to follow the model set by Ohio, which had banned its cities and counties from investing in corporations of any kind.[25] Lucas County's John Edwards proposed compromising by tethering the permissible amount of cities' and counties' corporate investments to the value of those jurisdictions' taxable property.[26] Des Moines County's Jonathan Hall stirred the pot still further by suggesting that local voters be allowed to decide for themselves whether to make certain kinds of corporate investments, but that the franchise often be limited to those who paid a significant amount in taxes or owned valuable real estate.[27] After much discussion of those and other suggestions, Lee County's Edward Johnston proposed that Section 4 serve only the narrow function of banning political and municipal corporations from holding shares in banking corporations.[28] Johnston's recommendation was ultimately accepted on a 30-to-2 vote.[29]

Apart from observing that Section 4's phrase "banking corporation" might encompass a broader range of entities than the same phrase covers in Section 9 (*Allen v. Clayton*, 1884), the Iowa Supreme Court has not addressed controversies concerning Section 4's meaning. Neither has the Office of the Attorney General.

Section 5.
Banking associations.

No act of the General Assembly, authorizing or creating corporations or associations with banking powers, nor amendments thereto shall take effect, or in any manner be in force, until the same shall have been submitted, separately, to the people, at a general or special election, as provided by law, to be held not less than three months after the passage of the act, and shall have been approved by a majority of all the electors voting for and against it at such election.

Section 5 states that legislation authorizing or creating entities "with banking powers" cannot take effect until it has been approved by the state's electorate. As Part I explains in greater detail, Iowa's 1846 constitution had barred all persons and entities from "exercising the privileges of banking, or creating paper

---

[24] *1857 Debates, supra* Article I, note 3, vol. 1, pp. 290–95.

[25] *1857 Debates, supra* Article I, note 3, vol. 1, pp. 297–98; *see also* Ohio Const. of 1851, art. VIII, § 6.

[26] *1857 Debates, supra* Article I, note 3, vol. 1, p. 295.

[27] *1857 Debates, supra* Article I, note 3, vol. 1, p. 303.

[28] *1857 Debates, supra* Article I, note 3, vol. 1, p. 343. Henry County's Rufus Clarke responded by suggesting that the delegates adopt a provision barring cities and counties from becoming indebted in an amount greater than five percent of their property's taxable value. *Id.* Clarke's suggestion ultimately found its way, in modified form, into Article XI, Section 3.

[29] *1857 Debates, supra* Article I, note 3, vol. 1, p. 419.

to circulate as money."[30] In 1884's *Allen v. Clayton*, the Iowa Supreme Court described that prohibition as "[t]he great evil of the constitution of 1846."[31] The public's dissatisfaction flowed largely from the fact that numerous other states did allow banks to issue paper (often called "bills," "drafts," or "notes") functioning as currency, but did not regulate those banks in a manner that effectively ensured the paper's value. When those banks' paper found its way into Iowa, buyers and sellers thus faced great uncertainty about its value. A distant bank might not have the resources to honor its bills at face value, and so those bills needed to be discounted when using them in transactions—but discounted by how much?

Many concluded that it would be preferable to allow paper-issuing banks to set up shop in Iowa; at least then, the reasoning went, lawmakers could regulate the banks and try to bring greater stability to the state's markets. Rather than widely swing open the state's doors to new banking activity, however, the delegates to the 1857 convention opted for the more cautious approach reflected in Section 5. With the notable exception of the "three months" provision (an addition proposed by Van Buren County's Timothy Day[32]), this was largely the path recommended by the Committee on Incorporations.[33]

Section 5 does not play a role in Iowa banking law today. In *Allen v. Clayton* (1884), the Iowa Supreme Court concluded that Section 5's reference to "corporations or associations with banking powers" encompasses only those entities that can "issue bills to circulate as money." After all, the court said, the desire to allow Iowa entities to issue bills for circulation lay at the heart of the rationale for adopting Section 5 in the first place.[34] In the 1860s, as part of an effort to establish a national currency and to build a network of federally organized banks, Congress imposed a ten-percent tax on the amount of all state-bank bills "paid out by" any state or national bank.[35] As a practical matter, that tax put state-chartered banks out of the business of issuing notes designed to function

---

[30] Iowa Const. of 1846, art. IX, § 1.

[31] The chief perceived problem was the bar on issuing paper intended to circulate as currency. Notwithstanding the 1846 ban on "exercising the privileges of banking," there were numerous enterprising individuals who established businesses that performed such banking functions as making loans, accepting deposits, and exchanging non-Iowa banks' circulating paper for specie. Erling A. Erickson, *Banking in Frontier Iowa: 1836–1865* (Ames: Iowa State University Press, 1971), ch. 4.

[32] *1857 Debates, supra* Article I, note 3, vol. 1, p. 406.

[33] *1857 Debates, supra* Article I, note 3, vol. 1, pp. 96–97 (sections 6 and 16 of the committee's proposal).

[34] The court reaffirmed this narrow reading of Section 5 in *State ex rel. Stone v. Union Stock Yards State Bank* (1897). In 1924, Attorney General Ben Gibson reiterated the court's judgment that this provision applies only to "banks of issue." Op. Iowa Att'y Gen., 1924 WL 60354 (Apr. 26, 1924) (replying to Governor Nathan Kendall).

[35] Act of Mar. 3, 1865, ch. 78, 13 Stat. 469, 484.

as currency.[36] Today, banks chartered under state law perform functions that are more familiar to modern sensibilities, such as accepting deposits and making loans. Because Section 5 is narrowly concerned with entities that perform a function that Iowa's banks no longer actually perform, it has long been rendered obsolete.

Section 6.
State bank.

Subject to the provisions of the foregoing section, the General Assembly may also provide for the establishment of a State Bank with branches.

Section 6 authorized the legislature to establish a multi-branch state bank. Iowa's 1846 constitution had not given the General Assembly this power, a deficiency that helped fuel the public's call for the 1857 constitutional convention.[37] At that convention, the Committee on Incorporations proposed authorizing the legislature to "charter a State Bank with branches, to be founded upon an actual specie basis," with each branch required to honor the other branches' "paper credit issued as money."[38] Committee member John Parvin explained that they wished to authorize the General Assembly to take either or both of two different approaches to ameliorating the state's banking woes: enact a general banking law under which others could establish banks (an option covered by Sections 5 and 8 of this article) or charter a bank on its own initiative pursuant to Section 5 and this provision. Parvin emphasized that, if the state opted to exercise the latter option, the state itself would not hold the stock—Article VIII, Section 3's bar on state shareholding would apply.[39] Lucas County's John Edwards added that, if the state established a bank, state officials could closely monitor its operations and governmental bodies could deposit their own funds there.[40] Marion County's Hiram Gibson and Scott County's George Ells worried that the "state bank" label would prompt many Iowans to assume, inaccurately, that the bank was financially backed by the assets of the state itself.[41] Ells nevertheless supported Section 6's adoption because he believed the state bank's bills would become familiar in appearance across the state and thus would be trusted more than the bills of lesser-known banks.[42] After debating the lessons to be learned from banking successes and failures in other states, especially Indiana and Ohio,

---

[36] Milton Friedman & Anna Jacobson Schwartz, *A Monetary History of the United States: 1867–1960* (Princeton: Princeton University Press, 1963), pp. 18–19.

[37] For more on this subject, see Part I of this book and the commentary on Article VIII, Section 5.

[38] *1857 Debates, supra* Article I, note 3, vol. 1, pp. 96–97.

[39] *1857 Debates, supra* Article I, note 3, vol. 1, p. 373.

[40] *1857 Debates, supra* Article I, note 3, vol. 1, pp. 380–81.

[41] *1857 Debates, supra* Article I, note 3, vol. 1, pp. 374–75 (Gibson), 384 (Ells).

[42] *1857 Debates, supra* Article I, note 3, vol. 1, pp. 390–91.

the delegates approved the bulk of the committee's proposal,[43] dividing the state-bank provisions between Sections 6 and 7.[44]

In 1858, the General Assembly opted to take both of the paths that John Parvin had described—it enacted a general banking law and it created a state bank.[45] The State Bank of Iowa endured only until 1865, when—as the commentary on Section 5 of this article briefly explains—Congress imposed a ten-percent tax on all notes issued by state banks and thereby made it economically infeasible for the State Bank of Iowa to continue to perform the chief function that had inspired its creation.[46]

Section 7.
Specie basis.

If a State Bank be established, it shall be founded on an actual specie basis, and the branches shall be mutually responsible for each other's liabilities upon all notes, bills, and other issues intended for circulation as money.

Building on the foundation laid by Section 6 of this article, Section 7 identifies two key requirements that had to be met if state lawmakers opted to establish a state bank: the bank's commitments had to be backed by gold and silver, and each branch had to honor the other branches' paper circulating as currency. Des Moines County's Jonathan Hall had argued, for example, that it was "essential" that the state bank's bills "at all times be convertible into gold and silver, when presented at the counter of the bank. Your banking system will not be worth a straw, if you have it so that the banks can suspend specie payment at any time."[47] For the origins and fate of this provision, see the commentary on Section 6 of this article.

Section 8.
General banking law.

If a general Banking law shall be enacted, it shall provide for the registry and countersigning, by an officer of State, of all bills, or paper credit designed to circulate as money, and require security to the full amount thereof, to be deposited with the State Treasurer, in United States stocks, or in interest paying stocks of States in good credit and standing, to be rated at ten per cent. below

---

[43] *1857 Debates, supra* Article I, note 3, vol. 1, pp. 375–91.

[44] *1857 Debates, supra* Article I, note 3, vol. 2, pp. 648–49, 785.

[45] Act of Mar. 22, 1858, ch. 114, 1858 Iowa Acts 215 (general banking law); Act of Mar. 20, 1858, ch. 87, 1858 Iowa Acts 125 (state bank). For a discussion of these historical developments, see *Allen v. Clayton* (1884).

[46] For more on the origins and fate of the State Bank of Iowa, see Erling A. Erickson, *Banking in Frontier Iowa: 1836–1865* (Ames: Iowa State University Press, 1971), ch. 6; Howard H. Preston, *History of Banking in Iowa* (Iowa City: State Historical Society of Iowa, 1922), ch. 6.

[47] *1857 Debates, supra* Article I, note 3, vol. 1, pp. 386–87.

their average value in the City of New York, for the thirty days next preceding their deposit; and in case of a depreciation of any portion of said stocks, to the amount of ten per cent. on the dollar, the bank or banks owning such stock shall be required to make up said deficiency by depositing additional stocks: and said law shall also provide for the recording of the names of all stockholders in such corporations, the amount of stock held by each, the time of any transfer, and to whom.

Section 8 authorized the General Assembly to enact a general law under which banks of issue—that is, banks authorized to issue paper designed to circulate as currency—could be established. Part I and the commentary on Sections 5 and 6 of this article explain the historical circumstances out of which the desire for such legislation arose. The Committee on Incorporations proposed largely the text that one sees here, with the exception of the two "ten percent" provisions.[48] Those two provisions trace their origins to suggestions made by Johnson County's William Penn Clarke,[49] Scott County's George Ells,[50] and Jefferson County's James Wilson.[51]

In *Allen v. Clayton* (1884), the Iowa Supreme Court determined that Section 8 refers "exclusive[ly] . . . to banks of issue." As explained in the commentary on Section 5 of this article, Iowa banks no longer issue bills designed to circulate as currency. Like Sections 5, 6, 7, 9, 10, and 11 of this article, therefore, Section 8 no longer plays a role in Iowa banking law.

Section 9.
Stockholders' responsibility.

Every stockholder in a banking corporation or institution shall be individually responsible and liable to its creditors, over and above the amount of stock by him or her held, to an amount equal to his or her respective shares so held for all of its liabilities, accruing while he or she remains such stockholder.

Aimed at incentivizing stockholders to closely monitor the activities of the banks in which they invested, Section 9 imposed double liability upon a bank's shareholders for liabilities that the bank incurred during the period when those shareholders owned the bank's shares. (For background on the constitution's treatment of banks, see Part I and the commentary on Sections 4 through 8 of

---

[48] *1857 Debates, supra* Article I, note 3, vol. 1, p. 96.

[49] *1857 Debates, supra* Article I, note 3, vol. 1, pp. 346–47, 419.

[50] *1857 Debates, supra* Article I, note 3, vol. 1, pp. 347–48.

[51] *1857 Debates, supra* Article I, note 3, vol. 2, p. 775; *see also id.* at pp. 1022–23 (putting Section 8 into its final form). In 1858, shortly after Iowa voters approved the new Iowa Constitution, the General Assembly enacted a general banking law pursuant to this provision. Act of Mar. 22, 1858, ch. 114, 1858 Iowa Acts 215. Because that legislation's requirements for creating new banks of issue were dauntingly stringent, however, no banks were established under it. Howard H. Preston, *History of Banking in Iowa* (Iowa City: State Historical Society of Iowa, 1922), ch. 5.

this article.) The provision still reads as originally proposed by the Committee on Incorporations at the 1857 constitutional convention, with one exception: the committee's initial draft lacked the closing language that appears today after the final comma. Instead, a semicolon appeared in that comma's location, followed by: "and in all cases where its stock shall be transferred, the liability of the transferer shall not cease, nor shall the liability of the transferee commence until the expiration of six months after such transfer shall have been duly recorded, as provided for by law."[52] Committee member Rufus Clarke explained that, as part of the delegates' effort to ensure that Iowa's new banks would be carefully operated, one of the committee's purposes was to ensure that bank stocks would not be swept up in unseemly speculation among investors. Johnson County's William Penn Clarke strongly objected to the committee's draft, arguing that shareholders' liabilities should terminate at the moment they sold their shares, and that bank stocks would be unattractive to investors under the proposed scheme. Jefferson County's James Wilson sought a middle ground, proposing an amendment that brought Section 9 largely into the form it takes today. Likening bank corporations to partnerships, he argued that banks' shareholders should be responsible for liabilities that the bank incurs on their watch. The delegates embraced Wilson's suggestion by a vote of 15 to 10.[53] In a subsequent session, they accepted minor modifications proposed by committee member John Parvin, thereby putting Section 9 into the form one sees above.

In *Allen v. Clayton* (1884), the Iowa Supreme Court determined that Section 9 refers "exclusive[ly] . . . to banks of issue."[54] As explained in the commentary on Section 5 of this article, Iowa banks no longer issue bills designed to circulate as currency. Like Sections 5, 6, 7, 8, 10, and 11 of this article, therefore, Section 9 no longer plays a role in Iowa banking law.[55]

Section 10.
Billholders preferred.

In case of the insolvency of any banking institution, the bill-holders shall have a preference over its other creditors.

---

[52] *1857 Debates, supra* Article I, note 3, vol. 1, p. 96.

[53] *1857 Debates, supra* Article I, note 3, vol. 1, pp. 363–64, 370–72.

[54] *Accord Andrew v. American Savings Bank* (1934); *Andrew v. City-Commercial Savings Bank* (1928); Op. Iowa Att'y Gen., 1961 WL 110096 (Feb. 7, 1961) (replying to William Lynes). For an argument that the *Allen* court interpreted Section 9 too narrowly, see Frank E. Horack, "The Banking Clauses in the Constitution of Iowa," 13 *Iowa Law Review* 293 (1928).

[55] For a discussion of *legislation* that imposed double liability on banks' shareholders, see Note, "Statutory Liability of Bank Stockholders in Iowa," 21 *Iowa Law Review* 611 (1936).

Section 10 was adopted to ensure that, when a bank collapsed and its remaining assets were being distributed, those holding its bills circulating as currency would have priority over those whose deposits the bank held. (For background on the constitution's treatment of banks, see Part I and the commentary on Sections 4 through 8 of this article.) The provision reads as originally proposed at the 1857 constitutional convention by the Committee on Incorporations.[56] Harvey Skiff, a banker from Jasper County and a member of the committee, explained Section 10's chief purpose:

> [T]he object [of] this section was . . . to make a distinction between bill-holders and depositors. The depositors generally reside in the neighborhood where the bank is situated. The bill-holders are scattered all over the country, wherever the bills circulate, and consequently they are not able to secure themselves so readily as depositors can.[57]

In *Allen v. Clayton* (1884), the Iowa Supreme Court determined that Section 10 refers "exclusive[ly] . . . to banks of issue." As explained in the commentary on Section 5 of this article, Iowa banks no longer issue bills designed to circulate as currency. Like Sections 5, 6, 7, 8, 9, and 11 of this article, therefore, Section 10 no longer plays a role in Iowa banking law.

Section 11.
Specie payments—suspension.

The suspension of specie payments by banking institutions shall never be permitted or sanctioned.

Reflecting the framers' conviction that bank bills circulating as currency should be readily convertible to gold and silver, Section 11 barred banks from suspending specie payments. (For background on the constitution's treatment of banks, see Part I and the commentary on Sections 4 through 8 of this article.) The provision was not controversial among the delegates to the 1857 constitutional convention.[58]

In *Allen v. Clayton* (1884), the Iowa Supreme Court determined that Section 11 refers "exclusive[ly] . . . to banks of issue." As explained in the commentary on Section 5 of this article, Iowa banks no longer issue bills designed to circulate as currency. Like Sections 5, 6, 7, 8, 9, and 10 of this article, therefore, Section 11 no longer plays a role in Iowa banking law.

---

[56] *1857 Debates, supra* Article I, note 3, vol. 1, p. 97.

[57] *1857 Debates, supra* Article I, note 3, vol. 1, p. 396.

[58] *1857 Debates, supra* Article I, note 3, vol. 1, pp. 403, 427; *id.* at vol. 2, p. 791.

Section 12.
Amendment or repeal of laws—exclusive privileges.

Subject to the provisions of this article, the General Assembly shall have power to amend or repeal all laws for the organization or creation of corporations, or granting of special or exclusive privileges or immunities, by a vote of two thirds of each branch of the General Assembly; and no exclusive privileges, except as in this article provided, shall ever be granted.

Section 12 reserves for a supermajority of the General Assembly the power to alter or repeal the state's laws governing the organization and creation of corporations, and declares the founders' opposition to granting corporations "exclusive privileges." At the 1857 constitutional convention, the Committee on Incorporations' initial draft of this provision was almost identical to what one sees here.[59] Two days before the committee presented that draft, the Committee on the Preamble and Bill of Rights had announced that it wished to add a clause to Article I, Section 2, declaring that "no privileges or immunities shall ever be granted that may not be altered, revoked or repealed by the General Assembly."[60] Scott County's George Ells suggested providing instead that "no special privileges or immunities shall ever be granted that may not be altered, amended or repealed, by the General Assembly by a vote of two-thirds of [each chamber]." Numerous delegates opposed both possible additions to Section 2, saying that both of them would discourage corporations from investing in railroads and other internal improvements, lest they begin costly operations only to have the legislature subsequently revoke the privileges that entitled them to undertake the work. Ells and others responded that, through their elected leaders, the sovereign people should retain the power to revoke corporate privileges in those rare instances in which the "privileged classes" abuse their legislatively granted powers. Henry County's Rufus Clarke said that he supported Ells's proposed addition but believed it would be better placed elsewhere in the constitution. After the delegates voted not to add Ells's language to Article I, Section 2,[61] the Committee on Incorporations—on which Clarke sat—proposed largely the text that one finds here in Section 12. Following a brief reprise of the debate that Ells and the Committee on the Preamble and Bill of Rights had previously provoked, and following some minor textual tinkering by Hardin County's Sheldon Winchester, the delegates approved the provision by an unrecorded margin.[62]

---

[59] *1857 Debates, supra* Article I, note 3, vol. 1, p. 97. The one notable difference concerned the phrase "granting of special or exclusive privileges or immunities"—the committee's draft lacked the words "or exclusive." That omission was rectified after James Wilson, a lawyer from Jefferson County, pointed out that it left the General Assembly without the power to repeal exclusive privileges. *Id.* at pp. 407, 412.

[60] *1857 Debates, supra* Article I, note 3, vol. 1, p. 101.

[61] *1857 Debates, supra* Article I, note 3, vol. 1, pp. 143–72.

[62] *1857 Debates, supra* Article I, note 3, vol. 1, pp. 407–12. Article VIII was ultimately approved in its entirety by a vote of 29 to 6. *Id.* at vol. 2, p. 1024.

Just one year after the new constitution's ratification, the Iowa Supreme Court determined that Section 12 applies "exclusively to corporations for pecuniary profit," and does not apply to municipal corporations (*Ex parte Pritz*, 1858). With respect to for-profit corporations, the court indicated in *St. John v. Iowa Business Men's Building & Loan Association* (1907) that Section 12 gives the legislature significant power:

> [A] corporation under our laws has no absolute right to do business in this State, and its articles of incorporation are at all times subject to amendment by the General Assembly. Conditions may at any time be imposed upon a corporation and enforcement thereof assured by revoking their privileges in the event of noncompliance.

Relying heavily upon *Des Moines Street Railroad Co. v. Des Moines Broad-Gauge Street Railway Co.* (1887), the court explained in 1991's *Northwestern Bell Telephone Co. v. Iowa Utilities Board* that Section 12 "only pertains to rights and powers that may be given to a corporation through its charter," and does not prevent the government from awarding a particular corporation exclusive operating rights for a reasonable period of time (such as the exclusive right to handle certain technological matters involving long-distance telephone calls in *Northwestern Bell*, or the exclusive right to provide a city's rail service on designated streets in *Des Moines Street Railroad*). With respect to corporations' charters, the power that Section 12 gives the General Assembly "is not absolute and is subject to limitations found elsewhere in both the Federal and State Constitutions," such as the limitations imposed by those constitutions' equal protection and due process provisions (*Chicago & Northwestern Railway Co. v. Fachman*, 1963). The bar on granting exclusive privileges applies only to "legislative enactments" and not to the actions of administrative officials, such as the state's director of revenue (*Moorman Manufacturing Co. v. Bair*, 1977).

Article IX

Education and School Lands

1ST. EDUCATION

Article IX contains two parts (commonly called "divisions"), the first dealing principally with a board of education and the second dealing principally with financial matters. Although never formally repealed, most (but, as shall be explained, perhaps not all) of the fifteen sections that compose the first division no longer have any bearing on the state's educational system and so are commonly omitted in printings of the state's constitution, just as they are omitted here.

How did these provisions become obsolete? The explanation is simple. Iowa's first constitution, ratified in 1846, directed the General Assembly to "provide for the election, by the people, of a Superintendent of Public Instruction" who would execute duties assigned by the legislature.[1] In Article IX's first division, the 1857 constitution shifted Iowa to a model under which the state's public schools would be managed by a newly created board of education.[2] But the division's final provision—Section 15—stated that, "[a]t any time after the year one thousand eight hundred and sixty three, the General Assembly shall have power to abolish or reorganize said Board of Education, and provide for the educational interest of the State in any other manner that to them shall seem best and

[1] Iowa Const. of 1846, art. X, § 1.

[2] Iowa Const. art. IX, div. 1, § 1.

proper." On March 19, 1864, the General Assembly did precisely that, abolishing the board of education and reinstating a superintendent-led system.[3] That legislation rendered most of Article IX's first division obsolete.[4]

There is one provision in Article IX's first division, however, that might still have life. Saying nothing about the board, Section 11 focuses on the only public university that existed in Iowa at the time of the 1857 constitution's adoption. Section 11 says: "The State University [commonly known today as the Iowa City-based University of Iowa] shall be established at one place without branches at any other place, and the University fund shall be applied to that Institution and no other." The 1846 constitution had authorized the legislature to establish multiple branches of the then-anticipated new university,[5] and the General Assembly had responded by laying the legislative groundwork for branches in the cities of Fairfield and Dubuque.[6] In Section 11, the delegates to the 1857 convention limited the university to a single location, believing that (among other things) the institution would suffer if its funds were scattered across multiple branches.[7] For many decades now, the state and other printers of the Iowa Constitution have regarded Section 11 as obsolete and thus have omitted it or otherwise flagged it as inoperative, just like the other provisions of Article IX's first division. The University of Iowa's leaders took that same view of Section 11 in early 2015 when they toyed with the idea of establishing a Des Moines branch.[8] But is the provision indeed out of play?

The question takes two forms, one constitutional and the other statutory. First, did Section 15 (quoted above) authorize the General Assembly to lift Section 11's ban on multiple branches? An affirmative answer is far from obvious. On what is arguably the most natural reading of the text, Section 15 simply authorizes the legislature to alter or abolish the board of education and to replace or supplement that board in a manner that serves the state's educational needs. Interpreted this way, Section 15 does not authorize the legislature to lift Section 11's ban on creating multiple branches of the University of Iowa, and so the ban remains in place today. On the other hand, perhaps Section 15's latter two comma-linked clauses should be read independently, with the first authorizing

---

[3] Act of Mar. 19, 1864, ch. 52, 1864 Iowa Acts 53. The legislation's enactment did not come as a surprise; tensions between the board and the General Assembly had begun to brew almost immediately after the new constitution's ratification. *See, e.g.*, *High School of Clayton County v. Clayton County* (1859); *District Township of the City of Dubuque v. City of Dubuque* (1858).

[4] Today, the state's educational system is governed by a *legislatively* created department of education and board of education. Iowa Code §§ 256.1 (department), 256.3 (board).

[5] Iowa Const. of 1846, art. X, § 5.

[6] Code of Iowa (1851), §§ 1029–40 (Fairfield), 1041–43 (Dubuque).

[7] *1857 Debates*, *supra* Article I, note 3, vol. 2, pp. 838–41, 953, 1029.

[8] *See* Jeff Charis-Carlson, "AIB to Be a Regent Center, Not a UI Branch Campus," *Iowa City Press-Citizen*, Feb. 6, 2015, at 6A.

the legislature to abolish or alter the board of education and with the second allowing the legislature to disregard *any* of the prior fourteen sections when doing so would advance the state's educational interests. Even if one should not read those two clauses as independent of one another, perhaps one could conclude that the power to abolish the board implicitly included the power to lift the ban on creating multiple branches of the university, due to the fact that other provisions in Article IX's first division gave the board managerial authority over the university.[9] If Section 15 did empower the legislature to push Section 11 aside, the next question is statutory: has the General Assembly enacted legislation that renders Section 11 obsolete? Neither in the 1864 legislation abolishing the board of education nor in university-focused legislation enacted two days later[10] did the General Assembly make any clear reference to the provision. Did the legislature's abolition of the board in 1864 implicitly authorize the university to establish branches in multiple locations? It is not clear why one should think so.

The Iowa Supreme Court has not yet weighed in on the question of Section 11's vitality. In at least three opinions—issued in 1967, 1964, and 1935—however, the Office of the Attorney General evinced the belief that Section 11 remained in force.[11]

■ 2ND. SCHOOL FUNDS AND SCHOOL LANDS

Section 1.
Control—management.

The educational and school funds and lands, shall be under the control and management of the General Assembly of this State.

Section 1 gives the General Assembly ultimate control over the state's educational funds and properties. Appearing relatively late in the drafting process at the 1857 constitutional convention,[12] the provision was a component of the delegates' effort to settle their disagreements about how power should be allocated between the General Assembly and the ill-fated board of education that they were creating in the first division of this article.[13] In *King v. State* (2012), the

---

[9] Iowa Const. art. IX, div. 1, §§ 1, 8; *see also* Revised Code of Iowa (1860), § 1928 (stating that the university would be governed by a board of trustees selected by the board of education).

[10] Act of Mar. 21, 1864, ch. 59, 1864 Iowa Acts 63.

[11] Op. Iowa Att'y Gen., 1967 WL 167018 (Feb. 14, 1967) (replying to Elmer Lange); Op. Iowa Att'y Gen., 1964 WL 121093 (Dec. 15, 1964) (replying to Elmer Lange); Op. Iowa Att'y Gen., 1935 WL 60843 (Sept. 30, 1935) (replying to the State University of Iowa).

[12] *1857 Debates, supra* Article I, note 3, vol. 2, p. 872. The provision was not controversial among the delegates. *See 1857 Debates, supra* Article I, note 3, vol. 2, p. 967.

[13] For a brief introduction to that ill-fated board, see the opening paragraphs of commentary on this article.

Iowa Supreme Court observed that "[w]hereas the first division [of Article IX] entrusted the 'educational interest' to the board of education, the second division made clear that funding would be the legislature's domain."

The Iowa Supreme Court has not yet resolved any controversies concerning Section 1's meaning, and the Office of the Attorney General has fielded only a few inquiries about it. In 2001, for example, the office concluded that Section 1 did not bar a city from condemning school property in order to obtain a right-of-way for a new street.[14] In 1939, Attorney General John Rankin determined that nothing in Article IX—including Section 1—exempted public schools from paying sales and use taxes on the library books they purchased.[15]

Section 2.
Permanent fund.

The University lands, and the proceeds thereof, and all monies belonging to said fund shall be a permanent fund for the sole use of the State University. The interest arising from the same shall be annually appropriated for the support and benefit of said University.

Together with Section 5 of this article, Section 2 was intended to secure a permanent financial foundation for the State University of Iowa, popularly known since the 1960s as the University of Iowa.[16] The state's 1846 constitution had directed the General Assembly to use the proceeds derived from thousands of acres of land—land that was given to the state by the federal government—to create "a permanent fund," the interest from which would be used to support a university.[17] As one of multiple steps that it took toward that end in 1847, the General Assembly declared that proceeds from the forthcoming sale of the federally donated land would be used to establish "a permanent fund, the interest of which shall be applied exclusively to the support of" the State University of Iowa.[18] At the 1857 constitutional convention, the Committee on Education and School Lands proposed that the delegates adopt the text that one sees

---

[14] Op. Iowa Att'y Gen., 2001 WL 1301432 (July 31, 2001) (replying to Andy McKean).

[15] Op. Iowa Att'y Gen., 1939 WL 77013 (Feb. 2, 1939) (replying to D.L. Murrow).

[16] For an explanation of the university's naming conventions, see David McCartney, "What's in a Name? For the University of Iowa, Lots of History and a Little Confusion," *University of Iowa Spectator* (Dec. 2010), available at http://spectator.uiowa.edu/2010/december/oldgold.html. *See also* Op. Iowa Att'y Gen., 1964 WL 121093 (Dec. 15, 1964) (replying to Elmer Lange) (concluding that the Board of Regents lacked the power to remove the word "State" from the university's legal name).

[17] Iowa Const. of 1846, art. X, § 5. For more on the University of Iowa's origins, see the commentary on Article XI, § 8, as well as J.L. Pickard, "Historical Sketch of the State University of Iowa," 4 *Annals of Iowa* 1 (1899).

[18] Act of Feb. 25, 1847, ch. 125, §§ 3, 7, 1847 Iowa Acts 188.

above.[19] The committee's proposal drew no historically documented opposition or debate. The fund—referred to within the university as the Permanent Land Fund—still exists and continues to generate income today.

The Iowa Supreme Court has not been called upon to resolve disagreements about Section 2's meaning.[20] Citing Sections 2 and 5 of this article, Attorney General Edward O'Connor advised the Iowa State Board of Education in 1936 that, after the board foreclosed on a mortgage that it obtained in exchange for a loan from the permanent fund, the board was authorized to use a reasonable portion of the permanent fund's principal to make improvements to the land.[21]

Section 3.
Perpetual support fund.

The General Assembly shall encourage, by all suitable means, the promotion of intellectual, scientific, moral, and agricultural improvement. The proceeds of all lands that have been, or hereafter may be, granted by the United States to this State, for the support of schools, which may have been, or shall hereafter be sold, or disposed of, and the five hundred thousand acres of land granted to the new States, under an act of Congress, distributing the proceeds of the public lands among the several States of the Union, approved in the year of our Lord one thousand eight hundred and forty one, and all estates of deceased persons who may have died without leaving a will or heir, and also such per cent. as has been or may hereafter be granted by Congress, on the sale of lands in this State, shall be, and remain a perpetual fund, the interest of which, together with all rents of the unsold lands, and such other means as the General Assembly may provide, shall be inviolably appropriated to the support of Common schools throughout the State.

By permanently securing certain funds for the state's "Common schools," Section 3 does for those schools what Sections 2 and 5 do for the State University of Iowa. With only tiny modifications made by the delegates to Iowa's 1857 constitutional convention, the provision was carried over wholesale from the state's 1846 constitution.[22] Hoping to ensure that Iowa's economically deprived children would receive a satisfactory education, Scott County's George Ells proposed that a clause be added to the end of Section 3, guaranteeing that the state's common schools would never charge tuition. The delegates rejected Ells's proposal,

---

[19] *1857 Debates, supra* Article I, note 3, vol. 1, pp. 78, 599. The committee's proposed version of Section 2 differed from the text one sees above in only one inconsequential respect. *See id.* at vol. 2, p. 771.

[20] A case that bears a subject-matter relation to Section 2, but is statutory in nature, is *Crum v. Cotting* (1867).

[21] Op. Iowa Att'y Gen., 1936 WL 68638 (Apr. 8, 1936) (replying to the Iowa State Board of Education).

[22] *Cf.* Iowa Const. of 1846, art. X, § 2. The provision was not controversial among the delegates to the 1857 convention. *See 1857 Debates, supra* Article I, note 3, vol. 1, pp. 78, 599; *id.* at vol. 2, p. 771.

however, by an 8-to-25 vote. Ells's opponents argued, for example, that his suggested addition was unnecessary because schools never turned away indigent children, that Ells's amendment risked unduly restricting local officials' ability to decide how to allocate funds between schools' winter and summer sessions, and that the state did not yet have the resources to guarantee all children a free education.[23]

In its most important ruling on Section 3 to date, the Iowa Supreme Court held in 2012's *King v. State* that the provision's first sentence (sometimes called "the education clause") merely gives the General Assembly the authority to allocate resources for education; it does not create judicially enforceable educational standards that the state's schools must meet. In *Kleen v. Porter* (1946), the court similarly concluded that Section 3's opening sentence gives the legislature broad power to allocate funds as it sees fit for the benefit of Iowans' education. In *Monona County v. Waples* (1935), the court relied upon Section 3 and other authorities when concluding that a mortgage given to Monona County in exchange for a loan from the state's permanent school fund was superior to a competing mortgage. Although the case was decided on statutory grounds, readers interested in Section 3's reference to the estates of individuals who die without wills or heirs might wish to read *McKeown v. Morrow* (1918), a case concerning the rightful owner of interest earned on estate funds that—absent the eventual appearance of the decedent's heir—would have been placed in the state's permanent school fund.

The Office of the Attorney General has issued opinions concerning Section 3 on only a few occasions. In 1939, for example, Attorney General John Rankin relied upon this provision and other authorities when advising a state senator that proposed legislation would impermissibly permit county officials to disregard their duty to preserve the state's permanent school fund.[24] Attorney General John Mitchell had provided similar advice two years earlier.[25]

Section 4.
Fines—how appropriated.

[Repealed.]

Section 4 concerned "[t]he money which may have been or shall be paid by persons as an equivalent for exemption from military duty, and the clear proceeds of all fines collected in the several Counties for any breach of the penal laws." The provision authorized the now-defunct board of education[26] to allocate

[23] *1857 Debates, supra* Article I, note 3, vol. 2, pp. 968–72.

[24] Op. Iowa Att'y Gen., 1939 WL 77084 (Mar. 16, 1939) (replying to Hugh Lundy).

[25] Op. Iowa Att'y Gen., 1937 WL 67691 (Mar. 4, 1937) (replying to L.H. Doran).

[26] For more on Iowa's first board of education, see the opening paragraphs of commentary on this article.

those funds among the state's counties pursuant to a prescribed formula. Iowans repealed the provision in 1974, thereby giving lawmakers greater flexibility.

Section 5.
Proceeds of lands.

The General Assembly shall take measures for the protection, improvement, or other disposition of such lands as have been, or may hereafter be reserved, or granted by the United States, or any person or persons, to this State, for the use of the University, and the funds accruing from the rents or sale of such lands, or from any other source for the purpose aforesaid, shall be, and remain, a permanent fund, the interest of which shall be applied to the support of said University, for the promotion of literature, the arts and sciences, as may be authorized by the terms of such grant. And it shall be the duty of the General Assembly as soon as may be, to provide effectual means for the improvement and permanent security of the funds of said University.

Together with Section 2 of this article, Section 5 aims to secure a permanent financial foundation for the State University of Iowa, commonly known since the 1960s as the University of Iowa.[27] The provision is virtually identical to one found in the state's 1846 constitution.[28] For an example of early legislation aimed at carrying out the charge that appears in Section 5's final sentence, see the legislation cited in the appended footnote.[29]

The Iowa Supreme Court has not been called upon to resolve disagreements about Section 5's meaning. Citing Sections 2 and 5 of this article, Attorney General Edward O'Connor advised the Iowa State Board of Education in 1936 that, after the board foreclosed on a mortgage that it had obtained in exchange for a loan from the permanent fund, the board was authorized to use a reasonable portion of the permanent fund's principal to make improvements to the land.[30] In 1935, O'Connor advised the board that it could purchase insurance on the real estate it held pursuant to this provision.[31]

---

[27] For more on the University of Iowa's origins, see the commentary on Section 2 of this article and on Article XI, Section 8.

[28] Iowa Const. of 1846, art. X, § 5. The one notable difference is that, unlike the provision one sees above, the 1846 text indicated that the university would have "such branches as the public convenience may hereafter demand." That phrase had already been removed when the Committee on Education and School Lands presented its first draft at the 1857 convention. *1857 Debates, supra* Article I, note 3, vol. 1, pp. 78, 599. The committee's draft was not controversial among the delegates. *See id.* at vol. 2, pp. 771–72.

[29] Act of Mar. 21, 1864, ch. 59, §§ 9, 12, 16, 17, 1864 Iowa Acts 63.

[30] Op. Iowa Att'y Gen., 1936 WL 68638 (Apr. 8, 1936) (replying to the Iowa State Board of Education).

[31] Op. Iowa Att'y Gen., 1935 WL 60791 (July 24, 1935) (replying to the Iowa State Board of Education).

Section 6.
Agents of school funds.

The financial agents of the school funds shall be the same, that by law, receive and control the State and county revenue for other civil purposes, under such regulations as may be provided by law.

Section 6 ensures that the same individuals who control state and county revenue for other civil purposes will be the same individuals responsible for school funds. With the exception of the clause that appears after the final comma, the provision still reads as initially proposed by the Committee on Education and School Lands at the 1857 constitutional convention.[32] The committee added the final clause on its own initiative later in the convention's proceedings.[33] The provision was not controversial among the delegates.[34]

The Iowa Supreme Court and the Office of the Attorney General have deployed Section 6 on only a handful of occasions. In *McColl v. Dallas County* (1935), for example, Section 6 was among the authorities that the court cited when concluding that certain property belonged to Dallas County and thus was statutorily exempt from taxation. In 1938, Attorney General John Mitchell concluded that Section 6 did not bar transferring custodianship of Iowa State University's endowment funds from the state's treasurer to the university's own treasurer.[35]

Section 7.
Distribution.

[Repealed.]

Section 7 stated that "[t]he money subject to the support and maintenance of common schools shall be distributed to the districts in proportion to the number of youths, between the ages of five and twenty-one years, in such manner as may be provided by the General Assembly." Iowans repealed this provision in 1984, thereby giving the legislature greater flexibility.

---

32 *1857 Debates, supra* Article I, note 3, vol. 1, pp. 79, 599.

33 *1857 Debates, supra* Article I, note 3, vol. 2, p. 872.

34 *1857 Debates, supra* Article I, note 3, vol. 2, pp. 967–68.

35 Op. Iowa Att'y Gen., 1938 WL 67285 (Dec. 27, 1938) (replying to M.R. Pierson).

Article X

Amendments to the Constitution

Section 1.
How proposed—submission.

Any amendment or amendments to this Constitution may be proposed in either House of the General Assembly; and if the same shall be agreed to by a majority of the members elected to each of the two Houses, such proposed amendment shall be entered on their journals, with the yeas and nays taken thereon, and referred to the Legislature to be chosen at the next general election, and shall be published, as provided by law, for three months previous to the time of making such choice; and if, in the General Assembly so next chosen as aforesaid, such proposed amendment or amendments shall be agreed to, by a majority of all the members elected to each House, then it shall be the duty of the General Assembly to submit such proposed amendment or amendments to the people, in such manner, and at such time as the General Assembly shall provide; and if the people shall approve and ratify such amendment or amendments, by a majority of the electors qualified to vote for members of the General Assembly, voting thereon, such amendment or amendments shall become a part of the Constitution of this State.

Complementing Section 3 of this article, which gives Iowans the opportunity every ten years to decide whether to hold a constitutional convention, Section 1 establishes a more targeted amendment method.[1] Modeled closely

[1] Various statutes concern Section 1's amendment process. *See,* e.g., Iowa Code §§ 49.43–.45, 49A. The U.S. Constitution similarly offers two different methods of launching the amendment process—one

on the New York Constitution of 1846,[2] this provision states that a proposed amendment becomes part of the constitution if it secures the approval of both houses of the General Assembly on two different occasions (with an intervening general election) and then is approved by the Iowa electorate. Under the state's 1846 constitution, there had been only one means by which the constitution's text could be changed: if the legislature decided that a constitutional amendment was in order, its sole recourse was to give Iowans an opportunity to vote on whether to call a constitutional convention.[3] When the 1846 text was placed before Iowans for approval, William Penn Clarke—a Whig who would later represent Johnson County at the 1857 convention—unsuccessfully urged voters to reject it, arguing (among other things) that the drafters had intentionally made their proposed constitution exceptionally difficult to change.[4] At the 1857 convention, in language substantively identical to what one sees in Section 1 today, the Committee on Amendments proposed that lawmakers and Iowans be given an additional amendment mechanism.[5] Although Clarke tried to change the committee's proposal in certain respects,[6] he was among the majority who ultimately concluded that the committee's draft struck the right balance between making a more streamlined amendment process available while nevertheless "guard[ing] . . . against any hasty changes in the fundamental law."[7]

In *Koehler v. Hill* (1883)—the Iowa Supreme Court's first and most important Section 1 ruling—the justices declared invalid an amendment purporting to bar individuals from manufacturing and selling alcoholic beverages in the state. The court identified two flaws in the path that the amendment had taken: in the legislature that first proposed the amendment, the house's journal did not recite the text that the representatives had approved, and the senate's journal recited a version of the amendment that was worded differently than the version approved by the next General Assembly and then by the electorate at large. The

by calling a convention and one by proposing specific amendments—but neither method calls for placing any matter before the electorate for a direct decision. *See* U.S. Const. art. V.

[2] N.Y. Const. of 1846, art. XIII, § 1; *see also 1857 Debates, supra* Article I, note 3, vol. 1, p. 616 (acknowledging the debt to New York).

[3] Iowa Const. of 1846, art. XI.

[4] *1844 and 1846 Fragments, supra* Article I, note 3, pp. 358–61. The editors of the *Iowa Standard* argued that the 1846 constitution's framers had intended to make it difficult for Iowans to remove the constitution's ban on allowing corporations and others to issue paper designed to circulate as currency. *Id.* at 365–67. For more on the currency debate, see Part I and the commentary on Article VIII, Section 5.

[5] *1857 Debates, supra* Article I, note 3, vol. 1, p. 603.

[6] *1857 Debates, supra* Article I, note 3, vol. 1, pp. 620, 639.

[7] *1857 Debates, supra* Article I, note 3, vol. 1, p. 603; *see also id.* at vol. 2, p. 1033 (recording the delegates' final vote). The delegates rejected numerous proposals to alter the committee's draft. *See id.* at vol. 1, pp. 603–22, 639.

reason why Section 1 requires the first legislature's two chambers to "enter [the amendment] on their journals, with the yeas and nays taken thereon," the court explained, is "to leave no reasonable doubt" about the proposed amendment's precise contents. It is not sufficient for either house of the first legislature merely to refer to the amendment in its journal "by title, or other descriptive words." In *State ex rel. Bailey v. Brookhart* (1901), the court struck down another amendment, finding that the first legislature's house of representatives had again failed to enter the amendment's text in its journal.

The court has found that Section 1 provides greater flexibility in other areas. In *Jones v. McClaughry* (1915), the court concluded that it is permissible for each house of the legislature to vote on a single resolution containing multiple proposed amendments; Section 1 does not require either house to vote on each individual amendment separately. In *Olander v. Hollowell* (1922), the second legislature to approve an amendment had not itself formally approved a resolution referring the amendment to the electorate; instead, the amendment had been placed before Iowa voters pursuant to the procedures specified in a previously enacted statute. The court held that Section 1's requirements had been met. "[I]t is entirely proper and legal," the court wrote, "for a legislature to provide by general, instead of special, legislation for submitting constitutional amendments to the people."

The Office of the Attorney General has issued several noteworthy opinions concerning Section 1. In 2000, the office concluded that, if Iowa voters reject a proposed amendment, that same proposal cannot be placed before Iowa voters again until it has once again been approved by successive legislatures.[8] In 1986, the office responded to a query which pointed out that one General Assembly had approved a resolution containing two amendments and the next General Assembly had approved only one of those amendments. Had the amendment approved by the second legislature met Section 1's requirement that it be approved by successive General Assemblies, even though it had been packaged in a resolution containing a rejected amendment? The office concluded that it had.[9] In 1968, Attorney General Richard Turner concluded that Section 1 requires that the full text of a proposed amendment appear on voters' ballots, but those ballots need not recite all additional language appearing in the resolutions approved by the General Assembly.[10] In 1933, Attorney General Edward O'Connor determined that the General Assembly has the power to approve proposed amendments at regular and special sessions alike.[11]

---

[8] Op. Iowa Att'y Gen., 2000 WL 33258472 (Apr. 3, 2000) (replying to Gary Blodgett).

[9] Op. Iowa Att'y Gen., 1986 WL 79955 (Feb. 20, 1986) (replying to Clay Spear, Linda Beatty, and Horace Daggett).

[10] Op. Iowa Att'y Gen., 1968 WL 172624 (June 24, 1968) (replying to Robert Landess).

[11] Op. Iowa Att'y Gen., 1933 WL 66203 (Feb. 17, 1933) (replying to the Senate Chamber).

Section 2.
More than one amendment.

If two or more amendments shall be submitted at the same time, they shall be submitted in such manner that the electors shall vote for or against each of such amendments separately.

Section 2 ensures that Iowa voters need not accept or reject a group of proposed amendments as an undifferentiated block; instead, they can choose individual winners and losers. The provision was not part of the set of proposals initially made by the Committee on Amendments at the 1857 convention.[12] Rather, it emerged from suggestions made by Des Moines County's Jonathan Hall, Henry County's Rufus Clarke, and Jefferson County's James Wilson.[13]

The Iowa Supreme Court's leading ruling on Section 2 is *Lobaugh v. Cook* (1905). The court in that case explained that Section 2 is based upon the acknowledgment that "[t]he elector, in voting for or against [a proposed amendment], is limited to ratifying or rejecting the proposition in its entirety, and cannot be put in a position where he may be compelled, in order to aid in carrying a proposition his judgment approves, to vote for another he would otherwise reject." In a passage worth quoting in full, the court described the line that must be drawn when trying to discern whether a proposed amendment containing multiple components violates Section 2:

> Modifications such as are merely incidental to the main purpose and object sought to be attained [by the amendment] are to be included, as essential to the preservation of the symmetry and harmony of the Constitution as a whole. Otherwise great confusion would be possible, from the adoption of some and rejection of other incidental changes necessary to accomplish the purpose proposed. It follows that, while an amendment can have but one main object, it should include such additional provisions as are essential, upon its ratification by the people, to render it consistent with other portions of the Constitution. Under the guise of accomplishing this, however, it cannot be loaded with matters not related to or necessarily connected therewith. . . .
>
> . . . If the amendment has but one object and purpose, and all else included therein is incidental thereto, and reasonably necessary to effect the object and purpose contemplated, it is not [vulnerable] to the charge of containing more than one amendment.

Applying those standards, the *Lobaugh* court concluded that a single amendment had permissibly addressed various matters relating to the amendment's central purpose of ensuring that all biennial general elections would be held only in even-numbered years. In *Jones v. McClaughry* (1915), the court similarly

[12] *1857 Debates, supra* Article I, note 3, vol. 1, p. 603.

[13] *1857 Debates, supra* Article I, note 3, vol. 1, pp. 618–19, 621, 626, 638–39.

concluded that the contents of a single amendment were all sufficiently related to the amendment's chief purpose of prescribing the ways in which criminal prosecutions may be launched.

A proposed amendment ran into conflict with *Lobaugh*'s principles in *Mathews v. Turner* (1931). In that case, Iowa voters were poised to cast ballots on a proposed amendment authorizing the state to issue $100 million in bonds for road and highway improvements. Beyond merely authorizing that indebtedness, however, the amendment also contained provisions that a voter favoring the bond authorization might oppose, such as provisions relating to the issuance and payment of counties' road bonds and provisions regarding roads' numbering and location. Because the proposed amendment contained "two or more propositions upon which a voter might desire to vote differently," the proposal would thus be invalid even if Iowa voters approved it. The court held that the forthcoming election should accordingly be enjoined.[14]

The Office of the Attorney General has issued a handful of significant opinions concerning Section 2, all of them drawing upon *Lobaugh*. In 1988, the office advised a lawmaker that a proposed amendment violated this provision because the proposal served "distinct and separate purposes" on which a voter might wish to split his or her ballot—namely, defining how the lieutenant governor should be selected and defining the duties that the lieutenant governor should perform.[15] In 1970, Attorney General Richard Turner advised a lawmaker that a proposed amendment did not violate Section 2; even though it would have the effect of changing multiple existing constitutional provisions, the entirety of the amendment concerned the single purpose of shifting numerous state officials from two-year terms to four-year terms.[16] Several days earlier, Turner had similarly given the office's blessing to a proposed amendment whose details all concerned "the privileges and duties of persons over the age of nineteen years."[17] (Turner's opinion in that instance exemplifies the difficulties of drawing lines in this area. Might not an Iowa voter have reasonably believed that persons nineteen years of age should have the right to vote but should not have the right to buy alcohol, or vice versa? Both of those rights, in addition to others, were encompassed by the proposed amendment.) In 1967, Turner concluded that two separate amendments were required to change the length of the lieutenant governor's term and to require candidates for the governorship and lieutenant governorship to appear on ballots as indivisible two-person teams.[18]

---

[14] Several months earlier, Attorney General John Fletcher had similarly concluded that the proposed amendment violated Section 2. Op. Iowa Att'y Gen., 1931 WL 69808 (Jan. 28, 1931) (replying to the Iowa House of Representatives).

[15] Op. Iowa Att'y Gen., 1988 WL 247788 (June 7, 1988) (replying to Rod Halvorson).

[16] Op. Iowa Att'y Gen., 1970 WL 207581 (Jan. 30, 1970) (replying to Minnette Doderer).

[17] Op. Iowa Att'y Gen., 1970 WL 207573 (Jan. 22, 1970) (replying to William Gannon).

[18] Op. Iowa Att'y Gen., 1967 WL 167015 (Feb. 6, 1967) (replying to Seeley Lodwick).

Section 3.
Constitutional convention.

At the general election to be held in the year one thousand nine hundred and seventy, and in each tenth year thereafter, and also at such times as the General Assembly may, by law, provide, the question, "Shall there be a convention to revise the constitution, and propose amendment or amendments to same?" shall be decided by the electors qualified to vote for members of the General Assembly; and in case a majority of the electors so qualified, voting at such election, for and against such proposition, shall decide in favor of a Convention for such purpose, the General Assembly, at its next session, shall provide by law for the election of delegates to such Convention, and for submitting the results of said Convention to the people, in such manner and at such time as the General Assembly shall provide; and if the people shall approve and ratify such amendment or amendments, by a majority of the electors qualified to vote for members of the General Assembly, voting thereon, such amendment or amendments shall become a part of the constitution of this state. If two or more amendments shall be submitted at the same time, they shall be submitted in such a manner that electors may vote for or against each such amendment separately.

Section 3 gives Iowa voters the opportunity every ten years (and on other occasions selected by the General Assembly) to decide whether to hold a constitutional convention for the purpose of revising or proposing amendments to the Iowa Constitution.[19] Under the state's first constitution, ratified in 1846, Iowans could cast ballots on that question only if the General Assembly opted to place it before them.[20] At the 1857 constitutional convention—a convention called pursuant to that 1846 provision—the delegates ensured that the convention question would be placed before voters every ten years with or without the approval of the General Assembly. To understand Section 3's drafting history, we need to draw a line after the phrase that appears midway through the passage, stating "shall provide by law for the election of delegates to such convention." Iowa voters added the text appearing after that imaginary line in 1964. In that same 1964 amendment, Iowans also made two changes to the text appearing before the line we have drawn: they established 1970 as the baseline year (replacing the 1857 text's reference to 1870), and they made it clear that a convention may propose amendments but cannot itself formally elevate amendments to constitutional status.[21] The remainder of the first half of Section 3 still reads as originally

---

[19] The General Assembly has adopted legislation concerning Section 3. *See, e.g.*, Iowa Code § 39.4. For a relatively early effort to describe the prevailing rules for (and mechanics of) constitutional conventions in Iowa, see John F. Sly, "Providing for a State Constitutional Convention," 19 *Iowa Journal of History & Politics* 3 (1921).

[20] Iowa Const. of 1846, art. XI.

[21] In contrast to what Section 3 says today, the 1857 version of Section 3 stated that, every ten years, Iowans would be asked "the question, 'Shall there be a Convention to revise the Constitution, and amend the same?'"

proposed by the 1857 convention's Committee on Amendments,[22] with one exception. Jefferson County's James Wilson pointed out that, under the committee's draft, a convention would be called only if a majority of all qualified voters in Iowa cast ballots in favor of doing so. At his suggestion, the convention lowered the bar, such that a convention is called if a majority of those actually casting ballots on the issue indicate that they wish to do so.[23]

Section 3 has not yet been the focus of appellate litigation. The Office of the Attorney General has issued only a few opinions concerning the provision's requirements.[24] In 1970, for example, Attorney General Richard Turner advised the Deputy Secretary of State that it is permissible for the convention question to be presented to voters on voting machines, rather than on separate paper ballots.[25]

---

[22] *1857 Debates, supra* Article I, note 3, vol. 1, p. 603.

[23] *1857 Debates, supra* Article I, note 3, vol. 2, pp. 1031–33. The vote on Wilson's proposal (18 to 14) was closer than one might initially expect. The opposition was driven by some delegates' belief that it ought to be very difficult to call a convention and that calling the 1857 convention had itself been contrary to the will of a majority of Iowans, even though a majority of those actually voting on the matter had favored it. *See id.*

[24] For an opinion on various statutory issues concerning Section 3 and campaign finance, see Op. Iowa Att'y Gen., 1980 WL 26087 (Nov. 18, 1980) (replying to Julia Gentleman).

[25] Op. Iowa Att'y Gen., 1970 WL 207617 (Mar. 13, 1970) (replying to Robert Landess). The office had reached the same conclusion ten years earlier. Op. Iowa Att'y Gen., 1960 WL 106900 (July 20, 1960) (replying to Melvin Synhorst).

Article XI

Miscellaneous

Section 1.
Justice of peace—jurisdiction.

The jurisdiction of Justices of the Peace shall extend to all civil cases, (except cases in chancery, and cases where the question of title to real estate may arise,) where the amount in controversy does not exceed one hundred dollars, and by the consent of the parties may be extended to any amount not exceeding three hundred dollars.

Section 1 defines the jurisdictional reach of justices of the peace. The delegates to Iowa's 1857 constitutional convention carried over the provision virtually verbatim from the state's first constitution, ratified in 1846. The one notable difference concerns the upper limit on the amounts in controversy that, with the parties' consent, justices of the peace are authorized to adjudicate: the 1857 convention reduced that ceiling from $500 to $300.[1] That figure, as well as the usual upper limit of $100, flowed from the delegates' belief that justices of the peace should be settling "neighborhood difficulties" (as Allamakee County's John Clark put it), rather than cases of "much importance."[2]

[1] *Cf.* Iowa Const. of 1846, art. XII, § 1.

[2] *1857 Debates, supra* Article I, note 3, vol. 2, pp. 795–98, 810–11.

Alas, the delegates' debate has no bearing on Iowa's judicial system today. The General Assembly abolished the position of justice of the peace in 1972.[3] For a quick sense of the many duties that holders of that office executed prior to 1972, one may scan the five pages devoted to justices of the peace in the index to the 1971 Iowa Code.

Section 2.
Counties.

> No new County shall be hereafter created containing less than four hundred and thirty two square miles; nor shall the territory of any organized county be reduced below that area; except the County of Worth, and counties west of it, along the Northern boundary of this State, may be organized without additional territory.

With the exceptions noted at the end of the provision, Section 2 establishes the minimum geographic size of Iowa's counties. The 432-square-mile minimum was first set by the state's 1846 constitution, then redeployed (with the addition of the exception-creating language that follows the second semicolon) at the 1857 constitutional convention.[4] The exception for Worth County and its neighbors was added at the suggestion of the humbly named Committee on Miscellaneous Subjects. Explaining the need for these exceptions, Johnson County's William Penn Clarke said that recent surveys had revealed that some of these counties contained fewer than 432 square miles, and the committee did not want to force them to reorganize with altered boundaries. Clayton County's Alpheus Scott urged the delegates either to omit Section 2 altogether or to allow regions to create smaller counties when they contained cities populated by 5,000 or more inhabitants. Scott argued that large cities were sometimes prone to impose heavy property taxes that burdened rural landowners for the benefit of urban projects, and that many rural communities thus would be better off if they and their nearby cities weren't compelled to share the same local governmental umbrella. Scott's motion was rejected by an unrecorded margin, and the provision remained otherwise uncontroversial.[5]

Citing Section 2's unambiguous requirements, the Iowa Supreme Court in 1871's *Garfield v. Brayton* struck down a statute purporting to create an undersized Crocker County. (The legislature had attempted to carve that area out of Kossuth County, which remains Iowa's geographically largest county today.) Section 2 has not otherwise been the focus of appellate litigation. The Office of

---

[3] Act of Apr. 20, 1972, ch. 1124, § 2, 1972 Iowa Acts 444.

[4] *Cf.* Iowa Const. of 1846, art. XII, § 2.

[5] *1857 Debates, supra* Article I, note 3, vol. 2, pp. 798–800.

the Attorney General has peripherally cited the provision in opinions concerning issues of county governance.[6]

Section 3.
Indebtedness of political or municipal corporations.

No county, or other political or municipal corporation shall be allowed to become indebted in any manner, or for any purpose, to an amount, in the aggregate, exceeding five per centum on the value of the taxable property within such county or corporation—to be ascertained by the last State and county tax lists, previous to the incurring of such indebtedness.

Section 3 caps the amount of debt that counties and the state's other incorporated political subdivisions[7] may incur, thereby complementing the limitation on *state* debt that one finds in Section 2 of Article VII. The provision's overarching purpose is "to prevent the general taxes of a political subdivision from becoming overburdened by obligations" (*Richards v. City of Muscatine*, 1975). Many of the state's municipalities, "while yet in swaddling clothes, had become overburdened with debt" (*N.W. Halsey & Co. v. City of Belle Plaine*, 1905). Like their counterparts in other states, Iowa's constitutional framers were especially troubled by "the reckless voting of benefits and bonuses to railway companies," which reduced the money available for other purposes (*Interstate Power Co. v. Town of McGregor*, 1941).

Section 3's drafting origins are rooted in the delegates' discussion of Section 4 of Article VIII, which declares that "[n]o political or municipal corporation shall become a stockholder in any banking corporation, directly or indirectly." As this volume's commentary on that provision explains, the 1857 convention's Committee on Incorporations had proposed expanding Section 4 to bar cities and counties from incurring more than $200,000 in debt.[8] That proposal sparked a lengthy debate, in the midst of which John Edwards—a lawyer from Lucas County—proposed that cities and counties be permitted to hold stock in non-banking corporations, so long as the aggregate amount of a municipality's stock investments did not "exceed ten per cent of the taxable property" in that city or county.[9] Later in that same debate, Henry County's Rufus Clarke proposed that cities' and counties' debts be capped at an amount equal to five

[6] Op. Iowa Att'y Gen., 1986 WL 79990 (Nov. 10, 1986) (replying to Berl Priebe); Op. Iowa Att'y Gen., 1979 WL 21073 (Sept. 14, 1979) (replying to G.A. Cady III).

[7] Section 3 applies to all incorporated political entities. The focus is usually on cities and counties, though in some instances the focus lies elsewhere. *See, e.g., Winspear v. District Township of Holman* (1873) (applying Section 3 to school-district townships). For convenience, this commentary often refers to all covered entities as municipalities.

[8] Prior to offering that proposal, the committee suggested leaving the question of municipal debt limits to the General Assembly. *1857 Debates, supra* Article I, note 3, vol. 1, p. 96.

[9] *1857 Debates, supra* Article I, note 3, vol. 1, p. 295.

percent of their property's taxable value.[10] The delegates ultimately decided to narrow Article VIII's Section 4 so that it serves only to bar municipal investments in banking corporations. When the delegates turned their attention to miscellaneous subjects here in Article XI, Edwards revived Clarke's proposal, offering language that is virtually identical to what one finds in Section 3 today. Without revisiting their earlier debate about municipal debt limits, the delegates approved Edwards's motion on a 19-to-16 vote.[11]

Section 3 has generated a large body of litigation, some of the details of which are beyond the scope of the overarching summary that follows. One important line of cases concerns what counts as a debt for purposes of this provision.[12] The Iowa Supreme Court has explained that a municipality creates a Section 3 debt only if the municipality has a "legally enforceable obligation to continue repayments in the future" (*Fults v. City of Coralville*, 2003). As the court put it in 1878's *Burlington Water Co. v. Woodward*, no debt exists if the existence of a legal obligation "depends upon some act of the city, or upon its volition to be exercised or determined at some future day." Bonds do not count toward a municipality's debt for purposes of Section 3 if they will be retired using revenues from municipal enterprises, rather than taxes (*Interstate Power Co. v. Town of McGregor*, 1941; *Wyatt v. Town of Manning*, 1933). Neither does a municipality create a Section 3 debt when it finances an improvement (such as a street) by giving the contractor the right to collect payment from those owning land adjacent to the improvement (*Corey v. City of Fort Dodge*, 1907; *Davis v. City of Des Moines*, 1887). When calculating its current debt, a municipality may deduct from its obligations all revenues (from taxes or from other sources) that it will receive during that fiscal period (*Banta v. Clarke County*, 1935; *French v. City of Burlington*, 1876), as well as the cash it already has on hand (*Miller v. City of Glenwood*, 1920). Section 3 does not insulate a municipality from tort judgments that push the municipality beyond its debt limit (*Fort Dodge Electric Light & Power Co. v. City of Fort Dodge*, 1902; *Thomas v. City of Burlington*, 1886). A municipality cannot evade Section 3's debt limit by dividing its general revenues into distinct pots of money and declaring that the municipality's liability for a given bond issue is limited to the funds in just one of those pots (*Richards v. City of Muscatine*, 1975; *Brunk v. City of Des Moines*, 1940).[13]

The Office of the Attorney General has similarly weighed in on how to calculate a municipality's debt in a given year. In 1972, for example, Attorney General Richard Turner determined that, when a city enters a multiyear lease

---

[10] *1857 Debates, supra* Article I, note 3, vol. 1, p. 343.

[11] *1857 Debates, supra* Article I, note 3, vol. 2, p. 812.

[12] Principles similar to those described here apply when determining whether the *state* has exceeded its constitutionally imposed debt limit. For those principles, see this volume's commentary on Article VII, § 2.

[13] *Accord* Op. Iowa Att'y Gen., 1989 WL 264892 (May 30, 1989) (replying to Allan Thoms).

for property it wishes to occupy, only the amount that the city owes for a given year of occupancy—and not the aggregate total of all payments it will make over the life of the lease—counts toward that year's existing debt.[14] Turner further concluded, however, that the rule is the opposite when the city is making multiyear installment payments toward purchasing a piece of property, rather than merely leasing it.

With respect to what counts as a city's or county's taxable property, the Iowa Supreme Court has determined that it includes both real and personal property (*Miller v. City of Glenwood*, 1920). In rulings that give municipalities greater debt-incurring freedom than they would have under a contrary arrangement, the court has said that the calculation required by Section 3 is based upon the full assessed value of a municipality's taxable property (as reflected on the municipality's most recent tax list), rather than any lesser portion of that full value that lawmakers may have decided to take into account when levying taxes (*Miller v. City of Glenwood*, 1920; *N.W. Halsey & Co. v. City of Belle Plaine*, 1905).

The General Assembly has enacted a detailed regulatory regime concerning county and city finances,[15] thereby rendering constitutional litigation regarding municipal debt less common than it was in earlier years.

Section 4.
Boundaries of state.

The boundaries of the State may be enlarged, with the consent of Congress and the General Assembly.

As Part I and the commentary on the opening section of the Iowa Constitution titled "Preamble and Boundaries" explains, issues concerning the state's borders played a leading role in the story of Iowa's entry into the Union. Proposed without controversy by the Committee on Miscellaneous Subjects at the 1857 convention,[16] Section 4 allows Iowa's current boundaries to be expanded, should any surrounding state find itself wishing to unload some of its territory and should the necessary approvals be obtained. The provision has never been the focus of opinions issued by the Iowa Supreme Court or the Office of the Attorney General.

Section 5.
Oath of office.

Every person elected or appointed to any office, shall, before entering upon the duties thereof, take an oath or affirmation to support the Constitution of the United States, and of this State, and also an oath of office.

---

[14] Op. Iowa Att'y Gen., 1972 WL 262444 (Sept. 26, 1972) (replying to Dennis Freeman).

[15] *See*, e.g., Iowa Code chs. 331 (counties), 384 (cities).

[16] *1857 Debates, supra* Article I, note 3, vol. 2, pp. 648, 800.

Section 5 requires all state and local officeholders to take oaths or affirmations before beginning to perform their jobs. Iowa's first constitution, ratified in 1846, had prescribed oaths for members of the General Assembly,[17] but had not required oaths of other state or local officials. Shortly after the 1846 constitution's adoption, the General Assembly enacted legislation requiring oaths of all civil officers.[18] At the 1857 constitutional convention, the Committee on Miscellaneous Subjects proposed precisely the language one sees here, constitutionally requiring oaths of all officeholders.[19] The committee's proposal was not controversial among the delegates.[20]

The Iowa Supreme Court has not squarely defined the term "office" as it appears in Section 5, and so it sometimes might not be clear whether an individual is required to take an oath or affirmation pursuant to this provision. In a possibly instructive case dating back to the close of the nineteenth century, however, the court identified criteria for determining whether a person is a "public officer" within the meaning of a legislative enactment (*State v. Spaulding*, 1897).[21] The court concluded that a person holds public office if his or her governmental position was created (and his or her duties were defined) by the constitution, by legislation, or by a board or commission lawfully acting pursuant to legislation, and if the person has been tasked with exercising some of the government's sovereign functions for the public's benefit.

The Office of the Attorney General has concluded that a person elected to fill a particular office creates a vacancy if he or she refuses to take the oath or affirmation required by Section 5.[22] Taking the required oath or affirmation, in other words, is the legal means by which individuals signify that they accept the offices that voters or others have offered to them.[23] In 1966, Attorney General Lawrence Scalise indicated that municipal law-enforcement officers must comply with Section 5's requirements.[24]

---

[17] Iowa Const. of 1846, art. IV, § 30.

[18] Code of Iowa (1851), §§ 320 (governor), 322 (judges), 331 (civil officers who are "required to give bond"), 332 (civil officers who are "not required to give bond").

[19] The committee's proposal tracked almost verbatim the corresponding provisions of the Indiana Constitution of 1851 and the Ohio Constitution of 1851. *See* Ind. Const. of 1851, art. XV, § 4; Ohio Const. of 1851, art. XV, § 7.

[20] *1857 Debates, supra* Article I, note 3, vol. 2, p. 800.

[21] The court subsequently relied upon *Spaulding* in *McKinley v. Clarke County* (1940), another statutory case.

[22] Op. Iowa Att'y Gen., 1996 WL 399717 (Apr. 16, 1996) (replying to R.K. Richardson).

[23] Op. Iowa Att'y Gen., 1905 WL 50245 (Dec. 29, 1905) (replying to Gov. A.B. Cummins).

[24] Op. Iowa Att'y Gen., 1966 WL 155330 (Oct. 6, 1966) (replying to C.F. Greenfield).

Section 6.
How vacancies filled.

In all cases of elections to fill vacancies in office occurring before the expiration of a full term, the person so elected shall hold for the residue of the unexpired term; and all persons appointed to fill vacancies in office, shall hold until the next general election, and until their successors are elected and qualified.

Section 6 establishes the lengths of time that those specially elected or appointed to fill vacancies will serve.[25] The 1857 constitutional convention's Committee on Miscellaneous Subjects proposed the provision without apparent controversy.[26] Various statutes supplement the constitution's treatment of vacancies.[27]

An office is vacant within the meaning of Section 6 not merely when the office's prior holder has died, resigned, or otherwise departed, but also when the office has been newly created (*Schaffner v. Shaw*, 1920).[28] With respect to all vacancies, no matter what their cause, Section 6 distinguishes between those vacancy-fillers who are chosen in special elections and those who are appointed. Regarding the former, the Iowa Supreme Court pointed out in *Wilson v. Shaw* (1922) that the elected individual serves the "unexpired portion" of the term that his or her predecessor did not complete.[29] Regarding Section 6's provision concerning appointments, the court has explained that the phrase "next general election" refers to "the next general election at which, in pursuance of law, a vacancy may legally be filled" (*State ex rel. Halbach v. Claussen*, 1933).[30] As Attorney General Richard Turner noted in a 1971 opinion, a person who is appointed to fill a vacancy might thus reach the end of his or her tenure prior to the end of the term that his or her predecessor was slated to serve.[31] Attorney General Dayton Countryman explained in 1955 that the reason for treating special-election-winners more favorably than appointees is that, while the former have secured voters' approval, the latter are to hold their jobs "only until the electorate has had an opportunity to make a selection."[32]

---

[25] Readers interested in issues concerning vacancies should also consult Article IV, Section 10, which gives the governor the power to appoint individuals to fill vacancies "[w]hen . . . no mode is provided by the constitution and laws for filling such vacancy. . . ."

[26] *1857 Debates, supra* Article I, note 3, vol. 2, pp. 648, 800–01, 811.

[27] *See, e.g.*, Iowa Code §§ 39.8, 46.5; ch. 69.

[28] *Accord State ex rel. Freeman v. Carvey* (1915) ("[W]henever an office exists and there is no incumbent to perform its functitons, there is a vacancy."). For an example of a vacancy arising due to lawmakers' creation of a new office, see Op. Iowa Att'y Gen., 1957 WL 95487 (Sept. 23, 1957) (replying to Gov. Herschel Loveless).

[29] *Accord* Op. Iowa Att'y Gen., 1974 WL 353744 (Apr. 5, 1974) (replying to Edward Wehr).

[30] For examples of this principle's application, see Op. Iowa Att'y Gen., 1961 WL 110146 (Feb. 16, 1961) (replying to Fritz Goreham); Op. Iowa Att'y Gen., 1960 WL 106915 (Aug. 5, 1960) (replying to C.F. Greenfield).

[31] Op. Iowa Att'y Gen., 1971 WL 240822 (Sept. 1, 1971) (replying to Murray Lawson).

[32] Op. Iowa Att'y Gen., 1955 WL 78386 (Jan. 7, 1955) (replying to Francis Fitzgibbons).

Section 7.
Land grants located.

The General Assembly shall not locate any of the public lands, which have been, or may be granted by Congress to this State, and the location of which may be given to the General Assembly, upon lands actually settled, without the consent of the occupant. The extent of the claim of such occupant, so exempted, shall not exceed three hundred and twenty acres.

Carrying the provision over from Iowa's 1846 constitution,[33] a slim majority of the delegates to the state's 1857 constitutional convention concluded that Section 7 was necessary to protect the rights of settlers who staked claims on federal lands.[34] Neither the Iowa Supreme Court nor the Office of the Attorney General has issued any published opinions concerning Section 7—and, given the provision's antiquated subject matter, they are unlikely to do so in the future. Although Section 7 did not play a role in the case's resolution, *Bellows v. Todd* (1874) illustrates the kinds of land disputes sometimes faced by those who settled on federal lands in the mid-nineteenth century.

Section 8.
Seat of government established—state university.

The seat of Government is hereby permanently established, as now fixed by law, at the City of Des Moines, in the County of Polk; and the State University, at Iowa City, in the County of Johnson.

Resolving one of the most famous geographic disputes in Iowa's early history, Section 8 permanently establishes the City of Des Moines as the state capital and Iowa City as the home of the State University of Iowa, popularly known since the 1960s as the University of Iowa.[35] Section 8's origins are briefly chronicled in Part I.

Section 8 has never been the subject of appellate litigation, but the Office of the Attorney General has issued several noteworthy opinions regarding the provision. In 1971, Attorney General Richard Turner determined that Section 8 would not bar the government from temporarily relocating the state capital during emergencies necessitating such a move.[36] In 1968, Turner noted that

---

[33] Iowa Const. of 1846, art. XII, § 3.

[34] *1857 Debates, supra* Article I, note 3, vol. 2, pp. 801, 811. A motion to entirely omit the provision failed by a 16-to-19 vote. *See id.* at p. 811.

[35] For an explanation of the university's naming conventions, see David McCartney, "What's in a Name? For the University of Iowa, Lots of History and a Little Confusion," *University of Iowa Spectator* (Dec. 2010), available at http://spectator.uiowa.edu/2010/december/oldgold.html. *See also* Op. Iowa Att'y Gen., 1964 WL 121093 (Dec. 15, 1964) (replying to Elmer Lange) (concluding that the Board of Regents lacked the power to remove the word "State" from the university's legal name).

[36] Op. Iowa Att'y Gen., 1971 WL 240829 (Sept. 30, 1971) (replying to Albert Maricle).

Section 8's phrase "seat of government" refers to the entire City of Des Moines, rather than to any specific collection of buildings, thereby giving state lawmakers significant flexibility in determining where within the city certain government offices should be located.[37] In 1935, Attorney General Edward O'Connor concluded that Section 8 did not bar the University of Iowa from accepting land on Dickinson County's Lake Okoboji to serve as a fieldwork site for the university's students and faculty.[38]

---

[37] Op. Iowa Att'y Gen., 1968 WL 172454 (Jan. 18, 1968) (replying to Stephen Robinson).

[38] Op. Iowa Att'y Gen., 1935 WL 60843 (Sept. 30, 1935) (replying to the State University of Iowa).

Article XII

Schedule

When ratified in 1857, Article XII contained fifteen enumerated sections. Most of those sections dealt with practical matters concerning the transition from the state's 1846 constitution to the new constitution. Section 3, for example, concerned criminal matters then pending in the state's courts and criminal acts committed prior to the new constitution's ratification; Section 5 concerned bonds that the state had issued; Sections 6 through 8 concerned the timing of the first elections for various governmental offices;[1] Sections 9 through 11 concerned transitional matters involving members of the General Assembly and executive appointees; Section 12 directed the General Assembly to divide the state into judicial districts; Section 13 set the parameters for voting on the constitution's ratification; Section 14 arranged for voters to weigh in on whether the racially restrictive word "white" should be stricken from Article II's description of those entitled to vote; and Section 15 dealt with matters particular to Mills County. Because those provisions are no longer relevant to legal issues arising today, they are commonly omitted in printings of the Iowa Constitution, just as they are omitted here.

One of the omitted provisions—Section 4—was formally repealed by Iowa voters in 1974, the same year that Iowans repealed Section 4 of the second

[1] For the delegates' sometimes heated debate about the appropriate timing of those elections, see *1857 Debates, supra* Article I, note 3, vol. 2, pp. 1036–48.

division of Article IX, which concerned certain matters involving fines and educational funds. Section 4 of Article XII stated that "[a]ll fines, penalties, or forfeitures due, or to become due, or accruing to the State, or to any County therein, or to the school fund, shall inure to the State, county, or school fund, in the manner prescribed by law."

This leaves only two sections of Article XII that merit discussion.

Section 1.
Supreme law—constitutionality of acts.

This Constitution shall be the supreme law of the State, and any law inconsistent therewith, shall be void. The General Assembly shall pass all laws necessary to carry this Constitution into effect.

By declaring that the Iowa Constitution is the state's supreme law, Section 1's first sentence serves a function comparable to the Supremacy Clause of the U.S. Constitution.[2] The provision's second sentence directs the General Assembly to enact any legislation necessary to put the constitution into operation. Section 1 in its entirety is framed precisely as originally proposed by the 1857 convention's Committee on the Schedule and was not controversial among the delegates.[3]

Iowa's courts are not quick to find that a law is unconstitutional and thus void. A court will strike down a law as unconstitutional only if the violation is "clear[] and palpabl[e]" (*Eckerson v. City of Des Moines*, 1908). As the court explained in *State v. Hernandez-Lopez* (2002) (internal citations and quotations omitted),

> statutes are cloaked with a presumption of constitutionality. The challenger bears a heavy burden, because it must prove the unconstitutionality beyond a reasonable doubt. Moreover, the challenger must refute every reasonable basis upon which the statute could be found to be constitutional. Furthermore, if the statute is capable of being construed in more than one manner, one of which is constitutional, we must adopt that construction.

How do the courts discern the constitution's requirements in a given instance? In *N.W. Halsey & Co. v. City of Belle Plaine* (1905), the Iowa Supreme Court summarized some of the factors it may consider:

> [W]e are required primarily to look to the words employed, giving to them meaning in their natural sense and as commonly understood. If necessary to a fuller understanding, we may place ourselves in touch with the makers of the instrument, and share in their view of the general subject by reading the constitutional debates; also the contemporary legislation, if any, having relation to the

---

[2] U.S. Const. art. VI, cl. 2.

[3] *1857 Debates, supra* Article I, note 3, vol. 2, pp. 914, 994, 1034–36.

> subject-matter; we may take note of the evil as manifestly sought to be remedied or guarded against, and of the conditions to be affected, then existing or reasonably to be apprehended in the future, and as disclosed by the authentic history of the state.[4]

This does not mean, however, that a court always applies constitutional texts in precisely the ways that the framers specifically anticipated. In 2009's *Varnum v. Brien*—the case in which the Iowa Supreme Court struck down the state's ban on same-sex marriage—the court explained that its job "is to protect constitutional rights of individuals from legislative enactments that have denied those rights, even when the rights have not yet been broadly accepted, were at one time unimagined, or challenge a deeply ingrained practice or law viewed to be impervious to the passage of time." In *Varnum* itself, the court found a degree of interpretive freedom in the fact that the constitution's framers knew that Iowans' understanding of fundamental principles of equality would evolve over time.

In *Godfrey v. State* (2017), the Iowa Supreme Court determined that Section 1's second sentence (directing the General Assembly to enact all laws necessary to put the constitution into effect) is not nearly as important today as its first. The *Godfrey* court held that, when a government official has violated a person's equal protection or due process rights (see Sections 6 and 9, respectively, of Article I) and the General Assembly has not created adequate statutory remedies for such violations, the person can bring a cause of action for damages against the government official. In reaching that conclusion, the court determined that Section 1's second sentence was intended simply to focus on the legislature's role in transitioning from the 1846 constitution to "this" 1857 constitution, and that the sentence "was not meant to dramatically undermine effective judicial enforcement of the Iowa Bill of Rights by making remedies dependent upon legislative whim." Justices Edward Mansfield, Thomas Waterman, and Bruce Zager argued in dissent that Section 1's second sentence is far more significant than that because, in their view, it gives the General Assembly—not the courts—the task of deciding whether to create causes of action for damages for constitutional violations.

Section 2.
Laws in force.

All laws now in force and not inconsistent with this Constitution, shall remain in force until they shall expire or be repealed.

Providing Iowa with legal continuity as it shifted to a new constitution in 1857, Section 2 states that all laws consistent with the constitution will remain in

[4] *Cf. Ex parte Pritz* (1858) ("In the interpretation of the Constitution, . . . we are to ascertain the meaning by getting at the intention of those making the instrument. What thought was in the mind of those making the Constitution—what was their intention, is the great leading rule of construction.").

effect until taken out of commission by ordinary means. The provision is framed precisely as originally proposed by the 1857 convention's Committee on the Schedule and was not controversial among the delegates.[5] The Iowa Supreme Court applied Section 2 according to its plain meaning on a couple of occasions early in the state's history (*Independent School District v. Miller*, 1920; *Warren v. Henly*, 1870). Given the passage of time and the massive growth in legislative enactments, revisions, and repeals, however, the provision no longer plays a prominent role in the life of the state. Section 2 does remain in place, however, should a rare case bring it into play.

[5] *1857 Debates, supra* Article I, note 3, vol. 2, pp. 914, 994, 1034–36.

■ BIBLIOGRAPHICAL ESSAY

The State Library of Iowa provides online copies of the draft constitution produced by the Territory of Iowa's 1844 constitutional convention, the constitution written and ratified in 1846, the constitution written and ratified in 1857, and the amended constitution as it stands today.[1] The State Library also provides a freestanding online collection of Iowa's constitutional amendments.[2] For a pairing of each constitutional provision with cases in which state and federal courts have interpreted it, see the first two volumes of *Iowa Code Annotated*, published by Thomson Reuters. Those two volumes also include brief references to opinions that the Office of the Attorney General has issued in response to questions concerning the constitution's meaning. Readers should not treat *Iowa Code Annotated* as if it were accurate and comprehensive in every respect; it sometimes omits noteworthy cases and opinions or includes cases and opinions with little interpretive significance.

The published opinions of the Iowa Supreme Court and the Iowa Court of Appeals appear in Thomson Reuters's *North Western Reporter*. For many years, the State of Iowa published the opinions of the Iowa Supreme Court in an annual volume titled *Iowa Reports*, but it discontinued that practice in 1968. The Iowa Supreme Court maintains an online archive of all of its published opinions from 1998 forward.[3] The Iowa Court of Appeals, created by the General Assembly in 1976, does the same thing.[4] Those looking for cases on a given issue of Iowa law—constitutional or otherwise—may consult the topically ordered volumes of *Iowa Digest*, published by Thomson Reuters. The opinions of the Iowa Attorney General from 1898 forward are available and readily searchable online.[5]

Documentation of the proceedings at the 1844 and 1846 constitutional conventions is thinner than one would like. The leading available resources

---

[1] *See* State Library of Iowa, "Constitutions," http://www.statelibraryofiowa.org/services/collections/law-library/iacon/iacons.

[2] *See* State Library of Iowa, "Amendments," http://www.statelibraryofiowa.org/services/collections/law-library/iacon/ioamend.

[3] *See* Iowa Judicial Branch, "Archive of Opinions for the Iowa Supreme Court," http://www.iowacourts.gov/About_the_Courts/Supreme_Court/Supreme_Court_Opinions/Opinions_Archive/.

[4] *See* Iowa Judicial Branch, "Archive of Opinions for the Iowa Court of Appeals," http://www.iowacourts.gov/About_the_Courts/Court_of_Appeals/Court_of_Appeals_Opinions/Opinions_Archive/.

[5] *See* Iowa Department of Justice, "Search Attorney General Opinions," https://www.iowaattorneygeneral.gov/about-us/attorney-general-opinions/attorney-general-opinions/.

regarding those conventions are *Fragments of the Debates of the Iowa Constitutional Conventions of 1844 and 1846*, ed. Benjamin F. Shambaugh (Iowa City: State Historical Society of Iowa, 1900); *Journal of the Convention for the Formation of a Constitution for the State of Iowa* (Iowa City: Jesse Williams, 1845); and *Journal of the Convention for the Formation of a Constitution for the State of Iowa* (Iowa City: Abraham H. Palmer, 1846). The State Library provides an online copy of the valuable but aptly titled *Fragments*.[6]

Materials for Iowa's 1857 constitutional convention are more comprehensive. These include *Journal of the Constitutional Convention of the State of Iowa* (Muscatine: John Mahin, 1857) and the two volumes of *The Debates of the Constitutional Convention of the State of Iowa* (Davenport: Luse, Lane & Co., 1857). A wide range of additional primary sources—many of them concerning Iowa's early constitutional history—are presented in the three volumes of *Documentary Material Relating to the History of Iowa*, ed. Benjamin F. Shambaugh (Iowa City: State Historical Society of Iowa, 1897). The State Library provides online copies of both volumes of *The Debates* and all three volumes of *Documentary Material*.[7] For editorials written in favor of or against ratification of the 1857 constitution, see "Contemporary Editorial Opinion of the 1857 Constitution," 55 *Iowa Journal of History* 115 (1957).

With respect to commentaries, a leading treatment of Iowa's early constitutional development is Benjamin F. Shambaugh, *The Constitutions of Iowa* (Iowa City: State Historical Society of Iowa, 1934). A number of book-length histories of Iowa and Iowa City contain materials that pertain to the formation of the state's 1846 and 1857 constitutions and subsequent amendments. One such source that I have found especially valuable is Leland L. Sage, *A History of Iowa* (Ames: Iowa State University Press, 1974). Additional useful histories that are similarly sweeping in scope include Richard, Lord Acton & Patricia Nassif Acton, *To Go Free: A Treasury of Iowa's Legal Heritage* (Ames: Iowa State University Press, 1995); Cyrenus Cole, *A History of the People of Iowa* (Cedar Rapids: Torch Press, 1921); the four volumes of Benjamin F. Gue, *History of Iowa* (Century History Co., 1903); William J. Petersen, *The Story of Iowa: The Progress of an American State* (New York: Lewis Historical Publishing Co., 1952); Dorothy Schwieder: *Iowa: The Middle Land* (Iowa City: University of Iowa Press, 1996); and Charles R. Tuttle, *An Illustrated History of the State of Iowa* (Chicago: Richard S. Peale & Co., 1876).

There are many additional, often more narrowly focused books of interest to those studying Iowa's constitution and sociopolitical history. Listed alphabetically by author, such books include Carrie Chapman Catt & Nellie Rogers

[6] *See* State Library of Iowa, "The Debates of the Constitutional Conventions of the State of Iowa," http://www.statelibraryofiowa.org/services/collections/law-library/iacon/iadeb/.

[7] *See* State Library of Iowa, "The Debates of the Constitutional Conventions of the State of Iowa," http://www.statelibraryofiowa.org/services/collections/law-library/iacon/iadeb/.

Shuler, *Woman Suffrage and Politics: The Inner Story of the Suffrage Movement* (New York: Charles Scribner's Sons, 1926), ch. 15; Robert Cook, *Baptism of Fire: The Republican Party in Iowa, 1838–1878* (Ames: Iowa State University Press, 1994); Robert R. Dykstra, *Bright Radical Star: Black Freedom and White Supremacy on the Hawkeye Frontier* (Ames: Iowa State University Press, 1993); Erling A. Erickson, *Banking in Frontier Iowa, 1836–1865* (Ames: Iowa State University Press, 1971); Ruth A. Gallaher, *Legal and Political Status of Women in Iowa: An Historical Account of the Rights of Women in Iowa from 1838 to 1918* (Iowa City: State Historical Society of Iowa, 1918); Margaret N. Keyes, *Old Capitol: Portrait of an Iowa Landmark* (Iowa City: University of Iowa Press, 1988); Louise R. Noun, *Strong-Minded Women: The Emergence of the Woman-Suffrage Movement in Iowa* (Ames: Iowa State University Press, 1969); Louis Pelzer, *Augustus Caesar Dodge* (Iowa City: State Historical Society of Iowa, 1908); Howard H. Preston, *History of Banking in Iowa* (Iowa City: State Historical Society of Iowa, 1922); Leslie A. Schwalm, *Emancipation's Diaspora: Race and Reconstruction in the Upper Midwest* (Chapel Hill: University of North Carolina Press, 2009); Benjamin F. Shambaugh, *The Old Stone Capitol Remembers* (Iowa City: State Historical Society of Iowa, 1939); Silvana R. Siddali, *Frontier Democracy: Constitutional Conventions in the Old Northwest* (New York: Cambridge University Press, 2016); Lowell J. Soike, *Busy in the Cause: Iowa, the Free-State Struggle in the West, and the Prelude to the Civil War* (Lincoln & London: University of Nebraska Press, 2014); Lowell J. Soike, *Necessary Courage: Iowa's Underground Railroad in the Struggle Against Slavery* (Iowa City: University of Iowa Press, 2013); and Frank J. Stork & Cynthia A. Clingan, *The Iowa General Assembly: Our Legislative Heritage, 1846–1980* (Des Moines: Iowa Senate, 1980). Attention is also owed to the fine essays that appear in the beautifully produced, image-intensive *Outside In: African-American History in Iowa, 1838–2000*, ed. Bill Silag (Des Moines: State Historical Society of Iowa, 2001).

For shorter treatments of Iowa's legal and political history, one can scan the tables of contents for the various issues of *Annals of Iowa*, the *Iowa Journal of History & Politics* (renamed the *Iowa Journal of History* in 1949), and *The Palimpsest*. While writing this book, I was aided by numerous articles from those three journals, including the following:

- On politics and political parties, see Jack T. Johnson, "The Election of 1842," 23 *The Palimpsest* 241 (1942); Louis Pelzer, "The History and Principles of the Democratic Party of the Territory of Iowa," 6 *Iowa Journal of History and Politics* 2 (1908); Louis Pelzer, "The History and Principles of the Whigs of the Territory of Iowa," 5 *Iowa Journal of History & Politics* 46 (1907); David S. Sparks, "The Birth of the Republican Party in Iowa, 1854–1856," 54 *Iowa Journal of History* 1 (1956); David S. Sparks, "The Decline of the Democratic Party in Iowa, 1850–1860," 53 *Iowa Journal of*

History 1 (1955); and Charles W. Wiggins, "Constitutional Convention Issue in Iowa (1960)," 40 *Annals of Iowa* 171 (1970).

- On Iowa's territorial and state capitals, see John E. Briggs, "The Removal of the Capital from Iowa City to Des Moines," 14 *Iowa Journal of History & Politics* 56 (1916); Peter A. Dey, "Recollections of the Old Capitol and the New," 7 *Annals of Iowa* 81 (1905); Marie Haefner, "The Capital at Burlington," 18 *The Palimpsest* 98 (1937); John C. Parish, "The Old Military Road," 2 *The Palimpsest* 33 (1921); Silvana R. Siddali, "'Principle, Interest and Patriotism All Combine': The Fight Over Iowa's Capital City," 64 *Annals of Iowa* 111 (2005); and J.A. Swisher, "Old Zion Church, Burlington, Iowa," 9 *Annals of Iowa* 524 (1910).
- On Iowa's name and geographic boundaries, see Erik McKinley Eriksson, "The Boundaries of Iowa," 25 *Iowa Journal of History & Politics* 163 (1927); Derek R. Everett, "To Shed Our Blood for Our Beloved Territory: The Iowa-Missouri Borderland," 67 *Annals of Iowa* 269 (2008); Carol J. Kraus, "A Study in Border Confrontation: The Iowa-Missouri Boundary Dispute," 40 *Annals of Iowa* 81 (1969); Jean Nicolas Nicollet, "The Nicollet Boundaries," 9 *The Palimpsest* 170 (1928); Benjamin F. Shambaugh, "Maps Illustrative of the Boundary History of Iowa," 2 *Iowa Journal of History & Politics* 369 (1904); and Benjamin F. Shambaugh, "The Naming of Iowa," 16 *The Palimpsest* 81 (1935).
- On issues of race, see Leola Nelson Bergmann, "The Negro in Iowa," 46 *Iowa Journal of History & Politics* 3 (1948); Arnie Cooper, "A Stony Road: Black Education in Iowa, 1838–1860," 48 *Annals of Iowa* 113 (1986); Ruth A. Gallaher, "A Colored Convention," 2 *The Palimpsest* 178 (1921); Louis Pelzer, "The Negro and Slavery in Early Iowa," 2 *Iowa Journal of History & Politics* 471 (1904); and Jacob Van Ek, "Underground Railroad in Iowa," 2 *The Palimpsest* 129 (1921).
- On voting rights, see Carl H. Erbe, "Constitutional Provisions for the Suffrage in Iowa," 22 *Iowa Journal of History & Politics* 163 (1924).
- On municipalities, see George F. Robeson, "Special Municipal Charters in Iowa, 1836–1858," 18 *Iowa Journal of History & Politics* 163 (1920).
- On corporations, see Frank Edward Horack, "Some Phases of Corporate Regulation in the State of Iowa," 2 *Iowa Journal of History & Politics* 485 (1904).
- On banking, see Ruth A. Gallaher, "Money in Pioneer Iowa, 1835–1865," 32 *Iowa Journal of History & Politics* 3 (1934).
- On state debts, see Carl H. Erbe, "Constitutional Limitations on Indebtedness in Iowa," 22 *Iowa Journal of History & Politics* 363 (1924).
- On the governor's veto power, see Jacob A. Swisher, "The Executive Veto in Iowa," 15 *Iowa Journal of History & Politics* 155 (1917).

- On the University of Iowa's early years, see J.L. Pickard, "Historical Sketch of the State University of Iowa," 4 *Annals of Iowa* 1 (1899) (written by one of the university's former presidents).
- On the militia, see Carl H. Erbe, "The Militia Under the Constitution of Iowa," 24 *Iowa Journal of History & Politics* 270 (1926).
- On constitutional amendments, see John F. Sly, "Providing for a State Constitutional Convention," 19 *Iowa Journal of History & Politics* 3 (1921).
- On individuals of particular significance to Iowa's story, see Erik McKinley Eriksson, "William Penn Clarke," 25 *Iowa Journal of History and Politics* 3 (1927); Ruth A. Gallaher, "Albert Miller Lea," 33 *Iowa Journal of History & Politics* 195 (1935); Ruth A. Gallaher, "N. Nicollet, Map Maker," 26 *The Palimpsest* 289 (1945); John C. Parish, "Robert Lucas," 3 *The Palimpsest* 233 (1922); and Edward H. Stiles, "Judge Jonathan C. Hall," 9 *Annals of Iowa* 18 (1907).

Both the *Iowa Law Review* and the *Drake Law Review* publish pieces from time to time on matters concerning the Iowa Constitution. Listed alphabetically by author, fine examples include Jerry L. Anderson & Christopher Poynor, "A Constitutional and Empirical Analysis of Iowa's Administrative Rules Committee Procedure," 61 *Drake Law Review* 1 (2012); Robert H. Bowmar, "The Anachronism Called Debt Limitation," 52 *Iowa Law Review* 863 (1967); Dan C. Dutcher, "Joinder of Parties and Actions," 29 *Iowa Law Review* 3 (1943); Frank E. Horack, "The Banking Clauses in the Constitution of Iowa," 13 *Iowa Law Review* 293 (1928); Note, "Iowa Constitution—Twenty-Year Limitation on Agricultural Leases," 39 *Iowa Law Review* 486 (1954); Rosemary Shaw Sackett & Richard H. Doyle, "History of the Iowa Court of Appeals," 60 *Drake Law Review* 1 (2011); Sam F. Scheidler, "Implementation of Constitutional Home Rule in Iowa," 22 *Drake Law Review* 294 (1973); and Harvey Uhlenhopp, "Judicial Reorganization in Iowa," 44 *Iowa Law Review* 6 (1958).

Less frequently, other states' student-edited or peer-reviewed journals address issues of Iowa law. For my accounts of recent judicial retention elections in Iowa, for example, see "Letter from Iowa: Same-Sex Marriage and the Ouster of Three Justices," 59 *Kansas Law Review* 715 (2011), and "Retention Redux: Iowa 2012," 14 *Journal of Appellate Practice & Process* 47 (2013).

■ TABLE OF CASES

A

B

C

D

E

F

G

H

I

J

K

L

M

N

O

P

R

S

T

U

V

W

Y

Z

INDEX

About the Author

Todd E. Pettys holds the H. Blair and Joan V. White Chair in Civil Litigation at the University of Iowa College of Law. He lives with his wife and daughter in Iowa City, Iowa.

Printed in the USA/Agawam, MA
October 25, 2017

661254.001